The European Seaborne Empires

The European Seaborne Empires

From the Thirty Years' War to the Age of Revolutions

Gabriel Paquette

Yale
UNIVERSITY PRESS
NEW HAVEN AND LONDON

Published with assistance from the Annie Burr Lewis Fund and from the foundation established in memory of Calvin Chapin of the Class of 1788, Yale College.

Yale University Press books may be purchased in quantity for educational, business, or promotional use. For information, please e-mail sales.press@yale.edu (U.S. office) or sales@yaleup.co.uk (U.K. office).

Set in Fournier MT type by IDS Infotech Ltd.
Printed in the United States of America.

Library of Congress Control Number: 2018958332
ISBN 978-0-300-20515-2 (hardcover : alk. paper)

A catalogue record for this book is available from the British Library.

This paper meets the requirements of ANSI/NISO Z39.48-1992 (Permanence of Paper).

10 9 8 7 6 5 4 3 2 1

Contents

Acknowledgments vii

Introduction 1

1. Definitions of "Empire" and Approaches to the Study of Its History 17

2. Western Europe in a World of Empires 31

3. The First Seaborne Empires: Portugal, Spain, and the Wider World before 1600 47

4. The Challenge to Iberian Dominance: The Rise of Britain, France, and the Dutch Republic as Competitor Imperial States after 1600 61

5. Consolidation, Conflict, and Reform in the Long Eighteenth Century 77

6. Law, Governance, and Institutional Frameworks 97

7. The Political Economy of Empire and Its Consequences 115

8. Imperial Migrations: Coerced, Forced, and "Free" 131

9. Labor Regimes 145

10. Creole Societies, *Mestizaje,* and the Regulation of Hybridity 160

11. Collaboration, Resistance, and the Fortunes of Empire 174

12. The Age of Revolutions 190

Epilogue: Continuities and Disjunctures 207

Notes 223

Bibliography 247

Index 285

Acknowledgments

The reader will share my awareness of this book's heavy reliance on the stellar research of hundreds of fellow scholars. I acknowledge their insights in the text itself and, especially, in the endnotes and bibliography. A synthetic and synoptic book, it should be baldly stated, does justice neither to the vast scholarly literature nor to the complexity of the subject itself. I can only hope that the reader's interest will have been sufficiently piqued to seek out and read the books and articles I have cited. As this book is designed as an introductory overview of the subject, however, I have sought to record my intellectual debts without cluttering the text with a distracting morass of notes. I have cited English-language works almost exclusively, given that the book's target audience is university students in the English-speaking world who may not have access to books in other languages.

I cannot deny or defend this book's inequality of proportions and lopsidedness. Some crucial themes are given far fewer pages than they deserve. There is more attention allotted, for example, to the Iberian empires than to either the Dutch or the French. Smaller seaborne empires, such as the Danish, are omitted altogether, chiefly for reasons of space. International relations and political economy receive greater attention than social history. Such emphases and asymmetries reflect my own understanding, knowledge of languages, and knowledge of historiographies, as well as my own tastes, inclinations, strengths, and shortcomings.

I have worked intermittently (and often unconsciously) on this book for more than a decade, in the course of teaching hundreds of undergraduates (and a handful of graduate students) at Wesleyan University, the University of Cambridge, Harvard University, and the Johns Hopkins University. I am profoundly grateful to each and every one of my students for unwittingly sharing some segments of this adventure with me. Several colleagues selflessly expended precious intellectual energy to read the original book proposal and/or draft chapters. I am grateful for their perspicacious insights and suggestions. In particular, I wish to thank Vijay Pinch, Matthew Brown, Manuel Lucena Giraldo, Richard Drayton, and the late Christopher Schmidt-Nowara. I benefited enormously from three readers' reports on the original proposal obtained by Yale University Press and from the two detailed reports on the full draft manuscript. I am grateful to my editor, Sarah Miller, for persuading me that this book was worth pursuing. She has been unfailingly patient and solicitous at all stages of the process. Her colleagues at Yale University Press likewise have provided invaluable and timely assistance.

The Department of History of the Johns Hopkins University, my scholarly home between 2011 and 2018, not only provided a congenial work environment but also furnished me with all manner of material support, for which I am profoundly grateful. The staff of the Milton S. Eisenhower Library dealt cheerfully with my innumerable requests. I wrote most of this book in the George Peabody Library. I thank librarians and curators Paul Espinosa and Earle Havens for providing me with a well-lit perch on the fourth floor of that magnificent library. This book was completed at the University of Oregon. I wish to thank the entire UO community for the warmth of the welcome extended to my family.

Several institutions and individuals granted indispensable permissions. Paul Espinosa arranged for the reproduction of several of the images included in this book from the Peabody, and I thank the Johns Hopkins University for granting permission to publish them here. I further thank Neil Safier, director of the John Carter Brown Library, for permission to reproduce images from that library's unparalleled collection. I am grateful to Bill Nelson for drawing the maps. Furthermore, I have been granted permission to reuse excerpts from the following previously published material: "Colonial Societies," in H. M. Scott, ed., *The Oxford Handbook of Early Modern European History, 1350–1750*, vol. II (Oxford: Oxford University Press, 2015), 280–306; and "The Reform of the Spanish Empire in the Age of Enlightenment," in Jesús Astigarraga, ed., *The Spanish Enlightenment Revisited*, Oxford University Studies in the Enlightenment (Oxford: Voltaire Foundation, 2015), 149–167.

My wife, Johanna Richlin, deserves more than the passing acknowledgment that I can offer here. Suffice it to say that whatever good is found in this book owes much to her love of and unstinting belief in its author. I dedicate this book to our daughter, Antonia, whose insatiable curiosity has done much to rekindle my own.

Introduction

To study the history of Europe's overseas empires is to enter into numerous and long-standing scholarly debates. A major source of these debates is a still prevalent set of assumptions about Europe and the non-European world. Though its influence has waned, historians have depicted Europe as in some way special or unique. Blessed with an array of endowments—cultural, intellectual, racial, material—that the non-European world purportedly lacked, Europe was portrayed as superior to the world's other regions.[1] The conclusion often reached is that Europe and Europeans ("the West") were privileged or exceptional whereas the non-European world and non-Europeans ("the Rest") were deficient or inadequate in some fundamental, insuperable way. They were incapable of traveling down the path blazed by Europeans. "Despotic Asian institutions," historian E. L. Jones wrote, "suppressed creativity or diverted it into producing voluptuous luxuries."[2] From this starting point, it is but a short leap to conceive of Europe's subjugation of the rest of the world—the formation and maintenance of "empire"—as something natural, inexorable, and good. This is a world divided between leader and follower nations, innovators and imitators, active agents and passive recipients.

These assumptions, and conclusions, have been assailed as the "colonizer's model of the world."[3] This model erroneously exaggerates the differences between Europe and the non-European world. Such hyperbole is rooted in prejudice. It rationalizes later European hegemony as inevitable and mistakes the result of Europe's dominance for its cause. The benefits derived by Europe from overseas empire were immense and came at the expense of non-Europeans. The exploitation of natural resources and labor set those world regions on a course toward "underdevelopment."[4] Whatever "breakthrough" Europe experienced may be attributed chiefly to factors extrinsic to it, to the benefits derived from empire.

There is nothing especially controversial in this statement. It has been recognized by commentators as diverse as Adam Smith and Karl Marx. "The Advantages which Europe, considered as one great country, has derived from the discovery and colonization of America, consist," Smith wrote in *The Wealth of Nations* (1776), "first, in the increase of its enjoyments; and, secondly, in the augmentation of its industry." Marx took a dimmer view of the proceedings. He highlighted forced migration, slavery, and the extraction of precious metals, instead of wealth derived from trade, as the indispensable factor in Europe's economic efflorescence. As he narrated in *Capital* (1867), "The discovery of gold and silver in America, the extirpation, enslavement and entombment of the aboriginal population . . . the turning of Africa into a warren for the commercial hunting of black-skins . . . these idyllic proceedings are the chief moments of the so-called primitive accumulation. . . . The treasures captured outside of Europe by undisguised looting, enslavement, and murder, floated back to the mother country and were there turned into capital." For Marx, then, overseas empire underpinned nascent capitalist institutions in Europe itself and accelerated their development. A contemporary historian operating in a non-Marxist paradigm, Kenneth Pomeranz, has disagreed with the assertion that Europe's development can be attributed chiefly to its access to colonial resources, but he concedes that the "fruits of overseas coercion" may account for the differences in the growth trajectories of European and Eurasian states after 1800.[5]

But even if the insights of Pomeranz, Marx, and Smith are accepted, many questions remain unanswered. How did vast swathes of the earth's surface come to be dominated by a small handful of parvenu states situated on the western periphery of Europe by 1800? How did Europeans obtain access to, lay claim to, and justify control over the territory, material resources, and labor of human subjects in the extra-European world? There are countless possible answers to these questions. The ultimate, and unsatisfying, answer is that myriad intersecting or overlapping causes explain this outcome, with some variables more important than others at certain times and in certain places. Historian John Darwin has termed this polyphony of causalities "chaotic pluralism," which neatly encapsulates the difficulty of settling upon a single model of causation.[6] In this book, I argue that three factors

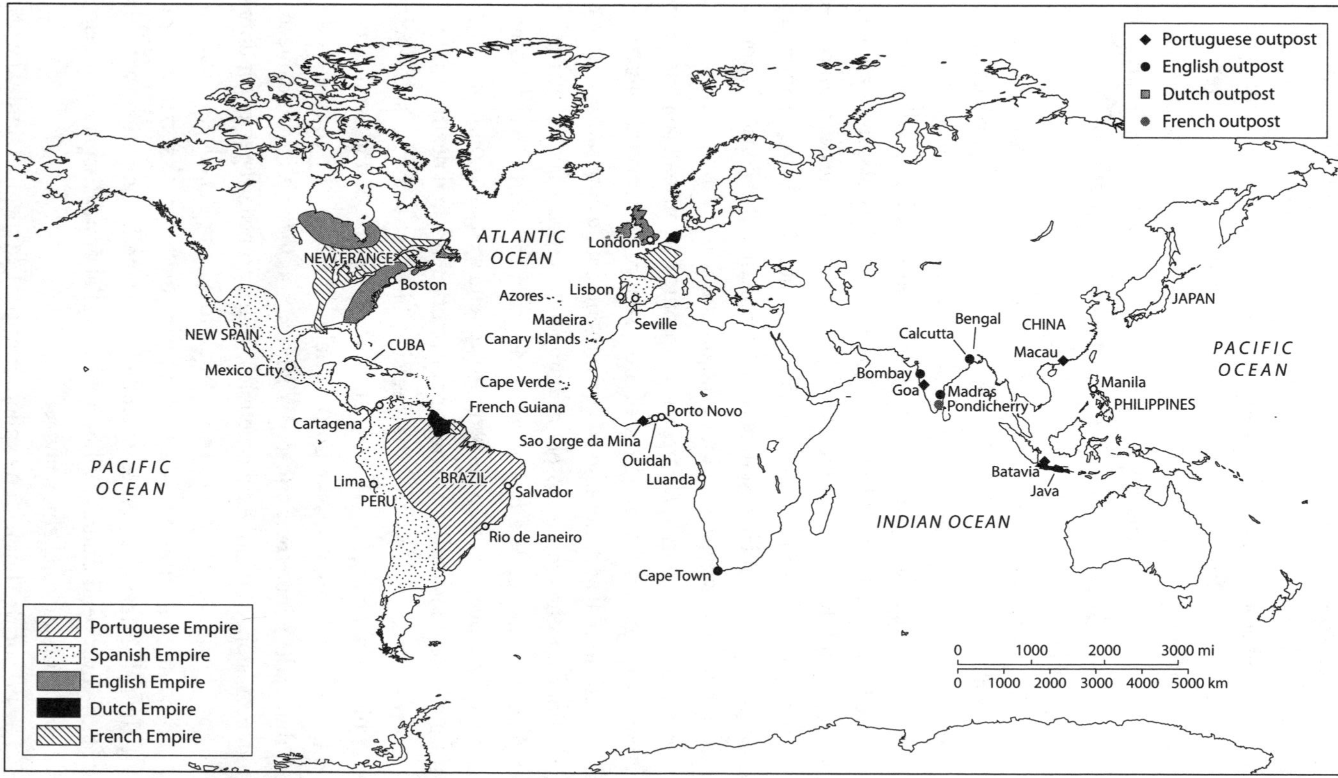

Figure 1. The European seaborne empires circa 1750

were most decisive: first, coercive violence was employed systematically by European states to pursue their objectives and embedded in the institutions they established overseas; second, the efficacious forms of governance and finance they developed enabled European states to project and retain power across vast distances, wringing notable advantage from both natural resources and native (as well as expatriate) labor in non-European territories; and, third, the collaboration of indigenous (and later "creole") elites—often for their own advantage—in the extension and consolidation of European control was indispensable.[7]

But the galvanizing force that set and kept these processes in motion was competition among European states. Various monarchies struggled for primacy within their own territorial borders and vis-à-vis one another. The conduct of European states in the non-European world is intelligible only against the backdrop of intra-European competition. Possession of an overseas territory and the exclusive access to its coveted resources was conceived as a precondition of survival in the bellicose, volatile landscape of interstate relations in Europe. Such resources also facilitated the consolidation of dynastic monarchies whose previous hold on political authority was tenuous and contested. The struggle for primacy at home and abroad spawned new repertoires of rule and techniques of governance. Rivalry among states ensured institutional and ideological convergence; state apparatuses came to resemble one another more closely as competition intensified. Viewing the states from a distance, one might conclude from the drift toward isomorphism that these purported rivals were in fact engaged in a common project for mutual benefit instead of a struggle for political life and death.

Interimperial rivalry was the decisive but far from the sole factor driving historical change. A second set of conflicts shaped the evolution of the empires European states sought to establish, chiefly the countervailing forces that undermined their efforts. Expansion was met with formidable and sustained resistance by indigenous peoples. The European capacity for domination ran up against very real constraints, including distance, population size, and communication networks. Within creole colonial societies themselves, the self-interest of elites eventually became incompatible with the aims of the European center. Willingness to collaborate dissipated; disassociation and ultimately rebellion ensued.

The title of this book is an explicit, if critical, homage to seminal works bearing similar titles published in the mid-twentieth century by historians

Figure 2. Western Europe circa 1720

C. R. Boxer and J. H. Parry.[8] My allusion to these works draws attention both to their enduring value and to the passage of time since their publication. Since then, scholars have thoroughly revised the contours, as well as the substance, of the narratives penned by Boxer and Parry. The ideological underpinnings, the range of labor regimes and migration, the forms of subaltern resistance and acquiescence, the diversity of roles undertaken by women, the development and application of racial theories, the Age of

Revolutions, and the transcontinental flows of goods and people are among the many historical subjects, themes, and topics imperfectly integrated into their narratives of Europe's seaborne empires. The triumphalism, awe, and, at times, apologetic nostalgia that characterized these books now appear misplaced and dissonant, even if their erudition, scope, and literary style continue to inspire and impress. There are evidentiary limits, of course, to revisionism. As anthropologist Michel-Rolph Trouillot noted, "Inequalities experienced by the actors lead to uneven historical power in the inscription of traces."[9] The archives on which historians must rely contain more insight into the aims and actions of governors, Crown officials, and municipal councils than the aspirations and sentiments of slaves, sailors, and indentured servants. Nevertheless, exciting advances in scholarship have resulted from the development and application of innovative methods. The resulting corpus of scholarship makes it feasible to reframe the traditional history of the seaborne empires for a new age.

If older narratives so desperately require thorough revision, why not simply jettison the archaic term "seaborne empires" and the now unfashionable scholarship, much of it written at the cusp of the Age of Decolonization, to which it is inextricably linked? Long before global and comparative history became fashionable, Parry and Boxer insisted on transcending national frameworks. The Portuguese, Spanish, British, French, and Dutch empires must be examined together, whether comparatively or in terms of their interactions, they contended. As Parry observed, "All [five empires were] active during the greater part of a 5-century period; all operated on several continents and in all of the major oceans; all acquired possessions of great territorial extent and diversity; and control over particular territories for long stretches of time."[10] These historians recognized how empires were more profitably studied over centuries than decades. They lucidly showed how empires intersected, collided, and, in the final analysis, were inseparable. Institutional history, high politics and geopolitical rivalry, and military history, which latterly has been shunned, were central features of their narratives. They should remain incorporated, robustly and without apology, in new narratives. Such a stance is not a defense of empire or to suggest that historians restrain expression of moral outrage, but merely to observe that such expressions must not foreclose scholarly assessment. Empire-phobes may hold assumptions as untenable as those cherished by empire-philes.[11] Even if a careful audit reveals exploitation to have been the defining feature of Europe's relations with the wider world, the structures through which this was attempted and achieved are no less worthy of study. Long-distance transportation, the mobilization of labor on unprecedented scale, the construction of vast cities, the functioning of complex and sprawling bureaucracies, the mapping and knitting together of vast territories, the integration of markets circling the globe, and the propagation of creeds across oceans are achievements (in a value-neutral sense) that must be understood and explained, even if ultimately maligned as vehicles or outcomes of oppression.

As to the modifier "seaborne," it usefully alludes to the mobility characteristic of the five Western European empires treated in this book. The connections they spun spanned multiple oceans. Their fortunes hinged on the density and constancy of maritime links conveying people and commodities from continent to continent. In the Portuguese Empire, for example, Africans from Angola sailed on vessels in the South China Sea, while Javanese sailors composed the crews of ships bound for Lisbon's wharves. The importance of seafaring increased as empires expanded. In the mid-sixteenth century, fewer than five thousand English subjects were employed as sailors and seamen. By 1750, sixty thousand Britons plied the waves, largely in the vessels of the merchant marine, but in the navy, too. Lives were led and livelihoods made (and lost) along ocean routes, marked by transcontinental flows of wealth and the cross-pollination of ideas. Elihu Yale's life offers a fine example of such a trajectory. A member of the English East India Company (EIC), he became governor of Fort St. George (modern Chennai, India) in 1687. Alongside his public duties, Yale also worked as a private trader, specializing in precious stones. This activity linked him farther afield, to the vast markets of China and the Philippines. Returning to England in 1699, Yale was persuaded by the Society for the Propagation of the Gospel (SPG) to patronize an initiative to elevate the Church of England's stature in North America. He donated a small fraction of his wealth to help realize a minor component of the SPG's grand project, the founding of a collegiate school in Connecticut. This school later became a university bearing Yale's name, whose press has published the book you hold in your hands (or, more likely, are reading on your laptop).[12]

The term "seaborne" has a further, practical advantage. It serves to delimit the subject of this book, confining it to the empires forged by the states situated on the periphery of Western Europe. In fact, to use the term "seaborne" is to concede the relative insignificance of these incipient entities. They were minor interlopers in a world largely divided among sprawling Eurasian and indigenous American terrestrial empires. The ambitious arrivistes often were confined to the edges of populous, administratively complex, affluent, sophisticated, massive polities. It is crucial, as historian Philip Curtin argued, to resist "the tendency to read backward from the clear pattern of dominance in the recent past, assuming that it was the case in the earlier period as well."[13] When set against the backdrop of these massive polities—Ottoman, Qing, Mughal, Romanov, Kongolese, Aztec, and Inca, among others—the Western European states described and analyzed in this book appear to be secondary and rather faltering actors in the unfolding global drama of power. Further, before metamorphosing into seaborne empires, these states were peripheral within Europe. The story of their ascent, then, is also one of how the commodities, precious metals, and capital accumulated in the extra-European world helped to transform formerly marginal enclaves into epicenters of geopolitical power.[14]

Armed with this revised understanding, historian Andre Gunder Frank has argued that the "alleged European exceptionalism and whole European miracle are no more than myths firmly based on Eurocentric ideology." He may be correct. Such ideas have undoubtedly infused the writing of European imperial history until recently.[15] While accepting the underlying veracity of Frank's insight, however, it is incontestable that the period from approximately 1620 to 1820, the chronological boundaries of this book, was marked by the explosive expansion of European influence—through trade, conquest, and occupation—at the expense of non-European empires, whether judged by control over territory, trade, or preservation of political sovereignty. The middle of the seventeenth century witnessed the emergence of the Dutch, British, and French as challengers to Iberian dominance in the Atlantic, Indian, and Pacific Oceans, the inception of interimperial rivalry that intensified until the end of the eighteenth century and drove much of the change recounted in this book. The decade of the 1620s also was marked by the quickening pace of the transatlantic slave trade, which galvanized the economies of the European seaborne empires and their successor states. The massive expansion of slavery in the newly independent United States and Brazil in the early nineteenth century, for example, continued well after the Age of Revolutions brought the formal history of the seaborne empires to a close. Brazil, for example, imported almost 2.4 million African slaves between 1800 and the abolition of the slave trade in 1850.[16]

While tracing the gathering strength of the seaborne empires from 1620 to 1820, we need to underscore the agency of those with whom Europeans came into contact. Far from simply accepting unilateral imposition of authority, non-Europeans were anything but passive bystanders or helpless victims. Through defiant resistance, subtle noncompliance, self-serving collaboration, and unilateral action they shaped the processes described in this book.[17] The form that colonialism assumed in a specific place depended on compacts reached, not the unilateral imposition of European power. The "real pattern of conquest," historian John Thornton noted, was a "'politics of alliance,'" which determined the cultural and political "maneuvering room" that indigenous peoples retained (and sometimes gained) after the purported "conquest." While violence always remained an option, and one Europeans availed themselves of habitually, authority was also imposed, retained, and circumscribed by negotiation, alliance, and collaboration. Only with this recognition can historians reinscribe non-European agency into narratives that narrowly victim-centered treatments erase or elide. Historian Gyan Prakash observed that "colonial categories were never instituted without their dislocation and transformation," for the "functioning of colonial power [was] a form of transaction and translation between incommensurable cultures and positions."[18] For this reason, unilateral imposition of power was impracticable. European and indigenous institutions existed side by side; a plurality of legal systems was common. Where compatibility permitted, hybridity was the norm; ideas and belief systems were syncretic; subjects were creolized. Far from stagnant, the societies with which Europeans came into contact often remained dynamic, changing in response to endogenous as well as exogenous stimuli, of which European contact and coercion was merely one among several factors.

By the same token, historians should exaggerate neither the agency nor the foresight of Europeans. The seaborne empires were not, generally speaking, planned enterprises. They were just as often products of weakness as of strength. This observation should not be confused with a claim that empires were acquired in a "fit of absence of mind."[19] It simply is a reminder that anachronism must be avoided; post facto assumptions of inexorability can be wildly misleading. If the arc of a narrative of empire follows a trajectory from first contact to apogee to decline to fall, such a narrative should be regarded with skepticism. Empires were unplanned and chaotic. For this reason, they must be approached ontologically and prospectively. "Rule" often was a belated attempt to profit from the unintended consequences of vast numbers of uncoordinated decisions taken by corporate bodies as well as individuals. When the appellation "empire" or "colony" was used, it often was an attempt to retrofit what had been achieved accidentally or extemporaneously to meet the burgeoning needs and heightened expectations of the metropole.

Not all forays into the non-European world were "imperial" in the strict sense implying intentionality. Spanish officials derided sixteenth- and seventeenth-century English raiders as "Lutheran corsairs." Sometimes, of course, piracy and plunder formed part of a broader geopolitical design. The infamous Henry Morgan, who sacked numerous Spanish Caribbean ports in the seventeenth century, transitioned from outlaw buccaneer to genteel Crown servant. He invested his booty in a Jamaican plantation, earned a knighthood, and eventually ascended to the post of lieutenant governor. Yet even though such a career progression was common, it nurtures a teleological view of European expansion that is simply misleading. In many cases, plunder was an end in itself, or else undertaken to weaken an enemy during war in order to gain a short-term advantage. As historian Kenneth Andrews contended with regard to the Caribbean prior to the mid-seventeenth century, European activities were "an affair of innumerable small ships, obscure promoters and anonymous seamen, so many particles of unorganized drift across the Atlantic." These activities remained "irregular, under-specialized, opportunistic and predatory." It was not the first step of a self-conscious policy of overseas territorial aggrandizement. In many cases, state action was unwieldy because it rested on the cooperation and coordination of private interests. A glance at the English Navy reveals the state's limited capacity to project power unilaterally. Before the eighteenth century, naval campaigns were largely the work of nonstate actors with fitful involvement from the Crown. Queen Elizabeth supplied a mere two of the twenty-five ships in Francis Drake's fleet during his Caribbean campaign of 1585. A mere one-sixth of the vessels that sailed against the 1588 Spanish Armada were Crown ships. Royal chartered companies, too, depended largely on private enterprise. As late as the 1680s, more than three-quarters of the English Royal African Company's ships were hired from private merchants. A similar story could be told for France, where much of the galley fleet before 1660 was provided by private entrepreneurs in exchange for payment. The Dutch, too, relied heavily on merchant ships in military conflicts.[20] Such examples serve to foreground the improvised, multifarious, limited nature of state action in the early modern period.

Even self-consciously "imperial" ventures quickly became extemporized exercises. Elaborate plans and firm intentions were scrambled by economic and political dynamics on the ground, which were animated by their own logics. The EIC's transition from a trading company to the suzerain of South Asia and a global narco-trafficker offers a case in point. The Company did not strive to expand its reach because it valorized territorial aggrandizement for its own sake. Rather, the fiscal demands resulting from its status as both a military despotism and a commercial company necessitated the maintenance of a hundred-thousand-strong army and sufficient Indian manufactures to remit to Britain to underwrite these activities. Indian land revenues paid for the army and counterbalanced the persistent deficit the EIC ran in its trade with both India and China. Before long, ordinary revenues proved insufficient to meet these ever-burgeoning demands. The Company resorted to shipping opium to China, where great profits were realized at the expense of an addiction epidemic. The size of the trade was enormous. Thirty thousand chests were imported into China in 1835, forty thousand a few years later. In the first half of the nineteenth century, opium accounted for up to 15 percent of the government of India's overall receipts.[21]

Europeans were far from omnipotent. They were repulsed from extra-European territories as often as they managed to establish a permanent presence. At least a few of these failures deserve mention, to give some sense of their ubiquity and to further erode any lingering appearance of the inevitability of empire or martial superiority. In North Africa, Spain lost its modest toehold in Tunis in 1574. Four years later, Portugal's King Sebastian mounted an ill-fated crusade in what is modern Morocco, resulting in his death and that of the scions of scores of noble families. Even when claims to territory seized were pressed, efforts were often clumsy and halting. England acquired Tangier in 1661 from the Portuguese but was forced to evacuate ignominiously in 1684, after massive expenditure. The North African (Barbary) regencies held an average of thirty-five thousand Europeans as slaves during the early modern period. In 1640, there were more English slaves in North Africa than there were African slaves under English control in the Caribbean. Even when Britain with its vaunted navy was ascendant, during the seventeenth and eighteenth centuries, more than twenty thousand Britons were taken captive in North Africa, who were released only upon payment of prodigious ransoms.[22]

In the Americas, Europeans seldom fared better. Spanish designs in Florida and the River Plate basin proved at first a dismal failure. Six expeditions to Florida failed between 1513 and 1565, and the first founders of a settlement along the River Plate resorted to cannibalism, failing to establish a permanent foothold until the 1580s. England had fleeting settlements at Roanoke (Virginia) in the 1580s, in the Amazon Delta in the early 1700s, and then at Darien (modern Panama) roughly a century later. In 1643, the Dutch fixed their gaze on Valdivia, in southern Chile, but indigenous people refused to supply them with food and thus forced a hasty evacuation. Between 1667 and 1674, a nascent French settlement in Madagascar was met with hostility from native rulers, and disease claimed the lives of more than two thousand settlers. French efforts to establish a viable colony at Kourou (Guiana) in 1763–1765 was a disaster of massive proportions, with nine thousand of the thirteen thousand settlers perishing from disease.[23] In the Caribbean theater, British forces were decimated by yellow fever and malaria as they sought to conquer territories of other European states. As historian John McNeill observed, "Spain's hold on the region was inexpensively buttressed by mosquitos and microbes." The toll of disease on invaders was ghastly. When Admiral Edward Vernon led twenty-nine thousand soldiers and sailors in amphibious invasions of Santiago de Cuba and Cartagena (1741), twenty-two thousand of his men were dead within a year, a mere one thousand of them battlefield casualties. In the 1762 capture of Havana (Cuba), British forces lost more than a thousand men, the vast majority of whom succumbed to disease, not battle-inflicted wounds, and less than half of the eleven thousand soldiers were fit for duty. Between 1793 and 1796, the British army in the Caribbean lost eighty thousand soldiers and sailors, with at least half of them dying from disease.[24]

The weakness of European states aspiring to dominion outside of Europe manifested in other ways, too. Even the territorial niches over which they exercised nominal sovereignty were dependent on the whims of non-European states. In the eighteenth century, the British colonies of Gibraltar and Minorca, seized from Spain, were provisioned by the non-allied states of Algiers and Morocco.[25] Europeans exerted force overseas only with great difficulty. In the Spanish Empire, for example, the number of regular soldiers sent from Spain to the Americas until the early eighteenth century remained minuscule. There were only six thousand regular troops in all of Spanish America in 1700, and the figure never exceeded fourteen thousand before

1750. The few full-time soldiers were either assigned to the garrisons in strategic port cities (Veracruz, Havana, and Cartagena) or else sent to *presidios*, frontier military outposts, in northern New Spain, southern Chile, and the unpopulated zones of the Río de la Plata (modern Argentina). In 1723, there were nineteen garrisons scattered along the northern Mexico frontier, with a total of a thousand men. The Spanish presence on the empire's southernmost frontier in Chile was slightly larger, where a string of forts manned by a standing force of two thousand faced the indomitable Araucanian Indians.

A further factor hindering empire was the reluctance and ambivalence of European states themselves. The desirability of overseas empire was far from unequivocally and universally supported. The vivid denunciations of Spanish colonial practices by conquistador-turned-bishop Bartolomé de las Casas in the sixteenth century were familiar to all Europeans. The Habsburg dynasty's purported pretensions to universal empire were considered abhorrent, too, but generally it was the misguided or faulty mode and methods by which imperial expansion was pursued that was criticized, not the endeavor itself. It posed a danger to the fragile equipoise of European politics. One can glean occasional glimpses into the crises of conscience accompanying imperial expansion. On a voyage to East Asia in 1690, for example, one Edward Barlow remarked, "But for nations to come and plant themselves in islands and countries by force, and build forts and raise laws, and force the people to customs against their true natures and people of said places without their consent, how will this stand with the law of God and the religion we profess, let the World judge."

Often those less enamored of empire bemoaned its deleterious effects on the metropole. Seventeenth-century Dutch commentators associated their republic's New World forays as generative of folly, vanity, incompetence, avarice, tyranny, and corruption. Earlier positive associations of America with the innocence they attributed to Amerindians, and with which they themselves had identified, dissipated.[26] Contemporary Spanish writers on economics, called *arbitristas,* connected overseas empire and metropolitan decline, both economic and moral. In the eighteenth century, leading European writers took up this theme. Montesquieu, for example, attributed Spain's alleged decline to its mania for precious metals, a mania stimulated by the conquest of the Americas. The situation had become so dire that Spain, he predicted, would soon be eclipsed by its American dominions. Leading *philosophes* Abbé Raynal and Denis Diderot defended a similar position with regard to Portugal. They contended that overseas conquest caused Portugal to lose "the foundation of all real power, which consists in agriculture," adding that all European nations seeking to establish overseas colonies "impair their own strength." Diderot and Raynal's contemporary Adam Smith pilloried the bountiful regulations controlling colonial trade, and the monopoly that each European state strove to maintain over its overseas territories. He derided these efforts as wrong-headed, "a dead weight upon the action of one of the great springs which puts into motion a great part of the business of mankind." They deprived states, both those with and those without colonies, of the benefits they would have derived from less-regulated trade. At the root of Smith's critique was that previous writers on economics had confused wealth with money. The single-minded quest of states for specie and a favorable balance of trade blinded them to the benefits of overseas commerce. Instead, the path they chose led them to empty their treasuries profligately to defend the overseas colonies they misguidedly coveted.[27]

There was a further, noneconomic critique of colonies that emerged in the mid-eighteenth century. Many commentators fretted that the exercise of dominion beyond Europe engendered political and moral corruption. Raynal and Diderot, among others, inquired whether imperial expansion had made humanity, Europeans in particular, happier, more peaceful, or better. Far-flung trade associated with empire aided economic improvement and material progress, they conceded, but the general answer to their rhetorical question was a curt no. Empire had probably left Europeans worse off. Peace, stability, and liberty had been endangered. Overseas, Europeans indulged in arbitrary government. Having found themselves with unchecked power, Raynal and Diderot averred, they arrogantly engaged in cruelty and despotism with impunity. Such conduct sowed the seeds of decadence and corruption at home. In decrying what he considered the abuses of EIC rule in India, parliamentarian and philosopher Edmund Burke declared that he was "certain that every means effectual to preserve India from oppression is a guard to preserve the British constitution from its worst corruption." His contemporary, Scottish historian William Robertson, lamented the "spirit of corruption" that infected European fortune hunters, which they repatriated together with their lucre and baubles: "Their sentiments of honor and of duty gradually relax . . . and [they] become unmindful of what they owe to their sovereign and to their country." Philosopher Jeremy Bentham defended a similar position. He decried the "uselessness and burthensomeness" of colonies. They were sources of corruption in the mother country and provoked conflict with other European nations, since "ill-gotten wealth [became] subject of concupiscence and invasion to swarms of depredators." The dissolution of empire, Bentham believed, would generate significant benefits for all parties involved. Political economist James Mill elaborated on this critique, blaming the quest for colonies for excessive military preparedness.[28] There were, then, many prominent voices within Europe itself critical of numerous facets of empire, if not opposed to it outright.

Recognition of intellectual ambivalence, military weakness, and multiple failures, the dispersed, decentralized, and contingent nature of what we latterly denominate "empire," does not imply exculpatory intent. Nor does it mitigate the depravities Europeans visited upon non-Europeans—whether through conquest, enslavement, or brutal violence—from the Thirty Years' War through the Age of Revolutions. Yet an anti-triumphalist and anti-apologetic narrative need not sacrifice complexity. Appreciation of such complexity does not make a narrative retrograde, atavistic, or neo-Whig in spirit. Instead this book seeks to transcend dualistic depictions of empire and offer a narrative with neither heroes nor villains. After providing a working definition of empire in Chapter 1 and situating Western Europe in a galaxy of formidable world empires in Chapter 2, I narrate the development of the Western European seaborne empires. In Chapter 3, I describe the rise of Spain and Portugal as imperial states before 1600. I then turn, in Chapter 4, to the challenges the Iberian empires faced from England, France, and the Netherlands in the seventeenth century. I seek to highlight interstate competition as the chief galvanizing force of overseas ambitions in the two-century period covered in this book. Chapter 5 continues the narrative into the eighteenth century up to the conclusion of the Seven Years' War in 1763.

Chapters 6 through 11 shift away from blow-by-blow narrative to a consideration of themes crucial to the study of early modern imperial history. I emphasize six themes: political and legal institutions (Chapter 6); political economy (Chapter 7); coerced and voluntary migration (Chapter 8); labor regimes, with an emphasis on slavery (Chapter 9); the creation of mestizo and creole societies (Chapter 10); and the role played by collaboration and resistance in shaping the trajectories of the seaborne empires (Chapter 11). Chapter 12 and the Epilogue return to the narrative mode, though with a sharp analytical edge. Chapter 12 describes the breakdown of the seaborne empires in the Americas and the ricochet effects of their demise across the globe. The Epilogue traces the transitions made by each of the seaborne empires during what was ostensibly an age of imperial contraction, describing how the Age of Revolutions paradoxically set the stage for a new phase of European empire, formal and informal, after 1820.[29]

1. Definitions of "Empire" and Approaches to the Study of Its History

To what extent is it accurate to denominate the Western European states and the overseas territory over which they claimed sovereignty as "empires"? Is "empire" a useful category of analysis? I contend that empire remains the apposite term and appropriate framework, even if it implies that European states exercised a degree of unchallenged authority that current scholarship has debunked. There is no shortage of definitions of empire. As historians John Gallagher and Ronald Robinson observed in the 1950s, "The Imperial Historian . . . is very much at the mercy of his own particular concept of empire. By that, he decides what facts are of 'imperial' significance."[1] In this book, I conceptualize empire as a political phenomenon. This approach goes against the grain of recent historical writing, which has shifted away from political and military history and toward cultural and intellectual history. I have sought to incorporate insights from the more recent historiography, particularly with regard to political culture and the intellectual underpinnings of forms of rule. My approach shies away, though not without misgivings, from what historian Philip Pomper has termed "'soft' Marxian-PostModernism . . . [which] finds in the myriad global transactions of modern capitalism and the cultural products sold by it something called 'empire.'"[2] This book thus can be only a fragment of a much larger history of empire studied from multiple perspectives.

Yet even when we confine our attention to the political aspects of empire, a single, succinct definition remains elusive. The challenge is largely attributable to the variety, range, and complexity of entities that have been designated "empires" by historians. There have been numerous efforts to arrive at a single definition. Here I mention in passing several of the more successful attempts. These tend to treat empire as emerging from overlapping processes involving the imposition of authority by one group upon another, focusing on the asymmetrical relationship established between them. Historian John Darwin argued that empire is "the assertion of mastery (by influence or rule) by one ethnic group, or its rulers, over a number of others." Political scientist William Doyle defined empire as "a relationship, formal or informal, in which one state controls the effective political sovereignty of another political society." Political scientist David Abernethy distilled empire into the "relationships of domination and subordination between one polity (called the metropole) and one or more territories (called colonies) that lie outside of the metropole's boundaries yet are claimed as its lawful possessions." Mastery, control, domination, and subordination are the prominent, common features of these definitions, with good reason. Historian Stephen Howe encompassed these features in a single definition: "An empire is a large, composite, multi-ethnic or multinational political unit, usually created by conquest, and divided between a dominant center and subordinate, sometimes far distant, peripheries."[3]

I find Howe's formulation to be a suitable working definition, provided that it is fleshed out and several caveats are made. First, one must remain cognizant of the violence and unremitting coercion to which subject populations were exposed following the entrenchment of European authority. Dispossession and resource extraction, slavery and other forms of forced labor practices, the suppression of precontact customs and the imposition of alien value systems are part and parcel of all empires. Second, asymmetries of political authority were the norm. Focusing on power differentials between "metropole" and "colonies," as Howe and others have, obscures the operation of what historians Jane Burbank and Frederick Cooper called the "repertoires of imperial power" within territories. These were "strategies empires chose as they incorporated diverse peoples into the polity while sustaining or making distinctions among them."[4] Individuals (and entire groups) could be excluded from participation in civil life, or taxed at varying rates, or made subject to distinct labor regimes on the basis of phenotype, provenance, or genealogy, for example.

Third, Doyle's notion of "control of effective political sovereignty," which is underplayed in Howe's definition of empire, must be foregrounded and nuanced. Indubitably, many European states aspired to such absolute sovereignty. In Jean Bodin's influential 1576 treatise *Les six livres de la république*, the notion of "shared" sovereignty was rejected. Bodin asserted that sovereignty could never be "mixed"; there must exist a single, undisputed center of authority in a political community. Legally, sovereignty meant jurisdiction, the authority over people, things, and territory. Such was the goal European states set for themselves, both within and beyond Europe. Yet centralizing monarchies seldom realized this aspiration: sovereignty was fragmented or shared among numerous groups, including the nobility and the clergy. Beyond Europe, as historian Lauren Benton elucidated, incipient European imperial states "did not claim or produce a monopoly on legal authority or on the assignment of political and legal identity." As a result, quite distinct conceptions of sovereignty operated in the global assemblages historians place under the rubric of empire. Sovereignty was routinely shared and rarely held as a monopoly. For example, the Dutch East India Company (VOC) conceived of sovereignty as a transferable commodity. As historian Adam Clulow argued, it was a "collection of rights—rather than a monolithic or indivisible whole—that could be split up and parceled out to more than one party."[5] Thus, in early modern empires, the partial cession of a "sovereign right" was commonplace, sovereignty was often divided within a single political community, and legal pluralism—simultaneously operating and sometimes overlapping systems of law—was the norm. It was only from the late eighteenth century (if then) that the state possessed the capacity to wield (or was brazen enough to claim) sole jurisdiction (and enforce that claim) where hybrid legal regimes or plural sovereignties had long existed.[6]

But how did those living in the historical period treated in this book understand the entities historians now classify as "empires"? Seventeenth- and eighteenth-century Europeans understood empire in terms of the precedents bequeathed by antiquity. In ancient Rome, as historian Anthony Pagden has explained, the word "imperium" implied "supreme power involving both command in war and the magistrate's right to execute the law." "Imperator" was a generic term to designate all Roman commanders until the second century C.E., when it was limited to refer to the supreme ruler of the Roman world. Until the eighteenth century, "empire" was almost interchangeable with "sovereignty," though it also could be used to classify a government exercising authority over vast territories.[7] In some senses, then, using the term "empire" to describe the vast entities examined in this book is anachronistic. Until the late eighteenth century, very few of the people who inhabited or even governed what today historians call empires understood themselves to be living in one. The term would have been a less than perfect fit. Even the lands over which Charles V (r. 1519–1558) ruled were not, as Pagden explained, "a single *imperium*, but a vast, sprawling cosmopolitan conglomerate, ruled over by an emperor who had no established capital. . . . [It] resembled a modern multinational corporation more than a state. . . . [There was] no common legal system and no single administrative structure."[8] In the centuries before 1800, for many Europeans there was but a single empire: the Holy Roman Empire (*Reich*) of the German nation.

To early modern European ears, the words "colonization" and "colonies" were less dissonant than "empire." Both derive from the Latin word "colere," which can be translated as "to cultivate," "to put to use," "to make of value." In antiquity, this word was used to describe the migration and resettlement of some portion of the population of a given polity to another territory, with the implication that the resulting settlement maintained connections—cultural, economic, political—with the sending community. Historians have devised typologies to differentiate between species of colony, from trading-base or military-base colonies to settlement colonies to colonies of rule. Yet many parts of the world that we understand to have been "colonized" by Europe were not conceived of in this way by contemporaries. For example, it might be remarked off-handedly that the various Spanish-speaking states composing Latin America were once colonies of Spain. Yet in the early modern period, these territories formed part of the "Hispanic Monarchy." Their inhabitants viewed themselves as residing not in a colony but rather in overseas kingdoms subject to the laws of the kingdom of Castile, with rights and duties commensurate with those enjoyed by the inhabitants of the Iberian Peninsula. For this reason, historians have begun to eschew "empire" as a framework of analysis. Increasingly, they prefer terms like "pluri-continental" or "polycentric" monarchy.[9] In addition to avoiding anachronism, there are advantages to such an approach. It dispenses with the center-periphery distinction that often distorts how empires functioned in practice. There were many interlinking "centers" that interacted with one another, not simply with a single metropole in bilateral fashion.

The notable disadvantage of an approach focused on structures and politics, however, is that it can divert attention from the systemic violence and exploitation without which empires could not function. It cannot be denied that "colony" and "empire" were rarely used in Spain, for example, until the end of the eighteenth century, and even then only in internal government documents and not in public decrees or proclamations. Yet nomenclature can be distressingly misleading. Historian Josep Fradera claimed that a focus on the belated and sporadic use of the word "colony" in Spanish produces unforgivable distortions. The organization of the colonial economy, built on forced labor, to say nothing of "annihilating, overpowering and subjugating enormous [indigenous] populations," suggests that the use (or not) of the word "colony" by contemporaries scarcely matters when assessing the character of Spain's empire.[10]

Terminology is merely one of the obstacles complicating the study of the European seaborne empires. Another is the prism of modern nationalism through which empires are often studied. Some historical writing gives the impression that empires were in some way "national" enterprises and followed a "special path" (in German, *Sonderweg*) distinct from the others. The notion of an imperial *Sonderweg* is deeply rooted in historical writing. As they sought to justify their aggressive actions against Catholic Spain (and Portugal) in the early seventeenth century, the nascent Protestant powers—the Dutch and English—constructed a narrative about Iberian conduct both beyond and within Europe that is referred to as the "Black Legend." The Protestant powers accused Spain, in particular, of aspiring to universal monarchy. It was a barbarous destroyer of America's indigenous peoples and, in the words of Pagden, an "inflexible, illiberal, and ultimately corrupting tyranny." This derogatory depiction has had a long afterlife, nurtured in various quarters. Through the end of the eighteenth century, the purported backwardness and barbarism of Spanish rule in the Americas was contrasted with Britain's allegedly enlightened posture. Britons conceived of their empire as commercial, based on trade and settlement. They distinguished this foundation from the brute force that they alleged characterized the Spanish Empire. Commerce depended on liberty, the argument ran, and commerce was the foundation of geopolitical greatness. Britain thus erected an empire on the foundation of liberty.[11]

In the nineteenth-century United States, writers as diverse as Washington Irving, George Tichnor, William H. Prescott, and Henry Wadsworth Longfellow depicted Spain as the antithesis of Anglo-America. Latin American liberals similarly looked aghast at the colonial heritage of their new nations and appropriated the Black Legend for their own purposes. Predictably, Spaniards rejected this portrayal and sought to replace it with an equally cartoonish and flattering characterization. Beginning in the late eighteenth century, Spain blocked the dissemination of histories written by foreigners that were believed to disparage Spain's conduct in the extra-European world. The Archive of the Indies (Archivo de Indias), in Seville, was established to compile documents from which a "true" history of the Spanish Empire could be written, an archive that all historians of colonial Latin America rely on to this day. This effort continued into the nineteenth century. As Spanish statesman and dramatist Francisco Martínez de la Rosa exclaimed in the 1840s, "Much of this glory [of spreading 'civilization'] belongs to Spain. This fact indemnifies my country against so many false accusations, so many calumnies propagated against her. Few nations have treated their colonies with such wisdom and kindness; few have ruled them with laws so favorable to the indigenous population."[12]

Such apologetics aside, the Black Legend won out and shows few signs of abating. It gathers strength in spite of scholarship demonstrating that Spanish "absolutism" in the Americas was more aspiration than reality. In a recent influential sociological study of the colonial origins of comparative development, the authors argued that Spanish colonialism "produced predatory states and dysfunctional markets," whereas British colonialism bequeathed "the rule of law, effective administration, and competitive markets."[13] More broadly, derogatory national stereotypes, tropes, and sometimes inaccurate overgeneralizations have thwarted the study of the European seaborne empires.

Yet the problem cannot be solved by shedding disparaging national stereotypes alone. It lies deeper, with the very use of the term "nation" in imperial context. Various "nations" and forms of "nationalism" were emerging, but these were far from fully formed. With regard to Britain in the eighteenth century, historian Linda Colley argued that it was a "patchwork in which uncertain areas of Welshness, Scottishness and Englishness were cut across by strong regional attachments and scored over again by loyalties to village, town, family and landscape."[14] When historians use the shorthand of "Britain," moreover, they must account for its permanent dynastic alliance with the German electorate of Hanover. Statements to similar effect could be made about Spain and France as late as 1800, and, to a lesser extent, of the smaller states of Portugal and the Dutch Republic, too.

It is misleading even to speak of "national" armies in the early modern period. They were "Noah's Ark armies," with soldiers drawn from across Europe and beyond. The bulk of soldiers in the late sixteenth-century

"Spanish" military, for example, were foreign mercenaries. When we turn to categorizing overseas territories, the situation is even more complex. Certainly, there were "English," "French," or "Portuguese" colonies in the sense that more or less well-defined territorial units were claimed by individual European states against the claims of their rivals. Yet within those territories, heterogeneity prevailed. Early "British" North America, for example, was inhabited by a "mixed multitude" drawn from many European territories and linguistic-cultural groups. Tangier, nominally an English colony, followed a similar pattern, with its multiplicity of nationalities, cultures, and religions. New Netherland (later New York), too, was marked by a hybrid population due to the diversity of languages and national origins there. In 1658, there were so many French speakers that official documents were printed in French as well as English and Dutch. By 1665, a full quarter of all marriages in the Dutch Reformed Church were exogenous ones. Many of the soldiers serving the Dutch East Indian and West Indian Companies were not Dutch. Foreigners often held key posts. The Dutch garrison in Luanda (modern Angola) in the 1640s was commanded by an Englishman, while in the late eighteenth century Batavia (now Indonesia) was defended by regiments of German and Swiss mercenaries.[15]

Borders and boundaries were often blurred, further complicating the study of empire in a hermetically sealed national context. In the interior of South America before 1750, the line separating Spanish from Portuguese territory was fuzzy. The frontier was, as historian Tamar Herzog noted, "chaotic, hazardous, and lacking a firm juridical basis." Border disputes were not handled by diplomats alone but often were determined by the accretions (and later formalization) of myriad quotidian actions, involving "who sent their horses to pasture where, who built a hut and who collected fruit." While eventually firm boundaries would be enshrined in treaties, the porosity of the frontier remained its defining feature. In this interstitial space, jurisdiction, sovereignty, and nation were destabilized. It often remained impervious to efforts to impose order. Sovereignty, as Benton convincingly noted, depended on "recurring proofs, including mapping, description, the founding of political communities, ceremonies recognizing new vassals, and administrative acts designed to support claims to discovery and possession."[16]

The polyglot, intercultural nature of the seaborne empires also resulted from the number of territories changing hands as a result of interimperial war and peace. The Caribbean islands of St. Croix and St. Lucia, for example, were swapped multiple times as chips in peace negotiations, while Jamaica was seized from Spain by England in the 1650s. The Dutch conquered and held the northeast of Brazil, as well as the Angolan littoral, for almost three decades in the seventeenth century before they were dislodged by the Portuguese. In the eighteenth century, the vast territory of New France passed from French to British control as a result of warfare, while other morsels, such as Louisiana, came under Spain's sway as compensation for its ill-fated alliance with France during the Seven Years' War. In all of these cases, the conflicts arising from differences in language, customs, and law were legion, and the transitions were often protracted and contentious.

Even in the regions over which Europeans laid claim and divided among themselves, their sway was far from absolute. Quite apart from the active resistance they encountered, described in Chapters 11 and 12, individuals routinely transgressed the official boundaries of empire or operated (and flourished) at their intersection. An important consequence of the relative weakness of governments' ability to enforce rules and norms prior to 1800 was that many lives and livelihoods were trans-imperial. Interimperial commerce, whether licit traffic or illicit contraband, was one such arena. The thriving Port and Madeira wine trade, for example, connected a range of producers, merchants, and consumers across the Atlantic Ocean, from the vineyard-laden valleys of northern Portugal to the dining rooms of patrician planters in the Chesapeake. This sort of activity transpired precisely in the period during which governments strove to limit the commercial undertakings of their subjects to their respective imperial systems. The aspirations of empires often exceeded their grasp. Even though it is accurate to imagine the early modern world as divided into empires, the considerable number of spaces, places, and people in between, who operated outside empires, or on their porous and sometimes overlapping boundaries, must be kept in mind. The multinational character of Europe's overseas territories persisted well into the nineteenth century, purportedly the age of national empires. Of the hundred thousand inhabitants of Algiers, capital of France's North African colony of Algeria, just under seventy thousand were Europeans, drawn from at least fourteen countries, of whom only thirty thousand were French.[17]

If demography and commercial circuits prod us away from anachronistic "national" frameworks, the features common to those empires examined here do, too. Many decades ago, historian Charles Verlinden remarked on the absurdity of studying medieval colonization through a "national" lens. Instead he pleaded for historians to recognize the prevalence of "reciprocal contacts and influences" and the "common origin, however diverse the nuances may be," of the Atlantic empires. Verlinden was referring chiefly to common Roman (and Greek) precedents and antecedents that structured the worldviews of the medieval empire builders he studied, but their influence did not fade. Far from it. As historian Thomas Dandelet argued with regard to the Renaissance, "Widespread dissemination of imperial literary, political and aesthetic ideals deriving from ancient Roman precedents created a common political culture and ambition throughout Western Europe" that undergirded overseas colonial ventures.[18] The shared repertoires of rule and common ideological taproot of the seaborne empires must always be kept in mind.

English Protestants and Spanish Catholics, for example, relied on similar discourses to justify their New World enterprises. They cited biblically sanctioned violence to vanquish demons and devils and thus conquer the newly encountered territories for their Christian God.[19] The world beyond Europe could be an inferno, but it also stoked hopes of finding an earthly paradise to redeem fallen humanity. It could be the site of utopian fantasies as often as a theater where deep-seated fears played out.[20] Yet claims to sovereignty ultimately were predicated on alleged inferiority of non-Europeans, and these justifications had a long pedigree. The ancient and medieval heritage included unflattering if not outright disparaging portrayals of the world beyond Europe. From Aristotle came the notion of "slaves by nature," that some groups are innately suited for perpetual servitude. Humoral, geographical, and climatological theories merged to reinforce Aristotelian ideas. It was widely accepted that inhabitants of regions marked by great heat or cold were inferior to those who lived in more temperate climates, like that of Mediterranean Europe. Deemed incapable of higher things, non-European peoples might justifiably be subordinated.[21] These ideas, prejudices, and notions were held in common and informed the enterprises of all five of the seaborne empires to a greater or lesser extent.

These preconceptions were forerunners of early modern notions of the extra-European world as characterized by arbitrary despotism, deviant sexuality and exotic eroticism, deformity, and unnatural monstrosity. Subsequently, eighteenth-century writers, like Georges-Louis Leclerc, Comte de Buffon, and Cornelius de Pauw, revived older theories concerning the effects of terrain, climate, and other environmental factors on the development of flora and fauna, including humans. Such theories, now with a scientific veneer, were deployed to account for the gap Europeans perceived between a supposedly torpid Asia and themselves, to say nothing of Amerindians' inferiority. Europeans' grandiosity was founded upon the belief that human societies beyond Europe remained mired in an earlier stage of human development. Some Europeans subscribed to what has been termed the "Four Stages Theory," the notion that societies progress consecutively through four stages of development, each of which is linked to a different mode of subsistence and concomitant political, legal, social, and moral orders. According to this model, hunting was the most primitive economic mode, whereas commerce was considered the most advanced. The previous high esteem Europeans expressed for Asian civilizations, particularly those of India and China, also waned by the late eighteenth century, as scientific and technological gauges came to inform and structure European assessments.[22]

Sharing a common intellectual taproot proved important, but perhaps of equal significance was the evolution of each empire in close proximity to its rivals due to geography, war and commercial competition, and intellectual connections. Persistent interpenetration, overlap, and repeated convergence have prompted some historians to contend that the histories of the various European empires are "entangled." They can be neither disaggregated easily nor studied as individual cases. As historian Eliga Gould explained with regard to British and Spanish America, it is crucial to "examine interconnected societies. Rather than insisting on the comparability of their subjects, or the need for equal treatment, entangled histories are concerned with 'mutual influencing,' 'reciprocal or asymmetric perceptions,' and 'intertwined processes of constituting one another.'"[23]

That competition was among the principal driving forces of European imperial expansion has already been noted. It often prompted a state to depict its rivals in disparaging terms, as the Black Legend suggests. Yet belligerence must not shroud how competition operated in practice. Rhetoric aside, it promoted the convergence of institutions across empires as much as it accentuated distinctions. As the eighteenth-century Portuguese statesman the first Marquis of Pombal admitted, "All European nations have improved themselves through reciprocal imitation; each one carefully keeps watch over the actions taken by the others. All of them take advantage of the utility of foreign inventions." Conflict, paradoxically, proved to be an impetus to the emulation of one state's institutions and policies by another. Historian

Richard Drayton revealed that British policy makers drew heavily on the ideas and practices of their French archrivals, especially in the areas of political economy and administration. Faced with mounting defensive and fiscal pressures, reformers in all states necessarily coveted, and sought to reproduce, successfully implemented policy innovations. Statesmen thus mingled cosmopolitan sensibilities with patriotic allegiance and were committed to employing the common European stock of ideas to bolster the position of their respective states.[24]

Interimperial cooperation was commonplace, even in the immediate aftermath of protracted war. Licit trade, not plunder or contraband, dominated relations between states in Europe itself. In the 1650s and 1660s, on the heels of eighty years of war against Spain, for example, the Dutch dominated the legal reexport trade within Europe of goods and products from Spanish America, including indigo, cochineal, and, above all, silver. Though the Dutch cultivated little sugarcane themselves, their merchants supplied half of the refined sugar consumed in Europe, whereas the Dutch West Indian Company's ships sold fifty-seven thousand African slaves to Spanish, French, and Dutch markets. If in the seventeenth and eighteenth centuries extra-European spaces were sites of seemingly interminable war among European nations, this situation changed in the first half of the nineteenth century. As historian David Todd argued, conflict gave way to a type of "cooperative emulation" that permitted European countries to use their military-technological superiority jointly to establish political dominance over, and to "civilize," the non-European world.[25]

Having developed a working definition of empire and having discussed several pitfalls to the study of empire, I should now describe the geographical parameters of the seaborne empires treated in the chapters that follow. This task is more difficult than it appears at first glance. As Pagden acknowledged, "'Europe' was, and always has been, a highly unstable term. No one has ever been certain quite where its frontiers lie." Some scholars have argued that such delineations are guided by ideology: "By positing a continental divide between Europe and Asia, western scholars were able to reinforce the notion of a cultural dichotomy between these 2 areas, a dichotomy that was essential to modern Europe's identity as a civilization." Regardless of the boundaries chosen and the reasons for choosing them, defining the extent of Western Europe's seaborne empires is distressingly confounding. Nominally European enclaves, coastal trading fortresses, territorial toeholds beyond continental Europe and its adjacent islands proliferated in the late fourteenth century, and their numbers exploded in the fifteenth century and thereafter. By the early sixteenth century, in part due to navigational advances and auxiliary innovations, such as shipboard cannon, they dotted the littorals of Africa and parts of Asia. But rarely did they amount to much more than trading posts with a garrison and a fluid constituency of merchants, artisans, seamen, and administrators. In Asia, for example, the Dutch VOC had eleven thousand employees at its zenith (c. 1690), with the lion's share based on the island of Java. But these employees were dispersed across the Indian and Pacific Oceans. The total number of soldiers, seamen, artisans, and administrators based at the largest fortress, Batavia, was 2,700.[26]

Of course, some of these outposts were anything but transient beachheads. Sometimes they exerted tremendous influence in the African and Asian societies with which they came into contact, whether through the slave trade or "legitimate commerce." Small islands and continental toeholds were often bitterly contested because of their great strategic value. After 1650, the Caribbean entrepôts of Curação and St. Eustatius enabled the Netherlands to defy Spain's trade regulations and establish robust commercial links with Spanish America. After 1700, territories Britain seized from rival empires—Gibraltar and Minorca from Spain, Cyprus and the Ionian islands from the Ottomans—were crucial in establishing the hegemony of the Royal Navy in the Mediterranean.

Yet in spite of their longevity and influence, smaller enclaves were marked by an impermanence of a different sort: the absence of government beyond executive fiat; scant cultural or institutional complexity; the presence of few women, children, or kinship structures; scarce territorial settlement; and paltry urbanization. These forays and beachheads, even those of long duration, are excluded from this brief survey. Occasionally, such coastal trading fortresses became launching pads for incursions into the interior and the foundation of colonies with more diversified social structures, larger European populations, multifaceted economic activities, elaborated customs, and other markers of complex societies. The case of the Dutch in South Africa offers a prime example of such an initially unplanned trajectory. The VOC primarily wished to create a refueling station to victual passing ships with fruits and vegetables. Not until 1707 were Dutch settlers (free burghers) designated the sole suppliers to Cape Town and the ships that anchored there en route to or from the East.[27] Another prime example is the EIC, which ultimately used coastal trading fortresses in South Asia as lily pads of territorial aggrandizement.

The territories claimed by European states in the Americas greatly exceeded their effective dominion, from the beginning until the end of the colonial period. Just after Columbus's landfall in the Caribbean yet prior to European contact with mainland northern South America, the Iberian monarchies, Spain and Portugal, divided the territories they believed they would find (but had not yet encountered) along a meridian 370 leagues (approximately 2,061 kilometers) west of the Cape Verde islands. According to the Treaty of Tordesillas (1494), Spain would exercise sovereignty to the west of that line of demarcation, with Portugal exercising sovereignty over territory to the east of it. After Portugal landed on the eastern coastal fringe of what became Brazil in 1500, South America was divided between Portugal and Spain. Spain's claims extended to North America, too, but its capacity to exert control over territories north of modern Mexico remained slight. The Iberian empires sought to found empires in Asia as well. Portugal established what became the Estado da Índia early in the sixteenth century, based at Goa, but with tentacles stretching into East Africa, Ceylon (Sri Lanka), and points farther east. Spain was absent from the Indian Ocean, but it considered the Pacific Ocean to be its own "lake," a *mare clausum*. The most significant possession was the Philippines, which would remain part of the Spanish Empire until the final years of the nineteenth century. In its early years, the Philippines were the transit point through which Mexican silver was funneled for trade with China.

Other European nations rejected these claims and contested Iberian hegemony, as Chapter 4 describes. The French supervised settlements in modern-day Canada (particularly Quebec) and also claimed several Caribbean islands, most notably Martinique, Guadeloupe, and Saint-Domingue. They established a string of forts along the waterways of what is now the Midwest of the United States. Following the Reformation, the ascendant Protestant powers, England and the Dutch Republic, launched their own imperial ventures in the New World. The more permanent fruits of a century of conflict were, for England, a chain of colonies along the eastern seaboard of North America, with population and economic centers in Virginia and Massachusetts, a string of islands in the Caribbean, of which the most important were Jamaica and Barbados, and a foothold on the northern coast of South America (Guyana). As for the Dutch Republic, transient conquests of the northeast of Brazil and settlements in what is now New York State had evaporated by the mid-seventeenth century, leaving it with several Caribbean islands, notably Curaçao, and a South American toehold, Surinam. The Dutch and English preyed on Portugal's Indian Ocean empire, expelling the Portuguese and installing themselves in their stead, chiefly through the mechanism of privileged trading companies, discussed in Chapter 7.

By 1700, the outlines of settlement were clearly defined. There was an Iberosphere in South America, Mesoamerica, and parts of what is now the North American West. There was an Anglosphere in the eastern fringes of North America, with a further zone of dominance to the north, in modern Canada, shared with France. And there was a Lusosphere across an enormous swathe of South America, though settlement was largely confined to the coast until the early eighteenth century. The circum-Caribbean in the eighteenth century was a territorial hodgepodge, with France, Spain, Britain, and the Dutch Republic holding a shifting portfolio of islands and mainland footholds. Tobago, Trinidad, Belize, Louisiana, Florida, St. Lucia all changed hands. Of course, grand claims to sovereignty could be misleading. Before 1750, European territorial settlement in North and South America was largely confined to the littorals and isolated population centers in the interior, usually developed around mines from which precious metals and stones were extracted. Whether due to Amerindian dominance, population scarcity, disease, or the absence of economic incentives, effective dominion eluded Europeans in many of the territories they claimed to rule. Outside the Atlantic, European claims were rather more modest until the eighteenth century, as described in previous paragraphs. With the exception of scores of coastal fortresses specializing in the slave trade, and a smattering of settlements in what is now Senegal (by France) and Angola (by Portugal), there was no significant African territory integrated into the seaborne empires. The situation was rather different in the Indian Ocean, where British penetration of the Indian subcontinent intensified after mid-century, and in the Pacific, at least after the British founded the penal colony at Botany Bay, Australia, in the final decade of the century. As late as 1750, however, European domination was far from complete and anything but secure. As Chapter 2 demonstrates, the European seaborne empires were dwarfed in scope and scale by the terrestrial empires of Eurasia until the dawn of the nineteenth century.

2. Western Europe in a World of Empires

In the seventeenth and eighteenth centuries, Europe's seaborne empires were comparatively minor players in a world dominated by the massive land-based polities of Eurasia. Except in the Americas, Europeans were relegated to the peripheries of the Safavid, Mughal, Ottoman, Romanov, and Manchu (and later Qing) empires, and sub-Saharan African polities. The world economic system then coalescing was centered on Asia until at least 1750. China and South Asia produced inexpensive, high-quality cotton and silk textiles, which Europeans and others (including Africans) fervently desired, to say nothing of their voracious demand for spices and tea. The interest was unrequited. Europeans produced nothing sought by South and East Asian consumers. As a consequence of the lack of reciprocity, Europeans were compelled to pay for Asian manufactured goods, spices, and tea in specie (gold and silver), the internationally recognized medium of exchange. Silver was the basis of the Chinese monetary system, and thus it has been argued that it was Chinese demand for silver that drove up its price. Regardless of whether it was demand for tea (and sundry spices) that caused Europeans to pay for it in silver or Chinese demand for silver that drove the transaction, China (and India) ultimately absorbed much of the silver extracted from the mines of Spanish America. As late as the eighteenth century, precious metals dominated Europe's trade with Asia. For example, they accounted for 70 percent of the value of cargoes sent by the French Compagnie des Indes to Asia between 1725 and 1769. New World silver thus bought Europeans access, but they remained bit players in the vast, variegated world of Asian trade. They were compelled to adapt themselves to the existing rules of the game.[1]

Silver was undoubtedly the indispensable lubricant in East-West transactions, but it must be remembered that Asian products were the very lifeblood of world trade. Sometimes they were valued more highly than specie. South Asian textiles, for example, were often a preferred medium of exchange. In Indonesia, the prices of spices were given in terms of length of Indian cloth, not precious metals. European states participated in Asian trade either directly or via intermediary trading companies, which are discussed in Chapters 6 and 7. The most important of these trading companies functioned as, in historian K. N. Chaudhuri's phrase, a "central distribution agency in marketing the commodities of Asia throughout the world." The Dutch VOC exemplifies how immense profits could be reaped without large-scale territorial conquest, chiefly by processing and then redistributing Asian products both to Europe and to other, secondary Asian ports. In fact, the VOC's business model was premised on intra-Asian trade. At its peak, the VOC sent twenty-five ships to Asia each year but dispatched forty ships along the Asian monsoon trading routes. They obtained and exchanged Asian, not European, products. This intra-Asian trade accounted for 90 percent of the VOC's total income in the late seventeenth century. The directors of the VOC—the Heren XVII (Seventeen Gentlemen)—called this trade "the soul of the company . . . if the soul decays the entire body would be destroyed." The British EIC's intra-Asian trade was similarly robust. Prior to 1650, it was a major supplier of coffee from Yemen to Persia and India, and sold this luxury consumable at an enormous profit.[2]

Trade was one thing, dominion quite another. Any aspirations to territorial expansion harbored by Europeans were thwarted by highly evolved, land-based empires in Eurasia. The realms of the Ottomans in western Asia and North Africa and of the Mughals in South Asia were agglomerations of heterogeneous territories, governed by dynastic rulers who derived much of their income from taxes on agriculture and, to a lesser extent, imposts on commerce. The Qing dynasty succeeded the Ming in the 1640s, following an extended period of administrative unraveling, and soon ruled vast swathes of East and Southeast Asia. The Qing state deployed an elaborate and sophisticated administrative apparatus that relied on myriad checks and balances to ensure obedience to directives from the imperial center. The empire was governed by a cadre of civil servants, drawn from across China, who had passed a series of intensely competitive exams and underwent rigorous training. Knowledge of diverse territories was enhanced by state-sponsored cartography, ethnography, and translation projects.[3] The Qing thus enjoyed

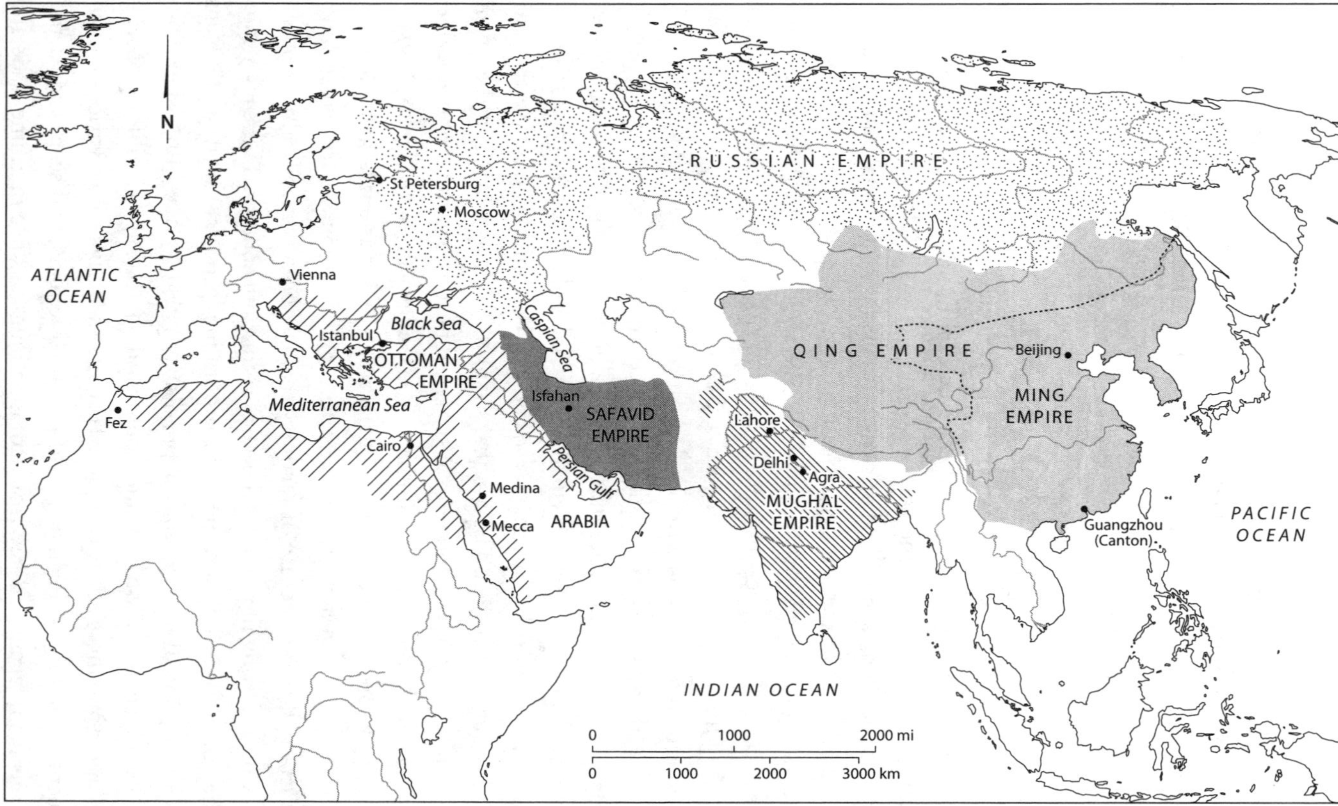

Figure 3. The Eurasian empires circa 1700

a level of uniformity, competence, and authority entertained by Western European statesmen in reverie.

For the two centuries before 1750, Asia's Muslim empires were in the midst of territorial expansion. Following the conquest of Constantinople in 1453, the Ottomans established themselves firmly in both the eastern Mediterranean and Central Asia. Under the rule of Sultan Suleyman the Magnificent (r. 1520–1566), the empire experienced a veritable golden age. Though it suffered a massive naval defeat—with twenty thousand dead and almost twenty ships either captured or destroyed—at the hands of a confederation of Catholic states at the Battle of Lepanto (1571), this loss proved to be a mere blip in what was otherwise a string of successes. In the century after Lepanto, Ottoman armies subdued much of Eastern and parts of Central Europe. They reached the gates of Vienna in 1683. Ultimately, the ninety-thousand-strong army lifted its siege of the Habsburg capital, but this defeat resulted from its own strategic missteps, not European military prowess or technological superiority. If anything, the rapidity and extent of its European conquests, especially those in the Balkans, overstretched the Ottoman state. The new dominions yielded less revenue than the cost of their retention and administration, creating long-term fiscal problems.

Other Asian states sought to exert control over new territories, people, and resources at the same time. The major rival of the Ottomans on their eastern frontier was the Safavid dynasty. Under Shah Abbas I (r. 1571–1629), the Safavids absorbed much of Iraq and imposed Shi'a Islam across the territories they controlled. The Mughal Empire, too, was waxing in the seventeenth century. When Emperor Akbar died in 1605, 110 million people lived within the borders of the Mughal state. Under Aurangzeb (r. 1658–1707), much of southern India was conquered, even if it was left largely unassimilated. The Qing state, tailor-made to mobilize resources for expansionist warfare, doubled the size of territory that had been controlled by its predecessor, the Ming dynasty, by the early eighteenth century. The Qing tripled the size of the population by incorporating peoples—such as Tibetans, Uighurs, and Burmese—never previously ruled by the Ming. The Qing encouraged the westward and southward migration of millions of Han Chinese into these newly conquered provinces. They offered various inducements to migrants, including land grants, free tools, and seed, and exemptions from taxation. They frowned upon long-distance maritime trade and, from the 1650s, explicitly forbade their subjects from engaging in it, a policy with profound consequences. This restriction notwithstanding, at its height the Qing ruled an empire of five hundred million people, with a standing army just shy of a million soldiers.[4] To give some sense of the enormity of this figure, bear in mind that in 1800 metropolitan Spain's entire population was 10.5 million, France's twenty-six million, Britain's (including Ireland's) fourteen million, and Portugal's three million.[5]

Another Eurasian empire embarked on a path toward territorial aggrandizement in the late seventeenth century was Russia, ruled by the Romanov dynasty from 1613. Before 1700, Russian influence chiefly spread westward into the Baltic, Poland, and Ukraine. The Romanov tsars relied on alliances with local elites, who essentially administered these peripheral regions in exchange for oaths of fealty (and contributions to the royal coffers). They were induced to cooperate in exchange for the recognition and protection of their privileges, property, and status. Unsurprisingly, given the success of this scheme, there were few systematic attempts at Russification, resulting in a de facto policy of religious and cultural toleration.[6]

Russian influence also spread eastward, expanding into Siberia. Perhaps a tenth of the annual revenues that accrued to the Kremlin in the seventeenth century were proceeds of the sale of hundreds of thousands of animal pelts shipped from Siberia. The ad hoc, extemporized nature of Russian empire building would change after 1700. Under Peter the Great (r. 1689–1725), Russia embarked on a multipronged, systematic program of administrative and military overhaul. He managed to rein in Russia's powerful landed nobility, long autonomous, and created incentives for its members to serve the increasingly centralized state. The principal mechanism was the "Table of the Ranks," introduced in 1722, which tied state service to social status. This somewhat meritocratic system also attracted ambitious commoners (though not serfs) who endeavored to ascend the ranks. In extraordinary cases, as a reward for exemplary service, whether military or civil, commoners could receive a heritable noble title.[7]

Deeply enamored of Western and Central European military technology and culture, the tsar signaled Russia's entry into European affairs by constructing a new, westward-facing capital, St. Petersburg. The Russian Army and Navy were revamped. During the Great Northern War waged against Sweden from 1700, Peter raised an army of four hundred thousand peasants, and over the course of his reign more than a thousand naval ships were built. War making was his chief concern, and military affairs consumed three-quarters of the state budget. Military might, and the need to generate revenues sufficient to maintain this strength, spurred territorial expansion and the absorption of a panoply of peoples across Central Asia. By the 1780s, ethnic Russians composed less than half the population ruled by the Romanov dynasty, a statistic that highlights the speed and scope of this territorial expansion because the ethnic Russian population itself nearly doubled over the course of the century.[8]

Elsewhere, beyond Asia, European advance was impeded by the presence of other empires—as well as microbes. In the early nineteenth century, much of West Africa was absorbed into the Sokoto Caliphate, which extended over four hundred thousand square kilometers, in which sharia law was administered by the thirty emirs who ruled its component units.[9] When the Spaniards reached central Mexico in 1519, they encountered the Aztecs at the height of their power, following their subjugation of most of the Valley of Mexico during the preceding two centuries. They had united these conquered territories through taxation and tribute. Resident tribute collectors constituted the very sinews of the Aztec Empire. Behind these tax collectors stood a formidable army to enforce the payment of tribute and suppress dissent within the empire. In Andean South America, the Incas were the dominant power by the fourteenth century. They exerted their authority along a network of twenty-five thousand kilometers of roads. Unlike the Aztecs, the Incas governed a decentralized empire, with no fewer than eighty provinces and 150 districts. On the subject people, the Incas imposed, a rotational labor system, called the *mit'a,* later adopted by the Spaniards. Labor was employed in various enterprises, from tending to agricultural lands held by the state to constructing roads, bridges, fortresses, temples, palaces, terraces, and the like. In North America, the Comanches were the "Lords of the South Plains," a territory that at its peak exceeded that controlled by Europeans north of the Rio Grande. Though largely decentralized, the Comanches nevertheless held the Spanish, British, and French at bay, obtaining considerable resources from them in the process. As historian Pekka Hämäläinen observed, the Comanches benefited from the presence of Euro-American colonists who lined the border with "formally autonomous but economically subservient and dependent outposts that served as economic access points" to European empires.[10]

The massive land-based empires of Eurasia and the Americas not only impeded European territorial expansion but also defined the terms of interaction and exchange. The scope of European activities was limited by the parameters those political entities defined, whether as traders, mercenaries, or missionaries. As previously noted, Europeans were interlopers in a well-established trading world. They boasted few desirable products of their own to trade besides precious metals (after 1500). Like the Dutch VOC, they necessarily turned to the coastal transshipment trade. European ascendancy, ephemeral in the most optimal of circumstances, remained largely contingent on the acquiescence, collaboration, or absence of non-Europeans. Even the Portuguese Estado da Índia, in one historian's phrase, was "no more than a collection of territorial niches and mercantile networks, the latter peopled by traders who were often anxious to keep the state at arm's length." European maritime activity was tolerated for the benefits it brought. Contact with Europeans opened new markets for Asian products, whether Iranian silk or Indian textiles. The Safavids benefited from a notable influx of silver as a result of this contact. It decreased their dependence on overland trade routes through the territory of their Ottoman rivals. The Mughals derived significant customs revenue from the export trade conducted by the British and Dutch East India Companies. To grasp how lucrative trade could be, consider that in 1678 alone the specie gained from taxing commerce with Europeans underwrote the maintenance of seventeen thousand cavalrymen.[11]

Nor were the Asian empires alone in deriving advantage from European commercial forays. Trade with Europeans could be used strategically to transform internal political dynamics, too. Permitting the establishment of European enclaves could bring advantages. In the 1560s, Kongo's King Álvaro I requested military assistance from the Portuguese to regain his throne after he had been deposed. The Portuguese, whose slave trade relied on their alliance with Kongo, dispatched six hundred soldiers and restored Álvaro. In early nineteenth-century Hawaii, Chief Kamehameha fomented trade in sandalwood and otter fur in exchange for European firearms but forbade land ownership by foreigners. He gained the upper hand over his indigenous rivals and united the archipelago in less than a decade. Non-European states could harness European coercive action to pursue their own objectives. As the British Navy sought to suppress the Indian Ocean slave trade in the first decades of the nineteenth century, the ruler of the Merina kingdom in Highland Madagascar, Radama I, exchanged a pledge to abolish the slave trade in his realm for the training of his military by the British. The resulting fighting force enabled him to exercise suzerainty over much of Madagascar.[12]

Europeans needed Asian rulers and merchants, not the other way around. Reliance was neither mutual nor reciprocal. From their earliest sixteenth-century incursions into Asia, European explorers and traders were held in low regard, if not contempt. At the Mughal court and elsewhere in Southeast Asia, the Portuguese were disparaged as a barbaric, uncouth, ill-mannered people. The officials of the VOC sought unsuccessfully to claim sovereignty in Japan in the early seventeenth century, but they were soon forced, in order to gain access to markets and products, to recast themselves as loyal, obedient vassals of the Shogun. Such views concerning European inferiority lingered well into the eighteenth century. As the Chinese Qianlong emperor bluntly put the matter in a letter to Britain's George III, "The productions of our empire are manifold, and in great abundance; nor do we stand in the least need of the produce of other countries. China in particular affords tea, earthenware, silk and other materials. All of these are in great request, both in your own and the other kingdoms of Europe."[13] Europeans were limited to operate in a special commercial zone outside the main port city of Canton (Guangzhou) after 1757, greatly limiting their influence and contact.

Only in the nineteenth century were Europeans positioned to stanch the flow of silver to Asian economies. In India-grown opium the British finally found a product Chinese consumers wanted, and they no longer obtained their tea with silver. Britain's burgeoning textile industry diminished demand for Indian finished cotton goods. Rather, their textiles flooded the South Asian market. Indian imports of cotton fabrics rose from one million yards in 1814 to fifty-one million in 1830. Britain's industrial revolution reversed the flow of trade and prompted the deindustrialization of India.[14]

But such a reversal lay far in the future. The Qianlong emperor's boast was well founded at the moment of its utterance. Porcelain, chintz, and lacquerware were the chief manifestations of a ubiquitous chinoiserie fad. European infatuation with Indian cotton textiles, too, approached manic proportions. It prompted Daniel Defoe to lament that imported textiles had "crept into our houses, our closets and bed chambers, curtains, cushions, chairs and at last beds themselves were nothing but calicoes or Indian stuffs." Though they were more proximate rivals than the distant Chinese, the Ottomans also fascinated Europeans, particularly in the eighteenth century, after the threat of military invasion abated. A fad for Turkish culture found expression in the rise of Ottoman-style coffeehouses. No fewer than thirty-seven London coffeehouses were named "The Turk's Head," and many of these doubled as *bagnios* or *hummums* on the Ottoman model. In opera, Handel's *Tamerlane* (1724) and Mozart's *Abduction from the Seraglio* (1782) were the best-known variations on a common theme, whereas in fashion, the taste for bright silks and billowing trousers thinly disguised their Ottoman inspiration.[15]

It must be emphasized that European fascination with India, China, and the Near East went beyond a preference for calicoes, a taste for tea, a fondness for chinoiserie, or a hankering after the *hummum*. Leading European thinkers, from Leibniz to Voltaire, favorably pointed to China as a model to emulate in areas of morality, law, and infrastructure. The Kang-Xi emperor, in particular, was hailed as a philosopher-king, committed as much to the welfare of his subjects as to the patronage of science and the arts. Demotic curiosity about the world beyond Europe also soared in the eighteenth century. In Britain, the rise of popular periodicals, like *Gentleman's Magazine* and *London Magazine*, regularly serialized travel narratives, giving accounts of "exotic" regions. Multivolume works on extra-European themes, such as William Robertson's *History of America* (1777) and Abbé Raynal's *History of the Two Indies* (1774–), East and West, were among the books borrowed most frequently from British libraries in the 1770s and 1780s. Raynal's *History* went through thirty editions across Europe in the two decades following its initial publication.[16]

In accentuating the relative weakness of European states, it must not be forgotten that European freebooters and state agents did seize control over numerous territories, usually small in size and conceived (at least at first) as bridgeheads for trade. Given the minuscule number of Europeans who faced vast, populous, and powerful polities, European accommodation was inevitable. Both in America and Africa, the Portuguese relied heavily on what have been termed "go-betweens" (in Brazil) and "trans-frontiersmen" (in Africa). These terms refer to Europeans who crossed frontiers and acculturated to the local dominant culture. In Brazil, European men who "went native" thereafter served as conduits between European and indigenous societies, often facilitating transactions for valuable commodities. Such go-betweens were largely responsible for the flourishing of the early Brazilwood trade, the mainstay of the early economy in what became Portuguese America.[17]

In Senegambia and the Upper Guinea Coast, such *lançados* were equally vital. Portuguese males—often fugitives from the law, religious persecution, or creditors—settled, married African women, and raised children, who would identify themselves as Portuguese. In Angola, such go-betweens, called *quimbares,* were equally influential, forming a population of Luso-Africans who occupied the liminal space between European and African societies. In East Africa, the activities of the Portuguese men who left the confines of the coastal fortresses were both ad hoc and largely unmonitored. Some of these individuals came to acquire land from various chiefs around the Zambesi, whether by outright purchase or in exchange for military service. These Portuguese then sought to bolster their proprietary claims by seeking the Portuguese Crown's recognition of their land title. The Crown complied, but it limited inheritance of the title to three generations and required a small quit-rent in addition to the right to press the owner's slaves into military service. These East African estates were called *prazos da coroa*. The *prazo* holders, however, became fully enmeshed in African society, through intermarriage, dependence on African auxiliaries for defense, and reliance on tribute from Africans residing in his territories in order to subsist. Over subsequent generations, though clinging tenaciously to the title of *prazo* holder, they steadily became integrated into African society. Their link to Portugal attenuated. Nor were the Portuguese alone in this regard. In the seventeenth century, EIC servants in India routinely became "renegades," voluntarily deserting for what they perceived were better conditions, superior compensation, and higher status. They were routinely absorbed into the wealthy, ethnically composite elites of India.[18] Even where small territories were claimed and settled in the non-European world, the gravitational pull of indigenous societies often resulted in European acculturation to them, and not the other way around.

At least before 1700, Europeans remained at the mercy of non-European states except where epidemic disease brought, unwittingly, from the Old World had decimated the population and left a territory susceptible to European designs. Most dramatically, the arrival of Europeans in the Americas provoked demographic disaster for indigenous societies, something that Europeans misattributed to divine will instead of microbial machinations. Depopulation, and the trauma and dislocation such annihilation brought in its wake, altered the dynamics of the formation of colonial societies. It explains how "conquest" was possible in the absence of numerical, technical, or other sources of superiority. Long before European settlements were definitively established, the epidemiological impact of cross-cultural contact reverberated throughout the New World. The vertiginous decline of Amerindian population was wrought by the introduction of new diseases which were not necessarily lethal in Europe, Asia, or Africa but which ravaged New World peoples without previous exposure, to say nothing of immunity, to them. At least five of these diseases—smallpox, measles, influenza, scarlet fever, and yellow fever—were unknown in the Americas, and some medical historians believe that mumps, rubella, pneumonia, anthrax, bubonic plague, malaria, and typhus, too, were introduced by Europeans and Africans.

The results of this contact with Old World diseases proved catastrophic. By the mid-seventeenth century, the Amerindian population in Spanish America had sunk to between 5 and 10 percent of levels in 1500, while the indigenous population of Brazil stood at no higher than one-quarter of its pre-1500 size. In the Caribbean, a minuscule percentage of the original Amerindian population survived. In North America, historians estimate that 90 percent of Algonquian speakers in Southern New England perished from epidemic disease by 1640, and perhaps half of all Hurons died from smallpox, influenza, and measles in the same period. Nor were epidemics merely the result of initial contact. In the middle decades of the eighteenth century, half of all Cherokees and half of all Catawbas died from smallpox. The introduction of alcohol and dietary changes due to trade and displacement also led to noticeable declines in fertility and thus hastened population decline. The transmission of disease was not unilateral. Syphilis was a disease of New World origin and ravaged European populations. From Europe, it spread to the world beyond the Atlantic. European sailors brought the venereal diseases of gonorrhea and syphilis to the South Pacific archipelagos, for example, with predictably catastrophic effects for the indigenous population. Among its direct consequences were weakened immunity, low birthrates, and high infant mortality rates.[19]

The Eurasian empires were slowly undermined in the eighteenth century, not by epidemic disease but by political and economic missteps and misfortune. For example, fiscal overstretch and currency devaluation made the Ottomans vulnerable to the ambitions of Europeans. A self-proclaimed "Holy League," led jointly by the Habsburgs and the Holy Roman Emperor, won victories in Hungary, Greece, and the Balkans by the end of the 1680s. By the Treaty of Karlowitz (1699), Ottomans receded Central and East

European territories—Croatia, Slovenia, and Hungary—to Christian states. Incipient Russian expansionism impinged on the Ottomans as well. By the mid-1770s, they had been forced to surrender control of the strategically situated Crimea, on the Black Sea, to the tsar. The perception of Ottoman decline fueled Napoleon's 1798 invasion (and ephemeral occupation) of Egypt. Further dismemberment of the empire followed in the late 1820s, when France, Russia, and Britain combined to support the independence of Greece, dealing a fatal blow to the Ottoman fleet at the Battle of Navarino (1827), thus exploiting the domestic crises plaguing the empire.

The Ottomans initially struggled to overcome domestic challenges, too. In the eighteenth century, the leaders of the Wahhabi movement, which sought a return to the purported primeval purity of early Islam and to expunge all allegedly un-Islamic practices, denied the political legitimacy of the Ottomans. They acted on this conviction, seizing control of much of central Arabia. With their political allies, they sacked and then rebuilt the Holy Cities of Mecca and Medina in the first years of the nineteenth century. Even if religious strife proved persistent, the Ottoman state responded to discontent on the periphery and sought out local allegiances. The Ottomans offered inducements, including greater political autonomy. Such flexibility and pragmatism paid off in the short term: tax revenues increased, and access to resources expanded. In the long term, however, the empowerment of local elites, who carved out what amounted to statelets of their own, threatened the empire's territorial and governmental integrity. It paved the way for insubordination on a grand scale, epitomized by Muhammad Ali, an Ottoman military official, who made himself master of Egypt in 1805 and defiantly clung to power until mid-century. The Ottoman state was decreasingly able to respond to such challenges to its authority because it lacked the fiscal means, which had been lost either due to military defeat or concessions to placate local elites. Expenses soon outstripped revenue, and the state was forced to borrow heavily. These setbacks, both internal and external, prompted reform, which gathered force from the late 1820s and culminated in the Tanzimat decrees inaugurating comprehensive reform in 1839.[20]

If European and Eurasian empires contributed to Ottoman decline, the fading fortunes of the Safavids and Mughals had few direct links to European actions. The Safavid state collapsed in the early 1720s, due to a weak military and incompetent leadership. By the 1790s, the dynasty's former territory was faction ridden and controlled by rival tribes. The factors contributing to the fragmentation of Mughal power in the eighteenth century are less clear-cut, but it appears that beneath the façade of centralized authority an unstable symbiosis lurked. The final push to stretch the empire's borders had caused great strain. Mughal rule more than ever depended on the cooperation and collaboration of numerous groups across the Indian subcontinent. These included local chieftains who had amassed great wealth, such as those of the Sikhs in the Punjab or the Jats south of Delhi (Agra), and the princely rulers who acknowledged Mughal overlordship through tribute but retained real authority in their respective realms. Another destabilizing force were the provincial governors appointed by the Mughals. While shying away from overt defiance, these local governors (nawabs) acted autonomously. They siphoned off revenues theoretically destined for Delhi. This trend was especially problematic in wealthy provinces, like Awadh, Hyderabad, and, especially, Bengal. By the mid-eighteenth century, nawabs there had effectively established ministates of their own, depriving the Mughals of the revenue they desperately needed. Historian Christopher Bayly astutely noted the paradox of this situation. The loose yet dynamic hegemony established by the Mughals had created the conditions for economic prosperity, but the new wealth and attendant social power now attenuated the ties that had bound the provinces to the Mughal state.[21]

Beset by recalcitrant rajas, upstart local chieftains, and ambitious Iranian and Afghan leaders, the political legitimacy and fiscal solvency of the Mughals were imperiled. Undoubtedly, the fracturing of authority was to some degree self-inflicted. Aurangzeb's quarter-century-long campaign to conquer the Deccan, for example, not only proved inconclusive but also spurred the rise of the Maratha kingdom, which by 1664 had captured Surat, the prized port in Gujarat. Other factors included factionalism at court, triggered in part by Aurangzeb's adherence to orthodox Islam, which led to the suspension of customs deemed to conflict with sharia law, the banning of music at court, and the dismissal of literary men from positions of authority they previously held. Whether by external or by internal forces, the Mughal Empire was in a parlous state of disarray by the second third of the eighteenth century. The Iranian king Nadir Shah was able to sack the capital Delhi in 1739, killing perhaps twenty thousand people in the process of plundering the city. This was a prelude to sack by Afghans in the 1750s.[22]

Following a period of rapid territorial expansion, the Qing, too, confronted internal difficulties. Some of these were inherent in an empire of such immense proportions, with its multiplicity of ethnicities, languages, and status groups. Certain emperors, such as the Yongzheng emperor (r. 1723–1735), sought to erase cultural differences and promote homogeneity by making vernacular Chinese (Mandarin) the lingua franca of the realm. Others, such as the Qianlong emperor, resisted such a policy and explicitly tolerated cultural and linguistic diversity. In the newly conquered western territory of Xianjiang, for example, the Muslim Uighur inhabitants not only were permitted to keep their religious leaders and follow their own dietary practices but were not required to shave their heads and grow the queue. Regardless of how their policies worked in specific places, overall it may be said that the Qing increasingly struggled to maintain the centralized, potent administration they previously had established, perhaps attributable to the errors of individual emperors. For example, the Kang-Xi emperor's conquests and economic policies produced remarkable abundance and, perhaps, engendered hubris. The bounty emboldened him to promise, as he basked in the afterglow of triumph, never to raise the basic tax rate on agricultural land. As a result, as historian William Rowe shrewdly observed, "Kang-Xi committed his successors to governing within a declining share of the realm's bounty despite facing an inflationary economy . . . by the nineteenth century, Qing central administration was permanently impoverished."[23] This situation might have been a contributing factor to the weakening of Qing governmental institutions in the late eighteenth century, signs of which included food scarcity, denunciations of endemic corruption, and the increased ferocity of bureaucratic infighting.

Before the nineteenth century, Europeans were unable to exploit the turmoil besetting these Eurasian empires, chiefly because their own weakness precluded it. One notable exception was in South Asia. The officials of England's EIC did not arrive as conquerors. The Mughal emperor Jahangir granted the English permission in 1617 to establish factories in several ports, notably Surat, but forbade their fortification. Even after the EIC was ensconced in "presidency capitals," its activities remained well within the limits defined by its Mughal hosts, upon whom it relied for protection. The number of British military personnel remained minuscule, with Indian troops under British command more numerous, thus giving little cause for alarm.[24] Missionary activity was restricted by the EIC, in an effort to avoid irritating its hosts. European reliance on native rulers continued unabated in the eighteenth century. Even after the victories at Plassey (1757) and Buxar

(1764), the EIC received the *diwani*, or land grant revenue rights, to Bengal, Bihar, and Orissa only as a reluctant concession from the Mughal emperor, Shah Alam II, in 1765.

Even in the aftermath of military triumph, the ascendancy of the British could proceed only by treaty, negotiation, and grant. They were compelled to rule within long-standing structures that conferred political legitimacy. The EIC never ceased paying homage to the symbolic authority of the Mughals. Persian, the official language of the court, was retained as the Company's official administrative language until 1835. Much more than feigned obeisance, the EIC considered its study and use as indispensable to its overall project, which encompassed (and perhaps was premised upon) cultural control. As the governor-general of British India Warren Hastings noted in 1784, "Every accumulation of knowledge, and especially such as is obtained by social communication with people over whom we exercise a dominion founded on the right of conquest, is useful to the state." Knowledge of languages enabled Company officials to police, collect taxes, and issue commands. But just as important, it enabled them to convert the Indian realities they encountered, yet often only dimly understood, into potent instruments of governance, from encyclopedias to statistical data. Such scholarly practices by Europeans, it should be added, were systematic and were applied far beyond India, an aspect of what literary scholar Edward Said called, for a later period, "Orientalism," "an accepted grid for filtering through the Orient into Western consciousness."[25]

This appreciation of Indian culture, however instrumental it ultimately proved, would ebb and flow in the nineteenth century. British officials came to deride South Asia as irredeemably backward, its cultural and social forms obstacles to be extirpated, inferior to those of Europe. In his 1818 *History of British India*, James Mill contended that a new law code imposed by the British would sweep away the dead weight of the Indian past. In the early 1830s, Company servant (and later renowned historian) Thomas Babington Macaulay proposed European-style education, both in form and content, as a precondition to the reform of Indian society and, in the distant future, self-government—"that by good government we may educate our subjects into a capacity for better government; that, having been instructed in European knowledge, they may, in some future age, demand European institutions." This position was supported by Governor-General Lord Bentick. It was fortified by Bentick's low regard for Indian civilization, which he maligned as a combination of "absurd history, absurd metaphysics, absurd physics and absurd theology." Such prejudice was shared by some Indian intellectuals, including Rammohun Roy, who protested the 1824 founding of the Sanskrit College at Calcutta, arguing that a European curriculum was what was needed in South Asia.[26]

As this analysis of Indian society percolated, it pushed observers such as Karl Marx to adopt a favorable attitude toward British imperial ambitions. In his view, British imperialism in India would jumpstart the motor of historical change. As Marx pithily put it, "England has a double mission in India: one destructive, the other regenerating—the annihilation of old Asiatic society and the laying of the material foundations of western society in Asia." The features to be annihilated were precisely the ones he diagnosed as impediments to the instantiation of capitalism's modes of production. Britain would "blow up the economical bases" of the "small semi-barbarian, semi-civilized communities." Just as the expansion of markets had precipitated the demise of feudalism in Europe, Marx contended that Britain's South Asian empire would pave the way for the region's integration into the world market and lay the basis for the "universal intercourse founded upon the mutual dependency of mankind."[27]

Marx was seemingly unaware of South Asia's position relative to Europe around 1500, when Europe was peripheral and comparatively backward. It was only from the final decades of the eighteenth century that European hegemony could be glimpsed, even if its realization still lay far in the future. For much of the preceding period, even after the early modern seaborne empires were launched and reached their apex, they remained comparatively minor players on the global stage their long-distance voyages helped usher into existence. The next chapter traces the evolution of the first two of these states—Portugal and Spain—poor polities on the western fringe of the European continent, from their initial maritime voyages in the fifteenth century to their encounters with Amerindian and Eurasian megastates in the sixteenth century and the first phases of the establishment of their overseas empires soon thereafter.

3. The First Seaborne Empires

Portugal, Spain, and the Wider World before 1600

Chapters 3 and 4 together provide an overview of the development of the five European seaborne empires treated in this book up to 1650. The basic contours of this narrative are the rise of the Iberian empires in the Americas and, to a lesser extent, the Indian and Pacific Oceans, followed by the emergence of rival states with overseas ambitions—England, the Dutch Republic, and France—in the first decades of the seventeenth century. These newcomers clashed with the Iberian states and succeeded in carving out their own empires, chiefly in those areas left unoccupied or poorly defended by the Iberian powers. Chapter 3 deals with Spain and Portugal, and Chapter 4 treats their parvenu competitors.

The rise of the Spanish and Portuguese Empires beyond Europe must be traced to the Christian struggle to gain control of the Iberian Peninsula. In the late fifteenth century, Christian conquerors managed to expel the Nasrid dynasty from Granada, the final Muslim foothold in the Iberian Peninsula, originally conquered in the early eighth century. Southern Spain, Al-Andalus, was the seat of the caliphate of Córdoba, which was the ruling authority in the Iberian Peninsula and suzerain of much of North Africa.[1] The so-called *Reconquista* (Reconquest) formed part of a wider and long-standing confrontation between Christian and Muslim states dating back to well before the Crusades. Wresting Granada in 1492, after centuries of spasmodic war, proved a pivotal moment in the centralization of the rest of the Iberian Peninsula, which was divided into several autonomous, nominally

Christian kingdoms. None of these had previously established its superiority over the rest. Portugal, situated on the western periphery of the peninsula, was independent of the larger polities surrounding it, specifically Castile and the agglomeration of territories attached, some more loosely than others, to the kingdom of Aragon, including smaller polities like Valencia and the Catalan *condados*.

Though the cities of Catalonia surpassed their Castilian counterparts in economic dynamism, Castile would establish its political primacy following its unification with Aragon in 1469. The marriage of Isabel of Castile and Ferdinand of Aragon was a dynastic union that laid the groundwork for the new polity of "Spain," embracing much of the Iberian Peninsula. As historian David Abulafia observed, the union "was not one of natural partners, nor even one of newly reconciled competitors, but of unlike with unlike." This apparent incongruity may explain the political evolution of Spain into a "composite monarchy," in contrast to a centralized one.[2] Numerous smaller entities were sheltered under a single sovereign. The Basque provinces, Catalonia, Navarre, Aragon, Valencia, and others became attached to the monarchy's Castilian nucleus in different ways and at different times. The circumstances by which this occurred were decisive. They determined the degree of independence of a given territory within the monarchy. Recently conquered Andalusia, for example, had never been a political entity apart and thus formed part of the Crown of Castile. For kingdoms with long-standing traditions of autonomy, the situation varied. Absorption into a larger political entity or unit did not portend relinquishing, or even modifying, existing laws, institutions, and customs. Each of these polities retained a hotchpotch of fiscal exemptions, legal immunities, spheres of unencumbered autonomy, and eclectic privileges. These had been negotiated, formally and informally, upon integration. Even after their union, each of the kingdoms continued to exist as a distinct political unit, maintaining its peculiar identity and status. Each was marked by a vast complex of corporate bodies, from the clergy to the nobility to merchant guilds, each of which zealously guarded its own bundle of rights and privileges, known as *fueros*.

The Spanish monarchy thus was a mosaic, characterized by legal pluralism and decentralization, even if all acknowledged the ultimate authority, or sovereignty, of the king. Such heterogeneity complicated the formulation of policies common to all of the component kingdoms. This situation proved especially vexing to the monarch when he sought to raise revenue through taxation. In fact, the monarch was required to consult and gain permission before new levies were imposed. In Spain (as well as in Portugal), the various estates or orders in society routinely came together as a representative body, known as the Cortes, to consult with the king on political and fiscal matters. Negotiation and compromise, not executive fiat, were the defining features of this political culture. As in other composite monarchies, there existed a permanent tension between the centripetal ambitions of the monarchs and the centrifugal tendencies immanent in the political system.

Compared to Spain, Portugal was a unitary kingdom, not a composite monarchy. Yet the authority of the monarch and his latitude for action were circumscribed by a powerful nobility.[3] Muslim authorities were vanquished and expelled from the southernmost region of Portugal, the Algarve, in 1249, thus preceding the Nasrid dynasty's capitulation in southern Spain by more than two hundred years. Portuguese independence from an expansionist Castile was preserved following the improbable military victory at Aljubarrota in 1385. Nevertheless, Portugal's position remained precarious, its independence tenuous and its economy far from robust. Overwhelmingly rural, its territory was subdivided among numerous overlords, from noble families to monastic orders, whose tenants scratched subsistence from farming small plots. The production of salt, the collection of seaweed (which was used as fertilizer), and fishing also were leading sectors of the economy. In spite of their limited extent and variety, Portugal's exports were in high demand in northern Europe, particularly its wine and cork. This export trade helped transform Lisbon, the capital, into a significant port, replete with Italian merchant houses, a mitochrondrion of global integration. It became a regular fueling station as well as a trading entrepôt for ships arriving from the Mediterranean and bound for the lucrative markets of northern Europe.

From the 1480s, the Portuguese monarchy strengthened its position relative to the nobility and the church. All land grants, titles of lordship, and confirmations of legal jurisdiction required royal confirmation. The members of the nobility were compelled to acknowledge the king as their superior, not merely a first among equals. The monarchy enhanced its capacity to raise revenue, appropriating taxes formerly levied locally for its exclusive use. Customs duties from trade also replenished the Crown's coffers, further fortifying its position. King Manuel's reign (1495–1521) coincided with the first epoch of Portuguese overseas exploration, a glittering period that has been called Portugal's Golden Age. The status and prestige of the monarch benefited greatly from its patronage of these voyages. Their success also stoked his megalomania. Manuel's chief objectives, ultimately unrealized, were the capture of Jerusalem and the destruction of Mecca. Manuel foresaw the subsequent expansion of Christendom into lands controlled by Muslim rulers, territory over which he intended to rule personally. The resources of the primordial Atlantic empire slowly taking shape, which will be discussed in the pages that follow, were welcomed as an adjunct to this larger spiritual mission. They remained subservient to this aim long after a flourishing overseas empire was founded. Thus, even on the westernmost fringe of continental Europe, whose shores were lapped by the Atlantic, the political, spiritual, and economic orientation remained eastward.

The fifteenth century witnessed the first stirrings of a policy of territorial expansion beyond the confines of Europe. Portugal and Spain were in the vanguard of this outward thrust. Spanish forays were predicated on earlier traditions of Catalan-Aragonese empire building in the Mediterranean. The Balearic Islands—Minorca, Mallorca, and Ibiza—had been colonized in the late medieval period. These efforts were themselves a palimpsest, building on and often intersecting with Venetian and Genoese settlements and trading outposts. The Catalan-Aragonese state also asserted itself farther afield in Sardinia, its influence extending to the eastern Mediterranean. Such efforts bequeathed several of the institutions historians now associate with Spain's global empire. For example, the office of viceroy was first established in the Catalan Duchy of Athens (Greece) in the fourteenth century. This institution offered a solution to the problem of royal absenteeism, making visible royal power when the monarch was not physically present in a given territory. The viceroy was fashioned as the king's alter ego. He carried out royal orders and governed territories far from the seat of monarchical authority.[4]

Mediterranean precedents such as these were crucial, but perhaps of greater direct relevance to the subsequent development of global empires were the voyages of exploration in the eastern Atlantic, particularly the colonization of the Canary Islands. Spanish and Portuguese ships, manned by polyglot multinational crews and funded by northern Italian merchant houses and banks, frequented the Canary Islands in the fourteenth century. The Canaries deserve mention in part because modern justifications of empire originate in their conquest. To be sure, the subject peoples of the Mediterranean empires were considered barbaric, like the Sards, or of dubious Christianity (like Orthodox Greeks, who were considered schismatic by Western European Christians). But the Canary Islanders (Guanches) were altogether novel, and Western European imaginations were stretched by the encounter. The planned conversion of the indigenous inhabitants soon was folded into a broader plan to incorporate other "pagan" peoples into Christendom's boundaries.[5] Rule over these newly encountered islands required papal approval. Unconquered islands were considered to be under the papal authority, entrusted to the pope for evangelization and good government. Lands untouched by Christianity remained his spiritual provinces to dispense to secular rulers. The papacy departed from earlier Christian legal precepts concerning the right of pagan rulers to govern themselves unmolested provided they abided by a loose set of precepts bundled together as "natural law." In this older view, non-Christian kingdoms that repudiated cannibalism, polygamy, wanton nudity, and other jarring practices could carry on without interference.

In an important shift, the papacy now claimed that, with the coming of Christ, pagan rulers had forfeited the right to self-rule. Rule over them would now be entrusted to Christians. From the eleventh century, the church had secured recognition of its authority over matters related to belief and practice, unencumbered by secular authorities. By the thirteenth century, the amalgam of church (or canon) law and remnants of Roman law was understood to form a corpus common to Christian territories, with which local or customary laws could not conflict. Viewed from Rome, regardless of the situation on the ground, Europe was a single legal regime, and, in its connection to non-Christian territories, the church was preeminent and claimed universal jurisdiction.

While the papacy might undertake the propagation of Christianity on a grand scale, it lacked the galleons and regiments to exert its authority. Secular rulers, like the monarchs of Spain and Portugal, could prove useful to the pope in this regard. In the wake of Columbus's first voyage, Pope Alexander VI issued a series of decrees, known as bulls, as well as sanctioning the *patronato real.* In 1493, the dominion of the Indies was conferred to Spanish monarchs, granting them exclusive right to proselytize the indigenous population; in 1501, control over the collection (and use) of church tithes from the Indies was granted; and in 1508, the Spanish Crown was granted the exclusive right to make appointments to ecclesiastical posts in the Indies.[6] Similar concessions were extended to Portugal. As a result, by means of the bulls and the patronato real, the Iberian monarchies became the papacy's willing subcontractors. Thereafter they could conduct their affairs within this framework. As for the non-European peoples inhabiting those territories, their rights were the subject of ceaseless polemic. Some prominent political writers, such as Francisco de Vitoria, averred that Europeans could only overthrow native rulers or wage "just war" against them if they were to violate fundamental tenets of natural law and prevent the Spaniards from proselytizing. Even then, war would be waged to bring them under European tutelage, such that "conquest" brought with it attendant duties of education, evangelization, and protection.[7]

Unsurprisingly, though they accepted the papal edicts, many in Spain and Portugal were dissatisfied with the papal donation alone. Spanish and Portuguese monarchs sought to demonstrate that the basis for their respective overseas dominions did not depend on the grant of another authority. The assault on the papal donation took several forms. Some writers, like Vitoria, rejected the view that the pope possessed special, unique rights over infidels, thus opening the door to alternative justifications.[8] In order to prevent conflict between themselves, deter potential rivals, and create a secular legal basis for their ultramarine enterprises, Spain and Portugal concluded the Treaty of Tordesillas (1494), by which they partitioned the world beyond Europe. This treaty did not materialize out of thin air. Already in the Treaty of Alcoçovas (1479), Spain and Portugal agreed to Castile's primacy in the Canaries in exchange for Portugal's right to establish sovereignty over unspecified territory in Africa. In the wake of this treaty, Portugal dispatched a fleet to construct a fort (which doubled as a commercial factory) on Africa's so-called Gold Coast, resulting in construction of São Jorge da Mina Castle, in modern Ghana, in 1482. The key feature of the Treaty of Tordesillas, signed fifteen years later, was the decision to draw a line of longitude running 370 leagues west of the Cape Verde islands that would demarcate Spain's sphere of authority from Portugal's. To the east of the line would be Portuguese territory, while to the West of it sovereignty would be wielded by Castile. It should be noted that the treaty was somewhat premature. In 1494, Columbus had made landfall in the Caribbean (Hispaniola, in particular), but no contact with continental South, Meso-, or North America had yet been made. Pedro Álvares Cabral's arrival in Brazil would occur six years later.

The conquest and colonization of the Canary Islands were an important spur to further navigation of the Atlantic. A nautical school was founded by Portugal's Prince Henry (dubbed "the Navigator") in the first decades of the fifteenth century in Sagres, a development indicative of the heightened interest evinced by Europeans in overseas exploration. Portugal also turned its attention to subjugating nearby overseas regions. It seized the port city of Ceuta, in North Africa, in 1415. The conquest was remarkable by the standards of its day. It involved one hundred ships, including two royal galleys, and nineteen thousand men. Historians have proffered several explanations for the motivations inspiring the Ceuta expedition: religious fervor; a place to vent the pent-up ambitions of the military class of knights, who were largely bereft of their occupation after the victory of Aljubarrota thirty years earlier; and the self-interest of Portuguese merchants and Crown, eager to obtain a share of the Morocco trade, which passed through Ceuta. In all likelihood, all of these elements were present, and their confluence proved decisive. For almost two centuries after 1415, the dream of a North African empire obsessed Portugal and, to a lesser extent, Spain. Spain established beachheads at Melilla (1496), Oran (1509), Bougie (1510), and Tripoli (1511). For individual knights, such excursions could prove uncommonly lucrative, whether through plunder or the taking of captives for ransom. A successful raid in 1511, for example, yielded a thousand head of cattle, three hundred camels and horses, and nearly six hundred prisoners.[9] But Portugal lacked the capacity—financial or military—to make these conquests permanent, whereas Spain lacked the political will to do so. To garrison, defend, and provision Ceuta would drain the royal treasury and, more to the point, exceeded the organizational capacity of the state. The enterprise was doomed to failure.

Indulging their crusading fantasy in North Africa did not preclude the continued exploration and settlement by Portugal of the eastern Atlantic. Portuguese sailors encountered and claimed several islands and archipelagos: Madeira (1420s), the Azores (late 1420s), Cape Verde (c. 1460), and São Tomé (c. 1470). Colonies of settlement were founded, and colonists experimented with various types of agricultural systems and labor regimes. Traditional wheat farming was attempted, and sugar plantations, relying on African slave labor, were also established. In São Tomé, large-scale sugar plantations (called *engenhos*) were worked by 150–300 slaves. Plantation agriculture in the eastern Atlantic archipelagos was a crucial forerunner of what Iberian adventurers and settlers later attempted in the Caribbean and in Brazil.

The Portuguese methodically explored the western littoral of Africa, too. They founded trading fortresses, called factories (*feitorias*, in Portuguese). Drawing on Mediterranean precedents, the factory was a military garrison guarded by a knight and operated by a civilian commercial agent (*feitor*). The agent conducted trade with African merchants or chiefs. The merchandise acquired was stored in the factory and then sold to the Portuguese fleets that periodically called at trading fortresses along the coast. The factories mainly sought to tap into the great trans-Saharan trading routes in order to secure gold, spices, and ivory. From the 1440s, enslaved Africans became a key export, usually transported to Lisbon and Cadiz. Enslaved Africans became domestic servants, urban laborers, herders, shepherds, and farmers throughout the Iberian Peninsula. Later, slaves would be exported to the eastern Atlantic archipelagos and their emergent sugar engenhos. It is estimated that as many as thirty-five thousand West Africans were sold into slavery in the Iberian Peninsula by the end of the century, and, in the mid-sixteenth century, almost 10 percent of the population of Seville, Spain's most important city, consisted of enslaved people of African descent.[10]

El Mina castle built by the Portuguese was conceived primarily as a trading fortress, not a beachhead for territorial conquest. It began as a Crown-directed enterprise, to be carried out by royal agents instead of contracted to private merchants. This decision presaged the later policy of employing revenues from overseas empire to strengthen the Crown's position in Europe, presaging later experiments in absolutism. Gold obtained in Africa through trade flowed directly into the royal coffers. Unsurprisingly, Portuguese contact and trade with Africa soon spilled out beyond the coastal factories. In the kingdom of Kongo, the Portuguese forged an alliance with the ruler, Manikongo. Christianity was soon embraced by Kongo's ruling elites, who also adopted Portuguese names, titles, coats of arms, and styles of dress. The kings of Kongo sent the sons of elites for education in Europe, and the son of King Mvemba Nzinga was consecrated in Rome as a bishop in the early sixteenth century.[11] By mid-century, however, the relationship soured. In 1571, the Portuguese Crown launched a grandiose scheme of conquest and settlement. Relations between Portugal and Kongo would vacillate between belligerence and alliance for the next two centuries.

North African military adventurism, eastern Atlantic exploration and colonization, and Central-West African trading fortresses did not divert attention from the legendary markets of India and China. Indeed, the exploration of the West African coast formed part of a larger aspiration to chart a route to these lucrative Asian emporiums. Identifying a sea route to Asia took on special urgency in the late fifteenth century. The Venetians had enjoyed a virtual monopoly over this eastern trade, but the overland route on which they relied was now blocked by the ascendant Ottoman Empire. Numerous voyages from diverse corners of Europe were undertaken. The Portuguese held an obvious advantage due to their extensive maritime experience and Crown investment in nautical knowledge and technology. At the southern end of Africa a ship captained by the Portuguese explorer Bartolomeu Dias rounded what became known as the Cape of Good Hope in 1487–1488, proving the existence of a maritime passage to Asia. This achievement spurred myriad other voyages, including the one devised and undertaken by Genoa-born Christopher Columbus. He had resided in the 1480s at various Portuguese factories on the West African coast, particularly El Mina. He secured the patronage of the Spanish Crown in the 1490s to seek a different sea route, the results of which are well known.[12]

Portuguese ships followed in the wake of Dias's voyage, most notably that of Vasco da Gama, who sailed into the Indian Ocean and reached India in 1498–1499. There Portugal revealed its predilection for trading fortresses, but it now sought to secure trade through military force. Portuguese conquests in the Indian Ocean occurred in rapid succession: of Goa (1510), Malacca (1511), Hormuz (1515), and Colombo (1518). Taken together, this constellation of coastal territorial or island footholds formed the Estado da Índia, a new kingdom to be ruled directly by the Portuguese Crown in western India.[13] No Portuguese harbored any illusion or pretension that these tiny bastions of Lusitanian power portended a territorial empire in Asia. As described in Chapter 2, the formidable wealth, institutional and military apparatus, and demographic heft of the Mughal Empire in India foreclosed this possibility. Furthermore, the profligacy of Portugal's sputtering efforts in its North African frontiers, particularly Ceuta, made apparent the absurdity of such a fantasy.

But the Indian Ocean was vulnerable to Portugal's designs. The land-based empires of South Asia had not extended their rule to the waves.[14] The Portuguese proclaimed themselves to be Lords of the [Indian] Ocean and sought to convert it into a mare clausum. Using its coastal nodes, the Portuguese transformed the Indian Ocean into an aqueous dominion with the trappings of a terrestrial state, administered by a vast fleet. Asian, African, and European merchants wishing to pass through Portuguese "territory" were compelled to obtain a pass, known as a *cartaz*, for which they would pay handsomely. A ship had to call at a Portuguese fort to pay customs duty before proceeding on its voyage. A trading vessel found without a cartaz automatically had its cargo confiscated and its crew harshly punished. The success of the cartaz emboldened the Portuguese to devise additional measures to regulate trade, including a convoy system known as the *cafila*. In this scheme, numerous local merchant ships paid for the privilege of sailing as a fleet guarded by Portuguese warships. The cafila was an early modern protection racket because the protection that was sold was from Portugal's own depredations.[15] Through these mechanisms, the Portuguese sought to monopolize the supply of spices entering Europe and to control and tax all types of trade in the Indian Ocean.

The benefits derived by Portugal from its bellicose approach to commerce were immense. The Estado da Índia was, like the factories in West Africa, a Crown enterprise: all participants were salaried servants of the Crown, who conducted trade for the king's account. The most lucrative goods—pepper, cinnamon, cloves, gold, ivory, and horses—were held as royal monopolies. Nevertheless, many people benefited from this trade in addition to the monarch. To reduce overhead, the Crown began to contract out the *carreira da Índia* (the voyage between Portugal and South Asia) to a consortium of bankers and financiers.[16] Great profits, too, could be made by merchants, for example, whether by reexporting precious items or selling them on the Portuguese domestic market. The nobility gained access to new posts, offices, and opportunities for glory seeking. The clergy encountered a new field of activity, with legions of pagan souls to catechize. In its initial phases, then, imperial expansion offered something for numerous powerful groups within Portuguese society, and provided incentives for cooperation. The Portuguese Crown came to play a coordinating role, calibrating and arbitrating, and thus enhanced its own authority. As historian Francisco Bethencourt elucidated, though it was decentralized "the system shows the constant presence of the crown in all spheres or organizational culture, distributing privileges, legitimizing nominations, ratifying decisions and establishing judicial and financial control."[17]

The Portuguese were scarcely more than aggressive interlopers, bullying themselves into a thriving trading world. They posed no threat to the Mughal Empire. If anything, the Portuguese acted as a convenient adjunct, ordering what otherwise was a semi-anarchic oceanic space. The Portuguese were content to remain inconspicuously on the periphery and to draw a handsome profit. If the epithet "parasite" fails to convey the symbiosis that resulted from the presence of the Portuguese, at least it avoids the error of magnifying their achievement. In South Asia, as well as West Africa, they aimed to be as unobtrusive as possible, for reasons of self-preservation. By and large, they left unmodified existing native property systems, customary modes of imposing taxes, and long-standing mechanisms for collecting taxes, a style of engagement subsequent European seaborne empires would emulate.

In one of the voyages that followed in Vasco da Gama's wake, a ship captained by Cabral in 1500 encountered a land previously unknown to European cartographers, which would become known as Brazil. Initially, the crew thought little of the land they surveyed. One of its members noted that Brazil might become "only a rest-house on the voyage to Calicut."[18] It might serve simply as a fueling station, or perhaps a trading fortress, en route to the ultimate destination: India. The Portuguese resorted to the factory system. For the first three decades (1500–1535), the principal economic activity was the extraction of brazilwood, which was obtained via trade with Amerindians. Amerindians also supplied manioc flour, which ensured the subsistence of the Portuguese traders confined to the coast. The trade grew rapidly, and coastal cities were soon established: Olinda (1537), Salvador (1549), Santos (1545), Vitoria (1551), Rio (1565), Sao Luiz (1612), and Belem (1616). Only in the eighteenth century would urban centers sprout in the interior. For the first two centuries, Brazil's cities and population remained "like crabs on the beach."[19]

Spain was not far behind Portugal in peering beyond the shores of the Iberian Peninsula. Recall that in 1479, the primacy of Spain in the Canaries was acknowledged in exchange for Portugal's rights over lands in Africa. Columbus's Crown-sponsored voyages of the 1490s expanded the field of Spain's ambition considerably. Columbus's voyages and early attempts to establish nodes of authority were largely frustrated, but voyages increased in frequency, and the period 1495–1520 saw the creation of areas of Spanish settlement in the Caribbean. In 1502, 2,500 Europeans were brought to the island of Hispaniola. Thereafter, activity accelerated: Europeans would crisscross the Caribbean, invading and colonizing Puerto Rico and Cuba between 1508 and 1511, and the Caribbean coast of Colombia (Tierra Firme) between 1509 and 1513. In 1513, Vasco Núñez de Balboa would cross the

Isthmus of Panama into the Pacific Ocean, ushering in a new theater of colonization.

Between 1519 and 1521, the Spanish landed and vanquished the Aztec Empire in Mesoamerica, under the command of Hernán Cortés. The conquest of the Incas in the Andes was led by Francisco Pizarro. When Pizarro—who had accompanied Cortés in his initial incursions into Mexico—began his invasion of Peru in 1530, he was aided by a favorable conjuncture of circumstances. Incan power had never been so fragile—from the 1520s, an epidemic (most likely smallpox) had swept along the trade routes of the Isthmus of Panama through the northern stretches of the Incan Empire, proving, as it had in Mexico, to be a formidable ally to European ambition. Though the Incas were overthrown and much of their territory subdued in an astounding five years, the conquistadors were enveloped in internecine strife. This intra-Spanish civil conflict ended in 1545. The end of division coincided with the discovery of silver in Potosí, in modern Bolivia. A full-fledged mining industry flourished by the 1570s.[20]

The story of the "conquest" of the empires of the Aztecs and Incas has been recounted innumerable times. Unfortunately, many of these accounts are often riddled with errors, both of fact and of interpretation. Historian Matthew Restall has summarized and debunked the myths infusing most of these narratives regarding Mexico.[21] When disease, the lack of unity of indigenous peoples (and more to the point, the fact that many collaborated with Spaniards, assisting them in all phases of subjugation), and technology are taken into account, then the "remarkable deeds" of conquistadors are diminished by a significant measure, and the swift pace of the overthrow of those empires can be better understood. Diseases such as smallpox, influenza, and measles decimated indigenous peoples in staggeringly high numbers, as they lacked the immunity of their Old World counterparts.

Few of the conquistadors were animated solely by the spiritual mission with which they had been entrusted by the king, and by extension the pope. Spaniards joined not in return for specified payment but rather in the hope of acquiring wealth and status. They were, in Restall's phrase, "armed entrepreneurs," "free agents, emigrants, settlers, unsalaried and un-uniformed earners of *encomiendas* and shares of treasure."[22] The conquistadors retained their private armies, at their own expense and under their personal command. This arrangement was at first welcomed by the Crown. It encouraged military service for the greater glory of the king without entailing an outlay of funds. These conquistadors acquired land grants and titles from the Crown, becoming *encomenderos*, with a right to Indian tribute and labor. Until 1582, encomenderos also were expected to supply certain forts and garrisons with men whom they paid. The encomenderos and their retinues did not constitute, then, a true army. Though the cost-cutting virtue of an inexpensive defense was extolled, high-ranking officials were acutely aware of the potential danger it posed. In 1615, the viceroy of Peru informed the king that "in any other area, these *soldados* would be regarded as dangerous vagabonds who posed a threat to public safety."[23]

In the late 1570s, Portugal suffered from a crisis of royal succession. In 1578, the young King Sebastian personally, and ill advisedly, led an army of invasion into Morocco. The king and the flower of the Portuguese nobility lost their lives at the battle of Alcácer Quibir and in the chaotic retreat that followed. Political crisis also followed on the heels of frequent outbreaks of plague in preceding decades, which claimed as many as thirty-five thousand lives in 1579 alone.[24] Philip II of Spain held and pressed a viable claim to the Portuguese crown (via his Portuguese mother's links to the ruling dynasty). The Portuguese nobility cooperated and recognized Philip as their monarch. Portugal was thus absorbed into Spain's composite monarchy, and would remain so for sixty years. Portugal was not ruled directly from Madrid but ruled by a governor, a common mechanism used throughout Spain's dominions to avoid antagonizing the local elite, placating them through the trappings of indirect rule. A Council of Portugal convened in Madrid. It supervised the actions of the governor and liaised with the court. Portugal maintained its own laws and institutions, including its representative body, the Cortes, even as it acknowledged Spain's sovereignty. Political and clerical offices held by Portuguese would be retained by them in the future. They also were eligible for appointment throughout Spain's empire, a considerable inducement to embrace the new political alignment, whereas Castilians were not granted reciprocal privileges.

Conciliatory gestures and concessions aside, however, Spain expected much from its new ultramarine possessions. One observer claimed that the incorporation of Portugal would make Philip II "the greatest king in the world," for "if the Romans were able to rule the world simply by ruling the Mediterranean, what of the man who rules the Atlantic and Pacific oceans, since they surround the world?"[25] Revenues of the Estado da Índia increased more than 20 percent in the quarter century following the union.[26] This was a clear sign of the Castilian Crown's intent to wring profit from Portugal's empire. For the next two decades, the dreaded prospect of a universal monarchy under the Habsburgs rallied Spain's opponents, as Chapter 4 narrates and explains, plunging Europe into warfare. Thereafter, from 1598 to 1621, Spain managed to avoid conflict in Europe, even if there were proxy battles of great importance in the emerging Atlantic theater. The so-called Pax Hispanica did not signal Spain's superiority as much as it signaled the growing parity among Europe's rival states.

4. The Challenge to Iberian Dominance

The Rise of Britain, France, and the Dutch Republic as Competitor Imperial States after 1600

The maritime discoveries, early settlement, and the material wealth they brought Spain and Portugal aroused the envy and fascination of other European states. Some of this interest was intellectual, sparked by the encounter with previously unknown peoples, societies, and lands. But of greater relevance here were the geopolitical implications of this attraction, and the competitive fire it enkindled. Spain's sprawling, resource-rich territorial empire in the New World upset the fragile balance of power in Europe. Many observers feared that the Habsburg dynasty had positioned itself to become a universal empire. Britain, the Netherlands, and France were influenced strongly by, and did much to develop and propagate, the Black Legend, discussed in Chapter 1.[1]

An emergent rivalry was fueled by, and helped to generate, massive changes in each of Europe's states, specifically the enlargement of the scope of their activities. The size of the government apparatus increased, as rulers sought to expand and centralize their authority. In France, for example, the number of salaried Crown employees leapt from twelve thousand to eighty thousand from 1500 to 1650. The size of the armies and levels of military expenditure of European states likewise increased, often outstripping the state's capacity to pay. In the 1540s, for example, England's Henry VIII spent nearly one-third of all revenues on fortifications, whereas Spain spent five times as much on fortifications in 1611 as it had in 1577. More generally,

European states spent half of their revenues on military expenditure during peacetime, rising to three-quarters in wartime. Steps toward centralization roused the ire of various privileged groups long accustomed, or legally entitled, to autonomy. The French Crown's decision to abolish the fiscal independence of the provincial estates in the 1620s provoked widespread revolt. Across the Channel, the English Crown's enactment of new policies in Scotland without securing the consent of local leaders instigated protests that eventually culminated in the overthrow of the monarchy.[2]

The conflicts between European states cannot be reduced solely to economic motivations. Honor, reputation, religious allegiance, and the ceaseless quest for *grandeza* intermingled with material calculations. Cardinal Richelieu and the Count-Duke of Olivares, who directed the foreign policies of France and Spain, respectively, in the early seventeenth century, epitomize the intersection of aspirations. In their minds, as historian John H. Elliott showed, "prestige brought power, power brought prestige; and prestige, if skillfully exploited, could sometimes make it unnecessary to resort to arms."[3] The Papal Donation and the Treaty of Tordesillas generated keen resentment. Other European states now possessed the strength to challenge Iberian claims to the world beyond Europe. To be sure, the wealth amassed by the Spanish Crown from overseas ventures was alluring. Nevertheless, the prestige that such wealth and global influence purchased was coveted at least as much as bullion.

This envy might have smoldered without consequence had it not been for another incendiary force. Anxiety concerning Spanish (and to a lesser degree Portuguese) global pretensions was stoked by the Reformation. Insurgent Protestantism, itself subdivided into myriad denominations, challenged the Catholic Church in spiritual as well as profane matters. Beginning in the 1530s, sectarian feuds unleashed turmoil, both within states and between them, across Europe. After incessant conflict, lasting more than a century, monarchs either reaffirmed Catholicism as the official religion of their respective states or else adopted and imposed a form of Protestantism. In England, Anglicanism was ascendant, though Catholic and Dissenting Protestant communities remained robust. In France, Catholicism ultimately prevailed following a long, sanguinary struggle.

The repercussions of the Reformation for the emergent seaborne empires were manifold, but at least two deserve mention. First, because

Protestant states rejected the authority of the pope, they refused to acknowledge the validity of the papal bulls. They scoffed at the arrogance (and unenforceability) of the pact made by the Iberian powers at Tordesillas. Claims to territory unsupported by settlement or fortifications would be rejected. Second, the Reformation transformed the dynamic of proselytization in the non-European world. The Catholic Counter-Reformation, a movement of renewal within the church, hastened by the Protestant threat, gave rise to a new type of church militant, emblematized by the Society of Jesus (the Jesuit Order). The Jesuits and the revamped regular orders conceived of the extra-European world as a battleground between the true faith and upstart apostasy.

The Reformation undermined European composite monarchies, too, sometimes tearing them asunder. The Dutch case offers an important example. The Netherlands was one of the constituent territorial parcels of the Spanish monarchy, the arch-champion of Catholic orthodoxy. Adherents of Protestantism gained ground, and majorities, in the seven northern provinces. As late as the 1560s, the Netherlands was an assemblage of towns and states, confederated in seventeen provinces, of Dutch, French, and Flemish speakers. By the 1640s, all of this had changed. The northern provinces revolted against Spanish rule, and, as a result of the decades-long war, marked by gruesome atrocities on both sides, gained their independence. They coalesced into the Seven United Provinces of the Free Netherlands. The ten southern provinces remained within the Spanish fold, due to a combination of military coercion and Catholic affinity.

By 1598, the Dutch Republic was effectively independent. Under the aegis of the Spanish Crown and, remarkably, during the protracted war for independence, the Netherlands had amassed prodigious wealth. Its principal cities, Antwerp and Amsterdam, were, respectively, the trading and banking center of northern Europe and the leading port. By the mid-seventeenth century, the Dutch Republic, as the Seven United Provinces became, was ruled by a burgher oligarchy, centered around the House of Orange-Nassau. It remained in most respects a decentralized state. Formally, sovereignty was vested in the respective provinces, though the *Stadtholder* exercised significant executive authority. The Dutch boasted a disciplined army. Their navy was formidable. Amsterdam continued its ascent toward dazzling affluence, a center of world trade, an achievement all the more remarkable because geographically the city was built upon low-lying and resource-poor land.[4]

A second major rival to Spain was England, another emergent Protestant power. The English did not at first participate robustly in the Age of Exploration. Several voyages embarked from the western port city of Bristol in the 1490s. These crews reached Newfoundland and exploited its bountiful cod fisheries. By the 1550s, London merchants commonly plied the northern sea routes to trade with Russia (Muscovy). But overseas expansion, save for commercial ventures and long-distance fishing, was confined largely to nearby lands, to France in particular, to the conquest and colonization of Ireland, and to incessant attempts to subdue Scotland. The latter two of these objectives were eventually achieved, but the process was protracted, occurring over several centuries.

The conquest of Ireland, first attempted in the second half of the sixteenth century, entailed a massive outlay of resources, the equivalent of total royal revenues for three years. Furthermore, it required an army of occupation in excess of eight thousand soldiers to sustain. Dispossession would occur in the aftermath of the 1641 Uprising. Forty-four thousand Irish Catholic landowners were deprived of their property, which was redistributed to Protestants. Like the Spanish, the English justified the conquest of Ireland by claiming that their aim was to convert its inhabitants to Christianity. They contended that this goal was impossible to realize so long as the Irish persisted in their barbarous ways. The English fashioned themselves as the new Romans who had come to civilize the Irish, just as the ancient Romans had once civilized the Britons. This historical vision bolstered the conviction that the Irish were culturally inferior to, and far behind, the English in developmental terms. Through subjection, the English colonizers reasoned, the Irish could be made fit to be free.[5]

Accompanied by less violence, though no shortage of coercion, the union of the English and Scottish Crowns was formalized in 1603. Success in Scotland and Ireland strengthened royal authority within England itself. Yet defense against foreign invasion and keeping domestic dissidents in check were priorities that precluded all but spasmodic official interest in the world beyond Europe.[6] Friction within Britain was exacerbated by the Crown's relentless attempts to impose religious uniformity. Anglicanism, a form of Protestantism, was the creed of the Church of England, itself subordinate to the monarchy. Dissenting Protestants as well as Catholics found themselves in a hostile environment. A considerable fraction of them abandoned England in the early seventeenth century, emigrating both to more hospitable states of continental Europe as well as to New World colonies. The drive for religious uniformity was exacerbated by tendencies toward royal absolutism, which threatened the equilibrium of the composite monarchy. As historian Mark Greengrass noted, "The English state was a pediment whose pillars rested on subcontracted powers to self-governing entities."[7] Political centralization and religious homogeneity sparked great protest. Ireland, overwhelmingly Catholic, was soon in rebellion. A Scottish army crossed the border into England, routed royal troops, and took the city of Newcastle without a siege.

In the meantime, the English Parliament made explicit its opposition to Charles I, a protest that eventually culminated in regicide and the establishment of a republic. Civil War raged, ultimately claiming the lives of a quarter of a million people, or 7 percent of the population. Under Oliver Cromwell, the monarchy was abolished, along with the House of Lords, and a republican commonwealth was established in its stead. Cromwell's armies reconquered Ireland (1649–1653) and defeated the Scots (1650, 1653). In 1657, Scotland was incorporated into the Commonwealth. After the restoration of the monarchy in 1660, a return to the status quo ex ante was inconceivable. The Crown exercised less power, and certain prerogatives were eradicated altogether. The new parliamentary monarchy, and Parliament's undivided control over taxation and expenditure, clarified where substantive authority and ultimate sovereignty now lay.[8]

After the Civil War, Britain remained far from a union of equals. Non-Anglican Protestants (Presbyterians, the majority in Scotland) and Catholics (who formed the vast majority in Ireland), as well as English dissenters (the Puritans, for example), were legally barred from office, effectively muting their participation in political life. England and Scotland would be joined permanently under the 1707 Act of Union, which dissolved the Scottish Parliament and instead gave the Scots seats in the English Parliament, which was transformed into the British Parliament. The Act of Union did not disturb preexisting religious organization and legal and education systems. But any semblance of political independence was eliminated. Following a major rebellion in 1798, resulting in at least thirty thousand casualties, Ireland was incorporated by an Act of Union, and, like Scotland a century earlier, deprived of its separate parliament.

By the final decades of the seventeenth century, France would achieve primacy in Western Europe. This result could hardly have been anticipated a century earlier, when the country was battered by a protracted civil war along confessional lines. Henry IV, who had been baptized a Catholic before converting to Protestantism and then switching back again to Catholicism, acceded to the throne in 1589. He swore to uphold Catholicism. Geopolitical crisis helped him to consolidate his position on the throne. In the 1590s, Spain invaded and occupied parts of France, and Henry deftly took up the mantle of defender of Europe against the ambitions of Philip II.[9]

But what kind of state did Henry rule? If not quite a composite monarchy, France was composed of heterogeneous, awkwardly compatible components. Some parts of the country, like Brittany, enjoyed autonomy due to custom, whereas others, such as the *pays d'état* in the South, retained significant control over their own affairs, wielded by entrenched local assemblies. Many nobles and inhabitants of major towns enjoyed exemption from taxation. This left peasants and residents of smaller towns to pay most direct taxes (*tailles*). The central government undermined its already circumscribed authority when it resorted to tax farming or venal office holding. Even so, nonpayment of taxes was widespread by the 1630s. Steps were taken to counteract this dismal state of affairs, strengthen royal authority, and expand its sources of revenue. Administrative innovations, such as the creation of intendants, clawed back some of what the Crown believed should fall within its purview. Unsurprisingly, the new assertiveness prompted a backlash, particularly among the *parlements* and the old nobility. Various rebellions in the 1620s and 1630s culminated in the Fronde in 1648. While the monarchy ultimately emerged stronger from these clashes with provincial elites, its finances were left in tatters in the short term. It declared bankruptcy in 1618. The economy's overall position was scarcely better. France was further devastated by food scarcity. In 1661, the price of bread in Paris tripled, while marriage and fertility rates declined precipitously. Religious strife, seemingly banished by the 1598 Edict of Nantes granting Protestants religious freedom, resurfaced. The 1685 revocation of the edict spurred the exodus of two hundred thousand Protestants (Huguenots) from France.[10]

The rise of the Dutch, British, and French represented a new threat to Spain's empire. Before the emergence of these new rivals, Madrid's overall contribution to defense of its American realm was insubstantial. Between 1535 and 1585, a mere five million ducats were expended to defend the entirety of Spanish America. This figure should be contrasted with the 2.5 million ducats squandered each year in the incessant, ultimately futile wars against the Dutch Republic. Ceaseless European warfare meant that Spain was hard-pressed to allocate funds to New World defense. Nor could the Crown borrow for this purpose: it was paying 49 percent interest on loans it had contracted in 1550. Upon his accession in 1556, Philip II was dismayed to discover that all future Crown revenues had been pledged to repay loans or interest for the next five years. Over the course of his reign, government revenue tripled, but public debt quadrupled. The impact was such that debt service absorbed nearly half of all revenues.[11] Penury of this magnitude portended that Spanish America would have to finance its own defense and civil administration. If the mainland was not especially vulnerable to foreign attack in the first half of the sixteenth century, the treasure fleet quickly became the object of every corsair's desire and was coveted by every monarch. Because external threats by sea had not existed previously, coastal fortifications were modest, at best. The defense of the Indies largely amounted to the protection of the treasure remitted to Spain from Mexico via the Caribbean and northern South American ports. The emergence of new threats meant that this older approach was untenable.

The establishment of Protestantism in England had geopolitical ramifications. It brought England into conflict with Spain. Like the Dutch, the English disregarded the papal bulls and insisted on the freedom to navigate the seas. A leading proponent of overseas expansion, Richard Hakluyt, insisted, "Seeing therefore that the sea and trade are common to the law of nature and nations, it was not lawful for the Pope, nor is it lawful for the Spaniards, to prohibit other nations from participation of this law." Armed with justifications of this sort, incursions into the Spanish Empire occurred with greater frequency, particularly during the reign of Elizabeth I (r. 1558–1603).[12] Sir Francis Drake's career is emblematic of these early irruptions into Iberian spaces, representative of the commingling of profit motive and religious conviction. Between 1577 and 1580, Drake and his crew circumnavigated the globe, plundering Spanish ships and towns and commandeering their bullion. In 1585, Drake launched a massive raid—boasting twenty ships and well over two thousand men—that exposed the inadequacy of Spanish America's defenses.

These bellicose excursions, including Drake's, were technically private enterprises, though they were undertaken with the Crown's furtive blessing. Individuals such as Sir Walter Raleigh and Sir Humphrey Gilbert, who had participated in the conquest of Ireland, were enamored of the idea of founding "plantations" in America, following the Spanish example. The first full-fledged attempt at establishing a colony was Raleigh's Virginia colony. In 1584, Elizabeth granted Raleigh a patent to discover and colonize new lands, which were soon dubbed "Virginia" after the Virgin Queen. In 1585, just over a hundred men landed in Roanoke on the southern shore of Chesapeake Bay. But this venture failed miserably: all of its members either died or returned to England. Interest thus shifted toward wresting territory in more fertile, mineral-laden Spanish America. Raleigh was again a galvanizing force, fixing his gaze on Guiana. It offered not only abundant fertile land for plantations, to be worked by indigenous labor on the Spanish model, but also a convenient base for piratical incursions into Spanish America. Raleigh's vision went unrealized in the short run, but it embodied a vision of empire in which plunder and agriculture were compatible, even mutually reinforcing, pursuits. In spite of this flurry of activity, the English state played little direct role. As Andrews observed, it was "unthinkable for [the government] to translate the dreams of ambitious courtiers and irresponsible sea-dogs into official policy." Eventually, English adventurers put down roots. Jamestown, Virginia, was founded in 1607, and a permanent settlement in Newfoundland was established three years later. A similar scene played out in Bermuda in 1612, to be followed several years later by the colony at Massachusetts Bay.[13]

It was under King Francis I that the French made their first forays into the Americas. Most notable was the 1534 voyage of Jacques Cartier, who explored Hudson Bay and the area that later became known as New France, although initial attempts to lay claim to or found colonies on the Atlantic coast came to naught. Exploration and colonization schemes were stalled by the civil wars that engulfed France. Under Henri IV, renewed interest in the overseas ventures was signaled by chartering a company for exploration, colonization, trade, and the administration of territories brought into the king's realm. In 1603, the French monarch gave the Huguenots a monopoly over the fur trade in Acadia, a region that included a portion of the present-day U.S. state of Maine and the Canadian province of Nova Scotia. Six years later, Samuel de Champlain founded the city of Quebec. In 1642 a French outpost was established on the site of the future city of Montreal. France's presence in the Americas, however, remained quite small. In 1626, the colony, which was called New France, counted a mere one hundred settlers, and this figure had increased to only three hundred by 1650. Still, with the assistance of the Jesuit Order, France explored and laid claim to the Great Lakes in the 1670s and

1680s, and Robert de La Salle journeyed the length of the Mississippi River to the Gulf of Mexico. While these northern territories held some appeal, it was the Caribbean that attracted French attention. The fertile soil and warm climate of the Caribbean furnished the requisite conditions for the cultivation of such tropical crops as indigo, tobacco, rice, cotton, and, above all, sugar. In the 1620s, the French government chartered companies to prospect for sugar islands and, in the 1630s, occupied St. Christophe (today St. Kitts), as well as Martinique, Guadeloupe, and, from the mid-1690s, Saint-Domingue (modern Haiti), the western half of the island of Hispaniola.

Initially, the incursions and forays made by Spain's rivals failed to break the brittle peace. But their recurrence and intensification stoked Spanish resentment. In 1588, Spain launched its infamous and ill-fated Armada to invade England. Approximately fifty ships were lost. This catastrophe permitted the English to sack the key peninsular port city of Cádiz in 1596. Two subsequent armadas sent against England, in 1596 and 1597, also failed, though the losses suffered are attributable to gale winds, not English maneuvers or prowess. After 1597, with the Spanish fleet in tatters, England's state-approved corsairs enjoyed a freer hand in the Atlantic, making feasible territorial expansion in North America and the Caribbean. Trade, plunder, and settlement were not mutually exclusive policies but inextricably linked.[14]

It was during and following the Thirty Years' War (1618–1648) that Spain's American empire received its most direct external challenge. The incorporation of Portugal and its colony of Brazil into the Spanish Crown from 1580 meant that Spanish territorial claims reached their greatest extent. But never had Spain faced so many rivals on multiple fronts, experienced comparable levels of domestic dissent, or been plagued by worse economic mismanagement than in the middle decades of the seventeenth century. Though most of the fighting took place in Central Europe, specifically the German-speaking lands, the worldwide conflict revolved around the Habsburg dynasty's supposed pretensions to universal empire. Between 1618 and 1621, Spanish involvement in Germany led, ultimately, to its effort to control the military corridors linking Vienna, Milan, and Brussels. These decisions also resulted in the resumption of hostilities with the Dutch. The expenditure necessitated by these excursions coincided with the sharp decline in remittances of American silver. New Spain's treasury spent one-third of its total revenue on defense, not counting its *situado* (subsidy) to the bullion-poor Caribbean colonies.

The acuteness of the shortfall compelled the Spanish Crown to identify new sources of revenue. Bureaucrats first surveyed Castile for untapped sources and, subsequently, extended their reach to other European parts of the composite monarchy, including Naples. The problem, as Elliott observed, was that each province "retained [its] own customary laws and representative assemblies, so that any attempt to extract larger financial and military contributions could well lead to disruptive constitutional conflict." Nevertheless, such a conflict proved exceedingly difficult to avoid. A high-placed observer complained that new kingdoms brought under the Spanish monarchy should not "appear to be separate nations[,] nor [should the subjects be] considered to be foreigners." Building on these ideas, Olivares recognized that the empire's diversity had to be replaced by uniformity, or at least with closer fiscal relationships between kingdoms befitting a supranational polity. In Olivares's far-reaching plan for a "Union of Arms" (1625), homogeneity was the prized object. It would entail the expansion of royal power and the curtailment of provincial customary rights, privileges, and constitutions. Their existence hampered the Spanish monarchy's capacity to respond punctually and decisively to geopolitical threats.[15] The unrelenting fiscal demands made upon the constituent kingdoms of the Spanish monarchy triggered unrest and then revolt. In the 1640s, Naples, Catalonia, and, as I shall discuss shortly, Portugal rose up, forcing the Spanish Crown to confront internal resistance as well as external foes.

Spain, including its Portuguese appendage, was most vulnerable beyond Europe. The Dutch, through their nimble, aggressive West India Company (WIC), struck at Iberian strongholds in the Americas. In 1624, they captured Salvador da Bahia, Brazil's most populous and wealthiest city. This success forced Spain to outfit an armada of fifty-six ships carrying more than twelve thousand men to expel the invaders, retake the city, and save face. But the Dutch threat did not subside. In 1627 alone, the WIC captured fifty-five Iberian ships, and in 1628 it captured the silver fleet sailing from New Spain. The value of the treasure was equivalent to two-thirds of the annual cost of maintaining the Dutch military. The impact on Spain's war effort, reliant on these regular infusions of American silver, was dire. For the Dutch, the fruits of this plunder would underwrite subsequent military and commercial ventures. The 1628 bounty buoyed the value of WIC shares on the Amsterdam Stock Exchange. This enabled the company to issue new shares, obtain fresh sources of credit, and undertake the conquest of

Figure 4. *A Topographicall Description and Admeasurement of the Yland of Barbados in the West Indyaes*. In Richard Ligon, *A True and Exact History of the Island of Barbados*. London: P. Parker and T. Guy, 1673. Courtesy of the George Peabody Library, The Sheridan Libraries, Johns Hopkins University.

Pernambuco, in the northeast of Brazil, several years later. There were symbolic expressions of this parasitism, too. Dutch raiders expropriated the bells of the Cathedral of San Juan, Puerto Rico, in 1627, later installing them in the First Dutch Church in New Amsterdam (today New York).[16]

With considerably smaller territory and a comparatively minuscule population, the Dutch managed to wage war across the globe and compete with their gargantuan rivals. Plundered silver indubitably was a boon, but Dutch survival was mostly attributable to the ingenious use of public debt. The payment of interest and redemption of loans were guaranteed by the government. A further inducement to lend was the high rates of return offered to those who purchased government-issued bonds. There was no shortage of lenders, and capital flooded into Amsterdam from across Europe. The Dutch were able, in effect, to borrow as much as they needed. In 1648, the Dutch Republic owed more than thirty times the amount it had in 1618, and yet it was never forced to declare bankruptcy.[17]

The English, too, seized advantage of the Thirty Years' War to pick off and occupy strategic island outposts and enclaves in the Caribbean: St. Kitts (1624), Barbados (1627), the Mosquito Coast of Nicaragua (sporadically, 1630s), and modern Belize (1642). By 1625, the English had laid foundations for colonies in Virginia, in New England, and in several smaller Caribbean islands that the Spaniards had not considered worthwhile to settle. These islands were initially conceived largely as entrepôts for contraband trade and plunder with continental Spanish America, not colonies of settlement. During the reign of Charles I (1625–1649), emigrants—both coerced and nominally uncoerced—flooded into North America and the Caribbean, transforming those islands into plantation societies. Roughly twenty thousand to twenty-five thousand Puritans departed for the New World in the 1630s. Population growth was stymied, however, by horrifically high mortality rates. Of the eight thousand men, women, and children brought to Virginia, a mere 1,218 were still alive a few years later. In 1622 alone, more than a thousand perished of disease, of starvation, or of the results of Native American attacks. In neighboring Maryland, infant mortality reached 30 percent, while 47 percent of the population died before reaching the age of twenty. Eventually, a less precarious food supply, strengthened immunity to disease, and the emergence of tobacco—a principal cash crop destined for export—gave rise to the conditions necessary for demographic stability and growth. Between 1640 and 1670, for example, the total European population in the Chesapeake leaped from eight thousand to 38,500, an annual growth rate of 7.5 percent. It was only once the colonial population had stabilized that England could pursue a systematic colonial policy as late as 1640.[18]

The union with Spain, perpetually embroiled in war, decimated Portugal's overseas empire. Besides the routine sacking of Cape Verde and São Tomé by English and Dutch corsairs, the WIC seized parts of the wealthy, sugar-producing northeast of Brazil. The Dutch also occupied Luanda, expelled the Portuguese from Ceylon, captured Ormuz in the Persian Gulf and Malacca, and blockaded Goa. Across the globe, Portuguese commerce was disrupted. The volume of shipping between Lisbon and Goa had declined significantly in the final decades of the sixteenth century, but the nadir was reached as a result of the Dutch assault. By the 1630s, the revenues of Portuguese India were inadequate to meet its basic defense. Slightly more than half as many ships embarked for Goa from Lisbon in the first half of the seventeenth century as had done so a century earlier. In the Atlantic, the

Dutch preyed on Portuguese shipping, capturing more than five hundred cargo ships between 1623 and 1638.[19]

Olivares's Union of Arms was the last straw. The previously supine Lusitanian nobility rallied around the Duke of Braganza and established his family as Portugal's ruling dynasty. The duke was an improbable figurehead for a revolt. He had been, until the late 1630s, a submissive vassal of Spain, for which he received significant emoluments, tax exemptions, and privileges. Much of the Portuguese nobility that supported him was thoroughly Castilianized through intermarriage. But the pulverization of the overseas empire and the onerous new tax burden imposed eroded the vaunted benefits of the composite monarchy. It made independence a desirable objective. Military victories against Spain followed. Portugal was effectively independent from 1648, even if Spain withheld formal recognition for another twenty years.[20]

How did the interloping, aspirant states justify their incursions into the Spanish and Portuguese empires? Unlike their Iberian counterparts, British and Dutch ideologues of empire rejected the notion that conquest itself conferred legitimacy and justified rule. The Dutch political writer and jurist Hugo Grotius distinguished the original acquisition of property through appropriation (*occupatio*), which existed before the establishment of civil society and as a natural right, from the notion of ownership (*dominium*) existing within civil society, regulated by the laws made by the appropriate public authority. In his famous *Mare liberum*, which formed part of his larger treatise *De Indis*, Grotius argued that states, like private individuals, could acquire goods and retain them as long they did not deny those goods to another state (or person) with a legitimate claim. A legitimate claim to ownership could be demonstrated by two actions: consumption and transfer to another entity. Grotius argued that Portuguese efforts to exclude the Dutch from the Indian Ocean could only be justified if Portugal could claim legitimate ownership over the sea as private property, which it could not.[21] The Dutch (and any other state) thus could not be excluded from trading in the Indian Ocean or, indeed, any other ocean.

Unlike the Iberian political philosophers, but like Grotius, English theorists of empire were at first unconcerned with their king's jurisdiction over native populations. Instead, they were preoccupied with justifying their occupation of lands to which they lacked title. In his *Second Treatise of Government* (1689–1690), John Locke asserted that ownership was acquired when a person had "mixed his labour with [it]; and joyned [it] to something that is his own." This statement was part of a larger argument that drew on the Roman law of *res nullius* (a thing belonging to no one), which held that all things without owners, which included unoccupied lands, remained the common property of all mankind until they were put to some productive use. This idea built on natural law jurisprudential traditions that justified agricultural colonies on the basis that those who brought land under productive cultivation had a stronger claim to it than those who had failed to do so. These notions spawned or melded with further justifications. Agricultural "improvement," as Drayton elucidated, "became a new criterion for responsible authority, and a mission toward which government might legitimately expand its powers."[22]

The arguments of Locke and Grotius formed the basis of most British and Dutch attempts to legitimate their presence in the New World, both against the claims of the Iberian powers, which appealed to the terms of the Treaty of Tordesillas, and against the protests of the native populations they dispossessed. America, Locke wrote, was in the same condition as that of the entire world before the founding of human societies, when "the inhabitants were too few for the country, and want of people and money gave men no temptation to enlarge their possessions of land, or contest for wider extent of ground."[23] Breaking from older Iberian tradition epitomized by Vitoria, the major conclusion of Locke's meditations was that Europeans could disregard all forms of government of aboriginals and, consequently, deny their status as nations. The British, by settling and cultivating the land, had acquired rights to possession that the native peoples had never enjoyed and, certainly, could not contest. In this manner, Locke's version of the res nullius argument was the most frequent legitimation of British presence in America and would later be amplified to justify the colonization of Australia and parts of sub-Saharan Africa.[24]

Res nullius arguments and the embrace of "improvement" as a justification for imperial expansion were closely linked to the pursuit and application of science in the extra-European world. Europeans were fascinated by the non-European world, and books on history, ethnography, natural history, travel narratives, cultural digests, and images circulated widely. This infatuation was a spur to exploration, which in turn generated scientific knowledge. To be sure, dispassionate inquiry and nonacquisitive curiosity were constant features of this interest in the world beyond Europe. European states sponsored scientific expeditions, but these were not undertaken for reasons untainted by geopolitical ambitions. In 1767, for example, France dispatched Louis-Antoine de Bougainville to the South Pacific. The motives underpinning this expedition were mixed, mingling traditional *raison d'état* yearnings (for example, to chart a new route to China, to encounter "unclaimed" territory ripe for colonization, and to identify new spices) with less utilitarian, "purely scientific" objectives. Britain's James Cook captained two voyages to the South Pacific (1768–1771 and 1772–1775) that charted the coasts of New Zealand and New Holland, added Hawaii to existing European maps, and skirted Antarctica. As with Bougainville's expedition, the artists and scientists accompanying Cook vastly expanded the boundaries of European knowledge concerning botany, zoology, and geology. Spain's Alejandro Malaspina led expeditions in the 1790s to the Americas and to the Pacific, which produced three hundred journals and log books, 450 albums of astronomical observation, fifteen hundred hydrographic reports, and sixteen thousand plants and seeds.[25]

These voyages aimed to enhance the sponsoring state's competitiveness in the international arena. Charles-Marie de La Condamine's 1735 expedition to South America, sponsored by France's Royal Academy of Sciences, was in part aimed at breaking Spain's monopoly on Peruvian bark trees, from which the antimalarial quinine was derived. Like its counterparts in Madrid, London, and Lisbon, as Londa Schiebinger and Claudia Swan noted, France's Jardin du Roi "worked hand in hand with the navy, outfitting ships with medicinal plants required for long voyages and, in turn, receiving specimens from around the world." Study of botany, astronomy, mineralogy, and so forth was not a dispassionate pursuit. Instead, as Drayton contended, it was at the foundation of a "faith that empire might be an instrument of cosmopolitan progress, and could benefit the imperialized as well as the imperializers."[26] Unsurprisingly, then, conduct and methods of European scientists reflected the outlook of the states sponsoring their activities. They often erased the contributions of indigenous collaborators who supplied the natural knowledge underpinning scientific advances. In historian Neil Safier's phrase, the precise roles of these collaborators were subsumed "under the guise of the exotic or expendable supernumerary." In Spanish America, as elsewhere, scientists sought to combine European and indigenous knowledge, privileging the concepts and categories of the former. For example, as historians Antonio Lafuente and Nuria Valverde argued, Linnaean botany could be converted into a form of "imperial biopower devoted to turning diversity, local variation and qualia into data."[27] In this way, science was empire's indispensable adjunct while at the same time being enhanced by the engagement with the non-European world of which imperial states sought to make themselves masters.

5. Consolidation, Conflict, and Reform in the Long Eighteenth Century

By the second half of the seventeenth century, England, the Dutch Republic, and France possessed their own steadily expanding and increasingly lucrative overseas empires, often carved from the margins of the Iberian empires. This chapter examines the position of the five seaborne empires relative to one another from the aftermath of the Thirty Years' War until the final decades of the eighteenth century. It traces efforts to consolidate control over and then reform the government and economy of their overseas empires, which occurred against the backdrop of unremitting interstate competition and conflict. The resources of overseas territories were a crucial determinant in the outcome of those clashes, all the more as ultramarine societies expanded demographically and prospered economically.

The Thirty Years' War proved catastrophic for the Habsburg dynasty, particularly for the Spanish branch of the family. Having hemorrhaged its treasury, exhausted its credit, alienated elites in its component kingdoms, and lost Portugal, Spain sought relief at the diplomatic bargaining table. It was compelled to concede as irrevocable the seizure of its territory by its European rivals during war. As Olivares advised the king, "In our present position, not only do we need a peace, truce or ceasefire, but we cannot go on without one." What is customarily referred to as the Peace of Westphalia (1648), which ended the conflict, resulted from two separate treaties, of Münster and of Osnabrück. Westphalia's transcendent importance often has been exaggerated in the history of international relations, but it did enshrine principles guiding the conduct of relations among states until the end of the eighteenth century. Building on the earlier peace treaties of Augsburg and of Cateau-Cambresis, Westphalia confirmed the principle of religious self-determination. Each state could determine its own religion without external interference. It also affirmed that sovereignty would henceforth be understood in terms of territory, not dynastic claims alone. Furthermore, all states would be considered independent and equal, regardless of differences in population size, geographical extent, and military strength. By secularizing politics and (in theory) elevating the principle of sovereignty over dynastic claims, Westphalia's architects sought to end the internecine and protracted conflicts that had plagued Europe for centuries. When fresh disputes arose, as they inevitably would, Westphalia's precedent established that congresses of states would be convened to resolve them before larger conflagrations immolated the Continent.[1]

Westphalia also confirmed Habsburg defeat and made indisputable Dutch and French ascendancy. Spain accepted Dutch control of all territory that the republic had occupied in America in exchange for a pledge to desist from trading illicitly with Spanish America. War with France did not cease after Westphalia but continued until 1659, albeit with slightly reduced intensity. France's chief minister, Cardinal Mazarin, refused even a truce. For him, Spain represented a mortal threat to France; it needed to be vanquished. In 1684, France and Spain finally suspended their protracted conflict, both within Europe and "beyond the line" in the extra-European world. Spain was not France's only enemy. France also perceived the upstart Dutch as insufferable rivals. Dutch commercial activities threatened France's *exclusif*, a form of trade monopoly. Already in the late 1660s the leading minister Jean-Baptiste Colbert had doubled tariffs on Dutch woolen goods and linen entering France. He raised the tariff on refined sugar, often carried by Dutch merchants, to a whopping 50 percent. In 1670, he pledged to "chase [the Dutch] from the West Indies entirely if it can be done without openly violating our treaties." These policies met with success. France had bettered its rivals. As the Great Elector put it in 1679, "France has already become the arbiter of Europe . . . henceforth, no prince will find security or profit except with the friendship and alliance of the king of France."[2]

France's empire was not restricted to the Americas. The first successful French settlement in Africa began in 1638 when an outpost was set up on the Isle de Gorée, off the coast of modern Senegal. In 1659, the French established a port city, christened Saint-Louis, on the mainland. The Indian Ocean also attracted avid French interest. Louis XIV chartered an East India Company in

1664. It was granted a monopoly over trade in India and the Indian Ocean as well as control over the territories it might occupy in Madagascar and India. Ultimately, France established three Indian Ocean colonies. In 1642, Île Bourbon (today Réunion) was seized. France also claimed neighboring Mauritius, an island originally occupied by the Dutch, in 1715. The colony prospered due to abundant arable land and one of the best harbors in the Indian Ocean. In 1756, France annexed the Seychelles archipelago. As on the other two Indian Ocean islands, trade, sugar, and cotton were favored. France aspired to dominion in India itself and held five Indian *comptoirs*, trading posts, by 1742.

England's Civil War (1640–1660) precipitated a major break in the nation's imperial policy. England renewed conflict with both Spain and the Dutch Republic. The foundation of a republican commonwealth marked a new stage in the struggle against Spain. The 1655 capture of Jamaica, part of Cromwell's Western Design, was the high-water mark of this aggressively expansionist policy, indubitably linked to the broader bellicose anti-Catholic and anti-Spanish sentiment percolating among the Lord Protector's followers. Spain, humbled in 1648, was vulnerable to such aggression. Britain could exploit its old adversary's weakness. Two hundred and seventeen new vessels were added to England's fleet between 1646 and 1659.[3] In 1670, according to the terms of the Treaty of Madrid, Spain reluctantly recognized England's annexations at its expense in the Caribbean. The Atlantic world, it must be added, was not the sole theater of action. It was matched by rising involvement in the Indian Ocean. In 1657, the British East India Company was given a new charter and put on a more durable basis.

Like France, England considered the Dutch Republic a fearsome rival. The 1651 Navigation Act, discussed in Chapter 7, was overtly pitched as an anti-Dutch measure. The mutual enmity between the two rising Protestant powers went far beyond narrow economic interest. As historian Steven Pincus explained, the Dutch "saw the English as perfidious regicides whose very state was illegitimate and whose religion was heresy. The English, by contrast, had come to see the Dutch as fallen brethren, men who had been seduced by mammon and monarchy."[4] Such disdain often bubbled over into belligerence and triggered a series of Anglo-Dutch Wars. In the third Anglo-Dutch War, fought in 1672, Britain and France were allied and poised to deal a fatal blow to the republic. Improbably, the Dutch repulsed a French army of 120 thousand soldiers, as well as a massive Anglo-French armada, and preserved their independence.

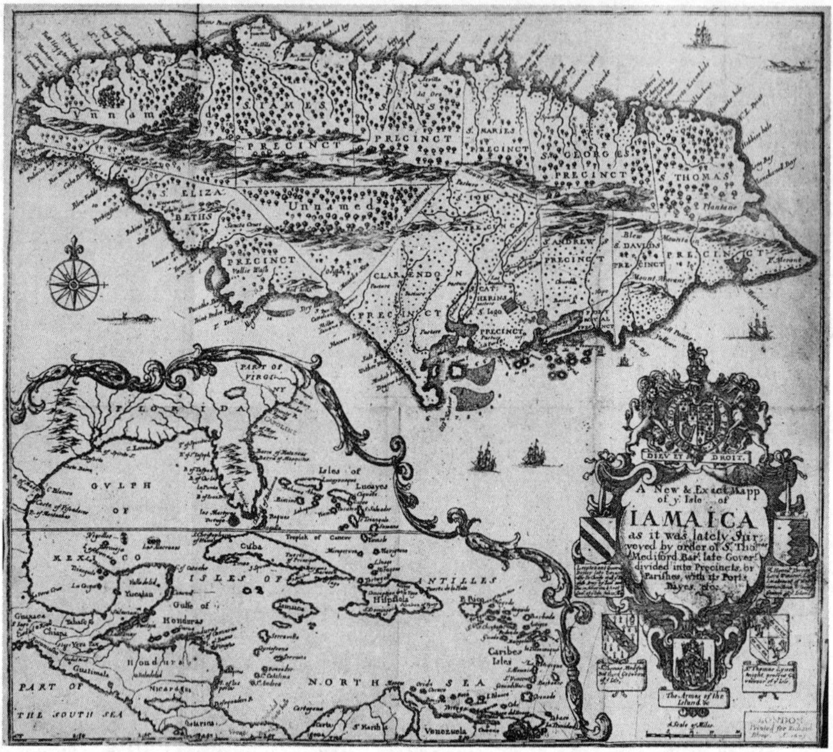

Figure 5. *A New and Exact Mapp of the Isle of Jamaica.* In Richard Blome, *The Present State of His Majesties Isles and Territories in America. . . .* London: Printed by H. Clark, for Dorman Newman, 1687. Courtesy of the George Peabody Library, The Sheridan Libraries, Johns Hopkins University.

Portugal squandered no time reclaiming sundry overseas territories and spheres of influence after regaining its independence from Spain. Bahia and Pernambuco in the northeast of Brazil were retaken, and the Dutch dislodged from Angola. Between 1648 and 1671, Portugal embarked on an aggressive phase of military expansion in Angola. The crucial moment was the 1665 Battle of Mbwila, in which the kingdom of Kongo's army was routed; the king, António I, was killed, along with almost five hundred nobles of various ranks. In Europe, Portugal fortified its international position, and the Braganza dynasty's tenuous political legitimacy, through a new alliance with England formed in the early 1650s, sealed by marriage between Charles II and Catherine of Braganza. Portugal was compelled to make significant concessions to its new ally, ceding Tangier and transferring Bombay. It also

Figure 6. Portuguese attack on a Dutch sugar mill in Brazil in 1645. "No. 2. Int jornael van M. vanden Broeck. fo. 5." In Matheus van den Broeck, *Journael ofte historiaelse beschrijvinge*. Amsterdam: Voor Gerrit van Goedesbergen, 1651. Courtesy of the John Carter Brown Library at Brown University.

granted England commercial privileges and paid a massive indemnity. In exchange, England maintained two thousand infantry soldiers and one thousand cavalry in Portugal. Crucially, it promised further military support in case of invasion. Subsequent marriage alliances secured the protection of France against potential Spanish aggression. Taken together, these alliances enabled Portugal to keep Spain at bay and to reach a peace settlement with the Dutch.[5]

The one region in which Portugal failed to recover its former authority was the Indian Ocean. There the Dutch remained ascendant and continued to make inroads against Portuguese positions, even as they relinquished territory in Brazil and Angola. The losses of Malacca and Ceylon were particularly damaging blows for Portugal to absorb. In 1652, Portugal possessed twenty major coastal toeholds across the Indian Ocean, but that figure had been halved a decade later. The situation was dire. In 1662, the governor of the Estado da Índia lamented that "the needs of this state are so many and so great . . . and there is not even a penny to help meet pressing and necessary expenditure." His pleas went unheeded. The Crown, aware that it could not wage war across the globe, deliberately concentrated its resources on Brazil. It sought to retain the Indian Ocean strongholds with minimal expenditure.[6] By the 1660s, a swing to the West in Portugal's imperial orientation was discernible. Brazil, the most lucrative, productive, and populous extraterritorial possession, became the sun around which the other territories, including Portugal itself, orbited. The Estado da Índia thus lapsed into a backwater. By the 1680s, revenue from its remnants amounted to a minuscule fraction of the treasury's overall receipts.

The fortunes of the Dutch overseas activity, both explicitly imperial and commercial, waxed and waned after 1650. Ejected from Brazil and Angola by the Portuguese, Dutch operations suffered a further blow in 1662, when the Chinese evicted the VOC from Formosa, which had been a center of lucrative trade for forty years. A further setback occurred in 1668, when the Japanese Shogunate embargoed the export of silver, thus slowing to a trickle a supply on which the Dutch depended. The encroachment of English trading companies displaced the Dutch in parts of West Africa, America, and Asia. As its geopolitical star waned, the republic's fiscal situation deteriorated, too. The aforementioned wars with France and England, even if inordinately successful relative to the republic's size, meant that state expenditures far outstripped revenues, even though tax levels had risen considerably. The state was forced to rely heavily on public credit, which previously had served the republic well. Borrowing now produced drastic consequences. By 1713, the debt service of Holland, the Dutch Republic's largest and most populous province, exceeded tax revenues.[7] If not foreshadowing decline, the disadvantageous fiscal position precluded a vigorous policy of expansion.

This plight, however, did not portend a retreat from empire or from extra-European trade. In fact, notable territorial gains were made in the Indian Ocean, at Portugal's expense. Following the successful siege of Colombo in 1655–1656, the Dutch controlled the entirety of Ceylon's cinnamon-producing zone. In the following years, the VOC forces overran scattered Portuguese enclaves in southern India. From the republic's remaining Caribbean possessions, Dutch merchants successfully, if illicitly, penetrated Spanish American markets. They supplied more than a thousand slaves to Spanish America between 1658 and 1729. Even amid political and fiscal turbulence, then, Dutch commerce retained certain advantages over its rivals. These included its robust merchant marine, low freight charges, capacity to transport bulky goods cheaply, and the attractively low interest rates Dutch merchants extended to their suppliers. The period 1680–1720, in fact, witnessed massive investment of metropolitan capital in the colonial trade, where greater opportunities for higher profit existed than in European markets.[8]

Viewed as whole, the Westphalian settlement failed to stem conflict among Western European states for overseas empire. Concessions, treaties, and nominal peace did not induce demobilization. There was no downward shift, for example, in Spain's military expenditure, which exceeded the remission of American bullion to the peninsula during the final decades of the seventeenth century. In Peru, the case was particularly stark: 95 percent of Crown revenues collected in the viceroyalty were spent there in the 1680s, chiefly to maintain fortresses, to rebuild the depleted fleet, and for other defensive measures. In a sense, self-sufficiency could be interpreted as a sign of the empire's durability in times of crisis, which did not unravel the entire system. Yet this was sorry comfort for many observers in Spain itself. For them, retention of empire was increasingly a dangerous liability or luxury, an albatross portending "decline." Spain's experience was extreme but not unique. The shared experience of interimperial rivalry, and the competitive emulation that characterized the empires' relations, had produced a convergence of war-making infrastructure across Europe. In the late seventeenth and early eighteenth centuries, France, England, and Russia devoted at least three-quarters of the respective revenues they collected to finance the military. Louis XIV's formidable wartime state employed roughly 10 percent of the adult male population of working age, the majority of whom served in the armed forces. In Britain, the military role of the state made it the most important single factor in the domestic economy. It was the largest borrower, spender, and employer.[9]

Historians have termed this phenomenon the "fiscal-military state," a new type of state designed to wage war. Economy and society were reorganized around the extraction of revenue. The first step to augment receipts was to impose new taxes, whether direct or excise taxes, and also to create state monopolies over valuable resources, including salt and minerals. In Britain, for example, revenue collection was enhanced by the expansion of a fiscal bureaucracy. Public credit also became a larger component of financing war than it had earlier. As historian John Brewer explained, by 1698 "it had become clear that public deficit finance was not an evanescent phenomenon but a long-term part of the workings of the English state." During the early eighteenth-century War of Spanish Succession, deficit finance accounted for

30 percent of the English state's expenditure, a figure that increased to 40 percent by the 1770s.[10]

The convergence was neither accidental nor coincidental. Each state emulated its rivals in areas of administrative, fiscal, or military policy in which its counterparts were comparatively proficient.[11] Emulation promised rapid improvement and mitigated the risk of failure associated with policy experimentation. Political writers and ministers, therefore, dissected, analyzed, and either lauded or rejected, the ideas, institutions, reforms, and character of rival empires. Such emulation was pragmatic, a scramble for viable models with which to compete with those same states whose policies were emulated or rejected. As foreign models were encountered, modified, and incorporated, the policy goals, content, and instruments of each seaborne empire increasingly came to resemble those of its rivals. Incessant war, mercantile rivalry, and the drive for power resulted in policy convergence and a movement toward institutional isomorphism.

Contemporaries were keenly aware that a spirit of emulation was pervasive. Emulation was contrasted with, and seen as the positive counterpart of, jealousy or envy throughout Europe. It could take many practical forms, including industrial espionage. For example, when the Spanish naval officer Jorge Juan was sent on a secret mission to England in 1749, he was instructed to observe practices as diverse as the use of steam power, port-sweeping methods, and the design of British warships, not to mention engage in the clandestine recruitment of English shipwrights. Anglo-French rivalry (and British ascendancy) did not prevent Britain from borrowing heavily from France. Britain's imperial reform of the 1780s took France's reforms after 1763 as a model, as Drayton elucidated. The assertion of Crown control over trading companies, the creation of free ports in the Caribbean to penetrate Spanish colonial markets, the emphasis on agrarian "improvement," and the recasting (and empowering) of the colonial governor as an "enlightened despot" were all manifestations of the spirit of emulation.[12] The growth of the fiscal-military state and the convergence of institutions across states, often attributable to emulation, then, were crucial features of the 150 years following Westphalia, accounting for the intensification of interstate conflict.

The Glorious Revolution in Britain (1688) decisively affected the trajectories of Europe's seaborne empires. It ended (for a time) Anglo-Dutch conflict, as the Dutch House of Orange-Nassau became Britain's ruling dynasty, replacing the exiled Stuart dynasty.[13] If it dissipated Anglo-Dutch enmity, the Glorious Revolution inaugurated a new phase of hostility toward France. An inconclusive nine-year war, ended by the Treaty of Ryswick in 1697, did nothing to abate the mutual antipathy. Nor would the Hanoverian Succession remove all rancor. Britain and France would find themselves at war for about half of the 126 years between 1689 and 1815, including several decades-long conflicts: 1689–1697, 1702–1713, 1739–1763, 1778–1783, and then almost constantly from 1792 to 1815.

The peace ending the War of Spanish Succession (1701–1713), enshrined in the Treaty of Utrecht, affirmed the ascendancy of France in continental Europe. It also ushered in the transition from the Habsburg to the Bourbon dynasty across the Pyrenees, in Spain. With the same royal family occupying both thrones (but not, crucially, under the same ruler), France and Spain formed a "Family Compact," an alliance that survived for the remainder of the century. The tightening bond uniting the Bourbon states pushed Portugal to embrace an even closer alliance with Britain. Under the terms of the Methuen Treaty (1703), Portugal made still further commercial concessions in exchange for British military protection. Utrecht has rightly been interpreted as a triumph for Britain. It established itself as a major power in the Mediterranean. It inflicted humbling naval defeats on Spain, highlighted by the conspicuously provocative occupation of Gibraltar in 1703 and the destruction of its fleet off Málaga a year later. Utrecht brought further concessions from Spain, including the transfer of the strategically situated Mediterranean island of Minorca to Britain. In this way, Britain's gains in the Mediterranean counterbalanced the advantages France derived from the War of Spanish Succession.[14]

Britain benefited from the Utrecht settlement beyond Europe, too. It gained commercial concessions in the Atlantic. The South Sea Company received the lucrative *asiento* contract. Previously held by the Dutch, the asiento gave the exclusive right to transport slaves to Spanish America for thirty years (1713–1739). This meant that British merchants could smuggle items on ships carrying slaves, but just as often they could establish networks of contacts for clandestine trade. A veneer of legality was provided in that the South Sea Company secured the right to introduce products into Spanish American markets once a year from 1716. In the Caribbean, Spanish communities obtained British manufactured goods in exchange for primary products, supplemented with bullion. Between 1748 and 1765, after the expiration of the asiento concession, at least three million pounds sterling worth of

Spanish bullion was received at British colonial ports, most of it at Jamaica.[15] The Spanish Empire thus hemorrhaged bullion, its strenuous efforts notwithstanding, and the frequency of such illicit commerce turned colonial monopoly into a farce. Burgeoning American demand, combined with the breakdown of the *flota* system, which barred non-Spanish ships from American ports, ensured that Madrid's pretensions to colonial monopoly were rendered farcical.

Nevertheless, in spite of innumerable concessions and high costs, Spanish America remained largely intact. Small enclaves and some entrepôts had been surrendered irrevocably, but the authority Spain exerted over both its less developed peripheries and its core viceroyalties was undiminished. The advent of the Bourbon dynasty was accompanied by a brief respite from war. Spain seized advantage of the pause, embarking on a naval reconstruction program, almost tripling the size of the fleet between 1720 and 1760. This facilitated a more robust Mediterranean policy. By 1746, Spain could station more than fifty thousand troops in Italy and pursue a range of military objectives in North Africa. Its navy lagged behind that of Britain even with these strenuous efforts. The persistent disparity necessitated a continued reliance on fortified ports in the Americas.[16] Although Spain would implement an elaborate coast guard system in a futile, belated effort to exclude interloping contraband traders, it studiously avoided battles at sea. Spain fought a single naval battle with Britain between 1713 and 1762, and that confrontation was triggered by an egregious attack on the silver fleet. Military reforms were accompanied by changes in civil administration and commercial regulations.

Portugal's American empire was transformed in the early eighteenth century. Before the 1690s, settlement was largely confined to Brazil's Atlantic coast. The sugar- and tobacco-producing regions of the northeast, centered on Bahia, dominated the economy. This geographical orientation would shift dramatically. In the seventeenth century, in the southern province of São Vicente (later renamed São Paulo), parties of so-called *bandeirantes* (or flag-bearing forces) pushed into the interior, in search of gold and Indian slaves. Precious mineral strikes occurred in the interior mountainous zone, subsequently christened Minas Gerais, beginning in 1695. These discoveries precipitated a massive influx of migrants into the interior. These new arrivals included fortune seekers, enslaved Africans, and legions of petty traders, merchants, and builders who galvanized formerly sleepy mountain villages into boomtowns. Slaves worked the mines, panned for gold in rivers, and scoured for diamonds. The mineral discoveries and population flows reoriented the Brazilian economy southward. The Atlantic port of Rio de Janeiro expanded rapidly in this period, and it became the seat of royal government in 1763.[17]

The state seized on the advantages of this mineral windfall. Portuguese gold underwrote a formidable palace-building and public works initiative in Lisbon and its environs. Several architectural jewels—the Lisbon aqueduct, the palace at Mafra, and the library of the University of Coimbra—were built in the first decades of the century. Mineral wealth also safeguarded the Portuguese Empire's independence. Its huge trade imbalance with northern European states, particularly Britain, compelled Portugal to pay for its imports from those countries in specie. Gold flowing from Brazil made its way into the hands of British merchants. Even in the late 1770s, after the productivity of the mines declined, Brazilian gold coins were among the most widely circulated in Britain and British North America.[18]

While such subservience guaranteed British protection, it generated long-term problems and dilemmas. The dynamism of Brazil's economy prompted high-placed officials to propose the transfer of the seat of the monarchy. As early as the 1730s, they recognized that Brazil's wealth, and its demographic weight within the monarchy, had surpassed that of Portugal. They reckoned that the colony would not long remain content in a subordinate position. Portugal slowly became extraneous to Brazil's economy, which was premised on the African slave trade and galvanized by slave labor. Brazilian merchants increasingly conducted bilateral trade between Angola and Brazil, thus weakening metropolitan control over both colonial economies. Of the ships arriving in Luanda, the major Angolan slaving port, between 1736 and 1770, less than a fifth had come from Portugal. The vast majority had set sail from Brazil's ports.[19] Yet these long-term structural problems, though palpable, were not acute. They could be ignored for several decades without causing disruption.

As previously noted, Britain and France were belligerents for much of the eighteenth century. The peace treaty of Aix-la-Chapelle (1748) failed to resolve their disputes, which increasingly centered on North America and India. In 1730, there were four hundred thousand subjects in British America and roughly a tenth of that number in New France. As the population of the British colonies expanded, designs on French possessions were pursued in

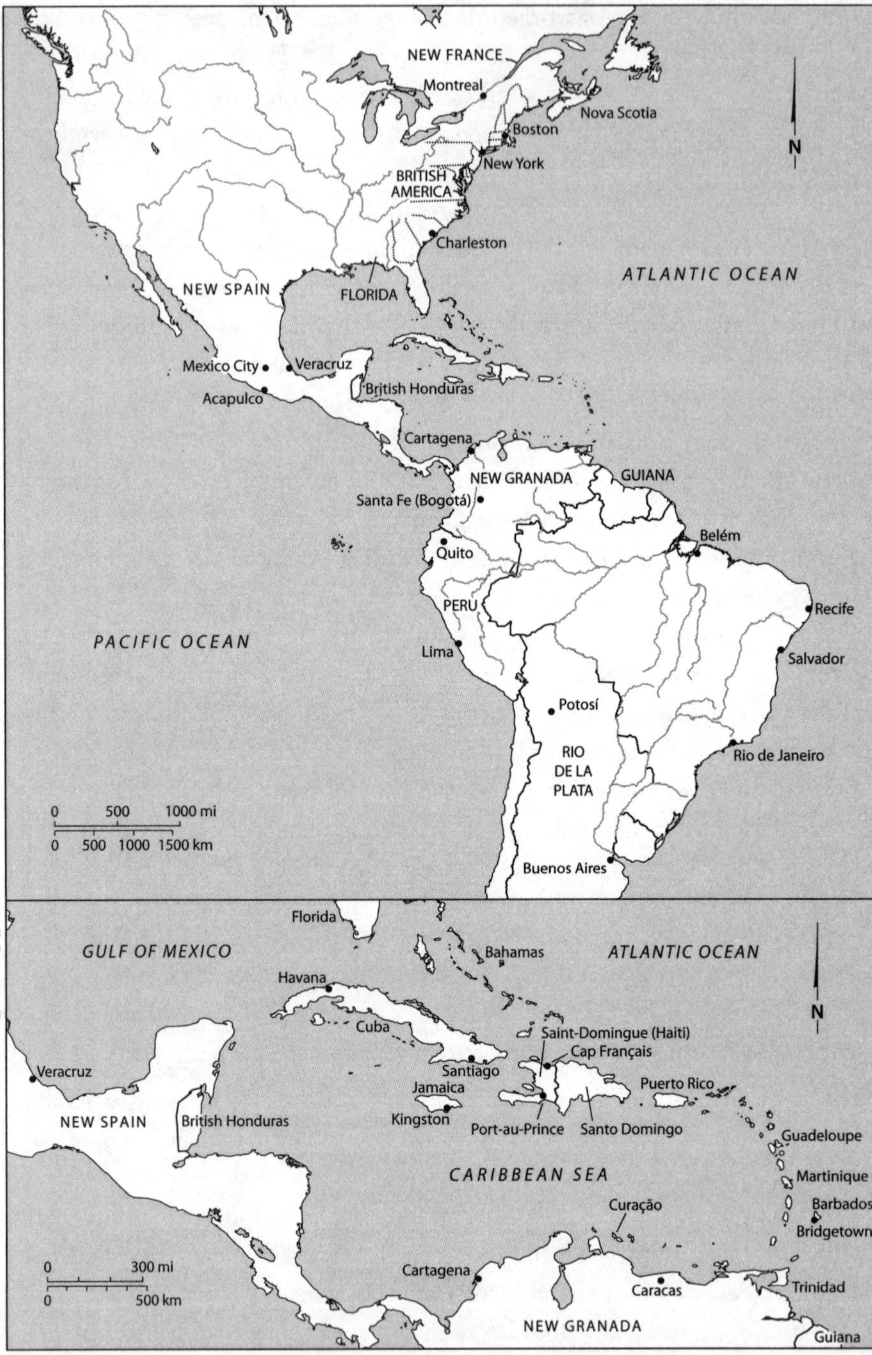

Figure 7. The Americas in the eighteenth century

earnest. Skirmishes in Europe and dynastic wars in Europe pitted the powers against each other on two continents. In the years before 1756, the French managed to check British expansion by sending military force into the Ohio Valley, where they constructed forts, expelled British traders, and forged alliances with Amerindians to counteract those enjoyed by Britain. France pursued a similarly aggressive strategy in South Asia, but with considerably less success.[20]

The Seven Years' War was the undeniable watershed of interimperial relations in the eighteenth century. The Americas were not the only theater, and the conflict was the outgrowth of a broader European conflict. In the simplest terms, the war confirmed British supremacy over the Atlantic sea lanes, the Caribbean, and North America above the Rio Grande. France surrendered French Canada (Quebec) to Britain, though it retained the most lucrative sugar colonies: Guadeloupe, Martinique, and, above all, Saint-Domingue. In 1770, at least thirty-five thousand French subjects lived in the Caribbean, most of them in Martinique and Saint-Domingue. Similarly, toeholds in South Asia, Pondicherry above all, were not forfeited. French statesmen were confounded by Britain's ascendancy. As the Duke of Choiseul declared in 1767, "I am completely astounded that England, which is a very tiny bit of Europe, is dominant. . . . I shall continue to hope that what is incomprehensible will not be eternal."[21] France would not accede complacently to British dominance.

Spain's entry into the Seven Years' War was belated and bungled. Buckling to French pressure to adhere to the terms of the Family Compact, Spain severely jeopardized its dominance in the Americas and in the Pacific. The British capture of Havana and Manila in 1762, a humbling defeat, underscored the inadequacy of existing fortifications, naval preparedness, and overall military strength. Though those two ports were later returned, the seizure shocked Spain and gave impetus to already stirring reform tendencies. Statesmen turned away from the sturdy and resilient composite monarchy structure. In its place, they sought to erect a unified nation-state, subservient to a centralized monarchy and capable of inculcating a new patriotic spirit. New viceroyalties were established as part of a wider reorganization of territorial administration. Older institutions and practices prone to abuse or misuse were modified. The *repartimiento* system was suppressed, and the practice of selling of offices was terminated. The navy was overhauled, the army and colonial militias expanded, coastal fortifications revamped, university education modernized, a less-regulated trade regime enacted, mineral yields boosted through new technology, export-led agricultural production incentivized, church property wrested away, and ecclesiastical patronage reclaimed for the state.[22]

Whether caused by these attempts or merely coterminous with them, there was remarkable urban, mercantile, and demographic growth in the Spanish Empire, particularly after 1770. This surge was sparked by export-led production of tropical commodities, galvanized by the dramatic influx of African slaves. Cacao and indigo made up 95 percent of the value of exports from Caracas (Venezuela) by 1795. The loosening of trade regulations clearly played a role, too, particularly the 1778 *comercio libre* (free trade) decree. There was rising demand for and consumption of European finished goods—cottons, linens, silks, but also agricultural goods such as oil and *aguardiente*—by Spanish Americans. The average value of exports from Spain to America was four times greater in 1796 than it had been in 1778. Bullion, of course, continued to dominate the economy, even as it was diversifying. It accounted for almost 80 percent of the assessed value of all shipments from the New World registered at Cádiz between 1717 and 1778. Other precious metals and minerals emerged, too. Gold continued to account for 90 percent of the value of exports from New Granada (modern Colombia) to Spain, and minerals in general still hovered around 60 percent for the empire as a whole.[23]

Spanish imperial resurgence was attributable not merely to the burgeoning commerce of the Atlantic ports and the lucrative extraction from the American mines. In the Andes, a combination of more efficient (and stringent) regulation and population growth caused the collection of tribute from indigenous communities to rise by as much as six times its previous level in several jurisdictions. In New Spain (Mexico), the Crown established monopolies on tobacco, playing cards, and gunpowder. The picture was not entirely rosy, of course. High-ranking Spanish officials, including the minister of the Indies, José de Gálvez, were keenly aware of imperial overstretch. In 1779, he warned that "to supply all the troops, military supplies and fortifications that peninsular Spain and its ultramarine empire would require would be an impossible enterprise, even if the crown had at its disposal all the treasures, armies and storehouses of Europe." Still, a valiant effort was made. Resources were redistributed to achieve these aims. A large portion of the silver, perhaps as much as 40 percent, in the royal coffers of

Figure 8. *A View of the Entrance of the Harbour of the Havana, Taken from within the Wrecks.* Engraving by Elias Durnford and Peter Canot. London: Printed for John Bowles, 1768. Courtesy of the John Carter Brown Library at Brown University.

Mexico was redirected to Caribbean ports, such as Havana, and the Philippines to defray the costs of garrisons and the fortification of coastal defenses.[24]

At mid-century, the Portuguese Empire was at a crossroads. Portugal had reached an uneasy détente with Spain. The borders fuzzily demarcated in the 1494 Treaty of Tordesillas were now clarified. The Treaty of Madrid (the so-called Treaty of the Limits), signed in 1750, guaranteed Spanish control of the Colonia de Sacramento (present-day Uruguay) and exclusive jurisdiction over the Río de la Plata in exchange for recognition of Portuguese supremacy in the Amazon, a swathe of territory on the eastern bank of the Uruguay River, and a mutual guarantee of support should either nation's American colonies suffer attack from a third nation. There were further causes for dispute, but most were resolved in the 1777 Treaty of San Ildefonso. If the prospect of a Spanish invasion was unlikely, additional threats to Portugal's sovereignty lurked. Recall that Portugal had cemented its alliance with Britain through the 1703 Methuen Treaty. Technically, it was a commercial treaty that granted privileges to Britain in the Portuguese and, by extension, the Brazilian market in exchange for low duties on the import of Portuguese wine into Britain. But the Methuen Treaty was an extraordinary trade agreement. Trade with Britain drained Portugal of its Brazilian specie. It also opened both Portugal and Brazil to cheaper British manufactured goods, against which nascent Portuguese manufactured goods were not competitive. This situation was tolerable so long as mineral yields were robust, but they declined significantly from mid-century, starkly revealing Portugal's deepening dependence on Britain.

As Portugal grappled with its geopolitical plight, catastrophe struck. In 1755, an earthquake and tsunami decimated Lisbon, killing between thirty thousand and sixty thousand inhabitants. It razed vast swathes of the city, including the royal palace. Sebastião José de Carvalho e Mello, better known to posterity by his later title, the Marquis of Pombal, rose to power in the wake of the disaster. His strident, yet efficient, emergency measures quickly stabilized the country. He brutally suppressed the social anarchy spawned by the disaster. He executed looters and fixed the prices of food, building materials, and rents. Having stabilized Portugal, Pombal turned his attention to Brazil. He enacted reforms to squeeze out more revenue, centralize administration, and mitigate the deleterious effects of unfavorable treaties with Britain. He chartered privileged trading companies to spur the economic activity in the north and northeast of Brazil. New crops—including cotton, rice, and cacao—were incentivized, for these were not regulated by the Methuen Treaty, and demand for them was rising in Europe. The colonial capital was transferred from Salvador to Rio de Janeiro. Contraband trade was curtailed, and the slave trade was stimulated. As described in greater detail in Chapter 6, the Jesuits, whom Pombal believed had surreptitiously formed a "state within a state" in the Americas and undermined royal authority, were expelled from Portuguese territory. The administration of Indians in their *aldeias* (villages) and missions, with a view toward their profitability, was assumed by the Crown.[25]

Though the Age of Revolutions is the subject of Chapter 12, the present account would be incomplete without some mention of the interaction of the seaborne empires in the aftermath of the Seven Years' War. France (1778), Spain (1779), and the Dutch Republic (1780) all entered the American Revolution, altering the nature of the conflict. Spain hoped to remove the ever-creeping British threat to its American empire, while France hoped to shift the balance of power within Europe in its favor. As the Count of Vergennes, the foreign minister, argued, "The separation of her northern

Figure 9. *A Picturesque View of the State of the Nation for February 1778*. Printed in the *Westminster Magazine* 66 (March 1778), 66. Courtesy of the John Carter Brown Library at Brown University. According to the John Carter Brown Library, British commerce is depicted as a cow; America as an Amerindian; Britain as a sleeping lion; the British public as a person in a state of despair; France and Spain as men holding bowls of milk; and Holland as a milkman.

colonies; her shrunken and diminished trade; her more encumbered finances, will proportionately reduce her power and make her less worrisome and less proud. She will be unable to kindle and feed the fire of division and discord among the great states of Europe."[26]

An enlarged army and revivified navy permitted Spain to join France in the war effort. The rebuilt Bourbon navies remained inferior to Britain's fleet in quality, but combined they were numerically superior and thus able to disrupt and undermine a British strategy that assumed mastery of the sea. For the revolutionaries, the Bourbon fleet provided the relief they needed at sea to secure victory on land. In 1781, for example, the French Navy blocked the entrance to the Chesapeake, preventing Britain from reinforcing its army, camped at Yorktown, and from laying siege to the rebels, which resulted in the capitulation that ended the revolution. The Bourbon Navy captured Grenada, St. Vincent, Tobago, and Minorca. Spain reoccupied West Florida and the Gulf Coast in North America, and Minorca in the Mediterranean. Britain was forced to abandon the Mosquito Coast in 1786 (in exchange for clear title in Belize). Spanish officials viewed these successes as a prelude to the repossession of the Malvinas (Falklands) and Gibraltar, though such hopes would soon be dashed. Unlike France and Spain, the Dutch Republic found its position weakened by intervention. The British Navy exacted revenge and decimated the VOC, reducing its fleet by half. Combined with other difficulties, the VOC's decline became irreversible. Expenses outstripped sales considerably, and loans to keep the VOC afloat drained what remained of its assets. In 1798, the state took over the Company's property and debts.[27] Like Spain and the Netherlands, France spent heavily in pursuit of its geopolitical ambitions. Naval expenditure quadrupled between 1778 and 1783, with ghastly consequences for state finances. Debt service rose from one-third of state revenue in the early 1770s to almost two-thirds of it by 1788. Though not a problem to dismiss lightly, the costs were offset by the satisfaction France gained from tarnishing Britain's prestige. Habsburg emperor Joseph II averred that the American War had demonstrated "just how much [Britain] has degenerated," revealing its "desperate and pitiable condition."[28]

Nevertheless, it must be underlined that though Britain suffered defeat, it was far from the total, debilitating defeat its adversaries sought (and expended) to inflict. Admiral Rodney's 1782 victory at the naval battle off Îles des Saints, near Guadeloupe, resulting in the capture of his French counterpart de Grasse, ensured territorial losses in the Caribbean were minimized. Rebel incursions into Canada yielded little, while Canada's link to Britain was bolstered by an influx of exiled loyalists who found the prospect of remaining in the nascent United States intolerable if not untenable. Nor had the Bourbon powers and the Dutch shaken Britain's position in Europe. Strategically situated Minorca was seized, to be sure, but Gibraltar was retained in spite of a protracted siege in 1781–1782. The French expeditions sent to India were repulsed, and rebellion in Ireland was averted.[29]

The second half of the eighteenth century witnessed the projection of British power across the globe, often at the expense of its rivals. In the Atlantic, Britain emerged as the indisputable victor in the Seven Years' War. Perhaps the most important development after 1750 involved the EIC, not the British state itself. The creation of a vast South Asian empire under the Company's aegis was largely unforeseen. The EIC had struggled for primacy even against other European powers in India as late as the 1740s. The French had captured Madras from the EIC in 1746, for example, though they returned it two years later. Soon thereafter, the Company established itself as the foremost European power in India. Between 1757 and 1765, the EIC acquired a vast territorial dominion. While the EIC's victory at the Battle of Plassey (1757) was undeniably of symbolic importance, signaling its status as a ruling power in what had been the Mughal Empire, the crucial military triumph was the Battle of Buxar (1764). As a result, most of eastern India came into the EIC's orbit, including Bengal, the richest province. The Company received and exercised several rights, privileges, and prerogatives traditionally associated with state sovereignty, both in South Asia and in Europe. The *diwani* was perhaps the most precious and lucrative of these concessions. Its possession, together with the exercise of additional monopolies, and the political stature they conferred, provided the EIC with something resembling dominion in South Asia. To secure its claim, the militarization of its presence was inexorable: Fort William in Bengal hosted a mere two hundred European troops in 1756, but sixteen hundred would be stationed there a decade later, to say nothing of the thousands of Indian soldiers under British command.[30]

As the EIC's revenues and territorial reach expanded, the role of India in the British empire and the relationship of the Company to the British state became pressing concerns. The government sought to curtail the EIC's autonomy. From 1773, it directly supervised the Company's activities. The 1784 India Act further strengthened Parliament's grip, establishing a Board of Control with jurisdiction over the territory administered by the EIC. A new class of official was created, and the new regulations forbade the officials' engagement in trade, in an attempt to disentangle political administration from commerce. Nevertheless, in spite of these innovations and the greater scrutiny it received from Parliament, the Company retained many of its older privileges. Its monopoly over trade, its revenue rights, and its control over appointments went untouched.[31]

By the Peace of Paris (1783), then, the seaborne empires, except the Dutch, remained formidable. They were indispensable sources of revenue and prestige for their respective metropoles, even if their demographic growth (and composition) and prosperity raised discomfiting questions about their future. As Chapter 12 details, the growing reliance on slave labor and revenue collection through fiscal and military coercion generated tensions that undermined the foundations of the seaborne empires. Such clashes, however, remained on the horizon in 1783. Still, contemporaries perceived clearly that overseas empire was a major component of the metropolitan economy and that the balance of power within Europe itself hinged on each state's capacity to harness the resources of its respective seaborne empire. As British statesman Henry Dundas observed in 1799, "Great Britain can at no time propose to maintain an extensive and complicated war but by destroying the colonial resources of our enemies and adding proportionately to our own commercial resources, which are, and must ever be, the sole basis of our maritime strength."[32]

6. Law, Governance, and Institutional Frameworks

Who made laws and dictated policy for Europe's seaborne empires? What were the main institutions through which these empires were governed? And how did the laws, institutions, and policies in overseas empires differ from those in Europe? To answer these questions, it is necessary to examine the principal forms of governance in the seaborne empires: royal government; charters given to individual proprietors and corporate bodies, specifically privileged trading companies; and the secular jurisdiction of the church. It is also crucial to analyze the limits placed on imperial power, whether juridical or in practice. Legal pluralism and hybrid sovereignty characterized these legal and administrative structures, even when European states sought to impose uniformity upon the heterogeneous assemblages historians denominate "empires."

Before delving into specific cases, it is imperative to describe the legal status of overseas territories relative to Europe. Historian John H. Elliott observed that "Spain's overseas possessions formed part, not of a colonial empire but of a worldwide monarchy composed of individual kingdoms and provinces." The Americas, or the Indies, as they were known, were considered to be an extension of the peninsular kingdom of Castile. The laws and institutions of the New World were modeled on those of Castile. Philip II summarized the relationship in 1571: "Because the kingdoms of Castile and the Indies belong to one crown, their laws and manner of government ought to be as alike as possible."[1] This goal remained constant, but laws would be modified in response to local conditions bearing scant resemblance to those of metropolitan Spain, such as the presence of large populations of Amerindians. By the late seventeenth century, many of the decrees, orders, and proclamations that applied only to the Americas were compiled and published. This *Recopilación* formed a body of law separate from, if purportedly consistent with, that of Castile. Thus, many of the same institutions existed, albeit in different forms, across the Spanish monarchy. There were viceroys both in Spain's European provinces and its ultramarine territories, for example. But the existence of the same offices and legal codes did not necessarily mean that they functioned identically across the constituent kingdoms.

The situation in Britain's empire was distinct from that in Spain's. In the absence of precedents, the Crown groped for a formula to establish its sovereignty. It had to legitimate its claims against enshrined prior claims, notably those in the Treaty of Tordesillas. It also would have to assert authority over its subjects who actually undertook the task of empire building and who were rarely, if ever, agents of the state in any strict sense. The 1606 charter for the colony of Virginia stated clearly that the inhabitants would enjoy "all liberties, franchises and immunities of free denizens and natural subjects . . . as if they had been abiding and born within this our realm of England." This may have accurately described the goal, but in practice numerous circumstances—slavery, border disputes with Amerindians, the allocation of land—prevailed in the New World concerning which English common law was silent or inapplicable. Each colony, therefore, through its respective local assembly, would devise its own laws to cope with an ultimately insuperable heterogeneity. Yet the room for maneuver was limited, and the Crown's sovereignty was aggressively asserted. The Virginia Charter, for example, reserved to the king the right to determine the colony's form of government, whereas the subsequent Massachusetts Bay Charter made explicit the Company's subordination to the Crown, also exacting a pledge that its laws conform to those of England. Nor did supervision stop with the issue of a charter. The colonies were monitored closely, first by the Privy Council, then the Lords of Trade from 1675, and finally the Board of Trade after 1696.[2]

The situation in Portugal's empire in theory resembled that in Britain's. A single law applied throughout the realm, whether European territory or ultramarine. The decisions of the high courts established in Goa and Salvador, respectively, could be appealed to the highest court in Lisbon, the *Disembargo do Paço*. In the Dutch Empire, legal regimes were hybrid. In Batavia, Dutch municipal institutions were replicated, but only VOC personnel could exercise public functions. This stipulation precluded many Europeans as well as mestizos from participating in public affairs. Furthermore, Dutch law was superseded by the VOC's law code. The Company established a high court that handled most matters, with minimal interference from or recourse to the metropole. Most strikingly, in stark contrast to the republican form of government in the Netherlands, the governor-general and his council wielded what amounted to dictatorial authority in Batavia.[3]

The principal form of government that European states sought to establish in overseas territories was royal government. The Spanish Empire offers the paradigmatic example. The Spanish monarch and the officials he appointed were the sole arbiters of most facets of government in each kingdom. From the very inception of its American empire, the Crown forced the leaders of the expeditions to enter into a contract, or *capitulación*, specifying the terms of the undertaking and unambiguously declaring the sovereignty of the monarch. The Crown sometimes incentivized exploration and conquest with a liberality it came to regret. The policy of granting the conquistadors in Mexico encomiendas, for example, was soon reversed. By 1579, the majority of Indians in New Spain were vassals of the king and not under the personal jurisdiction of the encomenderos.[4] Having clawed back authority, the monarch's capacity for patronage was formidable. The grant of ecclesiastical benefices, the sale of offices, the appointment of officials, and approval over the sale and transfer of feudal properties emanated directly from the monarch. The strategic distribution of these much-coveted plums guaranteed direct communication between the Crown and the beneficiaries of its largesse, not to mention the loyalty and service obligations that the acceptance of patronage entailed.

These ingenious devices of securing loyalty and subservience notwithstanding, the problem of linking the center of the Spanish monarchy with its peripheral kingdoms, whether in Europe or in America, remained and generated great anxiety. Several potential solutions were proposed. Councils were formed, composed of spokesmen for each kingdom. These met at court and consulted with the king, both directly and through his advisers. The importance of the councils should not be discounted. As a foreign visitor to Spain noted at the beginning of the seventeenth century, "What is surprising about Spain is that, though their government is absolute, their kings do nothing without the Councils."[5] How were the Indies, the Americas, to be fitted into this existing tangle of legal codes and institutions? Would it require an entirely new apparatus? A new Council of the Indies was formed between

1511 and 1519 and became a separate organ of government in 1524. The council combined the functions of a supreme court of appeal with those of an advisory body to supervise colonial affairs. It heard appeals, but administrative problems—naval defense, finance, indigenous policy—were entrusted to more specialized committees. The supervision of ecclesiastical matters also fell within the council's jurisdiction. The council similarly exercised broad powers of censorship. No book dealing with the Indies was allowed to be printed in Spain or in America without its previous inspection, approbation, and license. Likewise, no book could be introduced into America without its explicit permission.

The council received information from, and sent orders to, a viceroy who had been assigned to one of the peripheral kingdoms. In 1535, Charles I divided New World possessions into manageable administrative units. The viceroyalty of New Spain, which included the Philippines, was established in 1535; nine years later, the viceroyalty of Peru was created. In addition, smaller units, known as *audiencias*, discussed in greater detail below, were established in Charcas, Quito, Guatemala, and other important nodes. In each peripheral kingdom, except outlying frontier zones, the highest authority was the viceroy, the highest magistrate sent from Spain and, in most cases, a Castilian by birth. In his *Política Indiana* (1647), jurist Juan de Solórzano Pereira offered a justification for the institution. He explained that the position of viceroy was created "so that vassals who live and reside in remote provinces need not go seek their king, who is so far away, having his vicar nearby to ask for and get all those things they could expect and get from their king."[6]

Yet the viceroy was not omnipotent. He was compelled to work in conjunction with the aforementioned councils that sat in the Iberian Peninsula. The members of the councils were usually natives of the respective territory who responded vigorously to any perceived threat to their homeland (and, it must be said, their interests and those of their allies and retainers). Within well-defined limits, however, the viceroy maintained autonomy in directing the kingdom with which he was entrusted. His military authority was undivided.[7] He could issue proclamations (*bandos*) and measures (*ordenanzas*), though not laws in the strict sense. Although viceroys in the Americas shared some of the responsibilities of their European counterparts, including maintenance of domestic tranquillity, others were peculiar to the New World. These included protecting the promotion of evangelization and conversion, the negotiation of treaties with Amerindians, and responsibility for rewarding the descendants of the conquistadors and first settlers with sinecures and honors.

The viceroy and lesser officials in the Spanish Empire were not compelled to passively enforce the laws bearing the monarch's imprimatur. On the contrary, it was a firmly established principle that viceroys (and lower-ranking Crown officials) determined whether local conditions were propitious for enacting a given decree. The political writer Castillo de Bobadilla noted in his manual *Política para Corregidores* (1616) that royal provisions and decrees "contrary to justice" and prejudicial to the Crown's ultimate interests could be "obeyed but not executed" (*obdezco pero no cumplo*). By invoking this curious formula, a royal official reaffirmed his loyalty and subservience to the monarch while simultaneously indicating that the best expression of obedience was the nonenforcement of a decree until circumstances favored its implementation. This formula also reflected an appreciation of the hazards latent in imposing laws that failed to account for, in Philip II's words, "the diversity and difference of lands and peoples." Administration in Spain's overseas kingdoms, to borrow the historian John Phelan's phrase, thus was a "dynamic balance between the principles of authority and flexibility."[8]

The Portuguese case resembled the Spanish one, at least superficially. At the apex of the governmental hierarchy overseas stood the viceroy. While the viceroy was appointed by the monarch, imperial policy from the mid-seventeenth century emanated from the Crown-appointed Overseas Council (*Conselho Ultramarino*), which resembled Spain's Council of the Indies. The bulk of the council's membership was drawn from former colonial governors and magistrates, many of whom maintained close ties to territories they formerly administered. In contrast to the Spanish case, the Brazilian viceroy wielded few substantive powers. Only in wartime could the viceroy assume central control and direct military operations, organize supplies, and coordinate other logistics. For this reason, smaller political jurisdictions in Brazil retained significant authority, while centralized, viceregal authority remained weak.

The second form of government found in Europe's overseas empires was that established by charter, whether granted to a company (or corporation) or to an individual. It is crucial to recall that the seaborne empires generally evolved from private ventures, receiving varying levels of sponsorship and support from the state. In the case of the Iberian empires, the various papal bulls, together with the bilateral Treaty of Tordesillas, had sanctioned the monarchies of Spain and Portugal to divide the world between them. This meant that all actions undertaken by their subjects were pursued in their name and with their permission. Yet there was no implication that the state would actively involve itself, even as its agents compulsively sought to clarify and buttress their ultimate authority, or sovereignty. Early modern states lacked the material resources, personnel, and will to establish and supervise distant colonies. They were by default self-funded enterprises from the outset. Furthermore, until the eighteenth century, no government subsidies were offered to entice migrants to depart for and then remain overseas, where their subsistence was insecure.

Notwithstanding official parsimony, forays into the extra-European world were desirable from the state's point of view. The potential economic benefits were immense, as the Spanish and Portuguese cases amply attest. Mechanisms were devised to encourage private enterprise without relinquishing claim to any settlements that might be established. Instead, they endowed metropolitan nobles, merchants, and other entities with bundles of rights, privileges, and instruments of authority to undertake the task themselves, usually in exchange for some of the profits reaped from their enterprise. Portugal's policy in Brazil epitomized this approach. In the 1530s, the Crown issued hereditary land grants to several noblemen, called donatary captains. Fifteen such donatary captaincies were created, dividing Brazilian territory horizontally into strips of various lengths. These donatary captains became lords of vast stretches of the coast (as the interior was initially impenetrable). They exercised almost unimpeded authority. They levied and collected taxes and enjoyed fiscal privileges. Each captain was given the right to establish towns, to supervise the election of local officials, and to maintain a militia under his command. In order to spur economic activity and recruit settlers, he distributed lands to supplicants.[9]

In spite of this expansive authority and wide latitude for action, the donatary captain remained the king's agent and was subordinate to him. He acted within the framework laid out in the charter accompanying the initial land grant. This document defined relations between donatary captains and settlers, enumerated the obligations of the grantee, and specified the economic and political rights retained by the Crown. For example, the Crown retained its monopoly over the trade in dyewood (brazilwood). It claimed a fifth of all minerals unearthed and a tenth of commercial receipts collected. The king appointed an official directly to collect rents in each captaincy. Furthermore, the donatary captain was forbidden to enter into contact with indigenous peoples not yet converted to Christianity. Such relations remained the monarch's exclusive domain, derived from the *padroado*, the papal delegation of church authority to the monarch in the extra-European world. Yet in practice the charter was nearly impossible to enforce, and donatary captains, though legally subservient, retained significant authority with relatively little oversight.

Under this system, however, Brazil languished. In 1549, the Crown overhauled the colony's institutions, which was a complicated undertaking because the grants made to the donatary captains were, legally at least, perpetual and hereditary. Bahia de Todos os Santos (Bay of All Saints, later renamed Salvador), in Brazil's northeast, was chosen as the seat of government. A governor-general was appointed and was accompanied by several royal officials, including a treasurer and a chief magistrate. Soon the supremacy of the governor-general was established. Private initiative thus gave way to centralized (if still weak) royal government. The donatary-captaincy system was not abolished outright. Doing so would have tarnished the credibility of the Crown, making it appear to be an unreliable partner. Instead, royal authority was superimposed upon a heterogeneous, decentralized structure devised to encourage private initiative. Thus, in Brazil, as elsewhere, political authority was a palimpsest of numerous ideal models of governance.

The individual proprietor model was not unique to the Portuguese Empire, of course. Neofeudal models of territorial lordship were utilized in Britain's overseas dominions, too. In Maryland, for example, the royal charter given in 1632 to Cecil Calvert, Baron of Baltimore, not only presented him with an enormous territorial parcel but also endowed him with massive, nearly absolute administrative latitude with regard to land distribution, defense, and laws. In this sense, Baltimore's charter resembled the Portuguese system of donatary captaincies, but with considerably fewer restrictions. Baltimore's authority even extended to the choice of subjects, which prompted the influx of Catholics, then under duress in Britain. Even at the time of its issue, the colony's charter was perceived as anomalous. It relied on antiquated concepts of aristocratic and royal authority that the Stuart monarchy sought to revive. Yet even after such ideas had fallen out of official favor, in the aftermath of the Glorious Revolution, the 1732 royal charter for Georgia granted a board of proprietors jurisdiction over "all and every person and persons who shall at any time hereafter inhabit or reside within" the extensive boundaries of the new colony.[10] Anachronistic theories of absolutism thus held sway in the seaborne empires long after those same theories had been repudiated in Europe itself.

Besides Crown government and grants of territory to individual proprietors, a third yet related type of political authority existed in Europe's seaborne empires: the chartered corporation and privileged trading company. Under the terms of a royal charter, political-legal authority and property rights were delegated to a company in an overseas territory claimed by a given European state. In exchange for rights normally associated with sovereignty and exclusive economic access to a colonial territory, chartered companies pledged to foment emigration, construct forts, and man garrisons to protect the state's interests against the anticipated aggression of indigenous inhabitants and the malevolent designs of rival European states, and to conduct diplomatic relations with indigenous rulers. For settling four thousand Catholics in Canada within two decades, for example, the French Compagnie de la Nouvelle-France was granted a monopoly over all trade except fishing. It was authorized to distribute land to seigneurs, who in turn became responsible for recruiting additional settlers. These settlers would pay the seigneur feudal dues. In Berbice, Curaçao, and elsewhere in the 1620s, the Dutch WIC employed a similar method, called "patroonship," in which the work of colonization was outsourced to private investors (patroons), who assumed the burden of populating and administering the territory.[11]

Not all such arrangements worked in practice. The French Crown was dissatisfied with the Company's performance in Canada, for example. It reorganized the colony along military lines in the 1660s. Thereafter, there was a governor-general in Quebec City and local governors in the key towns, all supported by more than a thousand French regular troops. The governor-general's authority was, depending on one's perspective, reinforced or undercut by the presence of the royal intendant. This official controlled the administration of justice, finance, and civil affairs.[12] A comparable example in the British Empire was the Virginia Company. Colonies formed as chartered companies, however, often were converted into Crown-administered colonies. Charters given could be, and often were, revoked. Virginia was transmuted into a royal colony in 1629, with a Crown-appointed governor, who ruled in conjunction with an elected assembly. This swapping of company for Crown authority is reminiscent of earlier Iberian practices at the expense of the encomenderos and donatary captains, respectively. Unsurprisingly, colonies founded later, like New York and New Jersey, were not organized on the privately chartered or proprietary colony model.

Trading companies stood at the intersection of private entrepreneurial and state action. The two most important of these companies were the Dutch VOC (chartered in 1602) and the English EIC (chartered in 1600). Such companies often proved an attractive option from the state's perspective: they paid for their charters, thus bringing an infusion of revenue, and they undertook at their own (and their shareholders') expense enterprises that were desirable yet not urgent. In the seventeenth century, France's ambitious minister Colbert warmed to the idea. He viewed companies as particularly suitable for long-distance commerce in areas with meager commerce and where considerable risks were incurred. Earlier monopoly companies were consolidated into the Compagnie des Indes in 1719. The idea of privileged companies fell out of favor in France within a few decades, however, with the suspension of the Compagnie des Indes in 1769 marking the culmination of this trend. Newfound French aversion did not deter other European states from chartering companies, including Prussia (1683), Austrian Ostend (1722), and Sweden (1731). Portugal and Spain, too, experimented with privileged trading companies in the eighteenth century, though with mixed results. Pombal founded two companies and granted them monopoly over less-developed parts of the Brazilian north and northeast, including exclusive control over the slave trade to those areas. The companies encouraged the production of commodities for which there was increasing demand on the world market, including coffee and cotton. Cotton, in particular, proved to be a major boon. It helped to shift the balance of trade with Britain in Portugal's favor by 1800. Coffee became a mainstay of the Brazilian economy after independence from Portugal.

As previously noted, the VOC's charter granted it the right to conduct diplomacy, deploy force, and seize territory. War and trade were inextricable. As the VOC's governor-general informed the Company's directors in 1614, "You gentlemen ought to know from experience that trade in Asia should be conducted and maintained under the protection and with the aid of your own weapons, and that weapons must be wielded with the profits gained by the

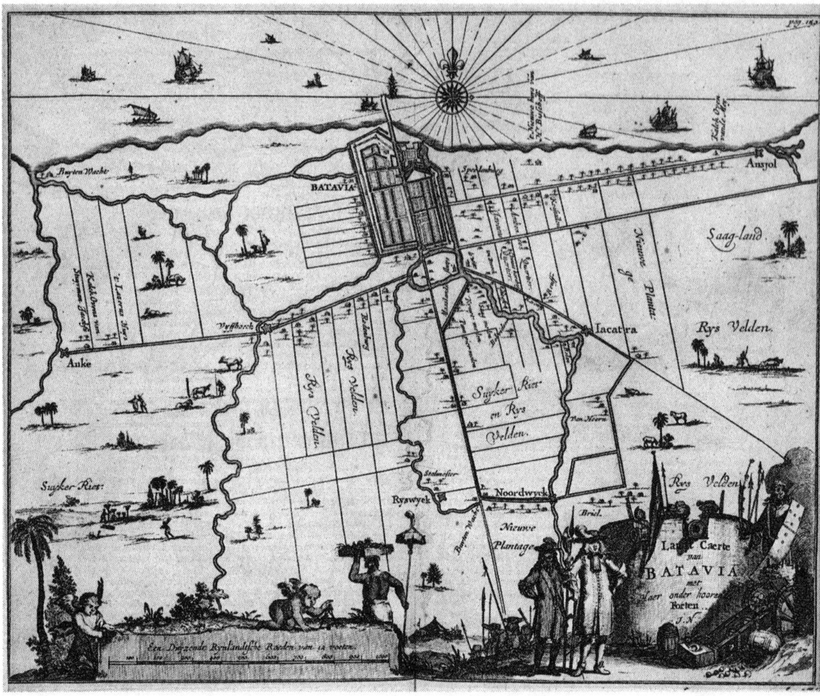

Figure 10. Map of Batavia and its environs. *Landt Caerte van Batavia*. In Johannes Nieuhof, *Gedenkwaerdige zee en lantreize door de voornaemste landschappen van West en Oostindien*. Amsterdam: Jacob van Meurs, 1682. Courtesy of the George Peabody Library, The Sheridan Libraries, Johns Hopkins University.

trade. So trade cannot be maintained without war, nor war without trade." Besides conducting itself like a state in its external relations, the VOC had notable autonomy over its internal affairs. The directors were officially the Company's ruling body, meeting in Amsterdam, but in the VOC's Asian empire, the Company was unsupervised. In Batavia, the center of its operations, the Company's court was the highest court. In matters of criminal law, defendants had no access to courts in the Dutch Republic. There was some ambiguity concerning whether the actions of the VOC and the wealth it amassed belonged to the directors or to the state that had issued its charter. The VOC did not mince words when it asserted its unqualified right to what it conquered. As the directors declared in 1644, "The places and strongholds [captured] in the East Indies should not be regarded as national conquests but as the property of private merchants, who [are] entitled to sell those places to whomever they wish, even if it was to the king of Spain, or to some other enemy of the United Provinces."[13]

With its outposts progressively dotting the Indian subcontinent over the course of the seventeenth century—with Surat (1612), Madras (1639), Calcutta (1690), and Bombay (1695) among the most significant territorial footholds—the EIC functioned similarly to the VOC, to the dismay of some observers. As Edmund Burke lamented, "The EIC did not seem to be merely a company formed for the extension of British commerce, but in reality a delegation of the whole power and sovereignty of this kingdom sent into the East." But that was precisely the point. As historian Philip Stern has elucidated: "The Company's models for governance derived not only from its function as an overseas chartered company but from its form as a joint-stock corporation, which in theory represented not a consortium of particular traders, but a conglomerate society of investors, who prosecuted trade on behalf of the whole as well as the English nation. Such a conception of the Company meant that, in Asia, Company officials understood their official business to be that of 'publique affairs.'"[14]

It would be erroneous to suggest that the state, settlers and merchants, and chartered companies were the sole political authorities in the seaborne empires. Particularly in the Iberian empires, the church and the state jostled for primacy both within and beyond Europe. Sometimes religious orders were embraced as indispensable adjuncts to state authority, while at other times they were loathed as a hindrance obstructing state action. The state's authority was circumscribed in different ways from that of each of the two types of clergy. The regular clergy, members of the Franciscan, Augustinian, Dominican, and other orders, took vows and lived according to monastic right in monasteries and convents. They could not be regulated by the state and were not subject to its judicial authority. The second type was the secular clergy, who staffed parishes and were supervised by bishops and archbishops. Secular clergy performed a wide range of public functions, from dispensing food to the indigent and running orphanages to maintaining the baptismal, marriage, and death records for the parish. The secular clergy therefore undertook many of the functions that now commonly come under the purview of the state.

Clerical authority was enhanced by the economic capacity and industriousness of both the regular order and the secular. In Spanish America, the regular clergy amassed great wealth both from the collection of tithes and from its real estate portfolio. The church lent its capital to a range of individuals, charging 3 to 7 percent interest. As a result of a loan to purchase land or construct a dwelling, for example, the church acquired a lien on that property, as a modern bank would. Convents pooled and invested dowries paid by the families of nuns upon their entrance into the convent. The church thus had a diverse property portfolio, from rural haciendas to urban rental properties to gold mines, which made it a major force in the economy. Its economic might conferred power in the secular realm.[15]

The various papal edicts presciently sought to anticipate and defuse conflict between the Iberian states while insinuating the church's political authority into the empires those states sought to establish. To some degree, the papacy achieved its objective, at least initially. In the Portuguese Empire, the secular authority of the church was subordinate to that of the state. The king enjoyed royal patronage. In exchange for receiving power to collect tithes and other duties owed to the church in Brazil as well as power over appointments to church offices there (with the exception of bishops, who were still appointed by the pope), the Crown guaranteed the protection of the clergy and assisted its efforts at evangelization, including the building of churches. The Portuguese king collected colonial tithes in his capacity as Grand Master of the Order of Christ.[16] The Spanish monarch enjoyed similarly expansive patronage powers and derived similar fiscal benefits. The authority of the Iberian monarchs over the church outside Europe greatly exceeded their authority over it in Europe.

Yet the patronato real and the padroado real came with significant strings attached, as the Iberian monarchs soon discovered. In Spanish America, the clergy supervised *reducciones,* which resettled Amerindians into towns, ostensibly for the purposes of evangelization and protection against rapacious colonists bent on extracting indigenous labor. In Brazil, the Jesuits established aldeias. The Jesuits differed from the regular orders in that their allegiance was to the pope alone, but nevertheless their zeal and resources made them an irresistible partner in evangelization efforts. They founded Amerindian villages under their order's auspices modeled on European communities. By 1562, there were eleven Jesuit parishes located around Bahia with thirty-four thousand Indians settled in them. In the seventeenth and eighteenth centuries, the Jesuits expanded the scope of their activities. From 1607, they founded missionary villages in what is today Paraguay. By 1739, there were thirty such villages. By the mid-1760s, there were over 200 Jesuit missions throughout the Americas, in which a quarter million Amerindians resided. Like the aldeias in Brazil, these missionary villages in Paraguay proved attractive to Amerindians. It offered some protection from colonists seeking to enslave or otherwise control Indian labor. In some places, like the Río de la Plata in the late seventeenth century, the missions accounted for a majority of the total population of a province.[17]

By the mid-eighteenth century, the position and power of the Jesuits had become anathema to the governments of Portugal, France. and Spain. As historian David Brading explained, "Their international character, the sheer élan of their expansion, their growing wealth and influence, and their resolute independence" made them a target of criticism. In the *Misiones*, land straddling Portuguese and Spanish South America, the authority of the Jesuits was uncontested. They supervised the labor of hundreds of thousands of Amerindians. For Iberian monarchs with absolutist pretensions, the autonomy and wealth of the Jesuits were unacceptable. They were accused of operating a "state within a state," effectively barring royal authority from what increasingly resembled separate dominions. Such autonomy was tantamount to a taunt, and the monarchies resolved to extirpate the Jesuits and colluded to bring about this result. Portugal, Spain, and France joined to expel them from their respective territories. Portugal took the lead in 1757, banishing a thousand Jesuit fathers. France followed suit in 1764, and Spain in 1767. The expulsions created a veritable Jesuit diaspora, mostly in Italy. The respective Crowns filled the vacuum with clergy from the regular orders or else direct state supervision. Spain divided the thirty Guaraní missions equally among the Mercedarians, Dominicans, and Franciscans. The logic apparently was that these mendicant orders were less venal and recalcitrant than the Jesuits. In 1773, the papacy succumbed to pressure and abolished the Society of Jesus altogether. The expulsions were deeply unpopular, especially in the Americas. In Mexico, for example, widespread uprisings ensued, including in the prosperous and populous cities of Guanajuato and San Luis de Potosí. The Spanish state suppressed these acts of resistance: nearly a thousand people were hanged, flogged, banished, or imprisoned. In the Paraguayan missions, the Guaraní rebelled against the Iberian states in order to preserve the reducciones that resettled Amerindians, anticipating that their dissolution would pave the way for onerous new forms of exploitation.[18]

Ecclestiastical authority sometimes worked in conjunction with that of the state. In Spanish America, the Inquisition was established by 1570.

Tribunals of judges, or inquisitors, operated in Mexico City, Lima, and Cartagena, with jurisdiction over all inhabitants except Amerindians. They investigated allegations of heresy and blasphemy, which extended to a range of social practices, from homosexuality to bigamy. In this way, the Inquisition regulated private behavior and social practices as a secular state might today. As historian Francisco Bethencourt explained, "Though they remained ecclesiastical tribunals, the status of the Iberian Inquisition was mixed, as they were also regarded as royal courts."[19] Inquisitors were appointed by the king, and their jurisdiction was superimposed over bishops in relation to crimes of heresy. In this way, church and state cooperatively enforced a shared vision of a well-ordered society.

Belief in and propagation of purportedly false doctrines fell under the purview of the Inquisition. This ambit was especially important in the Americas. There the interaction of different cultures and religions resulted in the emergence of syncretic religious forms and practices. Inquisitors routinely discovered that Europeans and creoles experimented with remedies from indigenous healers, whose powers derived, evidently, from non-Christian deities. Interestingly, in Spanish America, witchcraft was understood by the church to be a form of superstition. It was a minor sin, not an act of heresy, and this did not usually attract the Inquisition's attention. This approach differed dramatically from Protestant British North America, without an Inquisition, where those accused of witchcraft were hounded by authorities, and where persecution disproportionately affected women. Some 80 percent of those appearing in the infamous Salem witch trials of 1692 were women. The importance of the Inquisition in the Iberian world declined on the eve of the eighteenth century. The last public autos da fé in Madrid and Lisbon occurred in 1680 and 1683, respectively. In Portugal, the Inquisition was eventually taken over fully by the state. The distinction between new and old Christians was eliminated, and, though it would not be abolished until the 1820s, the Inquisition was a spent force.[20]

Privileged companies, conquistadors, and individual proprietors were useful initially, permitting European states to acquire overseas territories and administer them on the cheap. The church buttressed states' capacity to regulate behavior and eliminate irregular conduct among colonists. But as the scale of settlement and potential for lucre increased, states sought to supervise them more closely. Not infrequently, they indulged in absolutist decrees that they would not have dared to issue in Europe. In the early 1680s, for example, the British Crown liquidated the Massachusetts Bay Company and combined eight previously separate New England colonies into a single "Dominion of New England." It was administered by a governor-general wielding executive fiat, whose powers undercut local and municipal authority. He was empowered to raise new taxes without the consent of the colony's assembly, for example. After the Glorious Revolution, such egregious experiments in governance were discontinued, and the charters and assemblies were restored. But the colonies nevertheless would be monitored more closely than ever before. The revised charter for Massachusetts Bay, for example, established government by an elected assembly, supervised by a governor sent from Britain, and an appointed council. Supervising the various local governments from London was a body called the Lords of Trade and Plantations. It sought to guarantee the primacy of royal authority. A committee of the Privy Council, it functioned as an executive authority without parliamentary oversight on issues pertaining to overseas empire.[21] Colonists were painfully aware of the dilution of their authority and the contraction of their autonomy, even as they benefited from belonging to a polity, and market, spanning the Atlantic.

Creeping royal authority and centripetal tendencies were common features of all of the European seaborne empires, particularly from the early eighteenth century. But there were numerous countervailing forces, both statutory and customary, impeding royal authority's expansion. Various formal and informal mechanisms mitigated and counteracted it. For example, the political culture of Spanish America, in Elliott's phrase, "was postulated on the basis of a reciprocal process of negotiation between the monarch and his subjects. Lobbying and petitioning, compromise and counter-compromise, formed the everyday stuff of political life."[22] In Britain's empire, officials seldom interfered in matters other than trade before the late seventeenth century. Their latitude for action was circumscribed by vigilant assemblies, which continued to control finance, even as their authority was attenuated in other respects. Assemblies insinuated themselves into governance to a degree that far exceeded that of the House of Commons in Britain itself. In large measure, this resulted from the fact that the overall absence of a comprehensive, coordinated policy gave colonists ample leeway to conduct their own affairs.[23] French colonial administration was, as suggested earlier, highly centralized. Nevertheless, the majority of the Caribbean islands still possessed councils composed of colonists that could offer advice to the governor, though they could not legislate per se. The very existence of this institution, and the custom of consultation it engendered, put a brake on the more arbitrary proclivities of officials.

Spanish America, too, boasted an array of representative institutions. Perhaps the most important was the municipal council, the *cabildo,* which set policy on matters of local concern. These included adjudicating minor crimes, maintaining public order, ensuring that water and sanitation needs were met, and determining food prices. There was also indirect representation, as municipalities would send their agents to Madrid to lobby on their behalf. These agents requested special privileges or exemptions for their respective districts as a whole as well as for particular individuals. As historian Marcello Carmagnani argued, "The expansion of this custom was therefore vital to the smooth running of the colonial covenant." In the Portuguese Empire, the institution of the town council (*senado da câmara*) was ubiquitous. Councils possessed significant authority, though their decisions could be revoked if deemed injurious to Crown finances. Membership was coveted, since it brought legal immunity from certain types of punishment—notably torture and arbitrary arrest, recognition as members of the gentry, and exemption from military service. Councils were saddled with significant responsibilities. They functioned as a court of first instance; leased municipal lands; collected and then disbursed (on the Crown's behalf) payments to soldiers; arranged for the upkeep of jails, roads, and bridges; and regulated the prices of commodities and staples. Councils represented a formal institutional check on the authority of royal governors, not least because they held the right to correspond directly with the monarch in order to air grievances and seek remedies.[24]

States were attentive to the pleas and complaints of such bodies. In the Spanish Empire, for example, the Crown restricted the scope of viceregal authority in the New World. The vast wealth, great distance from Europe, and distasteful memory of disruptive recalcitrant comportment of several early conquistadors impelled the Crown to devise institutions to monitor the viceroy's activities. Instead of blurring lines of authority, the resulting mosaic of checks and balances mitigated the defects intrinsic to rule at a great distance. It betrayed the Crown's deep-seated distrust of its own agents posted beyond Castile's borders. Various legal restrictions and overlapping authority collided to limit viceregal authority. Of course, as the Spanish monarchs and their ministers fully realized, America could not be micromanaged from Madrid.

The difficulties of transatlantic communication left some patronage to the viceroy's discretion, particularly the authority to dispense minor appointments. Although subject to considerable oversight, the colonial treasury remained within the viceroy's purview, for example.

In Spanish America, the greatest limitation on viceregal authority was posed by the audiencias, the highest courts of Spanish America, of which thirteen had been established by 1661. The judges (*oidores*), appointed directly by the king, were empowered to correspond directly with the sovereign. The audiencias also retained attorneys (*fiscales*) responsible to the king for everything pertaining to the treasury. Viceregal autonomy was further checked by the *residencia*: at the expiration of their terms of service, all officials underwent a thorough evaluation of their conduct. Still another brake on viceregal power in Spanish America was a relatively short tenure in office. If in the sixteenth century the viceroy was appointed for an undetermined number of years, with the average length of service hovering around six years, after 1629 viceroys were appointed for three years with the possibility of a three-year renewal on the basis of merit. Such a short stint ensured not only that numerous ambitious men got a turn but also that a viceroy remained an outsider. His roots in the economy and society he administered were shallow by design.[25]

Governing overseas empires depended, in some cases and somewhat paradoxically, on leaving preexisting institutions in place, or adapting to the frameworks they established. Legal pluralism was the norm, not the exception. It was common for distinct systems of law to exist side by side, with different populations subject to distinct forms of justice. As historian Bianca Premo noted with regard to Spanish America, "Colonizers respected indigenous *usos y costumbres* as long as they did not conflict with Spanish law." The Crown created the Juzgado de Indios, a special tribunal to adjudicate disputes between Spanish settlers and Indians. Legal pluralism existed in British-controlled India, too. Officials strenuously asserted that the internal government of the territories should be regulated by some form of "ancient constitution." They combined elements of European and Asian law. Hindu and Muslim legal codes were retained, but now the courts were staffed with British judges and followed English judicial procedure. Furthermore, the court system was bifurcated. Civil matters were split between two courts, one for Muslims enforcing sharia and the other for Hindus enforcing Hindu law. Criminal courts, which applied to all Indian subjects, implemented

Muslim law. British-framed law codes for India would be instituted only in the early 1860s.[26]

Legal pluralism also emerged from the alacrity with which European states swapped, exchanged, and conquered one another's overseas territories. This inevitably complicated the legal framework under which the subject population lived. Far from sweeping away the preceding system of law, hybridity or pluralism was the norm. French law continued in force in Louisiana after it was ceded to Spain in 1763. Perhaps the best-known case is that of Quebec, which became part of British Canada in the aftermath of the Seven Years' War. French civil law continued to be used, but English criminal law was enforced. Unlike other colonies in North America, an assembly was not established, but there was no restriction placed on Catholicism. When British forces captured the Dutch Cape Colony in 1795, its new governor was instructed to keep "the laws and institutions that subsisted under the antient [*sic*] government of the said settlement."[27] Britain pursued the same strategy in Trinidad two years later when that island was seized from Spain.

In some cases, legal pluralism gave way to legal syncretism. In Angola, for example, the Tribunal de Mucanos was an African law court that was incorporated into the Portuguese legal system. African subjects who had been enslaved appeared before the tribunal to contest this status and seek their freedom. In Spanish America, each indigenous pueblo (village) had a cabildo, or town council. Yet despite its name, this cabildo really served, in the judgment of recent historians, as "merely a veneer over an ancient system of government by village elders." In the Mexican region of Oaxaca, for example, the combination of recurrent indigenous rebellion, legal wrangling, and everyday forms of mutual accommodation resulted in the interweaving of colonial institutions with what historian Yannis Yannakakis has termed the Indian "shadow system."[28] In this way, one system of law and institutional framework did not replace or supersede another altogether; rather, both coexisted and evolved in response to each other. The governance of the seaborne empires was thus in constant flux and marked by extreme heterogeneity. In some places, European public authority was entrenched, dominant, and effective. Much more common, until at least 1750, was the mélange of private and public jurisdictions, hybrid legal regimes, and spheres of autonomy for indigenous as well as creole subjects.

7. The Political Economy of Empire and Its Consequences

Adam Smith and Karl Marx in their different ways embodied eighteenth- and nineteenth-century observers' keen awareness of the impact of maritime exploration, intercontinental trade, and, ultimately, overseas empire on Europe's economy (and, by extension, European social structure and political order). By the mid-1500s, the proliferation of trade routes had woven a dense web facilitating commerce and migration across the earth. Smith's analysis focused on trade and the creation of new markets, whereas Marx highlighted imperial plunder, slavery, and resource extraction as building blocks of the "so-called primitive accumulation" underpinning capitalism. Smith's contemporary, the Abbé Raynal, added that overseas ventures had "given rise to a revolution . . . in the manners, industry and government of the whole world," signaling the cultural and political ramifications of Europe's interactions with the wider world.[1]

The political economy of empire thus is a vast subject. It may be approached from the various angles identified by Smith, Marx, and Raynal. These include, inter alia: the direct costs borne by the state to maintain and defend overseas empire; the revenues reaped directly by the imperial center; the material benefits (which might vulgarly be termed "profits") derived by private individuals from economic activities in the colonies, benefits that were often reinvested in the metropolitan economy with an often unacknowledged multiplier effect; the laws regulating commerce inside and outside empires; the foci of the productive capacities of a given empire (such as plantation agriculture and mining) and how they shaped its interaction with other parts of the world (for example, the "triangular trade"); the growth of internal markets within colonies; the economic benefits derived from investments in ports, roads, and shipyards; the cultural impact of colonial commerce in the creation of tastes, preferences, and fashions; the human costs of economic activities in the form of displacement and exploitation; and the geopolitical consequences (and financial expenditure) of bellicose rivalry over sources of colonial wealth.

This chapter focuses solely on the three aspects of the political economy of empire. First, the mechanisms by which each seaborne empire sought to retain the economic benefits of empire for itself to the exclusion of rival European states and, more generally, aimed for those benefits to accrue to the metropole. Second, the various approaches that might be employed to assess the economic impact of overseas empire on the metropolitan economy. Third, the environmental devastation wrought by the economic activities undertaken within European empires and how this ecological destruction was inseparable from wealth creation and capital accumulation.

The range of economic activities pursued within the seaborne empires was immense. Even if we confine our attention to products coveted by European consumers, the multiplicity is dazzling. A focus on export commodities—like sugar, tobacco, hides—and bullion can distract attention from this range. In the markets and wharves of eighteenth-century Lisbon, for example, a traveler would have encountered no fewer than 125 different Brazilian products, including twenty-four types of animal skin, forty types of wood, twenty-nine *drogas* (a capacious category that included resins, oils, gum Arabic, and balsams), and sundry curiosities such as whale baleen and tortoise shell.[2] In nineteenth-century London, sartorial fashions, such as the fad for whalebone corsets and sealskin hats from the Antipodes, were linked to the expanding imperial reach of the British state.

European trading companies sought to monopolize the items European consumers craved. In the East the Dutch VOC, for example, aimed to secure a monopoly on cloves, nutmeg, mace, and cinnamon, with mixed results.[3] The English EIC initially sought to regulate the flow of the same aromatic spices, plus pepper, but soon expanded its remit to include textiles (cotton and silk) from South Asia, coffee from Mokha (Yemen), and tea and porcelain from China. By the end of the seventeenth century, textiles, tea, and coffee composed almost half of the total value of Europe's trade with Asia. One million pieces of Chinese porcelain were imported each year by the EIC in the early eighteenth century. To luxury goods must be added the New World foods that enlivened the European diet. Maize, peanuts, potatoes, sweet potatoes, manioc (cassava/tapioca), squash, pumpkin, papaya, guava, avocado, pineapple, tomato, and chili were among the plants to expand Europe's palate. The embrace of cacao, the chief ingredient of chocolate, suggests the rapidity of the adoption of new foods. Tobacco also quickly became the rage in Europe and its colonial societies.[4]

It is important to appreciate the variety of products that long-distance trade and empire brought to European markets. The cornucopia that empire made possible shaped the fiscal strategies of European states. As late as 1760, for example, 40 percent of state revenues in Portugal were derived from its empire. Above all, European states (and their agents and subjects) sought bullion (chiefly silver) and a handful of high-value commodities (notably, sugar, tobacco, and hides) in those overseas ventures. From the seventeenth century, Spanish America, for example, was a silver-based empire. Silver remittances made up 80 to 90 percent of the value of all exports from Spanish America to the Iberian Peninsula. It routinely constituted a quarter of the state's overall revenues. Even as Spanish America's economy diversified, the actual value of precious metals extracted and shipped to Spain increased markedly. Ready access to American silver gave the Crown a source of liquidity, and thus room for maneuver, needed for waging war on multiple fronts, a decisive financial advantage vis-à-vis rival states without direct access to silver.[5]

Export-oriented monoculture was the economic foundation of many colonies without mineral wealth. In Maryland, for example, this dependence was acknowledged by the colonial assembly in 1697 when it bluntly stated: "The trade of this province ebbs and flows according to the rise and fall of tobacco in the market of England." European taste for sugar helped to spawn massive plantations in the Caribbean, Brazil, and beyond. The number of sugar mills (engenhos) in Brazil rose from sixty in 1570 to three hundred in 1645. Their number would continue to rise swiftly in subsequent centuries: in Bahia there were four hundred, while in Rio de Janeiro there were six hundred by 1800. Dutch Surinam saw a similar explosion in the number of plantations: by 1770 there were four hundred sugar and coffee plantations.[6] The establishment of large-scale agriculture was linked to increasing reliance on African slave labor, which is discussed in Chapters 8 and 9.

To retain the wealth wrung from overseas territories within their respective imperial systems, each seaborne empire developed regulations. Policies

Figure 11. Sugar production. *Sucrerie.* In Jean-Baptiste Du Tertre, *Histoire Generale des Antilles Habitées par les François. . . .* Vol. I. Paris: Chez Thomas Iolly, 1667. Courtesy of the John Carter Brown Library at Brown University.

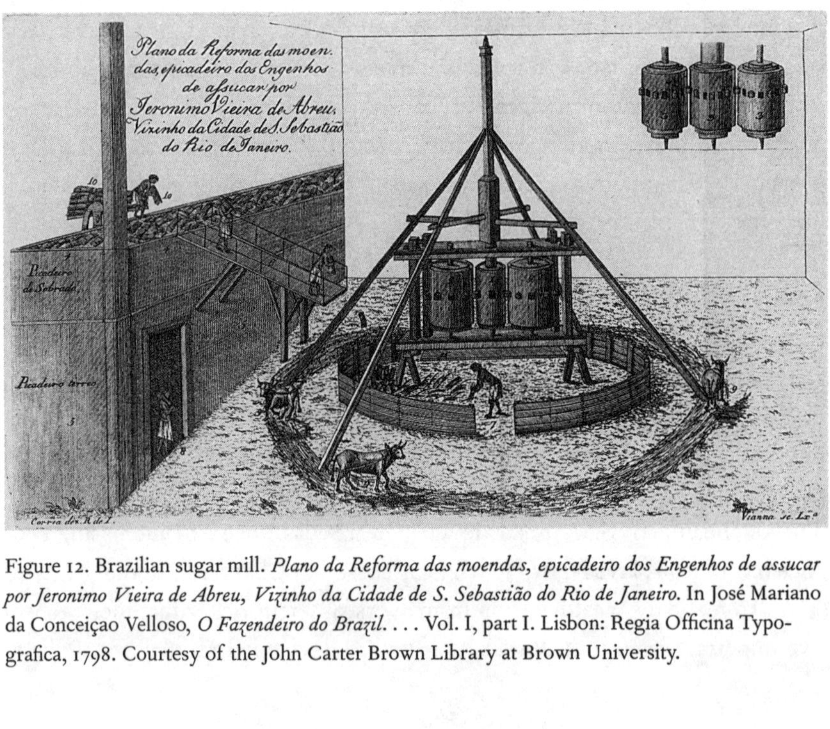

Figure 12. Brazilian sugar mill. *Plano da Reforma das moendas, epicadeiro dos Engenhos de assucar por Jeronimo Vieira de Abreu, Vizinho da Cidade de S. Sebastião do Rio de Janeiro.* In José Mariano da Conceiçao Velloso, *O Fazendeiro do Brazil. . . .* Vol. I, part I. Lisbon: Regia Officina Typografica, 1798. Courtesy of the John Carter Brown Library at Brown University.

of trade exclusion, grouped together somewhat misleadingly as "mercantilism," were rooted in the idea that a nation's wealth was inextricably linked to its geopolitical greatness, as measured by its balance of trade. Wealth was indispensable to achieve geopolitical power, and such power was the means to acquire or retain wealth. It is important to be wary of dismissing these ideas as founded on a fundamental misapprehension of abundance and scarcity, for scarcity was a consideration upon which geopolitical power hinged. The materials required to build and maintain a navy, for example, were in short supply. Timber was a precious resource, and its availability oscillated wildly. For example, the amount held in royal navy shipyards declined by 50 percent between 1783 and 1786. Global competition for hemp and flax aroused great anxiety. To its consternation, Britain relied on Russian hemp from the Baltic region. As an English EIC official put it in 1800, "Such a precarious dependence on a foreign power for an article on which our political existence so much depends is certainly too hazardous to be relied on, provided that we can remedy the evil by obtaining a supply from our own possessions."[7]

Colonies and extra-European trading posts fit into this broader mindset. The quest to maintain a favorable balance of trade spurred states to encourage exports while discouraging imports. The seaborne empires erected trade barriers to restrict the direct export of colonial products to other empires and to prohibit colonists from importing goods except from the metropole itself. As seventeenth-century political economist Charles Davenant wrote, "The principal care will be to keep [colonies] dependent upon the mother country and not to suffer those laws upon any account to be loosened whereby they are tied to it, for otherwise they will become more profitable to our neighbors than to us." This constellation of ideas was not an invention of the seventeenth century, of course. There were ancient, medieval, and early modern precedents for several of these regulations. In the British case, monopolies over wool sold abroad had been granted to cartels of merchants in the fifteenth century, while something resembling the Navigation Acts—restricting trade in and out of England to English-owned and -operated vessels—was in operation a century earlier. England also built upon Iberian precedents. The previously described cartaz, or pass, system established by the Portuguese in the Indian Ocean was an early and influential model. The first system of regulated trade in the Atlantic empires was the Spanish flota. It held that foreign commercial ships were legally prohibited from sailing to American ports. From 1526, Spanish merchant ships were forbidden to sail alone to or from the Americas. They were compelled to travel as part of a larger fleet. In 1537, a royal armada was dispatched to the Caribbean to secure the safe transport of gold and silver. By 1564, an elaborate convoy system was in place to escort merchant ships and other vessels laden with bullion to and from Spanish America. Two fleets per year embarked from Spain for Spanish America, the so-called Indies run (*carrera de Indias*), laden with goods for sale. In April, the ships would depart from Andalusian ports, protected by two heavily armed galleons, the so-called Armada of New Spain. In August, a second fleet of merchant ships embarked from Seville en route to the Isthmus of Panama, escorted by varying number of galleons, collectively called the Armada of Barlovento. Everything on these ships had to pass through Seville's House of Trade (Casa de Contratación), which became the "checkpoint, registry and customs collection agency for the incoming and outgoing fleets."[8] After 1720, Cádiz became the required port of call after the Guadalquivir River silted up, preventing ocean-going vessels from making their way to Seville. In spite of its inefficiencies, this fleet system long remained the dominant mode of crossing and recrossing the Atlantic. Until 1650, almost nine-tenths of Spain's transatlantic shipping was undertaken as part of a convoy. Though in altered form, some version of the flota survived until the end of the eighteenth century.

The expense of maintaining the convoy for the protection of navigation between Spanish America and the Iberian Peninsula was paid for by a series of levies on exports and imports. This levy might be as low as 6 percent, but it could sometimes reach 30 percent. Furthermore, to guarantee markets for Spanish exports, the development of manufactures was strictly forbidden in the colonies. Though it may appear arbitrary to modern eyes, such a policy was sensible: for Spanish merchants wisely sought to capture the markets of increasingly prosperous Spanish American cities, whose denizens clamored for European products, for their exclusive benefit. Annual rates of return on exports to Spanish America were between 8 and 15 percent, far more than profits skimmed from European trade. The problem for Spain was that merchants of other European states wanted access to its colonial markets, so contraband was rife. Yet even if the trade could be closely monitored, the benefit of that trade was diminished by Spanish reliance on products manufactured in other countries. In the early eighteenth century, 94 percent of manufactured goods leaving Seville for Spanish America were non-Spanish, European products.[9]

While Spain sought chiefly to exclude rivals from the prodigious mineral wealth it extracted from the mines of America and to retain populous Spanish America as a captive market for peninsular goods, the British, to their chagrin holding territories lacking precious metals, focused on the regulation of commerce. Designed originally to eliminate the Dutch as the principal shippers of English imports, the mid-seventeenth-century Navigation Act signaled a new approach toward government regulation of overseas trade. It placed the state in the service of national economic development. The act forbade the importation of plantation commodities from Africa, America, or Asia except on ships owned and operated by English subjects. The impact of this system of closed trading empires could devastate certain sectors of the colonial economy. Brazilian sugar's share of the European market shrank dramatically in the seventeenth century, for example. In 1630, 80 percent of sugar sold in London was Brazilian, a share that declined to a mere 10 percent in 1690, largely due to the Navigation Acts' privileging Barbadian and Jamaican sugar.[10]

The first Navigation Act was later amplified. Foreign agents or states were forbidden to engage in any facet of colonial trade, articles could not be shipped from the colonies to foreign nations, and colonial imports were limited to goods shipped from England. All of this combined to create a monopoly. The term "monopoly" was applied to any trade where there was a legal or legally sanctioned restriction on entry. The goal was to free England from its reliance on the importation of foreign commodities and to advantage English manufactures. Intraimperial trade was discouraged through prohibitions or high duties on commodities shipped from one colony to another. Furthermore, colonies were treated as captive markets for finished goods from Europe. The 1662 Staple Act stipulated that all goods, English and foreign, bound for the colonies had to depart from English ports.[11] Nor was Britain alone in erecting regulations of this sort. The French exclusif was designed with the same goal in mind.

European states experimented with (and sometimes relied on) a further type of monopoly: the privileged trading company. The Dutch VOC departed from earlier models of long-distance trade. Previously, merchants would pool their capital for an individual voyage and then share the profits or absorb the loss, in every case squaring their accounts and dissolving their partnership upon the completion of each discrete journey. By contrast, the VOC was a joint-stock company. This meant that all the owners of shares could sell them on Amsterdam's stock exchange without interfering with or disrupting the company's day-to-day operations. The VOC's management, the Heren XVII (the Seventeen Gentlemen), reinvested income from voyages back into the Company. In this way, capital reserves for future voyages were amassed. Income could also be redeployed to construct defensive fortifications and pay the salaries of VOC employees. The case for reinvesting shares was easy to make: the total dividend payments made by the VOC until 1650 were eight times the amount of the original investment. The VOC remained hugely profitable into the eighteenth century. Between 1715 and 1720, for example, annual dividends exceeded 40 percent. The English EIC was likewise highly profitable. Only in two years between 1709 and 1748 did it fail to pay dividends to its shareholders.[12]

Pursuit of the goal of imperial self-sufficiency through monopoly and an obsession with the balance of trade buttressed new institutions. If a state were to cultivate, harvest, and transport from its own overseas possessions those commodities previously obtained from its European rivals or non-European trading partners, the goal of imperial self-sufficiency was furthered. The rise of economic botany and scientific agriculture in the eighteenth century indicates how new forms of knowledge could bolster these imperial objectives. Botanical gardens, of which Kew near London is the best known, became a laboratory to which cuttings of exotic (and potentially lucrative) plants from across the world were sent, with a view to ultimately transferring them from the nursery to colonial plantations. For example, Britain commissioned H.M.S. *Bounty* to obtain breadfruit trees, a starchy yet nutritious staple, from the South Pacific. It was cultivated in the Caribbean to feed its burgeoning slave population. The Spanish government sponsored fifty-seven scientific expeditions to America in the second half of the eighteenth century alone. Naturalists sent plant cuttings to the Royal Botanical Garden in Madrid, which in turn collaborated with the physicians of the Royal Pharmacy to develop new medicines and cures that were then sold at great profit both within and beyond Spain's borders. Portugal adopted a similar approach.[13]

A favorable balance of trade at the expense of rival states was considered an inducement to engage in international commerce. If a European state could offload the surplus to its rivals, or even to neutral countries, the balance of trade (to say nothing of private profits) would favor the country supplying the goods. Colonies were deemed most useful when surplus commodities were shipped to the imperial center and then reexported. In this scenario, the state could tax the transaction twice, the merchants engaging in such reexport trade profited, and the balance of trade was improved. European states thus did not require all consumption to occur within their own borders; they merely sought to regulate and tax its flow. If higher prices could be fetched in other markets, reexportation was permitted. Merchants from northern Europe legally acquired tropical commodities arriving in Atlantic ports to meet demand there. In 1783, for example, more than a fifth of the sugar and almost half of the coffee arriving in Bordeaux, France, ultimately made its way to markets of the German port of Hamburg.[14]

Navigation laws, trade monopolies, and regulation of colonial products had unintended consequences. They pushed the market for coveted commodities, such as tobacco, underground. Restricted access produced artificial scarcities and raised the price on such commodities, thus encouraging contraband trade. By the middle of the eighteenth century, perhaps one-third of the tobacco consumed in France was illicit.[15] Across the Atlantic, contraband trade met genuine, urgent needs. Dutch Curaçao, close to modern Venezuela, is illustrative. Occupied in 1634 and blessed with a secure harbor, it was used by Dutch merchants to carry on a thriving clandestine trade with Spanish America. They supplied slaves and mules to plantations, together with high-quality manufactured goods, in exchange for bullion and valuable tropical commodities, particularly cacao, hides, and tobacco.

Yet at other times the tables were turned. The Dutch were simply unable to supply all their colonies at even subsistence level. British North American traders filled the void in places like Surinam. Massachusetts and Rhode Island merchants supplied equipment for nominally Dutch sugar mills, whereas their counterparts in New York brought small horses used as draughting animals to be used in those same mills. Investment in colonial agriculture and trade was often transnational, too. By 1760, for example, the majority of plantations in Dutch Demerara (in present-day Guyana) were owned by British investors, whereas the port of St. Eustatius was dotted with British-operated warehouses. In Danish St. Croix, Britons owned thirty of the largest seventy-five plantations around 1750. Something similar transpired in peripheral areas of the French Caribbean. Guadeloupe was bypassed by most French ships, which preferred to supply the more lucrative markets of Martinique and, especially, Saint-Domingue. Out of necessity, then, Guadeloupe's inhabitants disregarded the structures of the exclusif, and it is estimated that half of the archipelago's trade was illicit by 1770.[16]

To what degree did European states benefit economically from overseas empire? There are several ways of approaching this vexing question. One might attempt to calculate treasury receipts versus expenditure for overseas-defense warfare over a certain period of time. Or one might examine the fortunes of certain economic activities in the metropole and then seek to ascertain the degree to which they were galvanized by colonial activities. It might be possible to focus on a single family or a single firm and examine the degree to which overseas trade caused its fortunes to rise or fall. Quantitative analysis might appear, at first, to be an attractive approach, but imperfect and incomplete accounting practices in the early modern period leave historians in possession of only fragmentary data. It is difficult to extrapolate and reach broader conclusions from the paucity of available data.

Yet beyond the practical obstacles of data collection, aggregation, computation, there exists a deeper problem. As Drayton has elucidated, if one looks exclusively at profits or capital generated, it is easy to lose sight of the "dynamism [imperial economies] gave to world trade and the structures of capital, labor and production [they] mobilized."[17] Several examples may clarify this point. Tax regimes encouraged the processing of New World raw materials in Europe itself. In Britain, colonial imports gave rise to a series of secondary industries, from the refinement of coarse brown *muscavado* sugar to the dyeing of cloth with plantation-grown indigo to the manufacture of clay pipes to smoke Maryland tobacco. In France, there were twenty-nine sugar refineries (eight of them in Rouen) by 1683. One must therefore account for the multitude of often indirect economic processes to which an empire gave rise before one can determine if it was "profitable" or make some analogous pronouncement. As historian Nuala Zahedieh has explained, "The surge in colonial imports encouraged investment in production techniques which contributed to a major strengthening and diversification of its industrial base."[18]

The imperial economy was also an extensive field for investment, where complex financial instruments were devised and deployed. In the Dutch case, plantation mortgage-backed securities were common from the mid-eighteenth century. Under the system of the *plantagelening,* also known as *negotiaties,* aspiring planters contracted long-term loans from private investors to purchase land, equipment, slaves, and other essential inputs. As historian Jan de Vries described, these mortgages were then pooled together into a single unit trust. An investor could buy shares, usually earning an interest income of 6 percent. At least 241 such unit trusts were floated on the Amsterdam exchange between 1753 and 1794, three-quarters of which involved plantations in the sugar-frontier zones of Surinam and Guyana. Accounting for economic benefits derived is further complicated by the labyrinthine circuits through which finance flowed. Merchants in the French Atlantic ports of Nantes, La Rochelle, and Bordeaux, for example, owned sugar-producing estates in the Caribbean but did not reside there. They employed salaried agents as overseers and stewards. Determining where these estates fit into sprawling merchant portfolios is a significant challenge. Antillean commerce—including the trade in sugar, molasses, indigo, cacao, cotton, and coffee—composed half of France's reexports.[19] Colonial trade and European commerce may prove impossible in the end to disentangle and disaggregate.

The profits earned through the slave trade and slavery raise a similar tangle of issues. One might employ a case study approach, examining the profitability of specific firms, plantations, or individuals. But is this microscopic accounting the optimal manner to ascertain the broader economic impact of the trade? A better approach might be to examine how many livelihoods and businesses depended on the slave trade and slavery, from agents who insured the ships, to the captain and the crew, to the suppliers of the rations for the voyage, to the eventual slave owners and the middlemen who sold their slave-produced products. Seen from this broader perspective, the importance of the slave trade to the European economy was massive, embedded in all sectors of the economy across Europe, even in countries possessing neither colonies nor slaves, with multiplier effects impossible to trace, much less calculate.

Some historians, notably Eric Williams, argued that the vast fortunes drawn from slavery (including the slave trade) were the basis for Europe's Industrial Revolution. This position, construed narrowly, has been undermined by subsequent scholarship. Yet considered more capaciously, it retains notable cogency. Slavery should be viewed not simply as a labor input in the production of tropical commodities but rather as a system of property and a financial instrument. Ownership of slaves was a financial asset. It could be converted into an annuity, or turned into a legacy. In late eighteenth-century Britain, there was a "cadre of genteel rentier-slave owners," especially well represented among the gentry of southern England. Another way of grasping the multiplier effect of the imperial economy would be to examine the prodigious population growth of the ports whose fortunes were linked intimately to some aspect of the colonial trade or the slave trade (or both). In the eighteenth century, the population of Marseilles quintupled and Bristol's tripled. Liverpool, little more than a village in the seventeenth century, boasted a population of eighty thousand by the late eighteenth century, the heyday of the slave trade. Cádiz, too, went from a minor port in 1720 to a booming one with almost seventy thousand inhabitants by 1800.[20]

Returning to the notion of the imperial economy as a catalytic, galvanizing, dynamic force, it is clear that broader understandings of "impact," "benefit," and "profit" are needed. Privileged trading companies, like the EIC and VOC, which sometimes morphed into or served as handmaiden of colonialism, were an important innovation. The principles of joint-stock capital, national monopoly, and integrated corporate organization were not widespread instruments or concepts when the companies were chartered. Another revealing example is the sugar economy. Far from being limited to primitive resource extraction, as Marx and others averred, the operation of the sugar mill, for example, presaged and embodied the techniques and organizational principles generally associated with more advanced "capitalism" and economic modernity. The quest for efficiency and the romance of maximization encouraged planters to squeeze the greatest possible "outputs" from land and labor "inputs." As Drayton observed, sugar plantations were "at the cutting edge of capitalist civilization, whether we look at the size of the labor force attached to single enterprises, its task specialization, its subordination to time discipline, its alienation from its tools, its wholly expatriate character, the capital and machine intensive nature of sugar production, its extensive economies of scale, and its dependence on long-distance trade for inputs and for exporting its product." If sugar plantations bore the hallmarks of capitalist enterprise, so did the economic system that linked the rural haciendas, ranches, and mines of the Bajío region of Mexico with the cities and the wider world. Far from being a backwater, this rural economy was characterized by high levels of entrepreneurial activity, economies of scale, and social mobility.[21]

Any comprehensive accounting must address the political ramifications of imperial political economy. Access to American bullion, for example, buttressed if not underpinned the rise of royal absolutism (or at least pretensions to it) in the Iberian Peninsula. The Spanish Crown, and to a lesser degree the Portuguese, no longer depended heavily on the Cortes to access funds, as it previously had. The state now derived significant revenue from the colonial economy. The Portuguese case is illuminating. The Crown administered the monopoly on the spice trade in India and thus derived profits (and losses) from this enterprise. Where no monopolies were in place, the Crown collected the "royal fifth" on all gold that was mined. It also collected sundry tithes and fees. In Brazil, the Crown collected revenues on agricultural products, some of the proceeds of trade, bureaucratic office, or business, even down to cottage industries, such as beekeeping, cheese making, and liquor distilling. In his capacity as patron of the church, the Portuguese monarch collected a further tithe (*dizimos*), which was supposed to be used for upkeep of church properties but often was diverted to profane ends.[22] Such inflows of precious metals, and receipts from royal monopolies, decreased the fiscal burdens felt by elites in Europe while lessening the Crown's dependence on them. This shift may have made the elites more pliable and less resistant to increasingly bold royal incursions into previously unmolested spheres of social, economic, and political life. With colonial resources at their disposal, the Spanish and Portuguese monarchs summoned the Cortes infrequently. In Portugal it met for the last time in 1697–1698; in Spain it was seldom convened in the seventeenth and eighteenth centuries.

Imperial political economy was based on the exploitation of labor—indigenous and enslaved—and the extraction of resources, whether agrarian commodities or precious metals. While the human costs are increasingly recognized (and discussed in Chapters 9 and 10), the historical study of the environmental devastation wrought by the European seaborne empires remains in its infancy, as does the process by which ecosystem desecration was converted into capital that could be reinvested elsewhere. A snapshot of this broader history might include the following episodes. French traders exported two hundred thousand to four hundred thousand animal skins (chiefly beaver pelts) each year from Canada in the early eighteenth century, which equated to 70 percent of the value of exports from New France. A century later their British counterparts shipped fifty-four thousand deerskins per year between Charleston, South Carolina, and England. Rivers and streams were not spared, for the production of silver in purified form required mercury. At least sixty-three thousand tons of mercury was used in Mexico during the colonial period, and presumably as much in Peru. When the purification process was completed, the remaining mercury was dumped as waste, seeping into waterways and poisoning them irreparably.[23]

Landscapes were transformed when Old World animal species were introduced. Sheep devoured vegetation from Mexico to Australia, diminishing species diversity and promoting erosion, among other dire consequences. Humans did more than their share. Deforestation was a common effect of European colonial settlement. In the New World, the seemingly unlimited expanse of forest suggested an inexhaustible energy and timber supply. Although the quest for brazilwood certainly was a factor, export-oriented agriculture was more often the culprit. The cultivation of sugar, tobacco, and cotton led to deforestation, eroding the soil and depleting it of nutrients. In much of South America, land was cleared through slash-and-burn techniques, haphazardly and often on a grand scale. In Brazil, aspiring plantation owners would cut down lowland forest, the Mata Atlantica (Atlantic forest), let the slash dry, and then set the debris aflame. Sugarcane would be planted in these ashy fields, which afforded good yields for between ten and fifteen years. When yields (and profits) fell, cane growers would begin the cycle anew: there would be new incursions into the interior, leaving behind depleted soil.[24]

Not only were vast swathes of primeval forest felled for cane, further trees became the firewood that kept the sugar mill in operation. A sixteenth-century Brazilian engenho would consume eight cartloads of firewood a day. Two centuries later, as the size and capacity of the mills increased, this figure increased to fifteen to twenty-five cartloads a day. Firewood accounted for 15–20 percent of the operating costs of the engenho, an outlay exceeded only by that for slave labor. An eighteenth-century commentator described a Brazilian sugar mill in the following way: "These are actually consuming mouths that inhale wood from the countryside, black holes of perpetual fire and smoke giving lively images of the volcanoes of Mounts Vesuvius and Etna. One might almost say the furnace looks like Purgatory or Hell."[25]

The assault on the forest was not unique to the Iberian-claimed Americas. In Batavia, the Dutch VOC likewise sacrificed hectares of trees to fuel its insatiable sugar refineries. This led inexorably to soil erosion. In addition, the VOC dug numerous canals as well as constructed salt-evaporation flats. These proved to be a paradise for mosquitoes, and malaria devastated Batavia's inhabitants. From 1733 until 1795, eighty-five thousand VOC servants died of malaria, an average of almost fifteen hundred a year. Environmental degradation was not limited to the nakedly extractive cultivation of tropical commodities. The early freehold settlers of New England wreaked havoc through their spectacular consumption of firewood to survive the harsh winters. The typical household burned through a woodpile (thirty to forty cords) that amounted to an acre of forest each year. Between 1630 and 1800, 260 million cords of firewood were burned in New England, amounting to the equivalent of 6.5 million acres of forest. In addition, the British Navy increasingly came to depend on New World timber. Half of Britain's naval stores derived from its American colonies by 1715. The construction of a single European warship required between fourteen hundred and two thousand oak, elm, and birch trees.[26]

As in Brazil and Batavia, whether for firewood or warships, the consequences of such rapid and extensive deforestation in British North America were dire. Among the effects were increased runoff and silting, falling water tables, declining biodiversity, and temperature fluctuations. There is good reason to believe that climate conditions in the Caribbean shifted dramatically in the late eighteenth century. From the 1760s, the cycle of El Niño and La Niña currents produced more frequent storms, with heavier rainfall, but also drought conditions. Drought triggered crop failures, whereas rain worsened erosion. Violent hurricanes left behind great human suffering: more than nine thousand were killed in Martinique and six thousand in Guadeloupe in the early 1780s. Nor did the demise of that pillar of the colonial system, slavery, slow the pace of environmental degradation. In the aftermath of emancipation in the British and French Caribbean, freedmen were denied access to the best land, still controlled by their former owners. They therefore pursued subsistence agriculture in lands with poorer, less coveted soils, which accelerated erosion and deepened problems bequeathed by the sugar plantation complex.[27]

Though the expansion of empire was marked by environmental destruction in myriad forms, it also intersected with nascent environmentalism. As historian Richard Grove observed, ideas of forest protection, tree planning, soil conservation, climate preservation, and agricultural improvement were ubiquitous in the eighteenth-century British Empire. In Portuguese America, the efflorescence of natural history and economic botany combined with acute awareness of the environmental degradation wrought by resource extraction also gave rise to conservationist sensibilities and policies, including enforcement of the royal monopoly over the forest.[28] Such environmental consciousness and stewardship deserves recognition, even if it was ultimately outweighed in importance by destruction. The capacity of the seaborne empires to convert resources found in nature into capital is undoubtedly an aspect of the "primitive accumulation" that Marx understood as empire's contribution to the development of capitalism and that we understand as a crucial dimension of the political economy of the seaborne empires.

8. Imperial Migrations

Coerced, Forced, and "Free"

The transatlantic slave trade was the mode by which Europeans acquired captive Africans and sold them as slaves in the Americas. "Trade" may be a misnomer. As historian Walter Rodney observed, the "warfare, trickery, banditry and kidnapping" that produced "social violence" was part and parcel of the execrable traffic in human beings. Slavery was not the only form of migration involving coercion in Europe's overseas empires, for indentured servitude and convict transportation were ubiquitous as well. These forms of forced and quasi-forced migration brought laborers whose presence shaped the economic and social structures of the seaborne empires. Four out of every five migrants from Europe and Africa to the Americas before 1820 would endure some form of servitude. Of these migrants, three-quarters were enslaved Africans.[1] After surveying the varieties of forced and coerced migration, this chapter addresses nominally "free" migration from Europe to the various overseas empires. The word "free" is used warily. Much outward migration was attributable to conditions—including poverty, compulsory military service (notably naval impressment), evangelizing missions, religious persecution—that pushed individuals away from the societies into which they were born and involved factors other than volition.

Reliance on slave labor was not peculiar to European overseas empires. It was widespread in numerous African societies and in the Islamic states of the Middle East and Indian Ocean worlds. Before 1600, only a quarter of all

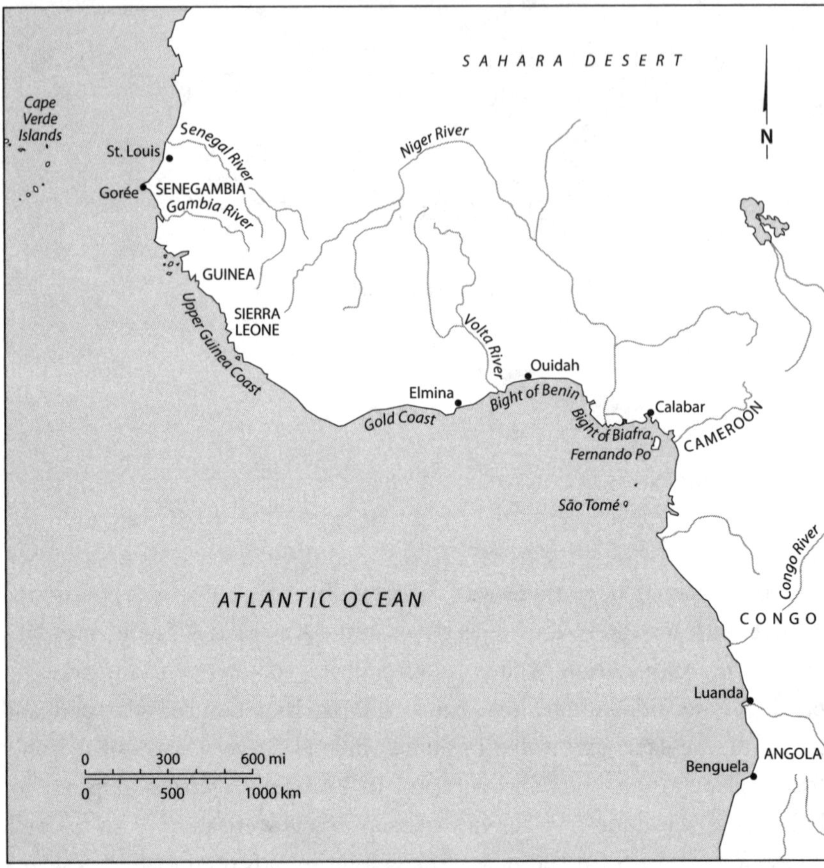

Figure 13. The West African coast in the era of the slave trade

slaves leaving Africa did so as part of the Atlantic trade. It was in the seventeenth century that the Atlantic slave trade came to dominate the overall African trade in slaves, accounting for two-thirds of the total number. It is not contentious, then, to observe that slavery existed in Africa long before the advent of the transatlantic slave trade. Yet to claim that Europeans merely siphoned off an existing supply of slaves, or that Europeans became participants in an already booming slave trade, would be highly misleading. Slavery in Africa existed on the margins of society. It was the entry and participation of European merchants that incentivized its expansion, galvanizing the transformation of a minor trade into a major one.[2]

More than twelve million Africans were embarked as slaves on ships from African ports bound for the Americas. Of these, almost five million were embarked at one of Portugal's Angolan ports—Luanda and Benguela, chiefly. Luanda was the port from which the greatest number of enslaved Africans were shipped, almost three million over the course of the trade. Of the American ports, those in Brazil received the greatest number, almost five million. Rio de Janeiro received almost two million and Salvador 1.5 million. By comparison, the ports of British and French America received many fewer slaves, though the numbers remain enormous: Kingston, Jamaica, 885 thousand; Charleston, South Carolina, just under two hundred thousand; Cap François, Saint-Domingue, slightly over four hundred thousand. Spanish America absorbed more than 1.5 million slaves, many of them destined for Cuba in the nineteenth century. The apogee of the transatlantic slave trade was the century spanning 1750 to 1850. An average of seventy-six thousand Africans were shipped as slaves each year, but in some years the figure exceeded a hundred thousand human beings. Over the course of the trade as a whole, the greatest number of Africans, two-fifths, were taken from West Central Africa, from what is today Angola. The Bight of Benin, the Bight of Biafra, and the Gold Coast were also major sources of slaves, together accounting for an additional two-fifths of the total. Over the course of the four centuries of the slave trade, three out of every four slaves sailed on a Portuguese or British ship. Almost half of all slaves were transported on Portuguese ships and slightly more than a quarter on British ships, with French, Spanish, and Dutch ships transporting lesser yet still sizable numbers.[3]

Europeans resorted to slave labor in the aftermath of the conquest of Constantinople by Christian crusaders in 1204. Before then, the institution of slavery had been in terminal decline across Western Europe. Subsequently, Genoese and Venetian merchants set up slave-trading posts dotting the coasts of the Black Sea. In fact, Black Sea ports furnished most of the slaves sold in the Mediterranean basin to work on various plantations, including those producing sugar in Cyprus and the Algarve region of southern Portugal. This early slave trade was not based on race, color, or religion. Even Orthodox Christians ended up as slaves in Western Europe. The number of slaves from this eastern Mediterranean trade was minuscule, however, no more than a thousand annually.[4] Slaves were expensive and scarce in this period.

The European slave trade soon extended to Africa. By 1450, well before the voyages of Cabral or Columbus, hundreds of enslaved Africans entered Europe each year. Before 1500 perhaps as many as thirteen hundred a year were transported to Europe and another five hundred to the Atlantic islands off Africa (Madeira, Cape Verde, São Tomé, and the Canaries). Cape Verde and São Tomé were uninhabited before the arrival of the Portuguese. Africans were brought as slaves from the mainland. The islands also were conceived as a dumping ground for Portugal's convicts (*degredados*) and other "undesirables." This slave trade, though, was a secondary outgrowth of Europeans' primary object: gold. It was gold, not slaves, that dominated Europe's trade with Africa at first. The advent of sugar cultivation changed everything. As many of the Atlantic archipelagos lacked an indigenous labor force, would-be planters turned to nearby African labor. By the 1520s, São Tomé imported almost two thousand slaves per year. The Portuguese system of factories, though not created for the purposes of the slave trade, easily lent itself to slaving. Factories functioned as a bridge between the hinterland, the coast, and foreign markets, whether in Europe or the Americas. The Portuguese Crown benefited handsomely from this incipient commerce. It sold licenses to conduct the trade, and by the early sixteenth century this concession accounted for 20 percent of royal income.[5]

Sugar cultivation required a large labor force engaged in ceaseless, strenuous activity, particularly during the harvest season. Forced labor was favored due to the intensity of sugar production. European free laborers shunned such work. Indentured servants and other coerced laborers thus undertook sugar production, but they often succumbed to the diseases endemic to the tropical climate in which sugar thrives. In the Americas, the Amerindian population numbers plummeted as a result of epidemic diseases transmitted by Europeans, who were thereby deprived of the indigenous labor force they coveted. The Spanish Crown's prohibition of Amerindian enslavement further impeded such exploitation. Europeans thus turned to Africa as a source of forced labor. As the next chapter makes clear, an array of racist, moral, theological, and political justifications were concocted to sanction the traffic of Africans.

The shift to African slave labor, and hence reliance on the slave trade, did not happen abruptly. Brazil offers an example of the protracted, uneven, and incomplete nature of this shift. African slaves and their descendants became the majority of the workforce on Brazilian plantations only after 1600, a hundred years after Cabral's initial landfall. Before then, Amerindians remained the principal labor force on sugar estates. The transition from Amerindian and European to African labor occurred even later in other empires. As late as 1690, there were more European and Amerindian bonded laborers than laborers of African descent in the British Caribbean. The seemingly late transition to a majority enslaved labor force of African descent is attributable in part to the fact that slave populations in the Americas were not self-sustaining, whether due to disease or the brutality of the slave regime. The number of deaths exceeded the number of births everywhere except in North America, and in Barbados after 1760. A steady supply of new captives was needed to sustain an economy premised on slavery.[6]

The supply, alas, proved steady, and it increased massively. The importation of enslaved Africans into Spanish America averaged just over a thousand a year in the sixteenth century, almost three thousand in the seventeenth, and nearly six thousand in the eighteenth century. In Brazil, an average of a thousand enslaved Africans a year disembarked in Portuguese territory in the sixteenth century. This number swelled to almost six thousand in the seventeenth, nearly nineteen thousand in the eighteenth, and twenty-four thousand in the first decade of the nineteenth century. In the British Caribbean, the transition to slave labor commenced in the middle of the seventeenth century. In Barbados, the number of white indentured servants declined from thirteen thousand to three thousand between 1650 and 1680, while the enslaved black population grew to three times the size of the total white population, both free and indentured, by 1700. In the French Caribbean, the massive, disproportionate influx of African slaves occurred slightly later. While in 1700 the number of black slaves was just slightly higher than the number of white inhabitants, slaves were four-fifths of the population by 1730. By 1790, the number of black slaves was ten times the number of white inhabitants.[7] On the British American mainland the disparity was not as stark, but nevertheless slaves accounted for a fifth of Virginia's population in the first decade of the eighteenth century.

European states sought to regulate the slave trade. They operated on the assumption that monopoly was the most efficacious mode of regulation. They used privileged trading companies to organize the slave trade. The Dutch WIC, the French Compagnie des Indes, and similar entities exercised a number of the functions ordinarily associated with states, such as building fortified trading posts on the West African Coast and conducting diplomacy with African polities. Companies ultimately served as middlemen, supervising private European traders and regulating their interactions with Africans. Not all European nations constructed such factories. Spain, for example, had forsworn claims to Africa according to the Treaty of Tordesillas (1494), and thus relied on Portuguese merchants to furnish its American empire with slaves until 1640. It later depended on Dutch, French, and British suppliers, often dictated by the vagaries of European geopolitics.

The goods Europeans sold in exchange for slaves varied. Textiles, often originating in South Asia, made up more than half of the total value of goods, but metal, alcohol, firearms, manufactured tools and utensils, and tobacco (for a time) also were common forms of payment. African blacksmiths coveted wrought iron to make all manner of instruments, from farm tools to weapons. The trade in weapons, too, was widespread, notwithstanding the misgivings of some Europeans. In 1718, for example, the Portuguese banned use of munitions in the slave trade. But the need to compete with rival Europeans soon eclipsed any misgivings they harbored. As an early eighteenth-century Dutch trader admitted, "We are obliged to [trade weapons] in order to remain at the same level as the foreigners and interlopers." Between 1750 and 1807, the annual quantity of guns shipped from Britain alone was between 283,000 and 394,000, to which must be added 384,000 kilograms of gunpowder sold each year. In the middle decades of the eighteenth century, the value of British exports to Africa quadrupled. It touched numerous sectors of the economy, from arms manufacturers to weavers to shipwrights. Insurance agents and bankers had a major stake in the slave trade.[8] Guns, textiles, and alcohol were not the only objects coveted. Indian Ocean cowrie shells also were frequently a component of the trade, as they were used as a currency instrument in much of West Africa. By the eighteenth century, Dutch and English merchants were importing forty million shells per year. It is estimated that in some parts of West Africa cowrie imports approached a third of the value of all goods.[9] The transatlantic slave trade therefore was more than a triangular trade between Africa, Europe, and the Americas. It was premised on a complicated multi-oceanic trade that stretched from the Pacific Coast of Peru to the Indian Ocean ports of South Asia.

Europeans rarely penetrated the interior of Africa in pursuit of slaves. They were confined to the coast by the military potency of African states and further deterred by lethal diseases. As Thornton concluded, "Europeans possessed no means, either economic or military, to compel African leaders to sell slaves." Most of the forts were leased by African rulers, in exchange for the payment of an annual rent, though some forts were seized by force, such as El Mina. Revealingly, El Mina was the only fort constructed of stone; most were built of mud and brick, the brick having been transported from Europe as ship's ballast. The use of brick and mud bespeaks the ephemerality (or at least fungible nature) of these posts and Europeans' clearly subordinate relation to African rulers. Africans controlled the onshore aspects of the trade, whereas Europeans were limited to shipping the slaves they acquired. African statesmen thus remained the ultimate arbiters of trade relations and controlled the fate of slaves. They required Europeans to pay significant taxes on the purchase and export of slaves. African agents were responsible also for the enslavement and the transportation of captives to the coast from the interior. War captives were a major source of slaves, but so too were individuals convicted of such crimes as murder, witchcraft, default on debt, and theft; those kidnapped or captured in raids; and those who fell afoul of local authorities, whether for political or religious reasons. European traders sought to curry favor with local rulers and encouraged them to send their children to study in Europe, as, in the words of Liverpool slaver merchants, "it not only conciliates their friendship and softens their manners, but adds greatly to the security of the trade."[10]

Europeans emphasized that their African counterparts were the legal providers of slaves. The trade thus could be presented as an arrangement freely entered into by two sovereigns. The charters of both the Compagnie de Sénegal (1681) and the Compagnie de Guinée (1685) made reference to "treaties made with Negro Kings [*les rois nègres*]." In one sense, this characterization was accurate, for local rulers sanctioned the trade and benefited from tax revenue. Yet the situation on the ground was more complex. It involved a great range of actors. The records of two ships trading at Ouidah (modern Dahomey) in the late eighteenth century reveal that of the 660 slaves purchased, a mere 10 percent were sold by the state. The lion's share, about 70 percent, were sold by a heterogeneous collection of large and small merchants. Individuals trading one or two slaves at a time made up the remainder.[11]

Many of the captives perished during the Atlantic crossing, the infamous Middle Passage. Epidemics could annihilate an entire ship, leading British opponents of the trade to designate the slave ship a "marine lazar house" and a "floating bier." The journey lasted between two and three months, depending on the ports of departure and arrival. British abolitionist William Wilberforce declared, "Never can so much misery be found condensed in so small a place as in a slave ship during the Middle Passage." Up to four hundred captives could be crowded onto a single ship. They were separated into three groups: men, grown boys, and women and children. Women were given light clothes to wear, but men were left naked in fair weather. Slaves were shackled together below deck at night. The rape of female captives by the crew and captain was rampant and went unpunished. The conditions were worse than squalid, but slave traders' tended dutifully to the amount of food and water the slaves consumed to protect their investment. Mortality rates averaged 12 percent over four centuries, notwithstanding the efforts of slavers to preserve the value of their cargo and maintain the health of the slaves for economic, not humanitarian, reasons. There existed a perverse belief among slave merchants that exercise would keep the captives healthy. They were forced to go on deck to sing and dance. They could be beaten for refusing to participate in such entertainments. But the enslaved died regardless of European pseudoscience, superstition, and sadism. Dysentery (called the "flux" or "bloody flux") and other intestinal diseases were the most common killer, but mosquito-borne illnesses like malaria and yellow fever, together with scurvy and respiratory ailments, claimed many lives. Piddling water rations exacerbated illness and resulted in widespread dehydration.[12]

Some of the enslaved worked aboard the ship, often undertaking menial tasks. This took several forms, including sanitizing the slave quarters below deck, caldrons of disease caked with fecal matter and other bodily fluids. Food preparation, especially by women, was also common, with rice, yams, and corn the staples of the diet. Occasionally the performance of such menial, if exhausting, tasks was rewarded with some form of preferment, from a small bit of liquor or tobacco to extra rations of food. Sometimes circumstances compelled slaves to take additional roles. During intra-European warfare, or when attacked by buccaneers, ship's captains armed the slaves, unfastening their chains temporarily and training them to handle weapons. Slaves frequently worked as sailors, including on voyages through the Middle Passage between Brazil and West Africa. In late eighteenth-century Brazil, one in six sailors involved in the slave trade was a slave.[13]

European crews, nominally free, did not escape the suffering of slave voyages. Traveling to the West African coast was, in their eyes, the worst of all possible fates. Those who signed up often did so out of desperation and the absence of better options. One eighteenth-century slave merchant referred to his crew as "white slaves," denigrating them as "the very dregs of the community." Half of all Europeans who traveled to West Africa in the eighteenth century perished, mainly from disease. Those who survived were pivotal contributors to the ship's management. They disciplined the enslaved, rooting out malcontents and administering corporal punishment below deck. The threat of slave rebellion was real and increased the overall cost of the voyage as slave ships carried larger than normal crews to guard against insurrection. Sailors also prepared the enslaved for sale, in what historian Marcus Rediker described as a "process of value creation and enhancement." As the ship approached its destination port, sailors were enjoined to remove shackles in order for chafing to heal, to clean and shave the men, to remove gray hairs (or to dye them black) to emphasize the slave's virility and youthfulness, and to rub down the body with palm oil to accentuate muscle tone. Those captives who disembarked were sold to a master, consigned thereafter to a lifetime of involuntary servitude, legally sanctioned violence, and myriad forms of degradation. Nor was this final, for there was a rampant internal slave trade in the Americas, which involved sale and transportation across vast distances. Of the nearly three million enslaved Africans brought to British America, about 15 percent boarded ships for other American ports, including the colonies of Spain and France.[14]

In addition to slavery, other forms of coercive labor practices girded the economic enterprises of Europe's seaborne empires. Indentured servitude was perhaps the most ubiquitous, though not universal. Dutch law, for example, did not recognize indenture as legal. While this institution existed in the Old World, its New World guise was significantly harsher, resembling, in some places, chattel slavery. In Barbados, for example, in historian Hilary McD. Beckles's phrase, planters "quite freely bought, sold, gambled away, mortgaged, taxed as property, and inherited in their wills indentured servants" before the implementation of a master-servant code in 1661. Contracts of indenture persuaded prospective colonists who could not support themselves financially to cross the Atlantic as well as secured a semi-stable labor force for the holders of the contract. These contracts gave the holder full right to a person's labor for a fixed period of time in exchange for subsistence, and sometimes stipulated a land grant at the end of the term of service as well. Perhaps 60 percent of the immigrants to Britain's American colonies traveled under some form of labor contract. In some places, like the Chesapeake in the seventeenth century, 75 to 85 percent of settlers were indentured servants, 40 percent of whom died before completing their term of service. Though not quite so numerous, indentured servants constituted the majority of French migrants to the Caribbean. Perhaps as many as thirty thousand to forty thousand such *engagés* arrived over the course of the seventeenth and eighteenth centuries. Most of these servants, primarily young men from the lower strata of society, between fifteen and thirty years of age, did not intend to settle in the Caribbean permanently. Some contracts of indenture even stipulated that payment for services would take place in France itself, not in the Antilles, suggesting the anticipated transient nature of their sojourn.[15]

Though the scale of indentured servitude diminished in the eighteenth century, arrangements resembling it lingered long after. Indentured labor persisted into the nineteenth century, and it experienced a resurgence after the abolition of slavery. There were forty-five thousand South Asian migrants in British-controlled Mauritius by the early 1840s, most hailing from Calcutta and Madras. At least twenty-two thousand were transported to the British colonies of Guiana, Trinidad, and Jamaica by the end of the same decade. In the Spanish Empire, the waning of the slave trade and the enhanced demand for forced labor led to a series of schemes resembling indenture. The first shipment of Chinese laborers to Cuba occurred in 1847. In the ensuing decades, 210,000 so-called coolies would be taken to Cuba (and the former Spanish colony of Peru) to work alongside, and sometimes replace, slave labor.[16]

In addition to contracts of indenture, European states resorted to other forms of forced migration to populate their colonies and secure an adequate labor supply. One of the most important was the forcible removal of convicts and other criminalized populations. The relocation of convicts from Europe to overseas empires is euphemistically termed "transportation" in English, but in reality it was a macabre affair akin to deportation. In the Portuguese Empire, for example, *degredados* (convicts condemned to exile or jail) were dispatched to various colonies. At least fifty thousand such degredados were shipped overseas before 1750. England had banished felons to America since at least 1615, but systematic foreign exile as punishment for serious crimes began somewhat later. After the Civil War (c. 1660), British political prisoners could be sentenced to transportation. Forced labor was a component of their sentence, a punishment that was extended by statute to religious nonconformists. Relatively few individuals were sentenced to transportation, however, until the early eighteenth century, when such punishment became increasingly common. Fifty thousand convicts were transported to Britain's American colonies over the course of the eighteenth century, including two-thirds of the felons convicted at the Old Bailey, London's chief criminal court.[17] Britain also sought to establish a penal colony at Cape Coast Castle (in modern Ghana) in the 1750s, but disease killed off the convicts landed there. Political dissidents could be banished as well and sometimes be pressed into military service beyond Europe. Prisoners from the 1745 Rebellion in Scotland, for example, were sent to the Caribbean to serve in local regiments as punishment.

Many prominent commentators opposed the establishment of overseas penal colonies as inadvisable, a faulty foundation for future settlement. Scottish historian William Robertson argued that "industry, sobriety, patience and mutual confidence are indispensably requisite in an infant settlement" and held that "the vices of those unsound and incurable members will probably infect the whole."[18] The warnings of Robertson and others went unheeded. Perhaps the greatest experiment in convict transportation occurred in the Antipodes. Botany Bay, Australia, received its first fleet carrying convicts in 1788. This experiment was animated by a spirit different to that of previous convict schemes. It relied on those convicted of property crimes, not felons. After serving their sentences, it was envisioned that they would become peasant proprietors, self-governing according to British common law, not administered by executive fiat and martial law. Because the nature of the crimes they had committed carried shorter sentences and pardons were fairly common, two-thirds of the five thousand colonists in Australia were free by 1800, a little more than a decade after disembarking from the first ships. Nevertheless, the transition toward a free society was forestalled by the steady influx of new convicts: eleven thousand alone arrived in the 1816–1820 period, and a further fifty-five thousand in the two decades that followed. When transportation to Australia was ended in 1852, 160,000 convicts had been transported, a mere one-sixth of whom were women.[19]

Australia was not the sole destination for convicts in the British Empire. There were various other outposts. At least nine thousand were banished to Bermuda between 1824 and 1863. The EIC transported Indian prisoners to the new penal colonies it began establishing in the 1790s. The links in the chain of this carceral necklace included the Andaman Islands (established 1793–1796), Penang (1790–1860), Malacca and Singapore (1825–1860), Mauritius (1815–1853), and the Arkan and Tenasserim provinces of Burma

(1828–1862). Increasingly, those identified as internal enemies of the state were targeted for extra-European transportation. Such a move was, as historian Miles Taylor has pointed out, "the cornerstone of the British state's containment of Chartism and of post-Famine disorder in Ireland." Emigration increasingly came to be a solution for political dissent and petty crime, not merely a response to domestic overpopulation and entrenched poverty. The use of colonies as dumping grounds for political dissidents was widespread. In the late 1820s, the Spanish government routinely banished liberals to the presidios it maintained in its North African beachheads. In the aftermath of the 1848 Revolution in France, Napoleon III deported fifteen thousand Parisians deemed to be politically disruptive to Algeria. One-third of these political convicts died of cholera, leading one commentator to remark: "Our colony in Algeria is nothing but a hospital contained within a prison."[20] Those convicted of nonpolitical offenses could find themselves transported to remote Guiana, which received its first contingent of two thousand prisoners in 1852.

It is crucial to foreground the various forms of forced and coerced migration that were part and parcel of European imperialism. Nevertheless, it must be conceded that a great portion of those Europeans crossing the Atlantic did so neither as slaves, servants, nor prisoners. In the absence of these strictures, it is tempting to consider these individuals as having decided to migrate, or emigrate, freely or voluntarily. There is some validity in such a conclusion, but it must be remembered that push factors were as decisive as pull factors as potential migrants contemplated leaving Europe's shores. There was great variation in nominally free migration patterns across empires. Perhaps 750,000 Spaniards voluntarily migrated to the Americas, with the vast majority migrating prior to 1650. It has been estimated that between one and 1.5 million Portuguese migrated overseas between 1500 and 1760. Perhaps as few as fifteen thousand persons migrated to Dutch colonial possessions in the Americas, the majority of them in the seventeenth century. This paltry figure contrasted starkly with the perhaps half million people who ventured to the Dutch East Indies, even if perhaps half of this figure was composed of "transmigrants," other Europeans who simply transited through the Dutch Republic on their way to Batavia. New France, as well as France's Caribbean possessions, initially failed to attract many voluntary migrants until the government offered inducements in the late 1660s. As late as 1680, there were a mere ten thousand European inhabitants in New France, whereas in the Antilles there were twelve thousand. In the first century following the foundation of Britain's Atlantic empire, 530 thousand migrants departed, amounting to at least twice and perhaps four times as many as forsook peninsular Spain for its New World colonies in the same period. Migration only accelerated thereafter. Between 1700 and 1775, 260,000 Britons left for America, most of them Irish, with Scots in second place.[21]

The social composition of the nominally free Europeans who populated the seaborne empires depended on the manner and mode of colonization. Almost all European states sought to lure sturdy laborers, skilled tradesmen, and earnest, God-fearing folk. Rarely did their target demographic demonstrate reciprocate the interest, at least before the eighteenth century. After 1760, for example, voluntary (or, at least, not legally coerced) migration of skilled men to British North America spiked. They were attracted to its burgeoning prosperity, robust employment prospects, and myriad opportunities for land speculation. Yet this rising interest caused great alarm. By 1773, Parliament contemplated a bill to ban all immigration to North America, reflecting a deep-seated fear of depopulation ubiquitous in early modern Europe. The final quarter of the eighteenth century saw a rising tide of migration, with a quarter of a million Europeans making their way to the nascent United States and Canada.[22]

Fears of depopulation, however, often were overblown. Imperial ventures were stymied by lack of interest from prospective settlers who were able to meet an impossibly high standard. This indifference compelled chartered companies, and other intermediary corporations European states subcontracted for the purposes of colonization, to resort to a less appealing demographic cohort. The Virginia Company, for example, recruited ex-convicts, the poor, decommissioned military veterans, and other perceived undesirables. Once such deplorable types had been induced to migrate, European states or their agents coerced them to stay in their new domiciles. What began as ostensibly voluntary migration could morph into something far from free. The English EIC, for example, struggled to attract and retain settlers. It was forced to introduce creatively coercive measures in the late seventeenth century. After 1671, for example, any man seeking a marriage license in Bombay was forced to sign a contract of indenture, pledging to remain in India for seven years. The poor, seeking relief from their poverty, were a vulnerable target in the Dutch Empire as well. As indenture was illegal in Dutch territories, the VOC relied on the façade of "voluntary" migration. It tapped into a network of private recruiters (*volkhouders*) who operated in port cities and propositioned unemployed men. These recruiters signed such poor souls up for service on a VOC vessel and provided food, clothing, and shelter until their ship sailed. In exchange, the recruiters received the first installment of a new recruit's wages. Such tactics earned these recruiters the moniker "soul sellers" (*zielverkoopers*), a disparaging epithet undoubtedly linked to the ghastly levels of mortality on VOC voyages. Upwards of one in seven migrants failed to reach Batavia. Two-thirds of those who left Europe never returned.[23]

Other vulnerable populations in Europe were similarly pressured to migrate to overseas territories. Young women and orphans were openly targeted. In New France, the Crown actively intervened to address the perceived dearth of European women. In the 1660s it recruited and transported seven hundred women—the so-called *filles du roi* (or "daughters of the king"), since their dowries were paid by the king. Eighty percent of these women were married within six months. The Portuguese state routinely dispatched orphaned girls to Brazil, to offset the imbalance between European men and European women, and to encourage procreation and hence population growth. More generally, the seaborne empires thus remained places where socially marginal types—absconding sailors, those without fixed domicile, refugees—gravitated. This remained true in the nineteenth century. A mid-nineteenth century French Army survey characterized one-tenth of the population of Algiers as "flottante," meeting the unflattering criteria above.[24]

Western European states peopled their empires from a variety of sources, from coerced laborer to nominally free migrants. In some cases, European migration was rewarded with social mobility and relief from either insalubrious cities or grinding rural poverty. Yet for most migrants, especially non-European ones, the experience was inseparable from enslavement, forced removal, and other forms of coercion. The seaborne empires relied on both types of migration, forced and free, ensuring that the trajectory of colonial societies would differ markedly from those of Europe. The stigmas attached to slavery and other forms of forced labor mingled with other prejudices, including racial ones, and reinforced the subordinate position of the colonies within a system of empire.

9. Labor Regimes

Several labor regimes existed simultaneously and overlapped in Europe's seaborne empires. While free labor—whether self-supporting urban artisan, plantation owner, or yeoman farmer—was the most common form in some societies, coerced labor predominated in others. The seaborne empires were also dependent on free, non-European labor. In EIC-controlled South Asia, the *lascars*, maritime labor gangs under command of *serangs* (headmen), were the sailors on the ships that plied the Indian Ocean, while thousands of dockworkers, porters, and vendors supplied and loaded the cargo into and out of their holds. In Spanish New Granada (modern Colombia), the navigation of the main fluvial artery connecting the capital and the sea, the Magdalena River, was coordinated by *bogas* (boatmen) who almost exclusively were free people of African descent.[1]

Forced or otherwise coerced labor was particularly prevalent where the economy was organized around extractive and export-oriented industries, like mining and plantation-based agriculture. Indentured servitude and convict transportation, discussed in the preceding chapter, were ubiquitous mechanisms of securing European labor. Forced labor was indispensable to the militaries that made empire possible. For centuries, convicts were forced to row in the galleys plying the Mediterranean. During the American Revolution (1775–1783) alone, eighty thousand Britons were impressed into naval service. Such coercion was vigorously resisted: hundreds of public brawls in British seaports pitted press gangs and their targeted victims.[2] More generally, the voracious demand by Europeans for labor in their overseas empires portended the invention of new oppressive labor regimes or else the survival, expansion, and (often) perversion of earlier practices.

Coerced labor took several forms. In Mexico, Amerindian slavery predominated at first and was built on indigenous foundations, as at least 5 percent of Aztec society was enslaved. Though the Spanish Crown soon prohibited enslavement of Amerindians, it did not foreclose other modes of accessing indigenous labor. The encomienda system, though derived from Iberian precedent, was recast in Spanish America. It allotted groups of Amerindians to an encomendero, typically a conquistador, who gained control over their labor and, according to the 1512 Laws of Burgos, was responsible for their spiritual welfare and protection. In spite of efforts to rein them in, notably through the 1542 New Laws that explicitly articulated Amerindians' free status, the largest encomenderos formed what amounted to a colonial aristocracy for the first decades after the conquest of Peru and Mexico. Hernan Cortés, for example, received encomienda right over 115,000 natives. The average size of an encomienda in the Valley of Mexico averaged six thousand in 1530. In Andean South America, the *mita* prevailed. Taken from a Quechua word, it referred to the annual labor service demanded by the Inca emperor and organized by local lords who were loyal to him. Spain continued this practice, though with more exacting brutality. They forced Amerindians to provide labor on a rotational basis in mines, agriculture, and textile factories. In the mines of Potosí, one-seventh of the adult population was forced to work one year out of every seven, which produced devastating population dislocations. The vast majority, around 80 percent, of laborers in the mines of Potosí and Zacatecas at the zenith of their productivity (1550–1650) were indigenous. Europeans devised other methods of extracting indigenous labor besides the encomienda, the mita, and tribute. The Jesuits' approach offers a prime example. In 1610, the Jesuits shifted their New World operations to Paraguay, where they attracted Amerindians fleeing from encroaching settlers bent on enslaving them. Amerindians sought and received refuge in the Jesuit missions. The Guaraní Indian mission population swelled fourfold in the second half of the seventeenth century. In exchange for accepting baptism and observing Catholic rites, the Guaraní received protection to cultivate family-size plots as well as to till communal fields. The main trade good of the Jesuit missions in the Río de la Plata was yerba maté, a local tea, sold regionally as well as in Europe, which accounted for the vast majority of their revenues in the region.[3]

Ready access to Amerindian labor, whether through the encomienda, the mita, or other coercive and semicoercive mechanisms, removed the incentive in Spanish America to purchase African slaves, at least at first. Even after the formal prohibition on Indian slavery in the 1540s, it persisted, as suggested by the fact that the Spanish Crown was compelled to issue a second decree to the same effect in 1679. In Brazil, a similar dynamic was at work. Amerindians were enslaved to labor in the sugarcane fields of the northeast. In a single year, 1575, twenty thousand Amerindians were abducted from the hinterlands of Bahia and enslaved. Even in less lucrative and extractive industries, exploitation of Amerindian labor was the norm. Colonists in Pará and Maranhão relied on Amerindian labor for the cultivation and harvest of basic foodstuffs. Even after the Portuguese Crown's 1609 ban on the Amerindian slave trade, at least one hundred thousand to two hundred thousand Amerindians were enslaved over the course of the seventeenth century, particularly in frontier zones, away from the colonial administration's watchful gaze. This figure does not account for the thousands of Amerindian "servants" who were regarded as property and whose condition differed little from outright bondage. Nor does it include the nominally "free," aldeia-settled Amerindians whom the state tapped to build fortifications and roads.[4]

French colonists also relied on indigenous labor well into the eighteenth century. In North America, the French plugged themselves into precolonial systems of enslavement and forced labor. Algonquian and Siouan peoples enslaved their enemies as a form of "symbolic domination" and then traded slaves to the French to cement their alliance. The trade thus emerged from interaction and contact with the French. Some of these enslaved Amerindians remained in North America, but many more were shipped to the French Caribbean as laborers in the burgeoning plantation system. Britain did not resist the temptation to enslave Amerindians either. In the 1650–1715 period, traders purchased more than twenty-five thousand indigenous slaves, the majority of whom were destined for the plantations of the Caribbean. The British also engaged in mass enslavement of Amerindians in the course of warfare. In the aftermath of King Philip's (or Metacom's) War (1675–1676) in New England, hundreds of vanquished Indians were transported and sold into bondage in the Caribbean.[5]

Amerindian slavery never disappeared from the seaborne empires. Nor did indentured servitude and convict transportation. Often these labor regimes existed simultaneously, in operation side by side in some cases. But there was a decisive shift toward enslaved African labor in the long term. How did it come to pass that some inhabitants of the European overseas empires were deemed fit to be subjects while others were subjected to slavery?

How was slavery, particularly of sub-Saharan Africans and their descendants, justified by those at the commanding heights of the seaborne empires? Some historians have called attention to functional factors, including the unusual skills that some Africans possessed, such as equestrian prowess or diving ability (in the pearl-fishing industry). Others have pointed out the colonial state's capacity to control, tax, or generate revenue from the slave trade to explain the preference for African labor.[6] Ultimately, however, the control over and exploitation of Africans was predicated on the creation of classificatory schemes to distinguish population groups from one another. Classification readily gave rise to hierarchies, placing one group in a position superior or inferior to that of the others, a positioning that could be used to justify discrimination.

While a full-fledged and comprehensive theory of race emerged only in the eighteenth century, and became increasingly rigid in the nineteenth, notions of race, and discriminatory actions based on race, have a much longer history. "Race" as a synonym for "caste" existed in the late medieval period. It was used with reference to flora and fauna. It was applied to human beings in the Iberian Peninsula, when Christians asserted that Muslims and Jews were affected by a heritable "impurity of blood" from the mid-1400s. As historian David Nirenberg has demonstrated, there was from this point forward an "increasingly widespread use of ideas about biological reproduction of somatic and behavioral traits." These ideas were then employed to "create and legitimate" social hierarchies and discriminatory practices. Following the voyages of discovery, such notions of race were applied to Africans and Amerindians. It is not coincidental that they were applied to those with darker phenotypes. In the early modern European imagination, blackness had sinister associations, ranging from disease to sin. In the 1300s and 1400s, Western European religious iconography was rife with images of black Africans as torturers and executioners, particularly in depictions of the Passion of Christ. Derogatory understandings of blackness and sin soon merged with the classical and biblical traditions that linked slavery with sin. Especially salient was Noah's curse of Canaan, his son Ham's son, in the book of Genesis. Ham sinned by looking on his father's nakedness, and Noah consigned Canaan (and by implication his descendants) to slavery.[7]

There were, of course, additional justifications for enslavement beyond phenotype. Heathenism had long been grounds for enslavement. A 1442 papal bull granted Portugal the authority to reduce to slavery "infidels" and others resisting proselytization. Inhabitants of the earth's so-called torrid zones were deemed inferior to those from more temperate climes. Often they were denominated "slaves by nature." But the association between black skin and slavery had become fixed and rigid by late seventeenth century, at least in the Americas. Morgan Godwyn, an Anglican missionary in Barbados, remarked in 1680, "These two words, *Negro* and *Slave* [are] by custom grown Homogeneous and Convertible; even as *Negro* and *Christian*, *Englishman* and *Heathen*, are by the like custom and partiality made opposites."[8]

Within the plantation system, the slave experience was quite varied. Phenotype mattered, and there was a hierarchy among slaves according to it. Proximity to the Middle Passage also factored. In Brazil, for example, there were at least three types of slave: *boçal* (recent arrival); *crioulo* (born in Brazil); and *ladino* (Portuguese speaker). Lighter phenotypes and those at greater remove from Africa were favored. Sometimes they could avoid consignment to the worst tasks. Field slaves were deemed the most menial, whereas domestic servants and some urban slaves could gain some status. The experience of plantation slavery was also shaped significantly by the crop under cultivation. In Jamaica, a major sugar-producing colony, monoculture never prevailed. As late as the 1770s, 40 percent of slaves were employed in some facet of production other than sugar cultivation. Half of the plantation was devoted to raising livestock and producing foodstuffs for local consumption. Neighboring regions of mainland British North America offer a glimpse into the differences in slave experiences resulting from the crop around which the slaves' labor was organized. In the South Carolina Low Country, large landholdings devoted to the cultivation of rice, a primary staple, which did not exhaust the nutrients of the soil, meant that slaves and their descendants had a greater likelihood of remaining on the plantation than they did elsewhere, in spite of the labor-intensive, backbreaking nature of the work. In the Chesapeake, by contrast, the cultivation of tobacco, which quickly exhausted the soil, often resulted in the breakup of slave families and communities. Planters either relocated in search of untapped lands to exploit or sold off their slaves when their land no longer yielded tobacco.[9]

In the northern mainland colonies, by contrast, though most slaves lived in the countryside, many worked in highly capitalized rural industries—tanneries, saltworks, and iron furnaces—and iron masters were commonly the largest slaveholders. Where slaves did work the land, it was on farms producing provisions for export to the Caribbean sugar islands. As the provisioning trade did not support the plantation regime found in either the Chesapeake or the Carolina Low County, most of these northern, farm-based slaves never labored in large gangs. Instead, they performed a variety of tasks, as hyper-specialization was less prevalent than it was farther south. The situation in the French Caribbean was similar. In Martinique and Guadeloupe, there were four times as many coffee and indigo cultivators as there were sugar planters. This is largely because these crops, along with cotton, did not require the same level of capital and slaves to establish and maintain. On a Saint-Domingue coffee plantation, for example, there were on average one-third the number of slaves, about thirty-three, there would have been on a sugar plantation. The cultivation of cotton required even fewer slaves, and thus presented a lower barrier to entry. On British St. Croix, cotton plantations required one-fifth the number of slaves needed by their sugar counterparts. Cotton possessed a further advantage over sugar: it could be grown in less fertile soil. Unsurprisingly, its popularity grew. Even before the advent of the cotton gin, cotton exports from the British Caribbean quadrupled in the 1780s, and in Saint-Domingue there were as many cotton as sugar planters in 1791. Elsewhere, some agricultural enterprises depended on slavery on a smaller scale. In South Africa, for example, almost half of the free male population owned at least one slave, even in what was chiefly an agrarian society. This meant that slave ownership trickled down the social ladder to holders of small plots. In the Caribbean, slaveholders with few slaves and no land had their slaves exploit the "commons." They dispatched their slaves to fish, hunt turtles, manatees, and whales, and engage in salt raking. They thus profited from slave labor without the capital investments of land and machinery.[10]

Though unrelenting, brutal, and dehumanizing, the nature of slavery and slave society varied widely across and within the seaborne empires. In the Spanish Empire, especially, urban slavery was ubiquitous. Between 10 and 25 percent of the populations of Lima, Mexico City, Quito, Cartagena, and Santa Fe de Bogotá were enslaved.[11] Urban slavery was also common to the middle colonies of British North America. Slaveholding became almost universal among the elite, and even within the reach of the middle classes, particularly in port cities like Boston, New York, Newport, and Charleston. By the 1760s, for example, Philadelphia's white artisans and tradesmen had become major slaveholders. On the eve of the American Revolution, three-quarters of Boston's wealthiest quartile of families were slaveholders. In all of these seaboard metropolises, slaves could be found both at the periphery of the urban economy, as servants in wealthy households, and at the center, laboring as workmen in the shops of artisans. In the Spanish American port city of Buenos Aires circa 1800, all manual professions relied on an integrated workforce, with enslaved and free laborers side by side. Some slaves were involved in the maritime economy. In Nevis and the Bahamas, for example, one in seven slaves worked in maritime occupations on the eve of abolition. The experience of urban slaves was different because of the possibilities for "self-hire." In towns like Bridgetown, Barbados, and Charleston, South Carolina, perhaps a fifth of all slaves engaged in this practice. They agreed to pay their owners a certain sum in exchange for permission to undertake paid work, usually as artisans. Sometimes self-hire arrangements could be quite lucrative, as suggested by the fact that many such enslaved artisans hired other slaves to work under their supervision.[12] Similar arrangements could be found in Brazil. Slaves could earn income by selling whatever surplus they generated from cultivating their own small plots. They were permitted to retain their earnings above their rental price. Furthermore, urban slaves could work on Sundays and holidays, nominally days of respite from the formal demands of slavery, and thus earn additional income.

Private individuals were not the only slaveholders in Europe's seaborne empires. The church and the state also played massive roles. In the Iberian world, convents, monasteries, and individual priests owned slaves. By the eighteenth century, the Jesuits owned more slaves than any other institution, business, or family in the Americas. Slaves worked alongside Amerindians under Jesuit tutelage to produce the wine, brandy, sugar, and yerba maté that was transported to distant markets and often underwrote the Society's educational activities, both in Europe and the Americas. The Jesuits were also the largest holder of slaves across the Atlantic in Portuguese-controlled Angola, where ten thousand slaves labored on fifty Jesuit-owned plantations in the late 1650s. Jesuit reliance on African enslaved labor was global in scope: the Jesuits in Portuguese Goa purchased slaves from Mozambique as late as 1750. The state too was involved in slave ownership. Some slaves were imported solely for military service. Between 1795 and 1808, the British government brought more than thirteen thousand male slaves from West Africa to fight in the French Revolutionary Wars. Parliament delayed the abolition of the slave trade to permit the army to make a final purchase of such captives.

Slaves sometimes gained their freedom by fighting in protracted global conflicts that entailed mass mobilization. The promise of freedom, or the desire to secure recently won freedom, lured slaves to serve as soldiers in imperial armies. As Napoleon Bonaparte mused about former slaves when he weighed reimposing slavery in post-emancipation Saint-Domingue, "They may make less sugar than when they were slaves, but they provide us, and serve as we need them, as soldiers. If we have one less sugar mill, we will have one more citadel occupied by friendly soldiers."[13]

The everyday experience of enslaved Africans in New World societies was marked by physical violence, rape, and dehumanizing terror. The cruelty, torture, and sadism entailed in the disciplining of black bodies was gruesome and has been explored at length by many historians. Here I focus solely on the various slave, or black, codes introduced in the Americas, which sanctioned violence and defined its legal parameters. The most notorious was the 1685 French Code Noir. It required masters to provide for the basic sustenance of their slaves, to tend to their baptism, and to ensure Sundays and religious feast days were free of toil. Most of the beneficent articles were blatantly ignored, whereas the stipulations regarding corporal punishment were assiduously enforced. It denied slaves civil status, thereby depriving them of rights enjoyed by whites to own property, to enter into contracts, to practice a trade, or to give evidence in a trial. The situation was only marginally less brutal in the British Empire. Slaves were defined as chattel, conveyable property, which means that they could be bought, sold, or inherited. The 1688 Slave Code of Barbados defined blacks as "of a barbarous, wild and savage nature," in need of special laws for "the good regulating, or ordering of them, as may both restrain the disorders, rapines and inhumanities to which they are naturally prone and inclined." Even self-hire and subsistence activities were highly regulated with stiff penalties for transgression. In the 1710s, the Jamaican Assembly prohibited slaves from owning livestock or selling meat, sugarcane, fish, or manufactured items without explicit permission. In the 1760s, St. Vincent prohibited slaves from selling or planting any crop that could be exported.[14] In the aftermath of revolts, slave codes were made even harsher. Following "Tacky's Revolt" in Jamaica (1760), for example, the movements and meetings of slaves were tightly monitored, as they would be in other Caribbean contexts.

In Spanish America, the situation of slaves was marginally better. As a result of the legacy of medieval Iberian law codes, themselves based on

Roman law precedent, particularly the thirteenth-century *Siete Partidas*, state and judicial institutions guaranteed slaves certain minimal rights. Slaves were recognized as Christians, with the attendant duties and obligations such classification entailed. The Portuguese analogue of the Siete Partidas was the *Ordenações Manuelinas* of the early sixteenth century. According to this code, killing a slave was a crime punishable by death. This was quite different from what prevailed in British colonies, where, until the end of the eighteenth century, the murder of a slave by an owner was punishable only with a fine. In the Iberian empires, slaves had access to the courts. This access had important ramifications. As historian Sherwin Bryant has noted, such legal action "produced formal changes . . . enshrining in law and legal practice the customary norms and practices that slaves negotiated with their masters."[15] Of course, laws were often honored in the breach, worth little more than the paper on which they were printed. In Brazil, for example, a 1710 royal order demanded that officials in the colony respond to legal complaints brought by slaves, but this went largely unenforced.

However much the de facto diverged from the de jure, slavery in the Iberian world differed markedly from Dutch, English, and French practice in a crucial respect. There existed a legal means by which slaves could become free: self-purchase. The right of self-purchase (*coartación,* in Spanish) was contingent on the owner's consent. A slave could make a down payment on his freedom, drawing on the Roman law concept of a *peculium.* A slave could accumulate personal wealth to purchase his or her freedom, even though such personal property was legally the property of the slave's owner. If slave and owner were unable to reach a mutually satisfactory price, Iberian law allowed a slave to request that a judge set the price of manumission. While not widespread, self-purchase was far from uncommon. As described previously, urban slaves in Brazil, for example, had ample opportunities through self-hire to earn funds with which their freedom might be purchased. Other routes to freedom included voluntary manumission, by which an owner freed a slave out of religious piety, ties of affection (toward a concubine or illegitimate child), or related motivations.[16]

Self-purchase or manumission by other means was rare in other slave societies, however. In the Cape Colony, Dutch settlers imported slaves at great expense from Madagascar, Mozambique, and the Indian Ocean littorals, treating these slaves purely as laborers. Unsurprising, there were few manumissions. Between 1715 and 1791, less than two-tenths of 1 percent of slaves were manumitted. In British North America, colonial legislatures barred faith-based manumissions in the mid-seventeenth century. Nevertheless, some opportunities for manumission existed. In extraordinary cases, the state manumitted slaves. In the aftermath of the aforementioned Tackey's Revolt, Jamaican authorities manumitted twenty "faithful" slaves (and duly compensated the owners), granting them an annuity for life.[17] In 1772, as a result of the verdict in the Somerset case, slavery was abolished in Britain itself, and slaves in Britain were therefore manumitted. In 1833 the Emancipation Act stipulated that all slaves in the British Empire would be freed in 1834. Other seaborne empires did not follow Britain's precedent. With the exception of short periods during the French Revolution, slavery remained legal in France until 1836 and in Spain until 1864.

Although it was the largest slave owner in Europe's seaborne empires, the Catholic Church somewhat paradoxically embraced the view that Africans possessed immortal souls. By and large, the church was committed to proselytizing among slaves, baptizing them, and granting time for worship. Cults of black saints flourished, as historian Erin Rowe has shown. The church also found ways to legitimate marriage and kinship of African origin according to Christian doctrine. Colonial Brazil recorded the highest number of legal marriages among the slave regions of Latin America, and less formal, long-term, stable connubial relations were even more common. Portuguese law provided some protection of slave marriages, and the ability of slave owners to separate husbands from wives was limited. Slaves could participate in religious rituals: saint's day celebrations and processions offered a respite from the drudgery of servitude. Indeed, it was within the church that slaves created collective organizations, established rituals, and developed practices that mitigated (to some degree) the suffering of enslavement. Fraternal organizations of slaves were ubiquitous in the Iberian empires, and godparentage also was sanctioned. Brotherhoods were established to ameliorate the plight of blacks (enslaved and free) and persons of mixed-race backgrounds. This sometimes included raising funds to purchase the freedom of kin who remained enslaved. Until the eighteenth century, there was no counterpart to Catholic Iberian practice in British North America. It was not until the Great Awakening of the 1740s and the religious revivalism in the South during the next two decades that large numbers of slaves were converted to Christianity. Missionary activity was undertaken not only by the Anglican Society for the Propagation of the Gospel in Foreign Parts but also by

Methodists, Baptists, Moravians, and Presbyterians. There were limits to such activity, of course. Across the New World, slave funerals frightened slave owners, who feared that burying and mourning the dead would be used as a pretext for conspiracy and revolt. From 1680, in British North America and the Caribbean laws were passed restricting the size and timing of funerals, with a small number of mourners and daytime funerals permitted by law.[18]

The transatlantic slave trade and, to a lesser extent, slavery itself came under attack in the eighteenth century. Britain abolished the slave trade in 1807, and the institution of slavery was legislated out of existence in 1834. The independence of Latin America augured the end of the slave trade everywhere except in Brazil, where it expanded on a massive scale, and in Cuba, which remained part of the Spanish Empire. The United States ended the Atlantic slave trade in the same year as Britain, but slavery itself (and an illegal Atlantic slave trade) continued until the eve of the American Civil War (1861–1865). The Dutch banned the slave trade in 1814, but not until 1863 was slavery itself abolished in Dutch colonies. Even then the recently emancipated were forced into labor contracts lasting another decade. France abolished the slave trade in 1818, but abolished slavery itself only thirty years later. Britain, Europe's chief maritime power, engaged in a prolonged campaign to compel Portugal, Spain (and Cuba), and Brazil to eradicate the trade. But the trade persisted, even flourished, during the nineteenth century. Finally, after two decades of stout resistance, Brazil bowed to British pressure in 1850, though slavery itself continued until 1888. Spain and Cuba held out for longer: the slave trade to Cuba was abolished only in 1867. Slavery itself survived there until 1886.[19]

These are the basic facts, but they offer little sense of why European empires turned, to a greater or lesser extent, away from slavery after having relied on it so heavily for centuries. There has been great debate over the causes of abolition in the British Empire. In the 1940s, the historian Eric Williams argued that while slavery had generated the capital that underwrote the Industrial Revolution in Britain, the onset of industrialization, combined with shifting ideas about wealth and the merits of free labor, decreased slavery's economic importance. Such a shift made abolition (and the moral and religious ideas underpinning it) a viable alternative, diminishing the political influence of the Caribbean slave owners who resisted it. Historian Seymour Drescher contested Williams's position and suggested, using trade statistics and price indices, that the abolition of slavery was a veritable "econocide" and must be explained by other factors. In recent years, the moral arguments against slavery, which Williams had considered of secondary importance, have been revived in sophisticated ways. As historian Christopher Brown has explained, "The origins of the [abolitionist] movement lay in the disastrous experience of the American [Revolution], which directed new attention to the character of overseas empire and fostered new efforts to bring colonial institutions in line with concepts of national virtue and English liberty."[20] In a recent intervention, incorporating the British case but with application to all of the seaborne empires, historian Robin Blackburn argued that "slavery was not overthrown for economic reasons but where it became politically untenable . . . in each case, slavery was politically vulnerable, not economically unprofitable."[21]

Moral ambivalence concerning slavery, which made it politically vulnerable, may be traced to various papal pronouncements from the fifteenth century. In 1462 Pius II encouraged owners to manumit their slaves, and in 1537 Paul III famously condemned (Amerindian) slavery as dissonant with Christianity's precepts. The Quakers voiced opposition to the slave trade in the seventeenth century. Slavery was increasingly condemned as an institution in the eighteenth century. Yet many European political writers and publicists were less assertive, sometimes pusillanimously so, when it came to the concrete matter of emancipating enslaved Africans and their descendants. Some leading *philosophes* skirted around the issue: Adam Smith condemned reliance on slave labor as uneconomical yet did not advocate abolition explicitly; Voltaire argued that Africans were inferior to Europeans; Montesquieu, while arguing that slavery debased master and slave alike, defended property rights, including the property rights of slaveholders, thereby defending an indefensible institution. Diderot's *Encyclopedia,* to its credit, condemned the slave trade in the strongest possible terms. Yet even its authors did not press for abolition. Condemning the hideousness of slavery did not foreshadow condoning the freedom of slaves or imagining a world without slavery.[22]

Nevertheless, the late eighteenth century witnessed certain challenges to and rejections of slavery. The aforementioned Somerset case established a free-soil tradition in Britain, thus ending slavery in metropolitan Britain itself. Portugal abolished slavery in the Iberian Peninsula even while encouraging its expansion in Brazil. In the Netherlands, where a weaker free-soil tradition existed, in 1776 the States-General declared that slaves retained their legal status for six months when brought to Netherlands by their owners, a policy that remained in place until a true free-soil principle was enshrined in law in the late 1830s. During the American Revolution, Vermont outlawed slavery in 1777, and the rest of the New England states and Pennsylvania had followed suit by 1784. Antislavery and anti–slave trade societies were founded in Britain and France in the 1780s on the eve of the French Revolution. In 1787, the London Abolition Society circulated a petition that garnered more than sixty thousand signatures. In 1791, five hundred separate petitions reached the House of Commons. And by 1791, anti–slave trade legislation was introduced in Parliament, though it was not passed at first. The massive outpouring of support for abolition was linked to shifting ideas about labor in Britain. As historian David Brion Davis noted, there was a "pressing need felt by both skilled workers and employers to dignify and even ennoble free labor." Even after Parliament abolished the British slave trade, public support for abolition of the slave trade by other states did not abate. Some 1,370 petitions, bearing more than 750,000 signatures, reached Parliament in 1814 in support of an international agreement to end the trade.[23] Having abolished the trade in its own empire, the British state coerced other empires, and the new Latin American as well as African states, to follow suit, often employing force to extract those commitments from reluctant polities.

The actual emancipation of slaves proved more elusive. Many of those who supported the abolition of the slave trade did not condone the abolition of slavery altogether. In fact, many proponents believed that the trade's demise would usher in a new era in slave management. Deprived of new imports, planters would now have to treat slaves more humanely, which in turn would boost plantation production. One response to the harsh brutality of slavery was escape. Very few slaves, however, managed to join the sort of fugitive communities described in Chapter 11. Large-scale slave rebellions, too, were rare, though they occurred with greater frequency in the Caribbean during the Age of Revolutions, including in the middle and latter phases of the Haitian Revolution. But everyday acts of resistance, including sabotage, work slowdowns, temporary absenteeism without permission—in short, a range of subtly subversive behaviors that are sometimes lumped together by historians as *petit marronnage*—were common. Their ubiquity is indicative of the complexity and durability of slavery in colonial societies during the early modern period.

The destruction of slavery was a major dimension of the Age of Revolutions. The cases of the North American and Spanish American Revolutions suggest how slavery could be weakened, if not demolished, in the course of a political revolution. Simón Bolívar, the most renowned Latin American independence leader, tied conscription to emancipation in northern South America, thus bringing his army the recruits he badly needed to wage war. This decree built on a promise he had made to Haiti's president Alexandre Pétion in 1816 while in exile there. Arms and supplies were exchanged for a pledge to eradicate slavery in the lands Bolívar's forces controlled. Yet the survival of slavery in some of the places where anticolonial revolutionary movements succeeded, whether the nascent United States or several Latin American states, suggests the social and economic limits of those revolutions. And the absence, or belated nature, of independence-seeking movements led by creoles in certain major slave societies, such as Cuba, the British Caribbean, and Brazil, suggests that many slaveholding elites believed that greater security existed within rather than outside the framework of empire.[24]

Slaves hastened their liberation through revolt well after the Age of Revolutions ostensibly ended. The massive Demerara slave uprising (and its brutal suppression) in the early 1820s mobilized antislavery forces in Britain. The 1831 Jamaican "Baptist War" involved sixty thousand slaves and was marked by extreme violence, the destruction of property, and the death of eighteen free whites and more than five hundred slaves. Although the 1833 Emancipation Act declared that the 750,000 slaves in the British Empire would be freed in 1834, they were to remain on plantations and in their owners' control until 1838. Twenty million pounds sterling was paid as compensation to slave owners in Britain. Determining the present-day value of this enormous sum is challenging, but consumer-price escalations place it at close to two billion pounds. If, however, the value is calculated relative to the size of the British economy at the time (c. 1834), the present value would swell to more than seventy-five billion pounds. As Drescher noted with regard to emancipation in the British Empire, "Civil liberty was to come at the expense of limited free labor for ex-slaves, increased prices for consumers, and higher taxes for metropolitans."[25]

All five of the seaborne empires were predicated on often intersecting forms of coerced labor. The enslavement of Africans and their descendants was the most prevalent form, but the extent of Amerindian slavery was notable and indispensable to European designs, especially in the early phases of colonization. A full audit of coercive practices would include indentured servitude and convict labor. Far from a pacific enterprise undertaken by plucky, intrepid colonists, wealth drawn from empire was inseparable from enslaved and otherwise coerced laborers. Though the Age of Revolutions was marked by the smashing of some slave regimes, many others would survive and shape the trajectories of the new postimperial states well into the nineteenth century.

10. Creole Societies, *Mestizaje*, and the Regulation of Hybridity

Whether through violence, accommodation, or uneasy coexistence, Europe's seaborne empires rapidly became mestizo societies. They gave rise to a variety of new cultural forms, often fusions of cultures that had never before come into contact with one another. Heterogeneity emerged from the mixing and melding pell-mell of diverse peoples of varied geographical and cultural provenance. From this chaotic milieu emerged new phenotypes and identities, which resembled and drew upon the original, precontact models while metamorphosing in unprecedented ways. The forging of colonial societies did not involve the mere replication and imposition of European models overseas. Hybridity went beyond exchanges of genetic material, diet, and customs, extending to the domain of religion, where syncretic practices often resulted from the collision of belief systems, chiefly through conversion efforts. Also contributing to the divergence of colonial societies from their original models, and from each other, were differences of terrain, climate, disease, and a host of other ecological and epidemiological factors, many of which were unknown in Europe and to which European colonists were compelled to adapt. In this chapter, social and cultural hybridity, and the regulation of these new forms forged in the crucible of empire, are examined and analyzed.

One of the most visible and enduring signs of hybridity is language. Empires summoned new languages into existence. Various African and European vocabularies and grammatical structures were merged, for example, in the creation of Papamiento, the language of the Dutch Caribbean colonies of

Curaçāo, Aruba, and Bonaire, and in the Kriolu of Cape Verde. There were at least twenty-five creole languages in the British Empire. In and around the Indian Ocean, one of the lingua francas employed Portuguese grammar with a lexicon that was a hybrid of Portuguese, Malay, Tamil, and Arabic. In the interior of Brazil, a *língua geral* evolved that combined elements of Tupí and Portuguese, which was for a time the most widely spoken language. Just as important, colonial societies were also polyglot societies, and this reality was reflected in the introduction into European languages of non-European loan words that have persisted long after the eclipse of formal empire. For instance, the word "shampoo," derived from a Hindi word for massage, entered the English language in the early nineteenth century. The plantation complex in the Americas proved conducive to linguistic borrowing. A range of African botanical and culinary words entered the English language in colonial Virginia, whether "banana" or "yam," derived from Mandinka and Wolof, or "goober," a term for peanut, taken from the Western Bantu language.[1] Not only were new languages created, new identities were conjured as well. Old World identities were not always retained and reproduced after crossing the Atlantic. The more than one hundred thousand German-speaking people from the Rhineland became "German," while the mixed, multilingual society of New Netherland became "Dutch."

Imperial authorities often sought to keep individuals of different geographical provenance, "race," or "ethnicity" separated from one another. This effort took several forms. The most sustained segregation initiative was that undertaken by the Spanish to divide their American subjects into two "republics": a Republic of Spaniards, which also included free and enslaved Africans and ethnically mixed *castas,* and a Republic of Indians. Initially, from the 1530s, Spanish colonizers sought to separate physically the two republics, often entailing the forced relocation of Amerindians into a *reducción* or *congregación.* The intention was to concentrate often-dispersed populations into clearly demarcated (and highly regulated) settlements. In all cases, these communities were situated a fair distance from the towns inhabited by Spaniards. They later became the pool of labor deployed for the extraction of commodities, chiefly silver. Eventually, the notion of the "two republics" was embraced by those who sought to protect Amerindians from the depredations of the conquistadors, and their descendants, and to hasten conversion to Christianity through the elimination of purportedly corrupting outside influences. A 1573 royal order, for example, declared that no Indian should enter a

Spanish city until it was completely built, "so that when the Indians do see it they are amazed . . . and they will fear [the Spanish] and will not dare offend them, and they will respect them and wish to have their friendship."[2]

Such prohibitions extended to other areas of society. In the Iberian empires, the secular clergy was open to non-Europeans, but entry into the more prestigious (and powerful) regular clergy was off-limits. It appears that indigenous nuns served in the convents of the Andes in the sixteenth century, but their presence was gradually eliminated. Efforts to establish a native regular clergy were abandoned in Portuguese Asia by 1580, whereas in Spanish Mexico and Peru mestizos could be ordained provided that they were "well-educated, properly qualified, and born legitimately in wedlock." The Jesuit Order, which did not admit people of color to its own ranks, did train them at its numerous colleges for entry into the secular priesthood.[3]

Yet efforts to cordon off Europeans from non-Europeans permanently, whether fueled by exploitative or paternalist ambition, were doomed to failure, even if they succeeded in specific instances. Spanish America offers a clear example of this failure. There the notion of the two republics bore scant resemblance to practice. Reliance on Amerindian artisans, construction workers, domestic servants, and vendors of staple goods necessitated frequent contact, and some quarters of certain cities, such as Lima, quickly became multiethnic. Laws separating the two republics were honored in the breach, particularly in the seventeenth century. In New Spain, where schools were established by Crown decree for the education of Indian youth, the curriculum specified instruction in reading and writing in Spanish, thus recognizing de jure the mixing that existed de facto. The situation in Spanish America was hardly unique. Efforts at segregation and sequester were omnipresent. In the Far East, the Dutch sought to isolate the Chinese community from the Javanese, while in the Philippines the Spanish sought to keep Chinese apart from both indigenous Filipinos and the growing mestizo population. In South Asia, the British laid out garden suburbs, to minimize the interactions between Britons and Indians.

Notwithstanding the strenuous efforts of colonial authorities, romantic and sexual relations, many of the latter involving various elements of coercion, frequently occurred across "ethnic" or "racial" lines (both remarkably slippery, unstable and perpetually shifting concepts and descriptions in the period covered in this book). Spanish America offers a clear illustration of these tendencies. Initially, it appears, exogamy was as much official policy as it was de facto practice, at least in part due to the preponderance of vagabond European men and the scarcity of European women. To justify and legitimate this practice, the Spanish Crown formally sanctioned interethnic marriage in the Caribbean in 1514. In some cases, marriage to women who were members of the indigenous nobility brought significant advantages, including authority over land and tribute. Conversely, mestizos who could trace their lineage to a conquistador were considered white and gained all the advantages associated with this association, regardless of phenotype. Elsewhere, such as in South Africa, the scarcity of European women encouraged Dutch authorities to remain silent on the marriages and extramarital conjugal relations between European men and free black women. The situation in Dutch Batavia was perhaps more pronounced, with a large population of Eurasian families due to intermarriage with the Javanese.

Similar patterns can be found across the fringes of the Portuguese Empire, including in São Tomé, where Portuguese traders and soldiers married African women. The Luso-African progeny described themselves as "children of the land" (*filhos da terra*). In Canada (New France), many French *coureurs de bois* (fur traders and trappers) married indigenous women, especially those who had converted to Catholicism. They became integrated into Amerindian kinship networks, and their *métis* children acted as cultural go-betweens. In both New France and Louisiana, such intermarriage received formal state approval. In the early British Chesapeake, marriage between blacks and whites was not uncommon. In New England, legal interracial marriage was possible everywhere except in Massachusetts, which banned it in 1705. In South Asia, a third of all wills filed in the British capital of Calcutta in the first half of the 1780s made reference to a native companion or concubine.[4] In short, across the seaborne empires, especially in the early stages and on the geographical periphery, interracial and interethnic unions were the norm and often met with acquiescence, if not grudging approval, from authorities.

In most places, however, the early policies of permissiveness that favored the emergence of a mestizo society gave way to proscriptive measures to achieve separation and exclusion. This shift often entailed attempts to curtail interethnic and interracial marital and sexual unions. Authorities increasingly sought to ban and punish such relations, often with great ferocity. In the French Caribbean, marriage between whites and blacks was forbidden by the 1730s, building on earlier legislation that penalized European men for fathering mulatto children. The previously lenient Dutch VOC periodically banned free burghers married to Asian women from traveling to Europe. In British America, "miscegenation" statutes were enacted by colonial assemblies. The 1662 Virginia act that defined children born of slaves as themselves slaves indirectly served as a deterrent to interracial marriage, setting a precedent that would be followed throughout British America. In 1691, the Virginia Assembly went further still: it threatened banishment of any free white person who married a black person. In South Asia, marriage to (or even cohabitating with) a native woman was considered transgressive by British authorities. Various regulations were enacted to curtail the practice. Many of these relationships—usually in the form of concubinage or informal marriage—only came to light after death, in the wills of European men who wished to bequeath property to a South Asian woman and thus recognize publicly a hitherto private relation. In Ibero-America, the absence of such prohibitory statutes, and the fact that civil status was matrilineal, encouraged exogamy. Enslaved men, for example, who married Amerindian or mestiza women, knew that their children would not grow up as slaves. This is not to say that authorities viewed this state of affairs favorably. Though never introducing a formal ban, Portugal's King Dom João V complained that Brazil's European inhabitants "are not in the habit of marrying . . . it is not easy to force them to renounce their black and mulatto concubines and for this reason every family is becoming tainted by the mixture of bloods."[5]

Soon ancestry became one of the major cleavages in colonial society. Intermediate legal categories were created to classify children born from interethnic and interracial unions. For example, in the Spanish colonial world the child of a Spaniard and an Amerindian was defined as a mestizo; a child whose parents were creole and black was a "mulatto"; the child of a union between someone of African ancestry and an Amerindian was a *zambo*. The permutations multiplied, but they were lumped together under the collective noun *casta*. This term referred to those of mixed parentage, but its connotation smacked of illegitimacy, or suspicion of it, due to African ancestry. The overall framework is known to historians as the *sistema de castas*. The first complete series of paintings depicting the children of interethnic unions, the castas, dates from 1715. The denigrating nature of this system of classification is suggested by the clear allusion to animals. The term "mulatto," for example, is derived from the word for mule, the offspring of a donkey and a horse; the term "cayote," the child of an Indian and a mestizo, is the Nahuatl word for prairie wolf. Derogatory terms had social repercussions. As art historian Ilona Katzew has argued, "The ranking of people according to their purported percentage of white, Indian or black blood [was] a form of resistance of the nobility against encroachment on its privileges and source of wealth."[6]

Similar racialized taxonomy existed in the Portuguese colonial world, where children of interracial unions were commonly marginalized socially and occupationally. There were more than 150 racial categories in early nineteenth-century Brazil. Official efforts at categorization of this sort were fraught with ambiguity: did the designation "mestiço" or "mulato" refer exclusively to perceived physical characteristics and features? Or did it encompass additional behavioral factors, such as judgments concerning the depth of commitment to Christian spirituality and piety? Prejudice related to behavior could be transferred from one group to another, adding a further layer of complexity. A clear example is the description of Brazilian Amerindians as *negros da terra* ("blacks of the land"), an allusion to the purported unflattering characteristics they shared with Africans.[7] Nevertheless, classification was increasingly based on phenotype, color specifically, and also ancestry, where relative "whiteness" defined one's place in the social hierarchy, determining access to education, occupation, and civic participation.

In the end of the eighteenth century, generations of intermarriage ensured that a large proportion of the inhabitants of colonies had at least some African or Amerindian ancestry. The supposed taint of lineage ("blood purity") or color foreclosed social advancement. Iberian purity of blood (*limpieza de sangre*) statutes originally used to discriminate against descendants of Jews and Muslims were expanded to encompass those with some degree of African descent. Increasingly, legal mechanisms were created to remove this taint. In the Spanish Empire, the Crown could extirpate (for a fee) the civil disabilities associated with nonwhite ancestry, paving the way for university attendance, to say nothing of ecclesiastical, military, or government careers previously beyond reach. This policy, known as a *cédula de gracias al sacar* in Spanish, had an analogue in British Jamaica. There so-called special bills were given to free people of color, mostly children of planters, that permitted them to serve in white militia units, vote in local elections, and hold public office.[8]

The concept of creole emerged early in the colonial period, creole identity somewhat later. Originally, it was derived from the Portuguese word "crioulo" (in turn derived from the verb "criar," to grow), which referred to descendants of Africans born in the Americas, distinguishing them from *boçales*, African-born slaves. From Portuguese, it was adopted in Spanish as *criollo*, where its meaning mutated. The first appearance in print of "creole" in a form resembling its core common modern usage was in Spanish royal chronicler Juan López de Velasco's *Geografía y descripción universal de las Indias* (1570), where the author claimed that Spaniards born in the Americas "who are called creoles [*criollos*] turn out like the natives even though they are not mixed with them [by] declining to the disposition of the land." Creole, though referring initially to children of Spaniards (and their progeny) born in America, thus carried unmistakably pejorative connotations. At first, however, in Spanish usage, it was less of a racial epithet than a geographical or cultural designation that referred to place of birth or habitation. Increasingly, however, as interracial unions produced children with darker phenotypes, creole came to connote someone of mixed racial ancestry as much as a Spaniard born in America, thus barring many creoles from bureaucratic and ecclesiastical posts. Nominally white North American colonists were quite sensitive to these tropes of degeneration and decay and contested them. In Virginia, future U.S. president Thomas Jefferson rejected ubiquitous claims of the innate inferiority of Amerindians (and by extension creoles). He asserted that "America, though a child of yesterday, has already given hopeful proofs of genius." He turned the critique around and contended it was the imperial wars Britain had waged that had triggered its decline. Its conduct did not "seem the legitimate offspring either of science or civilization," and "the sun of her glory is fast descending to the horizon. Her philosophy has crossed the channel, her freedom the Atlantic."[9]

Divergence between creole and European societies was hastened by metropolitan efforts to monitor and modify habits of consumption. Toward the middle of the eighteenth century, as metropolitan-periphery tensions escalated across the New World, there were attempts by authorities to regulate the consumption practices of colonists, including restrictions placed on luxuries, which had no counterpart in the Old World. In Brazil, for example, sumptuary laws were enacted prohibiting colonists from using velvet, gold, silk, or silver in their dress. In British North America, including the Caribbean, colonists emulated everything from metropolitan sartorial style to interior design fashion to alcohol preferences, perhaps in an effort to "anglicize" their societies. Toward the end of the colonial period, in the 1770s, this tendency gave way to a "creole" sensibility. Colonists displayed displeasure with the Navigation Acts and other restrictive mercantilist trade measures by rejecting imported tastes and striving to nurture a self-consciously distinct "American" style.

Throughout Ibero-America, sumptuary regulations fell more heavily on free people of African descent and slaves. In Brazil, not only were free blacks prohibited from carrying arms, those caught wearing silk, fine wool, or jewelry risked having those articles confiscated, were subject to a fine up to the full value of the confiscated items, and could be exiled to São Tomé, just off the coast of Africa. It appears that sartorial restrictions were not as extreme in the British and French Caribbean, where according to historian Robert DuPlessis "clothing enabled free people of color to visibly declare their membership in the social class commensurate with their economic position."[10] Nevertheless, restrictions to accentuate difference and status were widespread. In Barbados, slaves were forbidden to use stone in the construction of their huts and were subject to penalties for violating this prohibition.

Creolization also was engendered by topography and environmental conditions. Whether situated in cities, hinterlands, or distant peripheries, all colonial societies confronted comparable challenges. Faced with enormous differences in climate, flora, and fauna, most early colonists sought to reproduce closely European habits in the New World. Dietary and consumption preferences illustrate this tendency clearly. Spanish settlers, for example, sought to import or grow Old World foods in the Americas, particularly olive oil, wine, and wheat. Together with breeding European livestock to which they were accustomed (above all, pork and lamb), Spaniards believed that the consumption of such familiar foods would protect them against the hostile climate to which they were not yet inured. Spanish colonists also imported vast quantities of wine across the Atlantic before vineyards were established in Chile, Peru, and Argentina. During the sixteenth century, all ships leaving Spain for the Americas were mandated to carry animals, plant cuttings, and seeds in an effort to re-create Old World agriculture. Not all efforts of this type yielded results (camels, for example, failed to adapt), but most livestock (pigs and cattle, in particular) flourished in this new environment without natural predators, thus permitting colonists to purchase meat at lower prices in Mexico City than Spaniards could in Madrid. By the end of the sixteenth century, then, colonists could supply themselves with the staples previously acquired from Spain. They even engaged in import substitution *avant la lettre* by replacing olive oil with lard for cooking. A similar story, if on a smaller scale, could be told of the early activities of the English EIC, where a notable reluctance to embrace locally available cuisine was displayed. The Company imported hams, tongue, cheese, and butter from England, to say nothing of English clothes and European wines.[11]

As has been discussed, the creation of new societies in the seaborne empires brought into existence new social groups defined by the state—mestizos, creoles, *caboclos,* and other castas—without European counterparts or antecedents. One such group was free people of African descent in the Americas. Descendants of Africans who were forced to cross the Middle Passage to endure chattel slavery and who eventually gained release from enslavement, free blacks were identified chiefly by phenotype (though sometimes by lineage). Free blacks, who were often interracial persons, formed a sizable segment of the population in many colonial societies. For example, such *gente libre* composed approximately half the population of New Granada in the late 1770s. The population of free blacks expanded through both manumission and natural increase. In Dutch Surinam, free nonwhites outnumbered whites by a ratio of at least three to two.[12] In British America, where manumission was largely confined to urban areas, free blacks clustered in towns. In some places, such as Jamaica and South Carolina, up to two-thirds of free blacks resided in the port cities of Kingston and Charleston, respectively. A quarter of Peru's free population of color resided in Lima, and the majority of this population as a whole was based in urban areas. In some colonies, free people of color became significant owners of property. In Le Cap Français, French Saint-Domingue's principal city, free people of color owned a fifth of the houses in the 1780s. In 1832, free people of color in Jamaica owned about a fifth of all the island's slaves.

Even for nominally free blacks, including property holders, however, social and economic options remained severely limited. In the northern colonies of British America, a plethora of proscriptive statutes impinged on the liberties of free blacks, barring them from voting, militia membership, and jury service. There were even laws that threatened reenslavement of free blacks who lacked regular employment and were accused of loitering. In French colonies, interracial people were classified as black from the early eighteenth century, thus barred from service in tribunals or from practicing medicine. From the 1770s, in Saint-Domingue those with "white" family names were required to adopt a new surname designating "African" origin. Segregation became policy. Blacks and those of mixed racial ancestry were assigned separate seating in theaters, and all free people of color were required to carry papers verifying that they were legally free.[13]

The restrictions on free people of color in the Iberian empires resembled those of the French and British Caribbean. In Spanish Florida, free blacks had an earlier curfew than whites. They also were expected to undertake (paid) work on public works projects, something whites were spared. In Brazil, where the legally sanctioned possibility of self-purchase (*carta de alforria*) made it possible for a considerable number of slaves to gain their freedom, freedmen found to their chagrin that Crown decrees, gubernatorial acts, and local legislation undermined and diluted the freedom just acquired, treating all persons of African descent alike, whether enslaved or free. As a result, as historian John Russell-Wood observed, "the position of the freedman of color was ill-defined, ambiguous and insecure."[14] The mechanical trades were dominated by whites, and licenses were exceedingly difficult for free blacks to obtain. Iberian "purity of blood" statutes, initially aimed at Jews and Muslims in Europe, were applied to those of African descent in the New World, reducing blacks, both free and enslaved, to menial and low-prestige livelihoods, including that of "barber" (*barbeiro*), sanctioned to bleed, scarify, and apply leaches, presumably with the intention to heal. A barber could also obtain a further license as a tooth puller (*tiradentes*).

Though impediments were ubiquitous, military service offered free blacks the possibility for limited social mobility. In Spanish America, earlier restrictions, such as a 1551 law forbidding blacks to bear arms, were lifted in the face of the urgent need to defend coastal cities. In some regions particularly vulnerable to attack by either corsairs or foreign navies, there existed entire militia companies composed of free blacks, including at the officer level. Free, interracial soldiers made up 30 percent of the militia in late eighteenth-century Portuguese Angola. In Saint-Domingue, there were separate militia companies for whites, blacks, and interracial men. Militia service for free blacks was a possibility in the British Caribbean, too, but it offered none of the social privileges of Spanish militia service. Wartime exigencies pushed free black men into more important roles. The 1778 British occupation of St. Lucia, for example, was largely the work of a free black army regiment. As this discussion of military service implies, racial discrimination did not preclude free people of African descent from participation in the rich associational life present in many of the seaborne empires. The prevalence and key role of religious brotherhoods, or confraternities, in the Iberian empires has already been discussed, but the secular counterparts to such brotherhoods were ubiquitous, too. In Spanish America, these were called *cabildos de nación*, blending African and European cultural elements. This institution was widespread: there were at least twenty such confraternities in Havana alone in the middle of the eighteenth century. They organized processions, celebrations, and other public events.[15]

The place of religion in these mestizo and creole societies was front and center. Two aspects merit special consideration: first, the position of religion; and, second, the emergence of religious syncretism. To some degree, overseas empire was a place of refuge for religious minorities. In the Dutch colonies until the latter decades of the seventeenth century, the freedom to exercise one's religion did not exist, but freedom of conscience was protected. In Asia, the VOC expelled Catholic priests from Malacca and the Dutch-controlled zone of Ceylon, but lay Catholics were not persecuted. In New Netherland and the Cape, no other church was permitted to operate besides the Dutch Reformed Church. Only in 1659 was liberty of worship permitted in Curaçao.[16]

Nevertheless, the absence of an Inquisition in the Dutch and English seaborne empire was significant. Among the beneficiaries of the absence of persecution were Jews. Following their expulsion from Brazil, there were significant Sephardic Jewish communities in the Dutch Caribbean, with particularly robust congregations in Curaçao, St. Eustatius, and New Amsterdam. The Dutch congregations, as well as British islands, received an influx of Jews from the French Caribbean following their expulsion in 1685. Most Jewish congregations remained small, but that of Surinam was large enough in the final decades of the seventeenth century to warrant the construction of the large synagogue of Bracha Veshalom. In the late eighteenth century, there were more than one thousand Jews in British Jamaica, where they enjoyed freedom of worship, though religious tests ensured that they were forbidden to vote or to sit in the colonial assembly. Migrants to British North America were largely non-Anglican Protestants. There was no majority religion, and only two of the thirteen colonies—Connecticut and Massachusetts—had state churches. Maryland, Rhode Island, and Pennsylvania permitted liberty of conscience from their inception. Pennsylvania, which was governed according to Quaker principles, forbade coercion of conscience altogether.[17]

Though some religious groups, majority and minority, preserved precontact practices, the seaborne empires were also a theater of religious syncretism. Here elements of several religions were intermingled, often eclectically and haphazardly but occasionally more systematically, to produce novel forms. This is not to suggest that all of the aspects of precontact religious systems were preserved. Conversion to Christianity, even where non-Christian forms were retained (frequently furtively), often had gendered implications, diminishing the role of women in religious life. Where there had been female priests, shamans, and oracles in many precolonial religions, there were no female priests in Christian practice. Syncretism often emerged from evangelization, and the Iberian seaborne empires furnish some of the most paradigmatic examples. The awesome sway of the Catholic Church did not mean that pre-Columbian religious practices were eliminated. In spite of efforts to impose the sacrament of marriage, the effort to suppress the practice of trial marriage proved futile. Furthermore, Amerindians selected, in piecemeal fashion, those aspects of Christianity that were most congenial to them. In Mexico, Nahuas included Catholic saints on their household altars. They incorporated Catholic rituals into their own celebrations of kin on All Souls' Day, or the Day of the Dead. In the Andes, the Catholic St. James was linked to the mountain god (*huaca*) Illapa. The church campaigned to eradicate the pre-Columbian huacas, but its anti-idolatry efforts produced few results. Syncretism, or at least slippages between belief systems, was encouraged almost by the very nature of the evangelical enterprise. Clergy composed and published sermons, catechisms, and spiritual manuals in Nahuatl and Quechua, instead of forcing Amerindians to learn Spanish (or Latin). Enthusiasm for translating the message into indigenous languages subsequently waned, perhaps because of its tendency to promote the syncretic practices just mentioned. By the end of the seventeenth century, the Spanish Crown introduced legislation to ban the use of Amerindian languages in conversion.[18]

Syncretism may be observed in the slave societies of the Americas. This subject has long been debated. Did African culture, including religious belief systems, survive the Middle Passage? Or was the culture of African-born slaves and their descendants a "creolized" one, a new form that emerged in the New World and bore few traces to practices in Africa? These questions have given rise to competing answers. Recent research has suggested that in Brazil, at least before 1700, African kinship structures, religious rituals, dietary practices, and perhaps military techniques survived early phases of enslavement and were replicated in a reasonably intact form by future generations. Just as often, however, hybrid forms emerged, combining multiple African cultural and religious practices with indigenous Brazilian and European practices.[19] An uneasy coexistence of African religions and Christianity was prevalent. Slaves added and integrated Christian saints to African pantheons, rechristening them with new names and attributes. Sometimes, as in Brazil, it was Christians of European birth or descent who displayed interest in, and adopted, African and Amerindian religious forms, often to the dismay of religious authorities and, at certain times, the Inquisition. Here the ubiquity of the *mandinga* pouch, believed to ward off evil spirits, demonstrated the fusion of three religious cultures in the colonial context.[20] A similar eclecticism and refashioning may be observed in parts of Africa exposed to Portuguese influence, though here the power gradient in favor of Africans produced forms of syncretism distinct from those encountered in the Americas. In the kingdom of Kongo, where the capital, São Salvador, was recognized as an episcopal see toward the end of the sixteenth century, Christian doctrines of heaven and hell were rejected, but Jesus was worshiped as a powerful chief (*mfumu*), associated with a cult of the graves of chiefly ancestors. The tenet of faith concerning the Immaculate Conception was ignored, and the concept of salvation was transmuted into earthly protection. The Christian cross was ubiquitous and understood to ward off the effects of witchcraft. In Portuguese Angola, African Christians gravitated toward black-skinned saints like St. Benedict of Palermo. In the late seventeenth century, his saint's day was celebrated by twenty thousand Mbundu Christians in Luanda, and it was widely believed in Angola that his mother had been born in Africa.[21]

Empire involved unilateral, often violent impositions of authority, but the result hardly resembled the forms that agents of empire sought to impose. Evangelization was marked by compromise from the outset, resulting in syncretic religious practices and beliefs. Cultural forms were likewise hybrid, which generated acute anxiety for the architects of the seaborne empires, but were accepted almost as a commonplace by those resident in them. Similar statements could be made about legal, political, and economic institutions, for most exhibited mestizo traits. Historian Serge Gruzinski has observed that "since the indigenous version of reproduction was always accompanied by interpretation, it triggered a cascade of combinations, juxtapositions, amalgamations and superimpositions caught in the crossfire of mimicry and mestizo mechanisms." This unanticipated multiplicity meant that overseas societies diverged from those of the metropole from the outset. Heterogeneity and difference, far from being an obstacle to the designs of European imperial states, may have proved indispensable to their longevity, permitting alliances and collaborations that a less tolerant policy bent on uniformity would have precluded.[22]

11. Collaboration, Resistance, and the Fortunes of Empire

The history of the seaborne empires should not be framed solely as the unilateral imposition of European human, intellectual, economic, and political might on passive non-European subject populations. Empires could be neither established nor sustained without significant levels of collaboration. Though often in asymmetrical ways, Europeans entered into relations of exchange, partnership, and sometimes dependence to secure the resources they coveted. As Chapters 1 and 2 showed, the reach and authority of European agents seldom extended as far as their assertion of its extent. Even in the territories they claimed, Europeans often were confined to the margins, subservient to (and often at the mercy of) indigenous polities, or resorted to forms of indirect rule. They were limited and thwarted by the actions, strategies, and capacities of non-Europeans. If always tenuous and provisional, collaboration was necessarily the bedrock upon which European rule was erected. Its absence could be fatal.

By the same token, empires were undermined, and sometimes subverted, by the resistance of subaltern groups. Far from being placid and pacific, empires were marked by violence. The specter of violence stalked legal codes and informed urban planning. It was embedded in myriad ways to induce subservience and conformity. When that proved inadequate, physical force was employed. Even where such strategies appeared to succeed, where open resistance or defiance was absent, subject peoples found ways to avoid compliance. As historian William Taylor has shown for Mexico, they would use "the colonizer's laws and truth claims instrumentally, resist them non-violently or succeed in bypassing them rather than making a frontal assault." In fact, powerless populations studiously avoided "direct, symbolic confrontation," in political anthropologist James C. Scott's phrase. Instead of risking retaliation for ostentatious acts of subversion, they resorted to more prosaic weapons. These included "foot-dragging, dissimulation, desertion, false compliance, pilfering, feigned ignorance, slander, arson, [and] sabotage."[1] This chapter, then, surveys and analyzes different forms that collaboration and resistance took in the seaborne empires. The trajectory of empire often hinged on the success or failure of collaboration.

Collaboration with indigenous populations was the foundation of empire, as the Spanish sixteenth-century experience demonstrated. But such relations continued into the later period. The Dutch WIC, for example, employed Tupi auxiliaries, crucial in the conquest of Maranhão, in northern Brazil, in 1641. The Dutch even raised a Tupi regiment that crossed the Atlantic and participated in the capture of Portuguese Luanda in Angola and the island colony of São Tomé. The Tupi entered into alliance not only in exchange for payment in Dutch guilders but, what is more important, after having secured guarantees to respect their political autonomy. The Dutch allied with Pedro II of Kongo to expel the Portuguese from Angola, though this collaboration did not attain its objective. The Portuguese routinely used Amerindian troops as soldiers, guides, and auxiliaries in campaigns to disperse fugitive slave communities (*mocambos* and *quilombos,* discussed later in this chapter) and to reenslave their members. In South America, the Jesuits turned the Guaraní in their mission villages into a fighting force, but whether it was to protect the Guaraní against predatory colonists or to safeguard the Jesuits' property is hard to ascertain.[2]

On a significantly grander scale, across the globe, the English EIC's operations were handled by South Asians, not Europeans. In the 1740s, half of the ships servicing the EIC's foothold in Madras were Indian-owned. Suppliers, clerks, and administrators of all types were South Asian, not European. The Company's military capacity, too, relied heavily on indigenous soldiers. In 1777, Indian troops (known as sepoys) outnumbered European troops by a ratio of seven to one. These soldiers were deployed not only in India but increasingly as part of far-flung military operations, from South Africa to Egypt to Java. During the era of the French Revolution, the EIC boasted an army of twenty-four thousand Europeans and 130 thousand

Indians. Sepoys entered into EIC service as a result of an additional type of collaboration. Local rulers and landowners in India raised the men, incorporated them into regiments, and furnished the tax revenue required to support them. In exchange, the social and economic positions of these collaborators were confirmed, solidified, and reinforced under the regime. Control was also maintained through informants and the manipulation of the military intelligence they provided to thwart even glimmerings of resistance. As historian Christopher Bayly explained, the British "took over and manipulated the internal system of espionage and political reporting which had been employed by the kingdoms of the Indian subcontinent."[3]

Coercive labor systems, institutions, and social order were dependent on collaboration. In Spanish America, labor regimes were based on agreements struck with indigenous rulers. One of the clearest examples is the encomienda system in Mexico. It was premised on indigenous systems of authority, specifically the figure of the *cacique* (native leader). The Spanish encomendero would inform the local cacique of his labor requirements, and the cacique would activate pre-"conquest" labor and tribute mechanisms to meet the request. As historian Kevin Terraciano has argued, "The functioning of the *encomienda* depended on the indigenous community's maintenance of its internal government, land resources and tax-paying mechanisms." Collaboration played a key function in preservation of order in Andean Spanish America, too. The eighteenth-century Túpac Amaru rebellion never could have been suppressed without the native nobility's firm rejection of the demands of the rebel leadership. This nobility enjoyed special privileges and high status under Spanish law, both of which were unavailable to nonelite Amerindians. Some of these privileges or exemptions—such as a license to ride a horse or carry a sword or dagger—might appear trivial to contemporary eyes, but they were an integral part of situating oneself visibly in the legal and social order. Particularly in urbanized, more prosperous places, the notion of rebellion was anathema, since authority and status were inseparable from Spanish institutions and law. Whether in the Andes or in Mexico, elite and nonelite Amerindians were among the most ardent supporters of what some creoles pilloried as creeping royal absolutism. The Amerindians perceived a threat from unchecked local authorities and therefore regarded monarchical justice as the best safeguard of their rights, property, and lives.[4]

Material advantages accrued to Amerindians from commercial transactions. Trade between indigenous peoples and Europeans often brought mutual benefits even if there are ample cases in which it locked the indigenous into pernicious cycles of dependence. In British North America, Indians depended on whites for half of the tools they used in the seventeenth century. Such transactions could assist them in wars with rival indigenous groups. The Hudson Bay Company sold more than ten thousand flintlock muskets to the Cree Indians from 1670 to 1690. Tools, guns, and trinkets, however useful they might be, were not the only advantages of comity. The Algonquians who encountered French fur traders in the Great Lakes region in the 1650s perceived them as *Manidowek*, or *Manitous*, other-than-human persons. The Algonquians anticipated benefits from them that transcended trade, whether physical healing, martial prowess, or good fortune in the hunt. Even if these flattering sentiments went unreciprocated, European fur traders accepted and became habituated to the rules of the game made by Amerindians. They often had to abide by indigenous trade protocols, monitor and regulate prices to appease their trade partners, and cultivate alliances in order for trade to exist at all. The authorities in New France seemed to understand this frontier reality. By contrast, Spanish American authorities did not. The absence of intermarriage between Spaniards and Amerindians in the Texas borderlands, for example, in stark contrast to practice elsewhere, precipitated the exclusion of Europeans from certain types of trade, further marginalizing their position.[5]

Older imperial histories treated conquest as a discrete event, occurring once and thereafter irreversible. Subjugation had a clear beginning and end in this older depiction. Such a view is inaccurate. Capitulation, when it occurred, was never absolute, due to the feebleness of European authorities as well as the fighting capabilities of either resurgent or unvanquished indigenes. Conquest thus was a protracted, often incomplete process. In some cases, it was a reversible one. In Mexico, the 1680 revolt of the Pueblo Indians, for example, brought together more than seventeen thousand Pueblos and resulted in the death of four hundred Spaniards. Well north of the Rio Grande, King Philip's (or Metacom's) War in the 1670s was a key moment in English Puritan–Native American conflict. Perhaps 10 percent of colonists were killed, more than twelve thousand buildings were destroyed, and eight thousand cattle were slaughtered in southern New England.[6] Resistance on this scale disrupted European encroachment. It triggered a stream of refugees retreating to coastal towns. It demonstrated Amerindian mastery of European-style arms and the parity that could result from technological transfer. Nor was resistance a characteristic of the early colonial period alone. Pontiac's Rebellion (1763) served as a reminder of Amerindian military might. With the exception of Niagara, Detroit, and Duquesne (Pittsburgh), an alliance of several Amerindian nations attacked and occupied British forts in the Great Lakes region. Similar dynamics may be found in the Caribbean, where the English occupation of Antigua, Montserrat, and Nevis, for example, was contested by Carib Indians.

The Iberian monarchs made themselves lords of the Americas, but their mastery was never complete. Many Amerindians, however devastated by microbes and violence, remained beyond the grasp of the Spanish state altogether. They formed a society apart, never to be absorbed. On a turbulent and contested frontier, Amerindians remained autonomous. Even three centuries after the purported conquest, Spanish authority remained nonexistent in many territories. Independent Indians controlled more than half of the landmass of modern Latin America, from Tierra del Fuego to northern Mexico. It has been estimated that 2.7 million autonomous Amerindians lived within the boundaries of the territory over which Spain claimed legal dominion. As late as 1780, two-thirds of Chile's Araucanians did not recognize Spanish sovereignty. In Comanchería, in what is now the southwestern quadrant of the United States, also claimed by Spain, the Comanches carved out an empire the size of which exceeded the amount of European-controlled territory north of the Rio Grande. When Spaniards and Spanish Americans came into contact with them, they rarely dictated the terms of the interaction and often were treated as subjects, or potential subjects.[7]

Throughout Spanish America, Amerindian languages—Quechua, Aymara, Náhuatl, and others—were more widely spoken than Spanish. Far from seeking to suppress native languages, Spaniards' religious conversion efforts were premised on their preservation and ubiquity. These languages, Nahuatl in particular, remained the main conduit between Spanish settler and indigenous communities. In many parts of Brazil, the língua geral, a mixture of Portuguese and Tupi Guaraní, was more commonly spoken than European Portuguese.[8] The shortage of soldiers and funds, combined with the geographical enormity of the territories involved, routinely compelled European states to forgo schemes for aggrandizement and instead adopt policies of containment and accommodation.

In British and French North America, too, Amerindians remained beyond the boundaries of European control. The Iroquois retained both autonomy and sovereignty by maintaining a balance of power between the French and the British. Such a result could be achieved through neutrality, but often it necessitated an alliance with one of the two powers, to serve as a counterweight to the rising influence of the other. With few (if any) European regular troops in many places, Amerindians were indispensable cobelligerents. As a New England colonist recorded with dismay, Iroquois delegations were "courted and caressed like the potentates of the earth." This situation prevailed until the eclipse of New France, and of French power in North America, in 1763 following the Seven Years' War.[9]

Even after this turning point, however, the capacity of Amerindians to wage war and threaten European settlement did not escape the cognizance of the British government. In an effort to preserve a rapprochement in North America, and to deter Amerindian alliances with Spain, the British government established the Proclamation Line (1763), which forbade settlement west of the Appalachians. Licenses for land sales west of the mountain range were suspended. This policy was a conciliatory gesture. The proclamation read: "Great Frauds have been committed in the purchasing of lands of Indians to the great prejudice of our interests and to the great dissatisfaction of the Indians."[10] Yet such accommodation provoked the ire both of squatters of European descent on the contested lands and of wealthier land speculators, a further wedge driving apart the interests of the colonists and the metropolitan government.

The Iroquois, in particular, would suffer dearly for their alliance with the British during the American Revolution. Not only did their population plummet by a third, but the newly established United States in 1784 forced them to concede their status as a defeated belligerent now subject to U.S. authority. Largely left to their own devices in negotiating with the victorious rebels, the refugee Iroquois received from the British, their erstwhile allies, a substantial tract of land in present-day Ontario. Half of the Iroquois accepted this offer and migrated to Canada. The Iroquois were not the only indigenes to gamble on the outcome of the American Revolution and lose. Spain's ambitions were deemed compatible with those of the Chickasaws, Creeks, and Choctaws, who anticipated that Spanish resurgence in the Gulf Coast and Florida would check encroachment by English-speaking colonists in case of a rebel victory.[11] In the short term, this gamble paid off, but within a few decades the encroachment of settlers, now backed by the military might of the United States, precipitated the mass displacement of Amerindians in the southeast.

The foregoing account should not be pushed too far. Amerindian autonomy did not mean that indigenous communities were unaffected by European incursions. Beyond the omnipresent threat of violent dispossession (often accompanied by the imposition of coercive labor practices) and microbial menace, forces unleashed by European agents wrought more subtle transformations within Amerindian societies. It is true that some societies withstood these forces better than others. In the Yucatan, for example, the Maya preserved intact their basic cultural framework, adapting in response to Spanish coercion but preserving its overall design and principal features. But much more common was what transpired in Peru. There the monetization of the economy and privatization of property (marketization) provoked seismic shifts, most notably by triggering large-scale Amerindian migration to cities, where wage work could be found and onerous tribute avoided. In French and British North America, to offer a further example, the rise of the fur trade ultimately produced a deleterious effect on the Iroquois. The lure of the fur hunt disrupted well-entrenched patterns of shifting seasonal activities, particularly agricultural ones, and the division of labor within Iroquois society.[12]

European efforts to exert greater control over areas that had been "pacified" and were administered directly often sparked great resistance. Spanish America offers a clear example of how such a policy could backfire. The very entrenchment of Spanish rule often generated discontent. In the seventeenth century, efforts by local authorities to monopolize trade in regional products could spark a rebellion, as happened in Oaxaca in the 1660s. The late eighteenth century was a veritable "age of insurrection" in the Amerindian communities of the Andes. At least eighty-two local riots and revolts broke out between 1750 and 1780, culminating in a major rebellion (1781–1783). This rebellion was led by José Condorcanqui, better known by his neo-Incan title Túpac Amaru II. While discontent seldom manifested itself in a form other than local tax protests and ephemeral expressions of disgruntlement, the Túpac Amaru rebellion's scope, scale, and sweeping demands made it distinct. While refraining from a direct challenge to Spanish overlordship or Catholicism, the rebellion was galvanized by a novel combination of Incan symbolism, anti-European prejudice, and a political vision that foresaw the removal of meddling Spanish bureaucrats and the recovery of Amerindian political autonomy and territorial rights. Though ultimately suppressed, the rebellion claimed a hundred thousand lives.[13]

The tentacles of European states were rather stubby before the early eighteenth century. This permitted many groups to spring up, evolve, and operate widely with scant interference from authorities. On uninhabited islets and marshy estuaries in the Caribbean and the wider Atlantic, pirates flourished, especially during the "golden age" of piracy (c. 1650–1730), when up to two thousand roamed and wreaked havoc. Pirate crews were multinational and multiracial, bringing together escaped indentured servants, fugitive slaves, renegade sailors, and indigenes, among others. As Marcus Rediker has argued, they defiantly forged an alternative social order, one that brazenly subverted the concepts of justice, financial reward, and authority prevailing within colonial societies. Their range extended across the Atlantic, with slave vessels a frequent target. In the Indian Ocean, European pirates created a haven they called "Libertalia," purportedly governed by democratic codes. Yet pirates were not merely parasites (though they were that, too). In fact, their plunder contributed significantly to the "formal" economy of European states. Pirates based on the small island of St. Mary's, off the northeastern coast of Madagascar, for example, preyed on Asian-owned merchant ships, studiously avoiding those of the British EIC and the Dutch VOC. They exchanged their plundered goods for clothing, victuals, and other supplies to a New York–based merchant, who in turn sold them at northern European ports such as Hamburg. Local non-European pirate confederations also operated in the Pacific Ocean. They rejected Dutch and Spanish monopolies over certain types of trade and often wrested concessions from them. Ultimately, however, after Utrecht, when Britain had secured legal access to trade with Spain's American possessions, piracy lost its luster and became a nuisance. Britain thus worked to snuff out piracy, eliminating the liminal, interimperial spaces where it had flourished. Britain's Admiralty courts tried and executed more than four hundred pirates in the decade after 1716.[14]

Hoisting the Jolly Roger was not the only means of carving out a sphere of autonomy. Cattle ranchers of the rugged interior of the Brazilian northeast (*sertão*) throve. Their self-sufficiency and geographical isolation put them beyond the reach of the authorities sequestered on the coast. Some ranchers gained immense individual properties (*latifundios*), where they were a law unto themselves. In São Vincent (later renamed São Paulo), to the south, settlement quickly moved beyond the demarcated bounds of the colony. It was multinational (with Portuguese subjects intermingling with

Spaniards, Italians, and Northern Europeans) and multilingual. Extensive intermarriage between Europeans and Amerindians, tolerated intermittently and eventually endorsed in the mid-eighteenth century, resulted in a majority *mameluco* society. A similar situation obtained in Pará, in the far north of Amazonia. There were few populous towns, and scant currency meant that barter was common. Large landholders generally operated without state interference before the mid-eighteenth century.[15]

Slaves, too, often escaped the confines of the New World colonies into which they or their African ancestors had been forcibly brought and sold as chattel. A small minority, though still a substantial number, of slaves managed to escape captivity and form fugitive communities beyond the grasp of the colonial state. Such self-emancipating slaves were referred to by various names, but the Spanish term *cimarrón* or French *marron* and English maroon, the latter two derived from the Spanish, were the most common terms.[16] The communities they forged went by multiple names. In Spanish, such communities were referred to as *palenques, manieles, cumbes,* or *mocambos.* In Portuguese, there were four terms to designate such communities: *mocambos, ladeiras, magotes,* and *quilombos.* Of these, mocambo was the most commonly used, taken from a Mbundu word for "hideout."

In Spanish America, *palenque* communities remained beyond the reach of European authority. In the mid-sixteenth century, there were between two thousand and seven thousand maroon slaves in various *palenques* in Hispaniola. By 1720, there were twenty thousand maroons in Venezuela alone. They did not threaten Spanish dominance except insofar as they stood as symbols of defiance of law, serving as a beacon for slaves brutalized by the plantation system. It was only later, after the onset of the Haitian revolution in the 1790s, that maroon communities were perceived as a bona fide threat to peace, stability, and prosperity. In Brazil, fugitive slave communities varied widely in population size, from the eleven thousand to twenty thousand member quilombo of Palmares, located in the remote interior of the northeast, to a few hundred individuals, as in the case of the mocambos of southern Bahia. Most mocambos were situated close to farms and towns, but others, like Palmares, were located in inaccessible rural locations. Those closer to colonial settlements were, as historian Stuart Schwartz has noted, "often parasitic, based on highway theft, cattle rustling, raiding and extortion." Though sometimes evolving into agricultural communities, mocambos, under constant duress, rarely become wholly self-sufficient.

Figure 14. *Pacification with the Maroon Negroes.* In Bryan Edwards, *An Historical Survey of the Islands of Saint Domingo . . . Also, A Tour Through the Several Islands of Barbadoes, St. Vincent, Antigua, Tobago, and Grenada, in the Years 1791 and 1792* by Sir William Young. London: J. Stockdale, 1801. Courtesy of the George Peabody Library, The Sheridan Libraries, Johns Hopkins University.

They could, however, given the right circumstances, form complex political communities. Palmares's political organization relied heavily on forms of rule resembling, if not explicitly derived from, African models. Like many quilombos, Palmares was under constant attack. For almost a century, both the Dutch and the Portuguese sought to destroy it. Finally, it was overrun and razed at the end of the seventeenth century. Colonial authorities were rarely content to permit these communities to exist undisturbed. The Portuguese mounted harassment and extermination campaigns, relying on special units, headed by armed bands of "bush-whacking captains" (*capitães-do-mato*), themselves often free persons of color, to extirpate fledgling communities before they could put down deep roots. Punishments were often ghastly, involving a range of horrific forms of torture.[17]

These punitive campaigns notwithstanding, there were a surprising number of instances across the Americas in which European powers were forced to sue for peace with maroon communities. Treaties formally acknowledged the freedom that maroons had won and the territory they controlled, generally including a provision that they would not accept more refugee slaves. Britain reached terms with maroon communities in Jamaica (1739), St. Vincent (1773), and Dominica (1794). In the Jamaican case, the colonial government recognized the free and separate existence of the maroons as long as they did not aid and abet escaped slaves. In St. Vincent, the "Black Caribs," who called themselves Garifuna, descendants of intermarriage between indigenes of the eastern Caribbean and people of African descent, occupied prime land and withstood incessant attempts by British planters to dispossess them for almost three decades. In the early 1770s, their resistance resulted in roughly 250 British casualties and a compromise settlement. In 1797, however, they were overrun; five thousand Garifuna were deported to Roatan (in the Bay of Honduras).[18]

In addition to full-scale marronage and everyday subtle forms of resistance, slaves at times rebelled against their masters and the colonial state. The most famous of these rebellions before 1800 occurred in French Saint-Domingue. There it morphed into a revolution that culminated in the formation of independent Haiti, a precedent that rocked slave societies across the western hemisphere. But Saint-Domingue was far from an anomaly. Between 1638 and 1837, there were more than seventy aborted revolts or actual slave rebellions in the British Caribbean alone. One of the largest occurred in Jamaica. Known as Tackey's Revolt (1760), it spread across the island and involved up to thirty thousand slaves. It took a year to suppress and resulted in the deaths of more than sixty whites and an equal number of free people of color. Following Britain's acquisition of Grenada in 1763, six hundred to seven hundred escaped French slaves managed to retain their freedom for almost a decade, launching guerrilla strikes against the British. The Dutch Empire, too, was shaken by slave rebellions. The most notable rebellion occurred in 1763 in Berbice, where a significant portion of the colony was conquered by an army of slaves. In 1795, a revolt in Curacao involved two thousand slaves, a sixth of that colony's overall slave population.[19]

European empires encountered stiff resistance beyond the Americas as well. The British EIC faced serious challenges from the Mughal Empire's successor states in the second half of the eighteenth century. In Mysore, Hadar Ali and then his successor, Tipu Sultan, modernized the army, obtained European weapons and built their own armories, and constructed foundries to produce weapons the quality of which was easily equal to the Company's own. With its superior cavalry, Mysore campaigned against the EIC in the late 1760s. It nearly took Madras. The EIC was forced to sue for peace.[20] Threats came not only from without but also from within: mutinies of Indian sepoys as well as European and Eurasian troops were common. Resistance remained part and parcel of British expansion in South Asia. In Ceylon, the 1817–1818 Kandy Revolt was brutally suppressed, resulting in the death of ten thousand Singhalese, whereas on the subcontinent the 1857 rebellion would shake the empire to its foundations. The Dutch VOC's dominance in Java, too, was hotly contested. Prince Nuku of Tidore (one of the Moluccas Islands) united a wide range of discontented groups that opposed Dutch monopolies in the early 1780s.

Resistance to Europe's seaborne empires was not only offered by subaltern groups, whether indigenes or the enslaved. Long before the Age of Revolutions, colonists descended from Europeans ("whites") not only complained vociferously but also occasionally rose up in arms. In 1717 and 1723, there were fleetingly successful rebellions led by creoles in Martinique and Saint-Domingue, respectively. Sometimes there was resistance that transcended the color line that colonial officials sought to erect and protect. The British government feared that Irish indentured servants in particular might align themselves with black slaves and make common cause. Such fears were partially realized in the Virginia uprising known as Bacon's Rebellion in 1676. A tenth of Virginia's enslaved black population joined forces with indentured whites and marched on the capital of Jamestown. In Spanish America, the increasingly strident fiscal demands made by the Crown sparked numerous riots and rebellions among creole elites and plebeians in urban areas after 1750. The Quito Insurrection (1765) and the Comunero Revolt (1781) were the most prominent. The latter claimed to defend the "ancient constitution," the system of relations between Spanish Americans and the Crown that, rebels believed, new fiscal policies had imperiled.[21]

Though ubiquitous, the rising tide of discontent in Spanish America produced only paroxysms of protest, not translocal, empire-wide revolt, testament perhaps to the durability and malleability of its structures. Nevertheless, protests, revolts, and resistance demonstrated that imperial states could not disregard the rising expectations of their subjects. Republican political ideas that catalyzed unrest elsewhere eventually reached the shores of Portuguese America and permeated its political culture. The most renowned conspiracy, which was nipped in the bud, transpired in the province of Minas Gerais, Brazil, in the late 1780s. Free whites were not the only free people to test the limits of imperial authority. In the 1798 Tailors' Revolt in Bahia, free mulatto soldiers and artisans hatched plots based on the principles of the Haitian and French Revolutions. They called for independence, the declaration of a republic based on electoral democracy, the abolition of slavery, and full equality between blacks and whites.[22]

Chapter 12 digs into the history of those parts of Europe's seaborne empires that sought independence after 1770. But it is crucial to recall here that collaboration and compromise remained omnipresent even in a putatively revolutionary age. The familiar story of absolutist interference producing creole resentment and eventually revolution tends to foreground moments of conflict. In many places, however, creoles did not seek separation, or at least not at first. Brazilian elites, for example, were consciously co-opted by metropolitan Portugal. This strategy helped to defuse metropolitan-colonial tensions. Brazil's leading families sent their children to study at the University of Coimbra in Portugal. There they were groomed for positions in the imperial bureaucracy, from Goa to Angola to Pará. Almost nine hundred Brazilian-born subjects studied at Coimbra between 1772 and 1822. Many of these were recruited into government service upon completion of their studies.[23]

In the British Caribbean, as distinct from mainland North America, bonds between elite planters and metropolitan Britain were indissoluble. As in the Portuguese Empire, links were deepened through education. Between 1698 and 1776, more than two hundred West Indians attended elite Eton College and Harrow School in England. This figure dwarfs the fifty-four North Americans who matriculated there in the same period. Like Brazil, but unlike British North America, the British Caribbean had no university. Further binding agents protected against open expressions of discontent. In the British Caribbean, the unchallenged dominance of the Anglican Church reinforced political authority. Perhaps more important, fear of social revolution—from slaves or indentured servants—prodded island elites to cleave to the metropole. As historian Andrew O'Shaughnessy has argued, "Slavery reinforced metropolitan ties and made whites a besieged minority dependent on Britain for their ascendancy." Whites were outnumbered by residents of African descent, both enslaved and free, by a ratio of eight to one. From the 1770s, several assemblies in the British Caribbean—Tobago, Montserrat, Nevis, and St. Kitts—requested that more troops be stationed on their islands, even offering to pay for their maintenance, at the exact moment when their mainland counterparts were decrying the Quartering Acts, which mandated what the Caribbean elites sought.[24]

In the Age of Revolutions, it would be the mainland colonies of British America and Spanish America that pressed for independence from the metropole. What historians have termed "creole consciousness" coalesced in reaction to eighteenth-century reforms deemed imperious or supercilious, to be sure. Yet it must be recalled that British American and Spanish American creoles were far from deprived, languishing under an oppressive metropolitan yoke. On the contrary, culture, learning, and science flourished. Higher education was a hallmark of Spanish America and later of British America. The first university was founded at Santo Domingo in 1538, and several other universities, notably those of Lima and Mexico City, soon followed. There were nineteen universities in Spanish America by 1700, and by the end of the colonial period they had conferred 150,000 degrees. Mexico boasted a printing press by 1539, Lima had one by 1583, and fourteen cities had one by the eighteenth century. In British North America, the first printing press was installed in Cambridge, Massachusetts, in 1638, while the first two universities, Harvard College and the College of William and Mary, were founded in 1636 and 1693, respectively. By the 1760s, each colony north of Delaware possessed a university. Nine such universities would exist on the eve of the American Revolution. By the 1720s at least one newspaper was published in all major northern ports, and by 1750 some cities had three or more newspapers.[25]

Apart from universities and the printing press, the natural sciences and political economy were diffused through institutions resembling the academies and learned societies then flourishing in Europe. In Spanish American cities from the mid-eighteenth century, for example, so-called economic and patriotic societies, together with merchant guilds (*consulados*), provided venues for literate exchange and inculcated forms of sociability now associated with the Enlightenment. More informal access to new ideas in British America was gained through public as well as subscription libraries. Benjamin Franklin established the Library Company of Philadelphia in 1731, and it soon had a hundred subscribing members, leading Franklin to boast that "these libraries have improved the general conversation of Americans, made the common tradesmen and farmers as intelligent as most gentlemen from other countries." This model spread, and there were at least sixty-four subscription libraries on the eve of the American Revolution. British colonies after the Revolution were served both by public libraries and by missionary-founded libraries. The Society for Promoting Christian Knowledge had founded fifty lending libraries by the 1790s.[26]

These features of colonial life notwithstanding, other forces were attenuating the bond between creole elites and metropolitan governments. The Spanish Empire illustrates a phenomenon found to a greater or lesser extent in other European empires. Accustomed to handling their own affairs through their cabildos and participation in upper reaches of colonial bureaucracy (in the audiencia, for example), Spanish Americans perceived an unfair metropolitan bias, which equated difference with inferiority. Such bias often resulted in exclusion from offices and denial of privileges to which they previously enjoyed access. Particularly after the Seven Years' War, which proved a debacle for Spain, creole participation in public affairs was curtailed drastically. Simultaneously, peninsular-born officials flooded Spanish America and infringed upon the relative autonomy previously enjoyed by creoles. This manifested itself in various ways, from exclusion from representative bodies to subtler forms of control. In the aftermath of Lima's 1746 earthquake-tsunami, for example, creoles chafed at the new regulations restricting the height of new buildings and the number of façades permitted.[27] The accumulation of these perceived insults undermined the older notion of the Spanish monarchy as a conglomerate of coequal kingdoms. Instead creoles believed that they now inhabited a multitiered system with an overbearing metropole on the one hand and subordinate, exploited colonies on the other.

These shifts heightened a long-simmering, if not especially combustible, Spanish American and peninsular rivalry. It nudged incipient creole patriotism. Previously confined to innocuous expressions of local pride, an identification with place, and a vague sense of being distinct from Europeans, creole patriotism morphed and prodded some Spanish Americans to envisage a future outside empire. Such sentiments were further stimulated by the economic boom of the late eighteenth century, fueled not only by transatlantic trade but by the emergence of a robust internal market, too. Agitation and restlessness were stimulated by new ideologies swirling through the Atlantic world with hurricane force. Republicanism and political-economic critiques of the "old colonial system" spurred Spanish American creoles to imagine a new political arrangement. Sporadic conspiracies were uncovered, but, with the notable exception of the Comunero Revolt in New Granada, they did not threaten to tear down existing imperial structures. These conspiracies did, however, suggest that disruptive political ideas were in broad circulation. The nascent United States was held up as a potential model in some quarters. As a Bogotá intellectual noted disapprovingly in 1795, "All those who count themselves as enlightened are enthusiastic panegyrists for the way of thinking of [citizens of the United States]: the common coin of erudite discussion groups is to discuss and even form plans around the means of enjoying the same independence that they enjoy."[28] As similar ideas percolated in various empires, it was no longer far-fetched to imagine that a spark in one empire might produce a conflagration in another, or that a revolt might beget a revolution. Could such an uprising sever European states from their seaborne empires?

12. The Age of Revolutions

The century 1660–1760 was notable for the relative stability of political regimes in Eurasia, Europe, and Europe's overseas empires. There were exceptions to this generalization, as the dynastic changes and territorial swaps that settled the War of Spanish Succession starkly revealed. But it was only after 1760 that circumstances shifted decisively and imperiled the stability of the global Old Regime. This chapter narrates and analyzes the decisive period in the late eighteenth and early nineteenth centuries during which New World colonies separated from the Old World metropoles to which they had been linked for centuries. In particular, it examines imperial breakdown in British North America, French Saint-Domingue, vast swathes of Spanish America, and, finally, Portuguese America (Brazil). Thirteen of Britain's North American colonies had broken definitively with the metropole by 1783. France's wealthy, sugar-producing stronghold of Saint-Domingue (modern Haiti) was in the throes of a decade-long revolution by 1791. Spanish America was engulfed by civil unrest after 1808, largely as a result of the impact of France's empire-building project within Europe. The Portuguese Empire improbably weathered these revolutionary storms but eventually succumbed in the early 1820s. By 1825, the entire western hemisphere, with the crucial exceptions of Canada and much of the Caribbean, no longer formed part of a European seaborne empire.

The dissolution of these empires is often treated as part of an Age of Revolutions, for these political conflagrations were inextricably tied to, and strongly influenced by, a series of concomitant European revolutions, particularly in France. In the Americas, revolutions shattered empire, and the territorial shards entered the international system as new, nominally independent sovereign states. The Anglo–North American Declaration of Independence was merely the first of dozens of similar statements in the four decades after 1776. As historian David Armitage has elucidated, these declarations were "primarily assertions of external sovereignty within an expanding universe of other such sovereigns." Swiss jurist Emer de Vattel provided an influential definition of sovereignty in his 1758 *Law of Nations:* "Every nation which governs itself, under any form whatsoever, without dependency on any foreign country, is a sovereign state." Here the notion of absence of dependence is the key to understanding sovereignty: the defining feature of a sovereign state is its independence vis-à-vis other states.[1]

While the historical novelty of these processes warrants attention, it is equally crucial to bear in mind that these revolutions form part of the origin stories of the nations that emerged from the wreckage of empire. They are situated at the beginning of national history and are depicted as a break from the colonial past. Such an account may, in fact, be accurate in some ways, depending on the specific case under consideration. But such a telling distorts a more complex process and is tantamount to myth making. The American Revolution, for example, was not a "nationalist" revolt. In Armitage's epigram, "Revolution produced Americans; it was not produced by them." Yet most national histories treat independence as inevitable. They portray the colonial period as an extended prelude to a revolutionary struggle that inexorably culminated in statehood. Actions that challenged the legitimacy of the imperial system are foregrounded. They are treated as precursors to revolution. By taking revolution and the nation-state for their telos, they jumble the processes that generated these revolutions. As historian Jeremy Adelman has argued, "Revolutions did not begin as secessionist episodes . . . rather than assertions of national independence against empires, much more common in the complex breakdown of empires was the exploration of models of re-accommodating colonies into imperial formations, a groping for an arrangement that would stabilize, not dissolve, regimes."[2] Simply put, imperial subjects were not chafing at the bit to extricate themselves from empire. Many had more to lose—stature, position, economic resources, trading connections, defense, and so on—from disruption and dislocation caused by war than they stood to gain. When they did harbor grievances, they sought remedies within the familiar and often accommodating structure of empire. Political life in Europe's seaborne empires was characterized by negotiation, compromise, and give-and-take. These processes could defuse conflict, and various parties could be satisfied (or at least mollified) without toppling, or even endangering, the status quo.

What irreparably upset this equipoise, and made the existing political system untenable in the eyes of its participants, is a complicated, still contentious question. It is prudent not to lose sight of the myriad local processes and unpredictable contingencies that sparked the conflicts that morphed into full-scale revolutions and, ultimately, secession from empire. The explanatory weight of each factor differed by empire, of course. It even differed across the component parts of each empire. Nevertheless, imperial crisis arose from a combustible mixture of the same basic elements. First, metropolitan reform initiatives came to be perceived as heavy-handed, exploitative, exclusionary, and anachronistic. This was all the more intolerable as colonies became self-sufficient economically. Second, the spread of political ideologies imbued subjects with new notions of sovereignty, emphasizing self-government, which was out of step with the centralizing policies of imperial government. Third, an emerging "creole" consciousness of the vast cultural gulf separating Europe from America, with a valorization of America, created a sentimental and cognitive framework in which political separation was rendered intelligible. Fourth, particularly in the case of French Saint-Domingue, but also in many regions of Spanish America and Brazil, pent-up disgust with, and rejection of, the system of chattel slavery was both spark and tinder of the revolutions that followed.

Each of these four factors deserves examination in turn. First, revenue-starved imperial states, armed with new theories of absolutism, began to encroach on the relative autonomy—both political and fiscal—of their colonial subjects, particularly privileged groups. They did so out of a combination of ideology and also economic necessity. Increasing revenues entailed new taxes, hordes of royal officials scrutinizing minutiae of social life, the militarization of everyday existence, and the erosion of native-born status. This sharpening of the distinction between metropole and colony combined to foster new resentments and to deepen existing ones. As Elliott has observed, "The most effective grave-diggers of empire are usually the imperialists themselves."[3]

Second, the emerging set of political and economic ideas were in tension with, if not blatantly contradictory to, the institutional features and ideological assumptions of empire. Historian R. R. Palmer claimed that the resulting revolutions were "democratic." His criteria for denominating a revolution "democratic" are the following: "Confidence in the justice or reasonableness of existing authority is undermined; old loyalties fade, obligations are felt as impositions, law seems arbitrary, and respect for superiors is felt as a form of humiliation; where existing sources of prestige seem undeserved, hitherto accepted forms of wealth and income seem ill-gained, and government is sensed in as distant, apart from the governed and not really 'representing' them." Bayly showed how these political eruptions were not merely Atlantic revolutions but rather global ones. A common (or at least mutually intelligible) set of ideas could be found across the globe as a result of interactions among empires. The Spanish Constitution (1812), for example, was studied assiduously in the South Asian metropolises of Madras, Bombay, and Calcutta, and the revolutions in Goa and Rio de Janeiro in the 1820s shared the same political grammar and lexicon. When placed in the global framework, the revolutions appeared less "democratic" than "liberal," and mixed constitutionalism (constitutional monarchy, above all) was the norm.[4]

Third, resentments and new political ideas dovetailed with the coalescence of new identity, which might be termed "creole consciousness" or "creole patriotism." This eroded bonds of attachment and instead deepened the self-perception of the peculiarity of colonial societies and their incompatibility with empire. From their inception, the seaborne empires became laboratories, often violent and coercive ones, of new identities through processes of ethnogenesis, religious syncretism, and cultural hybridity. As their populations bloomed and their economies boomed, colonial subjects became increasingly self-sufficient. The gulf between metropolitan fiscal-military requirements (as well as the models of political authority prevailing in Europe) and colonial aspirations widened into an unbridgeable chasm.

Fourth, the great paradox of the Age of Revolutions was that it was also an age of reinvigorated slave systems. Increasing reliance on enslaved African labor ensured that doctrines concerning the rights of man and citizen, self-government, and the rational basis for organizing society were pockmarked with contradictions. Relative dependence on slavery often determined the trajectory of the revolutions; in Brazil, for example, monarchy was retained at least in part due to the pervasive belief that it was a bulwark against slave insurrection.

In North America geopolitical crises, and the government-reform programs they spawned, generated tensions between American-born subjects and metropolitan Britain, as it had in the Iberian empires. The Seven Years' War fueled the resentment of American colonists who felt restricted and hampered by trade regulations that precluded intercourse with their traditional markets. Colonial frustration was heightened by a spate of new taxes and trade regulations foisted upon them in the aftermath of the conflict. The 1764 Plantation Act reimposed duties on sugar; the 1765 Stamp Act sought to augment revenue by taxing business transactions; the 1766 Declaratory Act explicitly articulated Parliament's right to tax the colonies; and the 1773 Tea Act expanded the EIC's role as a direct supplier of tea to the colonies, to the chagrin of American middlemen. Some of the grievances colonists had stemmed from their belief that they had contributed heavily to the war effort, whether as soldiers or as providers of funds. According to the 1765 American Mutiny (Quartering) Act, they were taxed for the maintenance of a greatly increased contingent of soldiers garrisoned in the colonies.

In response to the indignant reaction such legislation provoked in North America, Britain imposed further punitive measures. Colonial elective assemblies had already endured the ignominy of neglect by Crown-appointed governors before the Seven Years' War. In the 1770s, as the conflict escalated, Britain substituted nominated assemblies for elected ones, including in Massachusetts. The trend was unmistakable. The 1774 Quebec Act (for recently acquired New France) installed a nominated for an elected assembly. It appeared to be a harbinger of things to come. Taken together, the British government's policies destroyed the illusion of a mutually beneficial and binding compact. As historian P. J. Marshall has elucidated, colonists believed that they were "entitled, as a matter of inherent right and not royal grant, to live under those provisions of the Common Law confirmed by certain English statutes that established the essential rights of all freeborn Englishmen." This clashed with the emergent British approach, which stressed parliamentary sovereignty over bundles of customary rights.[5]

The ensuing military conflict took several phases. In 1775–1776, British authority collapsed, and it appeared that the rebels would not only achieve their immediate objective of independence but also perhaps enlarge the size of their new polity by absorbing part of Canada. A rebel invasion of Canada failed, however, and the tide of the war drifted back in Britain's favor. The capture of the majority of North America's leading ports—New York (1776), Philadelphia (1777), and Charleston (1780)—and the dogged loyalty of subjects in Canada and the Caribbean suggested that the rebels would soon be subdued. Then the entry of France and then Spain into the war forced Britain to fight on multiple fronts, from the Mediterranean to the Caribbean, while bolstering the capabilities of the insurgents. Britain's defeat was attributable less to military strength than to its disregard for European diplomacy that had left it bereft of allies. As historian Brendan Simms has argued, "No amount of domestic mobilization, moral purity and naval prowess could replace the continental system of alliances on which British security, prosperity and imperial expansion had rested."[6]

The political upheaval in French Saint-Domingue was directly linked to the 1789 revolution in metropolitan France. The demographic composition of the island—with approximately half a million slaves, thirty thousand whites, and thirty thousand free people of color (of whom at least two-thirds were interracial)—had worried colonial officials fearful of a massive slave revolt. In the event, it was the free people of color whose actions precipitated the political crisis. Though Saint-Domingue was permitted to send representatives to the National Assembly in Paris, free people of color were understandably confused by their place in the new political order. The revolutionary rhetoric of liberty, equality, and fraternity rang hollow in the racially stratified Caribbean. In an address to the National Assembly, 15 percent of whose members owned property in the colonies, "Free Citizens of Color" claimed "the rights of man and citizen, those inalienable rights based on Nature and the Social Contract." The initial reluctance of the National Assembly to apply the doctrine of equality to race, which effectively excluded free people of color from the political process, brought a long-simmering conflict between whites and free people of color in Saint-Domingue to the fore. Even though the National Assembly ultimately reversed its position in 1792, the damage proved irreparable. In the meantime, a slave rebellion erupted in 1791 on the northern plain, near the city of Le Cap. Cane fields and houses were torched. Sugar-processing machinery was smashed. Interestingly, as historian David Geggus has documented, the slaves did not justify their actions using the new political language of rights; instead they employed a "conservative rhetoric of loyalty to Church and King."[7]

France's rivals, Britain and Spain, soon inserted themselves into the conflict, seeking to profit from the disarray. Britain in particular strenuously attempted to conquer Saint-Domingue from 1793. Faced with the prospect of foreign interference, the French government abolished slavery to rally slaves to its cause in order to repulse the invaders. As historian Laurent Dubois has

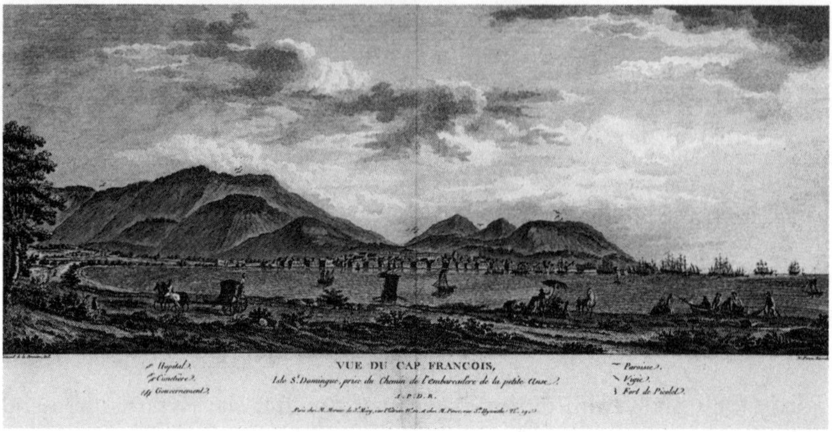

Figure 15. View of Cap François, Saint-Domingue (Cap Haïtien in present-day Haiti). *Vue du Cap Francois, Isle St. Domingue, Prise du Chemin de L'embarcadère de la Petite Anse.* In Nicolas Ponce, *Recueil de Vues des Lieux Principaux de la Colonie Françoise de Saint-Domingue.* Paris: Chez M. Moreau de Saint-Méry, 1791. Courtesy of the John Carter Brown Library at Brown University.

pointed out, this 1794 moment was pregnant with possibilities: "France and its colonies were united, in principle, under one set of laws understood as truly universal and applicable. . . . For a time, racial hierarchies were defeated by assimilationist universalism."[8] An army of resistance was raised, under the leadership of Toussaint Louverture, one of the free persons of color (now called *anciens libres,* to distinguish them from the newly liberated slaves). After repulsing the British and the Spanish, Louverture turned his attention to the governance of the country. Specifically, he aimed to revive the plantation system upon which the economy was premised. This proved nearly impossible to achieve without slaves, and he resorted to a forced-labor system. Though he and his officers were, for all intents and purposes, masters of Saint-Domingue, they carefully insisted on their unflinching loyalty to France, now ruled by Napoleon. The relative autonomy of Saint-Domingue within this new regime was not yet determined. Louverture pressed the issue by promulgating a constitution for the colony in 1801. While this charter stipulated Saint-Domingue's subordination to metropolitan France, this utterance was disingenuous. Consolidating power, Louverture declared himself governor for life, with the authority to appoint his own successor.

The political system Louverture had conjured into existence was closely linked to developments in metropolitan France. In 1802, irked by

Louverture's brazen defiance and separationist tendencies, Napoleon dispatched an army of reconquest. Although Louverture was captured (and would die in French custody, in the Jura Mountains of Switzerland), the invasion and, crucially, Napoleon's decision to reimpose slavery transformed the conflict. It now became a struggle for independence from France and for freedom from bondage. The French managed to reenslave freed people in other Caribbean territories—Martinique, Guadeloupe, and Guiana—but they failed in Saint-Domingue. After a brutal campaign, marked by atrocities on both sides, the French Army was expelled in 1803, having lost forty thousand troops (mostly to disease).

Under the leadership of Jean-Jacques Dessalines, independence was declared, and the abolition of slavery was confirmed. The name Haiti, the pre-Columbian Amerindian name for the island, was restored. White colonists were forcibly removed, in keeping with Dessalines's 1804 oath ("Never will any colonist or European set foot on this land as a master or proprietor"), subsequently enshrined in the 1805 constitution.[9] On the one hand, this charter was a radical document: it abolished slavery, established equality before the law, and eliminated distinctions based on color. On the other hand, it scarcely disguised the new state's character as a military autocracy, far from the republic that had been envisaged. Dessalines, now emperor, possessed the sole authority to make public appointments, to take decisions regarding the economy, and to direct foreign affairs. Only after his assassination, in 1806, would Haiti become a republic. Even then, however, Dessalines's former associate, Henri Christophe, would crown himself king of a breakaway state in the northern part of the country, and the new nation would only be unified in 1820.

It is impossible to overstate the impact of the Haitian Revolution. While planters from Virginia to Curaçao to Brazil trembled, the revolution never lacked for fervent admirers. William Wordsworth's elegy to the vanquished Louverture is suggestive: "Thou hast left behind / Powers that will work for thee; air, earth, and skies; / There's not a breathing of the common wind / That will forget thee." The French and Haitian Revolutions shook the Iberian empires, but they also created new opportunities. Brazilian sugar planters were poised to flourish when Saint-Domingue plunged into revolution. As production faltered, demand for, and the prices fetched by, Brazilian sugar on the world market soared. To meet this demand, Brazilian planters needed more slaves. Almost twenty-five thousand Africans were imported as slaves each year between 1790 and 1810. The influx of slaves coincided, too, with a massive increase in cotton exports from the north and northeast of Brazil to Britain. Coffee exports grew sevenfold in the decade before 1808. Overall, exports from Portugal and its colonial possessions (chiefly Brazil) quadrupled between 1789 and 1807. By the middle of the 1790s, then, Portuguese balance of payments had moved into surplus.[10] It appeared, fleetingly, that the Marquis of Pombal's grand scheme of imperial revivification, built on the foundation of new export commodities, had succeeded. The events of 1808, however, proved such prosperity a chimera.

Spain's negotiation of the revolutionary 1790s was disastrous in contrast to neighboring Portugal's. In the early part of the decade, regicidal France was a pariah state in Europe, which prompted Britain and Spain to put their ancient enmity aside and fight together for the preservation of the institution of monarchy. As the conflict evolved, however, Spain perceived greater benefits from an alliance with Napoleonic France, which provoked another diplomatic revolution, prompting the renewal of Anglo-Spanish conflict. The results for Spain and Spanish America were dire. The defeat of the Spanish fleet off Cape St. Vincent in 1797 foreshadowed Britain's three-year blockade of Cádiz. This blockade of Spain's principal Atlantic port irreparably disrupted the supply chain between merchants in the Iberian Peninsula and Spanish-American markets. The British Navy wrought further havoc by seizing the island of Trinidad in 1797. The centuries-old link between Spain and the Americas had been severed, then, well before the coup de grâce delivered in 1805 at Trafalgar, the naval battle in which most of Spain's warships were lost, an unexpected denouement of a century of imperial reform and revival.

Under these dire circumstances, the colonial economies were compelled to become either self-sufficient or reliant on contraband. The problem had been foreseen by many Spanish officials in the preceding decades. A Peruvian viceroy predicted that "on the day when [Americans] can supply themselves with all that is necessary, their dependence will be voluntary, and neither the military forces that we have there nor the gentleness of government nor the best-administered justice will be sufficient to secure our possession." They were drifting toward self-sufficiency. If in 1750 American-born subjects held just a fifth of all military commissions, by the beginning of the nineteenth century almost two-thirds of the officer corps was composed of creoles. Creoles jumped at the opportunity to purchase commissions, made available for purchase (and subject to loose standards and few procedures) from 1780 as a revenue-generating measure, and the cash-strapped Spanish treasury continued the practice thereafter, putting profit over principle as well as morale.[11]

None of this subversive activity, however, threatened at first to crescendo into a separatist rebellion. It was only when Napoleon betrayed his erstwhile ally and French armies occupied the Iberian Peninsula, from 1808, and deposed the Bourbon monarchy, that a crisis of legitimacy and sovereignty unfolded, which ultimately resulted in the independence of Spanish America in the early 1820s. In 1808–1810, each part of the empire devised ad hoc solutions to the problem of sovereignty. Most of these proposed solutions diverged from one another, and few were compatible with the older imperial framework. One idea that drew many adherents was the notion that sovereignty had reverted to the people, now conceived as belonging to, and being territorially rooted in, the various local regions in America, without connection to Spain.[12] Peninsular attempts to reintegrate these recalcitrant subjects by force failed, though only after a decade of unrelenting, disruptive warfare. Out of the wreckage of empire—indeed, forged in the crucible of separatist warfare and civil war—stumbled new nation-states of Latin America.

The British North American and French Revolutions had spawned a mania for written constitutions across the globe.[13] Even while rejecting the French invaders, Spaniards and Spanish Americans had embraced the idea of a written constitution in their dominions. While several of the constitutions devised in Spanish America were republican in character, and thus antimonarchical, the most influential constitution was the one framed, after intense debate, in Cádiz in 1812. With most of the Iberian Peninsula occupied by French invaders and the abdicated Spanish kings under house arrest in France, Spanish patriots clustered in Cádiz, its bay protected by British warships, to reframe the Spanish monarchy. The product of their deliberations was the Constitution of Cádiz (or the 1812 Spanish constitution). This constitution called for a mixed monarchy, with the king and an elected unicameral legislature jointly authorized to legislate for and govern Spain and Spanish America. The constitution also enshrined certain protections and rights in law. It went some distance toward destroying the political structure of ancien régime Spain. Perhaps most important, subjects were transformed into citizens. American colonists and peninsular Spaniards were to be governed by the same laws, with certain notable (and ultimately fatal) exceptions. The distinctions between American and Spaniard would be eliminated. Universal jurisdiction would replace the legal hodge-podge that characterized the composite monarchy.

The Cádiz constitution was implemented fitfully and fleetingly across the empire. In Spanish America, revolutionary movements animated by more radical political ideas (for example, a definitive separation from Europe, the destruction of monarchy, the abolition of slavery) precluded a more positive reception. In retrospect, the constitution's silence on slavery and its explicit barring of people of African descent from active political participation looms large in accounting for the frigid reception that an otherwise vanguard document received. In Spain itself, by the time the French armies were expelled from the peninsula, the restoration of the arch-absolutist Fernando VII provoked not only the suspension of the 1812 constitution but also the repudiation of its tenets, the prosecution of its advocates and adherents, and the dismantlement of the reconstructed imperial Spain on professed liberal principles. Such actions were consistent with the doctrines of the ascendant Holy Alliance, even if the actions of the vengeful Fernando were an extreme manifestation of the broader trend of political reaction. The end of Spanish dominion in America came only after almost two decades of warfare. Fernando sent an army of reconquest to America in 1816, but the lion's share of the sixteen thousand soldiers succumbed to tropical disease. Royalists clung to power in Peru before the decisive 1824 Battle of Ayacucho determined that Spanish America would be independent and republican. Shorn of its American empire, Spain held onto the lucrative sugar-producing islands of Cuba and Puerto Rico for the rest of the nineteenth century. But its dominance in the New World had come to a definitive end.

Portugal's empire largely avoided being swept up into the maelstrom of the Age of Revolutions. Before the reform initiatives of the iron-fisted Pombal in the 1750s, there had been few efforts to centralize authority and raise revenues. Local elites, particularly in Brazil, had been granted ample autonomy. Even if considerable leeway resulted from benign neglect and Portuguese weakness, elites had fewer reasons to resent metropolitan meddling than their counterparts elsewhere. The Brazilian viceroy, for example, wielded considerably less authority than his Spanish counterpart. Furthermore, the vast physical distances between population centers, uncooperative topography and prevailing winds, and sparse infrastructure made greater local autonomy almost inevitable. There also were conscious Crown efforts, as noted previously, to create a transatlantic governing elite through common education and training at the University of Coimbra and thus to nullify the peninsular-American antagonism that festered in the Spanish Empire. There were conflicts and conspiracies, including the important one that unfolded in Brazil's province of Minas Gerais. Despite stresses and strains, however, the center held, and things did not fall apart.

Portugal did not escape the tumult through its own agency and foresight alone. As previously mentioned, the 1790s were a boom time for Brazilian agriculture, since revolution in the Caribbean resulted in a vertiginous drop in sugar production, which Brazilian planters and merchants exploited. By 1805, Brazilian sugar accounted for 15 percent of world output. Furthermore, in contrast to what transpired in Spain, Portugal's alliance with Great Britain permitted its royal family to escape the French armies occupying the Iberian Peninsula by moving to the New World. Portuguese America was thus spared the crisis of authority that unraveled Spanish America. The prince regent, Dom João, was the first European monarch to set foot in the Americas when he disembarked in late 1807. He quickly endowed Rio de Janeiro with the institutions befitting its new status as interim capital of a global empire. He set up a parallel administration and sponsored a massive public works scheme. The new theaters, promenades, plazas, royal palaces, a botanical garden, and a bevy of government buildings led latter-day historians to dub the city "Tropical Versailles." New institutions needed personnel to run them, of course. Government posts proliferated and brought the transplanted regime new adherents, dependents, and clients. The Crown further ingratiated itself by creating new titles of nobility for particularly deserving (and obsequious) Brazilian subjects. The formation of a New World nobility, who enjoyed all of the trappings of social prestige previously the exclusive domain of their Old World counterparts, was an ingenious, innovative device to tighten the bond between the Brazilian elite and the refugee monarchs. It made the former deeply invested in the latter's survival and efflorescence.[14]

Even before the transfer of the court there was scant vocalized discontent with Brazil's status within the empire, let alone open resistance to Portugal's rule. The previously discussed late colonial conspiracies were swiftly and decisively suppressed. The relative tranquillity in the face of revolutionary headwinds is perhaps chiefly attributable to the notable cohesiveness of the ruling elite, fully conscious of the perils of living in a slave society and fearful of a Haitian-style insurrection in their midst. In 1800, Brazil's population was 37 percent slaves of African descent, 30 percent free persons of African ancestry or of mixed racial background (categorized then as "mulatto"), 30 percent "white" (a dreadfully imprecise and frequently misleading category), and 3 percent Amerindian. In such potentially combustible circumstances, elite dissent could produce unintended, revolutionary consequences. It was therefore scrupulously avoided.

In what was viewed as a dangerously topsy-turvy world, the royal family in Rio de Janeiro, far from being a burden, was refashioned into a powerful buttress to the existing social, economic, and political order. It was a prophylactic against the political chaos enveloping Brazil's Spanish American neighbors, in which older, ostensibly durable hierarchies seemed to be toppled almost daily. Political stability was deemed the indispensable precondition of economic prosperity.[15] By some measures, the decade of the 1810s, the heyday of Tropical Versailles, was an unequivocal success. The slave trade expanded, and the export of tropical commodities rose in tandem. The Crown even clawed back some of its forfeited prestige through a spate of territorial acquisitions: French Guiana was occupied in 1809; additional territory was snatched from Amerindians; and the consolidation of hotly contested claims to parts of southern Brazil and the Banda Oriental (modern Uruguay) proceeded apace as the Spanish Empire splintered.

The transfer of the court was justified as a wartime exigency. With, however, the defeat of Napoleon, the restoration of deposed kings to their old thrones, and the coming of a general peace in 1815, Dom João manifested little inclination to return to Portugal. It had been ravaged by war, and its economy was devastated. Its size and prosperity, furthermore, were vastly inferior compared with those of Brazil. Some argued that the court should reside permanently in Brazil, with Rio de Janeiro as the capital of a revamped empire. Such an arrangement would have reflected not only Brazil's economic might and Portugal's strategic vulnerability (as the French invasion had proven) but also the burgeoning slave trade, conducted between Brazil and Portuguese coastal enclaves in West Africa, chiefly though not exclusively from modern Angola.

Dispassionate analysis, of course, was not the only consideration. Self-interest was intimately involved in such counsel, as the return of the court to the metropole would have dissipated the parallel capital in Rio de Janeiro and reduced Brazil again to the status of a colony. Yet not everyone was enamored of the Crown's decision to tarry. Many resented the maintenance of a large, opulent court, for both fiscal and ideological reasons. Provincial elites, long accustomed to a modicum of self-government (or at least benign neglect), became increasingly alarmed by the unabashedly centralizing proclivities of Rio de Janeiro. In 1817, a revolt imbued with republican ideas broke out in Recife, Pernambuco. It was soon crushed, and the court showed few signs of returning to the Old World.[16]

The worst fears of Portugal's elite, eagerly awaiting the restitution of their preeminence, were confirmed in 1815 when Dom João elevated Brazil to the status of a kingdom, not merely an overseas dominion or colony but a territory coequal with Portugal. Already in 1808, he had thrown open the ports and markets of Brazil to merchants of all nations. These free-trade decrees had deprived Portuguese merchants of their monopoly over Brazilian commerce. It stripped Lisbon and Porto of their cherished (and lucrative) position as entrepôts for the reexport of Brazilian commodities to the markets of northern Europe. In 1820, a liberal revolution erupted in Portugal that sought to establish a constitutional monarchy, with Lisbon as its center. Though the king was compelled to return to Europe, he left his son and heir, Prince Dom Pedro, behind to serve as a counterweight to any political conspiracies. When the liberal Cortes demanded the prince return as well, he refused and, following a convoluted series of events, declared Brazil independent and fashioned himself into the monarch of an independent Brazilian empire. His swift actions were prompted not only by disdain for the insolent demands of the Portuguese liberals but also in order to preempt revolution from below. By opting for monarchy, retaining the same European dynasty on the throne, and calling their new polity an "empire," Dom Pedro and his supporters guaranteed that Brazil's future would diverge sharply from that of Brazil's Spanish republican neighbors. Independent Brazil was formally recognized by Portugal in 1825, and the same recognition was extended by other European powers soon thereafter.

Not all Brazilian regions (or populations) were satisfied with this monarchical-imperial settlement. Throughout the colonial period, the northern provinces of Maranhão and Pará had maintained closer relations with Lisbon than with the rest of Brazil, due to proximity, Atlantic currents, and large Portuguese-born merchant communities. Moreover, in northeastern provinces like Pernambuco and Bahia, whose economic halcyon days were long finished, the political ascendancy of Rio de Janeiro, with its centralizing pretensions, combined with the economic efflorescence of the southeastern provinces in general, caused consternation. There were half-hearted attempts to resist a union with Rio de Janeiro and instead retain a link with Portugal. But the derelict former metropole was in no position to pursue such a course of action with conviction, and a vague vogue for secession failed to gather momentum. Even those Brazilians who welcomed independence were unenthused by its high price: the survival of monarchy and the retention of the ruling Braganza dynasty proved distasteful. The recent precedent of the republican revolutions, from Boston to Buenos Aires, was their preferred model of political change. The stage was set, then, for a showdown between Dom Pedro with the provincial elites of Brazil's north and northeast. The suspicions of republicans, liberals, and proponents of regional autonomy were confirmed when Dom Pedro dissolved the assembly convened to draft a new constitution and issued a constitution in 1824. This "gift from the throne" was explicitly antifederalist. It established the legal architecture of the central government's dominance over the provinces.[17] Yet whatever disputes lingered (and there were many), they would be handled as domestic matters, without interference from Europe. With the establishment of monarchical Brazil as an independent empire, the Age of Atlantic Revolutions came to a close.

In triumphant accounts of revolutionary change, the defeated are commonly overlooked. In the British case, those who remained loyal to the Crown fled the nascent United States to join other British colonial societies. This loyalist migration to Canada, the Bahamas, Sierra Leone, India, and Britain itself presaged the subsequent reorientation of British colonial ambitions toward the Mediterranean, Indian Ocean, and Pacific worlds. Sixty thousand loyalists fled the former thirteen seaboard colonies, including thousands of former slaves who had fought for Britain and were emancipated as a result. More than half of the loyalists went to Canada, particularly Nova Scotia, New Brunswick, and Quebec, induced in part by generous land grants. In an effort to avoid a repetition of what had transpired south of the Great Lakes, the 1791 Canada Act ushered in a new constitutional arrangement in the British Empire. It provided for strong Crown government at the expense of the legislative assembly. Of the colonists who did not venture north to Canada, a sizable portion journeyed to Britain, whereas others, particularly slaveholders, relocated to the Caribbean, especially to Jamaica and the Bahamas. The British case was far from exceptional. More than thirty thousand refugees from Saint-Domingue arrived in Cuba in the 1790s. Tens of thousands of Spaniards were expelled from Mexico in the late 1820s in a spasm of xenophobic and ultranationalist policy making. Portuguese merchants were often attacked in Brazil after 1825, prompting a significant number to cross the Atlantic, far from the madding crowd.[18]

Historian Jack Goldstone has offered a general definition of revolution: "the forcible overthrow of a government by mass mobilization . . . in the name of social justice, to create new political institutions." Most of the revolutions of the period 1775–1825 do not conform to this definition. In the admittedly extreme case of Brazil, for example, there were no forcible overthrow and no mass mobilization, and no calls for social justice were heeded (slavery went untouched). What new political institutions were established enjoyed the Crown's imprimatur. More generally, as Bayly elucidated, the global revolutionary age was one of political and ideological compromise; mixed constitutionalism, combining monarchism with a modicum of representative institutions, predominated across Eurasia.[19] Mixed government even characterized the nascent United States, where a federal system took root, enshrined in the 1787 Constitution. With strong executive authority and a preponderance of authority invested in the central government, it appalled "Anti-Federalists" who preferred the controlling share of authority to be vested in the individual states.

Nor did revolutions and independence necessarily usher in new institutions, as the case of Latin America demonstrates. In Spanish America, preexisting patterns and latent forces, residues of the colonial era, reasserted themselves. They undermined the stability of the fledgling states for much of the nineteenth century. As the British consul in Colombia noted in the 1820s, the new government "left in existence and operation the old Spanish laws, with all of their multiplied imperfections, contradictions and confusedness, in all matters wherein their application and observance may not impugn against the new order of things."[20] Centralists vied with federalists for political primacy. The state's capacity to reshape society was undercut by entrenched local interests. Revolutionary promises of effective, equal citizenship for Indians, mestizos, and people of African descent went largely unfulfilled. Purportedly liberal regimes confiscated Indian land, with paltry compensation, in the name of progress and economic development. Republican institutions often were found lacking in republican spirit. In Brazil, the political settlement was marked by the apparent (though tenuous) triumph of monarchism over republicanism, of territorial integrity and a centralized administration over dispersed power and provincial autonomy, and of the expansion of a slave-reliant economy over free (or at least less coercive) labor regimes. When Brazilian independence was declared, the destruction of the Old Regime was incomplete, perhaps not even yet under way. Independence became decoupled from the dismemberment of the colonial system. In fact, independence, with its illusion of change, neutralized such efforts, depriving Brazil of the opportunity to convert the transition from colony to nation into a revolutionary overhaul of politics, society, and economy. Brazil may have been an extreme case, but it suggests how the end of empire did not necessarily entail the erasure or demolition of many of the institutions, practices, and ideas that had sustained it for centuries. Political revolution and social transformation could be decoupled, as those who lived in the twilight of this first age of decolonization could attest.

Epilogue

Continuities and Disjunctures

The Age of Revolutions brought a decisive phase in the history of the seaborne empires to a close. Yet it ultimately proved a prelude to the massive extension of Europe's authority to areas of the globe previously beyond its grasp. If in 1800 European states occupied, controlled, or laid claim to 35 percent of the land surface of the world, that figure leapt to 67 percent by 1878, and to 84 percent in 1914. The maritime dimension of empire did not fade away after 1800 but instead was enhanced by the advent of steam power, which annihilated distance. Steamships plied the world's oceans, making once interminable journeys possible. The average crossing between Britain and Halifax, Nova Scotia, was forty days in 1837, but it took a mere twelve days in 1852. Once the Red Sea route was opened, the London to Bombay voyage took a mere month. Within empires, new technologies permitted the integration of distant territories: regular steam service on the Ganges connected Calcutta and Allahabad as early as 1834.[1]

The maritime character of these empires was complemented and supported by new technologies and modes of communication—from railways to telegraphs—that made "seaborne" merely one of several modifiers to describe the empires of the nineteenth century. Littorals and port cities defined early modern European empires; after 1800, once impregnable hinterlands became vast terrestrial empires. European incursions into the continental interior of Africa, for example, had been precluded by dysentery, yellow fever, typhoid, and especially malaria. It was not known until the

1880s that malaria was caused by a plasmodium invading the bloodstream and until the 1890s that the vector of the disease was the Anopheles mosquito. But it had been known for centuries that chinchona bark (also known as "Jesuit bark") from the South American Andes was a cure for malaria. In the 1820s French chemists extracted quinine from chinchona bark, and by the 1830s it was manufactured in sufficient quantities for general use. Used during the occupation of Algeria, it contributed to the massive decline in mortality of French soldiers stationed there. By the 1860s, chinchona bark was cultivated on plantations in British India and Dutch Java.[2]

Given these shifts of scope, scale, and orientation, historians commonly distinguished between a "first," a "second," and a "third" Portuguese Empire, or a "first" and a "second" British Empire, as if these were distinct entities, abrupt transitions with scant continuity or overlap. In the British case, it was postulated that the American Revolution was an imperial watershed, after which the British state "swung to the east," to focus on India, and embraced "free trade" instead of "mercantilism."[3] Undoubtedly, empires morphed and transformed over time, often quite self-consciously, in pursuit of concrete aims, as the eighteenth-century reforms undertaken by all of Europe's seaborne empires indicate. In recent years, however, historians have concluded that to demarcate imperial transitions distracts attention either from continuities over time or from more macabre shifts in policy that imperial apologists were all too happy to ignore.

The most influential historian to contest the putative geographical and ideological reorientation of the British Empire after the American Revolution was Christopher Bayly. In his landmark *Imperial Meridian: The British Empire and the World, 1780–1830* (1989), he advanced the following argument: "The British Empire from 1780–1830 represented not simply a hiatus between irresistible waves of liberal reform, but a series of attempts to establish overseas despotisms which mirrored in many ways the politics of neo-absolutism and the Holy Alliance of contemporary Europe. These colonial despotisms were characterized by a form of aristocratic military government supporting a viceregal autocracy, by a well-developed imperial style which emphasized hierarchy and racial subordination. . . . The dominant ideological character of this Second British empire was aristocratic, autocratic and agrarianist." This new imperial style emerged during the French Revolutionary wars. Napoleon's overhaul of both the government of France and the European territories he conquered exceeded the scope and scale of eighteenth-century reform. The main features were a centralized bureaucracy, judicial system, and streamlined taxation. Unsurprisingly, Britain, like the other European seaborne empires, learned from, and adopted, some facet of the system of direct rule pioneered by Napoleon. He, in turn, had initially developed this system in Egypt, which he then applied in France and thereafter in the client states he established in Europe.[4] Whether in Trinidad (conquered in 1797), Sicily (occupied 1806–1815), or the Ionian Islands (1809–1814), the Napoleonic-style direct rule was embraced by the British government. When peace was restored in 1815, the experimental "proconsular despotism" was normalized, morphing seamlessly into what became known as "Crown colony" government. In practice, this meant that the Crown (not Parliament) appointed the governor, who held and exercised executive authority without oversight by now declawed local assemblies.

A second model of governance that emerged after 1815 was "responsible self-government," which was implemented initially in Canada (in 1841) and later extended to colonies with significant levels of white settlement, such as New Zealand and Australia (in 1852 and 1855, respectively). Here the Westminster model of government was reproduced on a miniature scale, with an elected assembly that resembled the House of Commons counterbalanced by a council appointed by the governor, an effective check on popular sovereignty. A third model, applied in parts of South Asia, was that of "protectorate," in which there was a local ruler who was acknowledged as the sovereign but whose actions were monitored and modified by the British, who offered his regime "protection." Less formal than a protectorate," but sharing many of its features, was the cognate strategy of "indirect rule." As historians Barbara and Thomas Metcalf have argued, "The continuation of princely rule also helped the British veil their power behind the rulers whose ceremonial and ritual authority remained visibly intact." Of course, the authority retained by native rulers was severely circumscribed: they could not maintain their own armies or enter into diplomatic relations with other states.[5]

The Age of Revolutions witnessed the creation of dozens of new polities out of the carcasses of the seaborne empires, chiefly in the Americas. But independence, the departure of European armies and administrators, and the erection of a new political order did not signify the end of coercion or influence customarily associated with empire. The various mechanisms, usually based on unfavorable terms of trade, through which powerful European states undermined and eroded the sovereignty of, and reaped significant advantages from, newly founded states may be grouped together as "informal empire." Britain's relation with Latin America after 1820 is a paradigmatic case. In exchange for diplomatic recognition, Britain demanded commercial concessions, notably free access for British shipping and "most favored nation status" for exports. Well before independence, British foreign secretary Robert Stewart, Viscount Castlereagh, argued in 1807 that "England should create and support an amicable and local government, with which those commercial relations may freely subsist," while his successor, George Canning, confided in 1824 that "Spanish America is free, and if we do not mismanage our affairs sadly, she is English."[6]

The extension of credit and the expansion of commerce were principal features of relations between Britain and the new Latin American states. Their governments needed access to credit following decades of war and before new institutions could replace those of the defunct Spanish Empire. Elites sought foreign investment and credit, and Britain provided them with alacrity. Financiers and merchants arranged loans to the governments of Colombia, Chile, Mexico, Peru, and Brazil totaling twenty million pounds sterling between 1822 and 1825, in some cases before these states had gained formal diplomatic recognition. These loans were traded as bonds in London. The entire enterprise was a fiasco from the start. First, the borrowing nations received only 60 percent of the face value of the loans they had contracted, after fees, discounts, and other deductions were accounted for. Many of these loans were used for military expenses, not to fortify nascent civilian institutions. In Mexico, two-thirds of its 1824 loan was funneled to the military.

Unsurprisingly, reliant on debt and ruling precariously over impoverished wartorn territories with few ready sources of revenue, Latin American states failed to repay their loans. By 1829, nearly nineteen million pounds' worth of these bonds were in default. Not only did thousands of individual investors in Europe suffer drastic losses, the new states were deprived of access to credit. The range of fiscal options was circumscribed: unfavorable commercial treaties meant that customs and tariffs could not be used as instruments of economic salvation. The states were forced to depend on rather thin domestic resources. These soon proved inadequate, especially as many powerful sectors scoffed at taxation. By 1830, for example, Brazil had borrowed four times its annual revenue and had no recourse to direct taxation of the landholding rural oligarchy. Default was an infraction that carried significant penalties and ultimately infringed upon the sovereignty of the borrowers. British free trade and commercial penetration, then, quickly turned coercive. To create an environment conducive to lending and investment, stable and complaisant governments proved most suitable. It is therefore crucial to recognize, as Gallagher and Robinson observed long ago, how British "political action aided the growth of commercial supremacy, and how this supremacy in turn strengthened political influence."[7]

Historians A. G. Hopkins and Peter Cain perceived in these early interactions with independent Latin America the first hints of a subsequent feature of British imperialism. As they argued, "The drive to create an international trading system centered on London and [was] mediated by sterling. World trade was to be financed by short-term credits; world development was to be promoted initially by long-term loans to foreign governments and subsequently through direct investment. The whole package was to be tied together by a regime of international free trade, which would encourage specialization, cut transaction costs and create an interlocking system of multilateral payments."[8] The mutual strengthening of commerce and politics, of the preference for coercive pressure to achieve objectives instead of formal territorial control, may be seen nakedly in British pressure to eradicate the slave trade in the early nineteenth century. Britain had routinely bullied Portugal to take gradual steps to end the slave trade, threatening to withhold loans and military support if it failed to comply. The independence of Brazil, by then the largest recipient of African slaves, caused conflict, as it was not incumbent on Brazil to honor treaties signed by Portugal. Canning wished to make diplomatic recognition contingent on the abolition of the slave trade ("[Brazil] should be purged from its impurity before we take it into our embraces"), but he ultimately offered recognition in exchange for the promise to end the trade within five years.

In any case, commercial treaties and anti-slave-trade agreements were negotiated together and seen as inextricable in the subsequent decades. From 1825 until 1850, the British government used its navy to clamp down on the slave trade to Brazil, much of which was conducted from Portuguese Africa. Vessels captured on the high seas were tried in international tribunals, called Mixed Commissions, or sometimes British Vice-Admiralty courts. In Mixed Commissions, representatives of the powers involved sat in judgment of the captured ship, its crew, and the slaves on board. If the ship was found guilty, the enslaved were liberated and, in some cases, the crew tried as pirates. The most efficacious year was 1837, when nine thousand Africans were liberated. While an effective deterrent, the Royal Navy captured a fraction of the ships engaged in the slave trade. Britain therefore took more direct action, sending warships to patrol Guanabara Bay, Rio de Janeiro, and compelling the Brazilian government to abolish the slave trade in 1850.[9]

Such pressure was applied not only in Latin America but in Africa, too. British suppression of the slave trade aimed to foment so-called legitimate commerce, premised on "free trade." Among the many ironies that accompanied this effort was the fact that coercion intensified the use of slave labor in Africa itself to produce the very items to be exchanged. In West Africa, imports of palm oil into Britain increased thirtyfold between 1810 and 1850, whereas the quality of finished cotton textiles shipped from Britain to West Africa increased by the same magnitude in roughly the same period. Palm oil greased the wheels of Britain's industrial machinery and furnished the essential ingredient for soap and candles. But palm oil was not acquired with textiles alone; commerce was rarely sweetly pacific. Long after the abolition of the slave trade, Britain continued to ship staggering quantities of guns to West Africa: fifty-two thousand arms in 1829 and eighty-four thousand in 1844, with even higher numbers in the second half of the century. When trade alone failed to produce the desired outcome, force was employed. Britain bombarded Lagos, in modern Nigeria, to compel its compliance with slave trade treaties, foreshadowing its annexation as a colony in 1861. This transition from informal to formal colonialism was not an aberration or non sequitur. Indeed, as historian Richard Huzzey has observed, "Disrespect for African sovereignty and territoriality, combined with a civilization hierarchy of diplomatic protocol, established the moral and legal basis for European expansion."[10]

European states, particularly Britain, acted aggressively to impose their will concerning matters other than the slave trade, often enshrining coercive tactics by treaty. As a result of the 1830 Treaty of Balta Liman, Britain forced Egypt, then ruled by Muhammad Ali, to abolish state monopolies and to lower external tariffs; both concessions deprived the state of its major revenue streams. Gunboat diplomacy was common. As Lord Palmerston, a progenitor of this approach, observed, "It may be true in one sense that trade ought not to be enforced with cannon balls, but on the other hand trade cannot flourish without security, and that security may often be unattainable without the protection of physical force." A key example is British policy toward China. Incapable of conquering China, and resentful of the Qing dynasty's efforts to block entry of its South Asian–produced opium, Britain resorted to military aggression in the early 1840s to shift the terms of trade. Its leverage was limited. Britain remained dependent on China for tea; not until the late nineteenth century would Britain obtain more than 10 percent of its tea from India. Military force shifted the equation. Britain captured the city of Canton (Guangzhou), forcing the Chinese to sue for peace. By the resulting Treaty of Nanjing (1842), China paid Britain an indemnity and was forced to open additional ports (such as Shanghai) to foreign merchants, to restrict Chinese duties on British goods to a paltry 5 percent, and, crucially, to cede Hong Kong to Britain until 1997. European influence would expand still further during the political crisis that engulfed China for fifteen years from 1851. The Taiping Rebellion claimed more than twenty million lives and decimated the finances of the Qing dynasty, leaving it poorly equipped to repel aggressive European states.[11]

It would be misleading to suggest, however, that those steering policy in nineteenth-century Britain *solely* aspired to "informal" empire. As previously mentioned, massive territories were acquired in South Asia, with the Sindh and Punjab, part of contemporary Pakistan, conquered in the 1840s. Territorial occupation and population of Australia and New Zealand, discussed below, was a prominent aspect of British geopolitical ambitions. It is therefore unsurprising that the first half of the nineteenth century witnessed an acceleration of the global distribution of Britain's military power. Most of Britain's army regiments were based in the empire by the mid-1830s, whereas only a tiny majority had been based outside Britain a century earlier. While this shift deserves notice, it must be observed that many of the nodes absorbed into the "formal" empire aimed at the expansion of commerce in markets that Britain had already penetrated. For example, Singapore, Penang, and Malacca, which together formed the Straits Settlements from 1826, were established to serve as a bridge between Indian and Chinese markets.

European powers began to use long-held colonies in new ways, too. In Java, following successive periods of occupation by British forces, the Dutch implemented what was called the "cultivation system" after 1830. This policy forced native farmers to set aside a portion of their land, generally a fifth, and to cultivate lucrative commodities for export, including cochineal, tobacco, cotton, indigo, and sugar, at the expense of staples, like rice. Unsurprising, food shortages and widespread famine ensued. But the benefits for the Dutch were quick to appear. By the mid-1830s, revenue flowed from Indonesia into the Dutch treasury. It amounted to a quarter of all Dutch government expenditure in this period. In the 1840s and 1850s, the proportion increased to half of total government revenue.[12]

France's Caribbean and Indian Ocean colonies also recovered from the collapse that had accompanied the final throes of the Napoleonic Wars. By the 1820s, colonial imports reached 15 percent of all French imports. More dramatically, France revived its sugar economy on the backs of slaves. By 1826, Guadeloupe, Martinique, and Réunion produced the same amount of sugar as Saint-Domingue before its revolution. French imports from the colonies and the number of ships involved in the colonial trade doubled between 1816 and 1829. The abolition of slavery across the French Empire in 1848 triggered, predictably, a massive decline in sugar production and exports. In Guadeloupe, thirty-eight thousand tons of sugar were exported in 1847, but that figure plummeted to thirteen thousand by 1849. In the 1850s, under the new Bonapartist regime, slavery was not revived in the Antilles, but other coercive measures were enacted to generate a large, disciplined labor force for the cultivation of tropical commodities. The legal freedom of former slaves, who were classified as "cultivators" and not citizens, was linked to compulsory service, whether agricultural or military. France also resorted to other sources of labor. One source was a pool of contract laborers (*engagés*) from its colony in Senegal, of whom sixteen thousand were transported to the Caribbean.[13] Additional laborers were shipped from France's remaining comptoirs in South Asia.

But the major pivot in French overseas ambition was toward North Africa. Algeria was conceived of explicitly as a colony of settlement, as a vent to relieve pressure in overcrowded cities, with their entrenched poverty and disconcerting revolutionary tendencies. Vast emigration to Algeria was encouraged by the government, and its advocates were drawn from across the political spectrum. Conquest and colonization proved more challenging than anticipated. France met with formidable resistance. Emir Abd-el Kader possessed weapons as effective and up to date as those used by the invading French Army. He defeated French forces in successive military confrontations in the 1830s, largely confining European settlement to the coast. By 1840, France had expended vast sums on the pacification of Algeria. More than thirty-five thousand of its soldiers had succumbed to disease and

Figure 16. Disembarkation of the French Army in Algeria. *Débarquement de L'Armée Française à Sidi-Feruche (14 Juin 1830)*. In A. Berbrugger, *Algérie Historique, Pittoresque et Monumentale, Première Partie: Province d'Alger*. Paris: Chez J. Delahaye, 1843. Courtesy of the George Peabody Library, The Sheridan Libraries, Johns Hopkins University.

combat-related mortality. Besides reviving the economic fortunes of its Caribbean and Indian Ocean colonies, and its policy of territorial conquest in North Africa, France used a third prong in its imperial strategy. This was the seizure and maintenance of coastal enclaves and small islands as an adjunct to its commercial activity. Such *points d'appui* or *points de relâche* were established in Gabon (1839), the Marqueses Islands and Tahiti (1842), and New Caledonia (1853). There was rising interest in overseas empire: an Institut d'Afrique was founded in 1839, with a membership drawn from across social strata, a forerunner of later French designs in sub-Saharan Africa.[14]

For Spain, the "loss" of America triggered profound national introspection. Economically, some historians estimate that Spain suffered a total fall in foreign trade of 75 percent. It no longer had access to many American imports, some of which (for example, raw cotton, cacao, indigo) it had refined in the peninsula and then reexported to northern Europe. Peninsular trade with Spanish America, which had received 40 percent of exports, collapsed. The great trading port of Cádiz was devastated.[15] There were several responses to this multifaceted crisis. The first was the reorientation of Spain's economy and culture toward continental Europe, which occurred gradually over the course of the nineteenth century. The second response, sometimes in conflict with the first, was to focus energies and assets on the remaining lucrative colonies, Cuba and Puerto Rico above all. Consonant with the revanchist despotism in Spain itself, the revamped colonies were governed by martial law. In Puerto Rico, for example, the governor was endowed with almost dictatorial powers, and he smothered incipient separatist tendencies.

The economic ideas animating eighteenth-century "enlightened reform," a combination of agrarianism and highly supervised if less-regulated trade, had not been snuffed out in nineteenth-century Spain. Deprived of its terrestrial empire, Spain partially opened its ports, bringing Cuba and Puerto Rico's commodities, chiefly sugar, to world markets. This commerce also brought customs receipts to the cash-strapped Spanish treasury. At the same time, in the name of "national economy," colonial markets remained protected. Cuba, in particular, received roughly a fifth of all Spanish exports. Using new technologies, Cuban planters initiated a period that historians have termed the "second slavery." Slavery expanded, rather than contracted, in the putative age of abolition. The use of steamships, steam-powered sugar mills, and railways combined to ramp up sugar production. Latin America's first railway line, opened in 1837, connected the sugar-producing hinterland with the port of Havana. Steam-driven sugar mills reduced the need for scarce and expensive wood, bolstering efficiency and profits.[16]

The demand for slaves was voracious. Almost eight hundred thousand enslaved Africans disembarked in Cuba and Puerto Rico between 1791 and 1870. Furthermore, it appears that, at least until 1835, the vast majority were transported on Spanish ships, thus giving Spain a material stake in that facet of the slave economy as well. By 1870, Cuba produced two-fifths of the sugar consumed on the world market.[17] When the supply of slaves did not meet the voracious demand for them, authorities turned to other coercive forms of labor. In Puerto Rico, at mid-century, the *libreta* (workbook) system was introduced, which forced free peasants to work in plantation-based agriculture. When local labor proved inadequate (or intransigent), planters resorted to East Asian contract laborers, so-called coolies, of whom approximately 140,000 disembarked in Cuban ports in the 1850s and 1860s.

After it established constitutional monarchy in 1834, Spain renamed its "overseas provinces" (*provincias de ultramar*). But they did not enjoy legal equality with the metropole. This inequality was a flagrant violation of the liberal principles the government professed. To escape this contradiction, and also the discomfiting paradox of slavery's persistence, Spanish politicians argued that slavery made Cuba and Puerto Rico heterogeneous and therefore in need of "special laws." These were enacted in the late 1830s. Deprived of parliamentary representation, governed by executive fiat, and increasingly reliant on slave labor, the Caribbean "provinces" were in limbo. They operated neither within the flexible, often advantageous pre-1808 institutional framework nor within the liberal state's juridical and administrative structures. It should be noted that the fashion for special laws to govern overseas territories was not peculiarly Spanish. Writing on French administration of Algeria in the mid-1830s, Alexis de Tocqueville exclaimed, "We must give up this taste for uniformity that torments us, and . . . realize that it would be as dangerous as it is absurd to apply the same laws to [Algeria]."[18]

The prosperity of Cuba and Puerto Rico, and Spain's reliance on them, emboldened politicians to entertain visions of lost grandeur regained. Military adventurism was a feature of the political landscape after 1850. Successive governments fought a jingoistic (and superficially victorious) war in Morocco (1859–1860). Spain (re)occupied Santo Domingo between 1861 and 1865, though it was compelled to withdraw after a force of more than forty thousand Spanish soldiers failed to quell a rebellion there. It joined French expeditions to Indochina and later supported its installation of a puppet state in Mexico (1864–1867). And it fought a war against Peru and Chile (1864–1866), largely over bird droppings: the guano-rich Chincha Islands.[19] Soon, however, from 1868, Spain found itself on the defensive as revolution broke out in Cuba.

Brazilian independence deprived Portugal of its largest and most lucrative colony. It lost the territory that had contained the capital of the entire empire from 1808 to 1821, one that had been raised to the status of a kingdom coequal to Portugal in 1815. Shorn of Brazil, Portugal was left with a tenuous hold on coastal zones in Angola and Mozambique, and more secure possession of Goa, Cape Verde, and Guinea. In 1820 the population of the Portuguese Empire was 7.3 million; in 1850 it stood at a mere 1.65 million.[20] After the Portuguese Civil War ended in the mid-1830s, the government identified these neglected backwaters of empire as a national priority. It reached this conclusion because Portugal, taken alone, was an impoverished, primarily agricultural state, with precious little industry and few prospects for advantageous trade within Europe. Economically, for all intents and purposes, it had been reduced to the status of a semicolony of Britain. Its very viability as an independent state was called into question. As unification projects in Italy and Germany gathered momentum, some favored an analogous Iberian Union, with Portugal absorbed into a peninsular constitutional monarchy with Spain. The fantasy of a revamped empire, with Africa reimagined as a latter-day Brazil, was embraced as the most promising path to economic prosperity and national self-preservation.

Imperial projects proliferated in the 1840s, but the internecine strife plaguing Portugal's domestic politics ensured that few were undertaken. A further obstacle was the circumstances of Angola, where the Portuguese-controlled areas were dominated by the slave trade to Brazil and Cuba. Portugal had pledged to eradicate the slave trade, a pledge enshrined in various treaties with its chief ally, Britain. It was only after Brazil abolished the transatlantic slave trade in 1850, as a result of British gunboat diplomacy, that shifting the basis of Angola's economy could be contemplated. The second half of the nineteenth century was marked by experiments with settler colonialism and export-oriented agriculture, a prelude to the more vigorous imperial expansion undertaken in the twentieth century.[21]

With the loss of America, Britain scavenged for a new dumping ground for convicts. In the middle decades of the eighteenth century, British explorers had reconnoitered the Pacific, gaining knowledge of New Zealand and Australia. Botany Bay in Australia was selected in 1788 as the site of a new penal colony.[22] The advantages of this locale were its proximity to the Dutch East Indies, access to southern whaling—which provided oil not only to lubricate machinery but also to light London's street lamps—and ample stores of timber and flax, which were used for the Royal Navy's masts, sails, and ropes. Convict labor galvanized Australia's economy, which increasingly was based on sheep. Sheared wool would be shipped to Britain and then processed in the mill towns. There were four million sheep grazing on Australian pastures in 1840, and almost thirteen million a decade later. The majority of convicts were assigned upon arrival to masters, most of whom were themselves ex-convicts. The duties of these masters were few, limited to their charges' rudimentary subsistence. The convicts thus served out their sentences, without pay, their brawn undergirding the burgeoning pastoral economy and ensuring its profitability.

Of course, this economy relied on transhumance, and the shepherds drove their flocks far beyond the coastal settlements of Botany Bay, deep into the interior. The British government may have claimed the right to settle and govern territory beyond the littoral, but it had no substantive presence there. Shepherds and would-be settlers encountered, and soon displaced and dispossessed, the Aboriginal inhabitants. The settlers responded to scattered Aboriginal resistance by unleashing terror, of which the 1838 massacre at Mayall Creek, in northern New South Wales, and the 1843 atrocity at Warrigal Creek, in Victoria, were but two manifestations of the same sordid phenomenon. On the land they expropriated, these antipodean conquistadors established a warren of personal jurisdictions, which the British state would have to sort through, confirm, or contest in subsequent decades. At least in the early decades, the situation in New Zealand differed from that in Australia. The numerical superiority and martial capacity of indigenous Maoris kept would-be British settlers at bay. As historian Keith Sinclair argued, "The European towns for a decade or more were mere encampments on the fringes of Polynesia; the settlers held their land on the doubtful tenure of Maori sufferance."[23] In fact, the British were compelled to reach accommodation with the chiefs in the Treaty of Waitangi (1840), which swapped Maori recognition of British sovereignty for a guarantee of the lands and property they possessed.

A convict-dependent economy and expansionist settler ethos proved less than conducive to civil government in Australia. It was ruled as a military despotism, albeit one with enlightened pretensions. Under Lachlan Macquarie in the 1810s, the city of Sydney was laid out anew, and public works programs were undertaken. But this convict society was under constant surveillance. The government actively intervened to enforce its vision of public morality: the Sabbath was to be observed, and houses of ill repute regulated. Behavior considered transgressive was punished. Besides flogging and other forms of corporal discipline, relocation to special penal colonies was common. Convict transportation peaked in the 1830s, with more than fifty thousand brought to Australia, more than during the previous two decades combined.[24]

Slowly, as more land was expropriated from Aboriginal groups, and as free members of Australian society grew as a proportion of the overall population, new measures were taken. Transportation of convicts to New South Wales ended in 1840 and was abandoned for Australia as a whole in 1849, except for Van Dieman's Land (now Tasmania), where it was continued for another four years. In the place of convicts, Britain subsidized the migration of settlers. Of the hundred thousand British subjects who immigrated to Australia and New Zealand between 1837 and 1846, eighty thousand received subsidies. Their arrival was fueled in part by a broader pro-emigration ideology, which some historians dub "settlerism," that gained adherents in the Anglo-American world in the middle decades of the nineteenth century.[25] In 1842, more than fifty years after its founding, New South Wales was granted a partly elected legislative council; a constitution would be granted in the 1850s. Besides pro-emigration ideology and the dispensation of a modicum of self-government, newly discovered precious metals lured Britons. In 1851, gold strikes in Victoria sparked a gold rush on the same scale as that unfolding in California at around the same time. It attracted five hundred thousand migrants within a decade.

Similar dynamics played out in other parts of the British Empire, though with important differences. The transfer of the Cape of Good Hope from the Netherlands to Britain was followed by an influx of British settlers. More than ten thousand arrived in the 1820s, and they soon clashed with Afrikaners, or Boers, descendants of the Dutch. The new system of private landownership squeezed poorer Boers, while the "free" labor policy and abolition of slavery only fueled the Boers' disaffection. In 1835–1837, disenchanted Boers undertook the Great Trek, which resulted in the settlement of eastern South Africa. After military victories over the Zulu, particularly the 1838 Battle of Blood River, the Boers seized control of half of the territory of Zululand. There they established their own republic, Natal, separate from the Cape Colony, and later would establish other independent polities in the interior, notably the Transvaal (1852) and the Orange Free State (1852).[26] Conflict between Boers and the Cape Colony was a permanent feature of the nineteenth century. Beginning with the British annexation of Natal in 1843, tensions would simmer, exploding in the Boer Wars at the end of the century. Other settler initiatives were pursued by European states in West Africa. New colonies in Africa were founded by freed slaves from the British Empire, including Sierra Leone (reestablished as a Crown colony in 1808). The French would found Libreville in Gabon (1849) along similar lines, while the independent United States got into the act as well when the American Colonization Society helped to found Liberia (1822).

As the nineteenth century wore on, culture was deployed to further European ambitions, a dimension of informal empire that relied on the formation of habits and the inculcation of norms favorable to control. Gunboats were not enough in the long run. Sports, for example, were consciously spread by British officials in overseas empire to co-opt native elites and keep settlers in check. A golf course in Calcutta opened in 1829. Cricket clubs opened in Sydney and Bombay in 1826 and 1849, respectively. According to historian Ronald Hyam, the diffusion of sports was imbued with ideological purpose: "Through its apolitical nature, sport was seen as a cultural artifact, and improving agency, capable of shaping shared beliefs and attitudes between rulers and ruled, subliminally transmitting notions of discipline and decorum."[27] To sport must be added, inter alia, the episteme privileged in colonial education, asymmetrical treaties, and myriad forms of "soft" and apparently anodyne forms of power that complemented the naked violence that accompanied empire.

The European empires of the nineteenth and twentieth centuries cultivated their fruits in well-tilled soils and with tools whose efficacy was well established. Writing of the abolition of slavery in the British Empire, the historian Eric Williams remarked that "the ideas built on [those] interests continue long after the interests have been destroyed and work their old mischief, which is all the more mischievous because the interests to which they corresponded no longer exist."[28] This insight might be extended to the long-disappeared early modern seaborne empires surveyed in this book. They bequeathed repertoires if not arsenals of concepts, prejudices, techniques of (mis)rule and orientations, to say nothing of inequalities and inequities that have shaped Europe's interactions with the wider world until the present day. The seaborne empires made possible globalization, understood as the "progressive increase in the scale of social processes from a local or regional to a world level."[29] With this shift in scale and intensified contact emerges not only shared appetites for consumer goods across the globe but also perhaps the preconditions of human emancipation and solidarity to overcome the manifold suffering and injustice bequeathed by the long-forgotten seaborne empires.

Notes

Introduction

1. Mid-twentieth-century historians attributed Europe's rise to a peculiar set of cultural endowments and characteristics. While acknowledging the importance of access to overseas resources, historian William McNeill argued that Europe ("the West") gained a "clear margin of superiority over the other great civilizations of the world," primarily due to the "internal tensions arising from its own heterogeneous cultural inheritance," which produced a "veritable social explosion." The catalyst, in other words, was intrinsic, not extrinsic, to Europe. See McNeill, *Rise of the West*, 578.
2. Jones, *European Miracle*, 231.
3. Blaut, *Colonizer's Model of the World*, 1, 10–11, 42; see also Abu-Lughod, *Before European Hegemony*.
4. Rodney, *How Europe Underdeveloped Africa*, 14.
5. Smith, *Wealth of Nations*, vol. II, 591; Marx, *Capital*, vol. I (1867), quoted in Renton, *Marx on Globalisation*, 50, 52; Pomeranz, *Great Divergence*, 4.
6. Darwin, *Empire Project*.
7. For the purposes of this book, historian Jack Goldstone's definition of the "state" is adequate: "institutions of a centralized, national-level, rule-making and rule-enforcing power, including the individuals who controlled these institutions when acting in their official capacities." See Goldstone, *Revolution*, 4.
8. Boxer, *Portuguese Seaborne Empire* and *Dutch Seaborne Empire;* Parry, *Spanish Seaborne Empire;* more recently, see Jeremy Black, *British Seaborne Empire*.
9. Trouillot, *Silencing the Past*, 48.
10. Parry, *Trade and Dominion*, 7.
11. Roca Barea, *Imperiofobia*.
12. Russell-Wood, "Ports of Colonial Brazil," 209; Rediker, *Devil and the Deep Blue Sea*, 290; ODNB, "Yale, Elihu."

13. Curtin, *The World and the West,* 3.
14. I am indebted to Professor Richard Drayton for this insight.
15. Frank, *ReOrient,* 21.
16. Calculated from the Transatlantic Slave Trade Database (www.slavevoyages.org), last accessed November 14, 2017.
17. For example, as historian Toby Green showed, "Africans not only made use of pan-Atlantic links but developed them themselves, working both within and alongside imperial structures, and through their forced and autonomous migrations back and forth." See Green, "Beyond an Imperial Atlantic," 118–119.
18. Thornton, *Cultural History of the Atlantic World,* 160–161; Prakash, "After Colonialism," 3.
19. In Seeley's famous late nineteenth-century formulation, "We seem, as it were, to have conquered and peopled half the world in a fit of absence of mind." In Seeley, *Expansion of England,* 8.
20. Michael Craton, "Reluctant Creoles: The Planters' World in the British West Indies," in Bailyn and Morgan, *Strangers in the Realm,* 323; Andrews, *Spanish Caribbean,* 252; Brewer, *Sinews of Power,* 10; Zahedieh, *Capital and Colonies,* 148; Anderson, *War and Society,* 27.
21. Spence, *Modern China,* 151; Bayly, *Indian Society,* 105, 116.
22. Davis, *Christian Slaves,* 15; Eltis, *Rise of African Slavery,* 57; Colley, *Captives,* 44; on Europeans held captive by Amerindians in Spanish America, see Operé, *Indian Captivity.*
23. Restall, *Seven Myths;* McFarlane, *British in Americas,* 38; Fisher, *Economic Aspects,* 86; Rothschild, "'A Horrible Tragedy,'" 77; though Kouro was an extraordinary disaster, it was not anomalous: over half of the six thousand migrants to French New Orleans between 1717 and 1720 died either en route or shortly after their arrival. See Havard and Vidal, *Histoire,* 206.
24. McNeill, *Mosquito Empires,* 136, 166; McNeill, *Atlantic Empires,* 104; Crosby, *Ecological Imperialism,* 140; Charters, *Disease, War and the Imperial State,* 66, 72.
25. Colley, *Captives,* 122.
26. Barlow quotation in Rediker, *Devil and the Deep Blue Sea,* 40; Schmidt, *Innocence Abroad,* 197, 275, 289.
27. Outram, *Enlightenment;* Montesquieu, *Spirit of the Laws,* 393, 396; Raynal, *Philosophical and Political History,* vol. I, 132; Smith, *Wealth of Nations,* vol. II, 592; Winch, *Classical Political Economy,* 3–13 passim; it should be emphasized that Smith was not against empire altogether but rather against the manner in which European states conceived of and pursued overseas empire.

28. Muthu, *Enlightenment against Empire,* 106; Burke quotation in Pagden, *Peoples and Empires,* 97; Robertson, *History of America,* vol. III, 352; Bentham, "Rid Yourselves," 114; Winch, *Classical Political Economy,* 25–34, 105.
29. Brown, *Informal Empire;* Brown and Paquette, *Connections after Colonialism.*

1. Definitions of "Empire" and Approaches to the Study of Its History

1. Gallagher and Robinson, "Imperialism of Free Trade," 1.
2. Pomper, "History and Theory of Empires," 4; for an influential example of this approach, see Hardt and Negri, *Empire;* on the relationship between imperial history and postcolonial theory, see (among others) Kennedy, "Imperial History and Post-Colonial Theory."
3. Darwin, *Unfinished Empire,* 7; Doyle, *Empires,* 45; Abernethy, *Dynamics of Global Governance,* 19; Howe, *Empire,* 30.
4. Burbank and Cooper, *Empires in World History,* 2, 8.
5. Bodin quotation in Koenigsberger, *Europe in the Sixteenth Century,* 338; Benton, *Law and Colonial Cultures,* 258; Clulow, *The Company and the Shogun,* 214–215.
6. On this shift, see Ford, *Settler Sovereignty,* and, above all, Benton, *Search for Sovereignty.*
7. Pagden, *Peoples and Empires,* xxii; Pagden, *Burdens of Empire,* 2; We must bear in mind Lauren Benton's observation that Roman law was a "source rather than a script" in the early modern era: agents of empire were flexible and creative in their construction of legal arguments in specific contexts. See Benton, "Possessing Empire," 19.
8. Pagden, *Peoples and Empires,* 44.
9. Reinhard, *Short History of Colonialism,* 3–4; Cardim et al., *Polycentric Monarchies.*
10. Timothy Anna, "Spain and the Breakdown of the Imperial Ethos: The Problem of Equality," in Armitage, *Theories of Empire,* 326; Pagden, *Spanish Imperialism,* 91; Fradera, "Spain," 52–53, 56.
11. Pagden, *Lords of All the World,* 87, 116; Armitage, *Ideological Origins,* 8, 141–143.
12. Jaksíc, *Hispanic World,* 2–6; Kagan, "Prescott's Paradigm"; Martínez de la Rosa quotation in Costeloe, *Response to Revolution,* 22; on Spanish efforts to write histories contesting the Black Legend in the eighteenth century, see Cañizares-Esguerra, *How to Write.*

13. Cañizares-Esguerra, *Puritan Conquistadors,* 232; Irigoin and Grafe, "Bargaining for Absolutism"; Mahoney, Lange, and vom Hau, "Colonialism and Development," 1414.
14. Colley, *Britons,* 17.
15. Hale, *War and Society,* 70; Elliott, *Europe Divided,* 24; Bailyn, *Barbarous Years,* xiv, 261; Boxer, *Dutch Seaborne Empire,* 80.
16. Herzog, *Frontiers of Possession,* 42, 49, 68, 60; Benton, *Search for Sovereignty,* 23.
17. Hancock, *Oceans of Wine;* Clancy-Smith, *Mediterraneans,* 90; Michael Heffernan, "French Colonial Migration," in Cohen, *Cambridge Survey of Migration,* 35.
18. Verlinden, "Transfer of Colonial Techniques," 3–4, 32; Dandelet, *Renaissance of Empire,* 3.
19. Cañizares-Esguerra, *Puritan Conquistadors,* 9–12.
20. Elliott, *Old World and the New.*
21. Wey Gómez, *Tropics of Empire;* Davis, *Inhuman Bondage,* 55.
22. Schmidt, *Inventing Exoticism;* Gerbi, *Dispute of the New World;* Metcalf, *Ideologies of the Raj,* 6, 14; Meek, *Social Science and the Ignoble Savage,* 2; Adas, *Machines as the Measure of Men,* 3.
23. Gould, "Entangled Histories, Entangled Worlds," 766.
24. Pombal quotation in Maxwell, "Pombal," 608; Drayton, *Nature's Government;* for an extension of Drayton's insights to Spain, see Paquette, *Enlightenment, Governance, and Reform.*
25. De Vries, "Dutch Atlantic Economy," 7–8; Todd, "French Imperial Meridian," 162, 185; Todd, "Transnational Projects," 277.
26. Pagden, "Europe: Conceptualizing a Continent," in Pagden, *Idea of Europe,* 45; Lewis and Wigen, *Myth of the Continents,* 26; Fernández-Armesto, *Before Columbus;* VOC is the Dutch acronym for the *Verenigde Ostindische Compagnie;* Israel, *The Dutch Republic,* 939.
27. Elphick and Giliomee, "The Origins and Entrenchment of European Dominance at the Cape, c. 1652–c. 1840," in Elphick and Giliomee, *The Shaping of South African Society*, 530–531.

2. *Western Europe in a World of Empires*

1. Drayton, "Globalisation of France," 427; Frank, *ReOrient,* 134, 147, 184–185.
2. Asher and Talbot, *India before Europe,* 159; Chaudhuri, *Trading World of Asia,* 455; Leonard Blussé, "Northern European Empire in Asia: The VOC,"

in Scott, *Oxford Handbook*, 245; Prakash, *European Commercial Enterprise*, 96, 102; see also Scammell, *World Encompassed*, 406–407; Frank, *ReOrient*, 282; Cowan, *Social Life of Coffee*, 59.

3. Rowe, *China's Last Empire*, 38–39, 48; Perdue, "Empires and Frontiers," 97.
4. Rowe, *China's Last Empire*, 1, 32, 92; Perdue, *China Marches West*, 526–527; note that much of this empire was tributary, meaning that fringes, like Southeast Asia, paid tribute in acknowledgment of Chinese political dominance. As a result, Qing influence was immense, but much of the empire was not governed directly.
5. Doyle, *Old European Order*, 5–6.
6. Kappeler, *Russian Empire*, 103–104; Kappeler argued that status/class, not religion/nationality, mattered most in the Russian Empire before 1700: "A loyal noble was as a rule accepted by the Russian government, no matter if he was a Lutheran Baltic German, a Catholic Pole or a Muslim Tatar," 104.
7. McNeill and McNeill, *The Human Web*, 175; Engel and Martin, *Russia in World History*, 54.
8. Perdue, "Empires and Frontiers," 124–132; McNeill, *Plagues and Peoples*, 216; Rieber, *The Struggle for the Eurasian Borderlands.*
9. Iliffe, *Africans*, 174.
10. Fernández-Armesto and Restall, *Conquistadors*, 16–18; Rostworowski and Morris, "The Fourfold Domain," 822–844; Hämäläinen, *Comanche Empire*, 4.
11. Subrahmanyan, *Portuguese Empire*, 276; Metcalf and Metcalf, *Modern India*, 47.
12. John K. Thornton, "Firearms, Diplomacy and Conquest in Angola: Cooperation and Alliance in West Central Africa, 1491–1671," in Lee, *Empires and Indigenes*, 173; Matsuda, *Pacific Worlds*, 154; Edward Alpers, "On Becoming a British Lake: Piracy, Slavery, and British Imperialism in the Indian Ocean during the First Half of the Nineteenth Century," in Harms, Freamon, and Blight, *Indian Ocean Slavery*, 49.
13. Clulow, *Company and the Shogun*, 16–19; Jorge Flores, "Floating Franks: The Portuguese and Their Empire as Seen from Early Modern Asia," in Aldrich and McKenzie, *Routledge History*, 40–41; Qianlong quotation in Rowe, *China's Last Empire*, 146–147; an exception appears to have been European clocks, which were in high demand in imperial China; see Mungello, *Great Encounter*, 39.
14. Kennedy, *Rise and Fall of the Great Powers*, 148; for an argument against commercial policy as leading to Indian deindustrialization and in favor of

"the profound political re-ordering that accompanied British rule" as an explanation, see Parthasarathi, *Transition to a Colonial Economy*, 5, 147.

15. Berg, *Luxury and Pleasure*, 55; Defoe quotation in Beckert, *Empire of Cotton*, 33; Cowan, *Social Life of Coffee*, 115–116; Wolff, *The Singing Turk;* Quataert, *Ottoman Empire*, 9.
16. Adas, *Machines as the Measure of Men*, 79–88; Marshall and Williams, *Great Map of Mankind*, 52, 56; Muthu, *Enlightenment against Empire*, 72.
17. Metcalf, *Go-Betweens*, 59.
18. Newitt, *Mozambique*, 126, 129; Dalrymple, *White Mughals*, 18–19.
19. Amy Bushnell Turner, "Indigenous America and the Limits of the Atlantic World, 1493–1825," in Greene and Morgan, *Atlantic History;* Bailyn, *Barabarous Years*, 500; Calloway, *New Worlds for All*, 20; Igler, *The Great Ocean*, 70.
20. Quataert, *Ottoman Empire*, 50; Barkey, *Empires of Difference*, 194–200, 257; Hanioğlu, *Late Ottoman Empire*.
21. Dale, *Muslim Empires*, 248–249; Metcalf and Metcalf, *Modern India*, 30–31; Asher and Talbot, *India before Europe*, 247–249; Bayly, *Indian Society*, 11.
22. Dale, *Muslim Empires*, 257–261; Asher and Talbot, *India before Europe*, 227, 255.
23. Rowe, *China's Last Empire*, 66–69; Spence, *Modern China*, 97.
24. Metcalf and Metcalf, *Modern India*, 47–48.
25. Asher and Talbot, *India before Europe*, 287; Hastings quotation in Adas, *Machines as the Measure of Men*, 96; Cohn, *Colonialism and Its Forms of Knowledge*, 4–5, 21; mapping played a similar function; see Edney, *Mapping and Empire;* Said, *Orientalism*, 6.
26. Macaulay quotation in Metcalf, *Ideologies of the Raj*, 34; Wesseling, *European Colonial Empires*, 58–59.
27. Karl Marx, "The Future Results of British Rule in India" (1853), in Avineri, *Karl Marx on Colonialism*, 125; Marx, "The British Rule in India" (1853), in ibid., 88; Marx, "Future Results," 131.

3. The First Seaborne Empires

1. Harvey, *Islamic Spain*.
2. Abulafia, *Western Mediterranean Kingdoms*, 236; Elliott, "A Europe of Composite Monarchies"; Koenigsberger, "*Dominium regale*."
3. This section on Portugal draws on Disney, *History of Portugal*, vols. I and II; Oliveira Marques, *History;* and Newitt, *Portugal*.

4. Abulafia, *Discovery of Mankind;* Fernández-Armesto, *Before Columbus;* Elliott, *Imperial Spain;* Cañeque, *King's Living Image*, 25.
5. Abulafia, *Discovery of Mankind*, 72–73.
6. Benton, *Law and Colonial Cultures*, 33–37, 79–82.
7. Gil Pujol, "Spain and Portugal," 428.
8. Tuck, *Rights of War and Peace*, 72–73.
9. Newitt, *Portugal*, 50, 52; also Newitt, *Portuguese Overseas Expansion;* Russell-Wood, *Portuguese Empire;* Disney, *Portugal*.
10. Newitt, *Portuguese Overseas Expansion;* Garofalo, "Shape of a Diaspora," 28; Wheat, *Atlantic Africa*, 183.
11. Sundkler and Steed, *History of the Church in Africa*, 51–52.
12. Abulafia, *Discovery of Mankind*, 30.
13. Newitt, *Portuguese Overseas Expansion;* Disney, *Portugal*.
14. Recent historians have shown that Asian rulers did exploit and regulate the ocean as part of their realm. They have contested the notion that there was a vast gulf between European and Asian conceptions of sovereignty and space. See Prange, "The Contested Sea." Nevertheless, there is little doubt that the nature and extent of the regulatory regime installed in the Indian Ocean by the Portuguese was genuinely a departure from the norms in place prior to their arrival.
15. Subrahmanyan, *Portuguese Empire in Asia;* Pearson, *Indian Ocean*, 121; note that the Ottomans challenged Portuguese efforts to dominate the Indian Ocean, as recounted in Casale, *Ottoman Age of Exploration*.
16. Newitt, *Portuguese Overseas Expansion*, 194–195.
17. Francisco Bethencourt, "Political Configurations and Local Powers," in Bethencourt and Curto, *Portuguese Oceanic Expansion*, 200.
18. "Letter of Pedro Vaz da Caminha," in Schwartz, *Early Brazil*, 9.
19. Frei Vicente do Salvador, quoted in Lockhart and Schwartz, *Early Latin America*, 229.
20. Burkholder and Johnson, *Colonial Latin America;* Thomas, *Rivers of Gold;* and Thomas, *Conquest*.
21. Restall, *Seven Myths*.
22. Restall, *Seven Myths*.
23. Quotation in Campbell, "Changing Racial and Administrative Structure," 117.
24. Newitt, *Portuguese Overseas Expansion*, 174–175.
25. Hernando del Castillo quotation in Parker, *Empire, War and Faith*, 21.
26. Newitt, *Portuguese Overseas Expansion*, 195.

4. The Challenge to Iberian Dominance

1. Elliott, *Old World and the New;* Maltby, *The Black Legend in England.*
2. Hale, *War and Society,* 233; Tallett, *War and Society,* 177; Parker, *Europe in Crisis,* 54–55, 61, 75.
3. Elliott, *Richelieu and Olivares,* 85.
4. Boxer, *Dutch Seaborne Empire;* Israel, *Dutch Republic*
5. Nicholas Canny, "The Ideology of English Colonization: From Ireland to America," in Armitage, *Theories of Empire,* 193
6. Parker, *Global Crisis,* 381; Andrews, *Trade, Plunder and Settlement,* 11.
7. Greengrass, *Christendom Destroyed,* 656.
8. Black, *British Isles,* 150.
9. Elliott, *Europe Divided,* 342.
10. Munck, *Seventeenth-Century Europe,* 31, 46, 148–150; Collins, *State in Early Modern France,* 24, 73, 86; Parker, *Global Crisis,* 316–321.
11. Parker, *The Military Revolution,* 63; Parker, *Philip II,* 178–179.
12. Hakluyt quotation in Darwin, *Unfinished Empire,* 18; there are dangers of oversimplification here: Philip II had twice (in 1561 and 1563) personally intervened to prevent the pope from excommunicating Elizabeth. He did so because his grand strategy was premised on Anglo-Spanish entente. See Elliott, *Europe Divided,* 171.
13. Andrews, *Trade, Plunder and Settlement,* 11; McFarlane, *British in the Americas,* 43–44.
14. Glete, *Warfare at Sea,* 163; Andrews, *Trade, Plunder and Settlement,* 256.
15. Elliott, *Richelieu and Olivares,* 63–64; Spanish economic reformer and royal secretary Pedro Fernández Navarette (1564–1632) quotation in Gil Pujol, "Un rey, una fe, muchas naciones," 64; Elliott, *Count-Duke of Olivares,* 193–197.
16. Israel, *Dutch Republic and the Hispanic World,* 197–198; de Vries, "Dutch Atlantic Economies," 4; Klooster, *Dutch Moment,* 257.
17. Parker, *Military Revolution,* 63; Greengrass, *Christendom Destroyed,* 551.
18. Berkin, *First Generations,* 6–7; Bailyn, *Barbarous Years,* 111, 170; McFarlane, *Britain in the Americas,* 87.
19. Parker, *Empire, War and Faith,* 34–35; Bethencourt, *Racisms,* 185; Furber, *Rival Empires,* 27.
20. Monteiro, Ramos, and Vasconcelos e Sousa, *História de Portugal;* Valladares, *Portugal y la monarquía Hispánica.*
21. Tuck, *Rights of War and Peace,* 85–89.

22. Locke quotation in Anthony Pagden, "The Struggle for Legitimacy and the Image of Empire in the Atlantic to c. 1700," in Canny, *Oxford History*, vol. I, 42; David Armitage, "Literature and Empire," in Canny, *Oxford History*, vol. I, 108; Drayton, *Nature's Government*, 89.
23. Pagden, "Struggle for Legitimacy," 43.
24. Fitzmaurice, "Discovery, Conquest and the Occupation of Territory."
25. Fernández-Armesto, *Pathfinders*, 306; Bleichmar, *Visible Empire*.
26. Schiebinger and Swan, *Colonial Botany*, 1, 5; Richard Drayton, "Knowledge and Empire," in Marshall, *Oxford History*, vol. II, 250.
27. Neil Safier, "Fruitless Botany: Joseph de Jussieu's South American Odyssey," in Delbourgo and Dew, *Science and Empire*, 219; and, more generally, Safier, *Measuring the New World;* Lafuente and Valverde, "Linnaean Botany and Spanish Imperial Biopolitics," in Schiebinger and Swan, *Colonial Botany*, 141; Antonio Lafuente, "Enlightenment in an Imperial Context: Local Science in the Late Eighteenth-century Hispanic World," in MacLeod, *Nature and Empire*, 166.

5. Consolidation, Conflict, and Reform in the Long Eighteenth Century

1. Olivares quotation in Parker, *Europe in Crisis*, 256; McKay and Scott, *Great Powers*, 3–6; there is a less triumphant reading of Westphalia, which dismisses it as a breakthrough and contends that it instead marked "the recognition and regulation of the international—or, to be more precise, inter-dynastic—relations of absolutist, dynastic polities." See Teschke, *The Myth of 1648*, 2–3.
2. Findlay and O'Rourke, *Power and Plenty*, 245–246; Colbert quotation in Williams, *From Columbus to Castro*, 161; Frederick William (Elector of Brandenburg and Duke of Prussia) quotation in McKay and Scott, *Great Powers*, 36.
3. Brewer, *Sinews of Power*, 11.
4. Pincus, *Protestantism and Patriotism*, 75.
5. Boxer, *Dutch in Brazil*, 190–191; Thornton, *Kingdom of Kongo*, 73–76; Boxer, *Portuguese Seaborne Empire;* Disney, *Portugal*.
6. Quotation in Ames, *Renascent Empire*, 12; on the decision to focus on Brazil, see Winius, "India or Brazil?" 8–9.
7. De Vries and van der Woude, *First Modern Economy*, 117–119; Holland contained 40 percent of the population and accounted for 60 percent of the wealth of the Dutch Republic in the late seventeenth century. See Price, *Dutch Republic*, 69.

8. Israel, *Dutch Republic,* 936; Klooster, *Illicit Riches,* 1–14 passim; de Vries and van der Woude, *First Modern Economy,* 428–429.
9. Fisher, *Economic Aspects,* 87–88; Parker, *Military Revolution,* 62; Collins, *The State in Early Modern France,* 199; Brewer, *Sinews of Power,* 27.
10. Brewer, *Sinews of Power,* 154; Scott, *Birth of a Great Power System,* 16.
11. For an overview and analysis, see Reinert, *Translating Empire.*
12. Drayton, *Nature's Government,* 91–92, 99.
13. On the Glorious Revolution, see Pincus, *1688.*
14. Disney, *Portugal;* Kennedy, *British Naval Mastery,* 86.
15. P. J. Marshall, "Introduction," in Marshall, *Oxford History,* vol. II, 22.
16. McNeill, *Atlantic Empires,* 68; Storrs, *The Spanish Resurgence;* Kuethe, *Cuba,* 4–5.
17. Bethell, *Colonial Brazil;* Boxer, *Golden Age in Brazil.*
18. Boxer, *Portuguese Seaborne Empire;* Russell-Wood, *Portuguese Empire,* 185.
19. Boxer, *Golden Age in Brazil,* 323; Alencastro, *Trato dos viventes,* 250–251, 324–325, 354.
20. Black, *British Seaborne Empire;* and Black, *Fighting for America.*
21. Quotation in Tombs, *That Sweet Enemy,* 154.
22. Paquette, *Enlightenment, Governance, and Reform;* Andrien and Kuethe, *Spanish Atlantic World.*
23. Brading, "Bourbon Spain," 416; Andrien and Kuethe, *Spanish Atlantic World;* McFarlane, *Colombia before Independence.*
24. McKinley, *Pre-Revolutionary Caracas,* 37; McFarlane, *Colombia before Independence,* 151; Thomson, *We Alone Will Rule,* 247; Brading, *Miners and Merchants,* 29; Gálvez quotation in Weber, *Bárbaros,* 162; Marichal, *Bankruptcy of Empire,* 257.
25. Maxwell, *Pombal,* 24; Maxwell, *Conflicts and Conspiracies.*
26. Vergennes quotation in Tombs, *That Sweet Enemy,* 162.
27. Dull, *Diplomatic History;* Ferreiro, *Brothers at Arms;* Quintero Saravia, *Bernardo de Gálvez;* Gaastra, *Dutch East India Company,* 148, 170; de Vries and van der Woude, *First Modern Economy,* 455.
28. Blanning, *Pursuit of Glory,* 594 (quotation), 602; Collins, *The State in Early Modern France,* 311; Soll, *Reckoning.*
29. Black, *British Seaborne Empire,* 137–139; Jasanoff, *Liberty's Exiles.*
30. This account draws heavily on Bayly, *Indian Society,* 44–47; Jasanoff, *Edge of Empire,* 31.
31. Levine, *British Empire,* 67–68.
32. Dundas quotation in McAleer, *Britain's Maritime Empire,* 9.

6. Law, Governance, and Institutional Frameworks

1. John H. Elliott, "Iberian Empires," in Scott, *Oxford Handbook*, 211; Philip II quotation in Haring, *Spanish Empire*, 5–6.
2. Ford, *Settler Sovereignty;* Virginia Company quotation in Darwin, *Unfinished Empire*, 69; not all commentators concurred, including William Blackstone, the preeminent British jurist of the eighteenth century, who considered the American colonies conquered or ceded countries and thus not incorporated into the common law of England. See Gould, "Zones of Law," 497–498; Darwin, *Unfinished Empire*, 68; Elliott, *Empires of the Atlantic World*, 143; Steele, *English Atlantic*, 230.
3. Leonard Blussé, "Northern European Empire in Asia: The VOC," in Scott, *Oxford Handbook*, 236, 245; Furber, *Rival Empires*, 190–191; This distinction between Europeans and non-Europeans sharpened in the British Empire as well. From 1793, the EIC determined that all civil appointments, except the most menial, would be held by "covenanted" servants, all of whom were of European origin.
4. Hernández Chávez, *Mexico*, 38.
5. Quotation in Thompson, "Castile," 87.
6. Elliott, "Spain and Its Empire in the Sixteenth and Seventeenth Centuries," in Elliott, *Spain and Its World*, 15; Solórzano quotation in Cañeque, *King's Living Image*, 17.
7. Phelan, *Kingdom of Quito*, 124.
8. Castillo de Bobadilla quotation in Haring, *Spanish Empire*, 114–115; Phelan, "Authority and Flexibility," 47–65.
9. This and the following paragraphs draw on, inter alia, Skidmore, *Brazil;* Lockhart and Schwartz, *Early Latin America;* Burkholder and Johnson, *Colonial Latin America;* Disney, *Portugal;* and Newitt, *Portuguese Overseas Expansion.*
10. Bailyn, *Barbarous Years*, 123; quotation in Ford, *Settler Sovereignty*, 16.
11. Eccles, *French in North America*, 29–30; Lehning, *European Colonialism*, 23; de Vries, "Dutch Atlantic Economy," 15.
12. Steele, *Warpaths*, 73–76; Havard and Vidal, *Histoire*, 101.
13. Governor-General Jan Pieterzoon Coen quotation in Parker, *Military Revolution*, 132; Ward, *Networks of Empire*, 16–17; directors' quotation in Boxer, *Dutch Seaborne Empire*, 45–46.
14. Burke quotation in Thomson, *Mercenaries, Pirates, and Sovereigns*, 32; Philip J. Stern, "Company, State and Empire: Governance and Regulating Frameworks in Asia," in Bowen, Mancke, and Reid, *British Oceanic Empire*, 135; more generally, see Stern, *Company State.*

15. Susan Elizabeth Ramirez, "Institutions of the Spanish Empire in the Habsburg Era," in Holloway, *Companion*, 106–123; Lynch, *New Worlds*, 108; Lane and Restall, *Riddle of Colonial Latin America*, 105.
16. Boxer, *Portuguese Seaborne Empire;* Newitt, *Portuguese Overseas Expansion;* Disney, *Portugal.*
17. Burkholder and Johnson, *Colonial Latin America;* Sarreal, *Guaraní and Their Missions*, 1, 3; Boxer, *Portuguese Seaborne Empire;* Cohen, *The Fire of Tongues;* Alden, *Making of an Enterprise.*
18. Brading, *First America*, 183, 467; Weber, *Bárbaros*, 119; Thomas Cohen and Emmanuele Colombo, "Jesuit Missions," in Scott, *Oxford Handbook*, 265.
19. Bethencourt, *Inquisition*, 441, 35.
20. Ruth Behar, "Sexual Witchcraft, Colonialism and Women's Powers: Views from the Mexican Inquisition," in Lavrin, *Sexuality and Marriage*, 200; Berkin, *First Generations*, 46; Schwartz, *All Can Be Saved*, 237; in Spain, the Inquisition was abolished only in 1834, though the Cortes of Cádiz had abolished it in 1813.
21. On the doctrine of "repugnancy," see Darwin, *Unfinished Empire*, 74; Pettigrew, *Freedom's Debt*, 24.
22. Elliott, *Empires of the Atlantic World*, 133.
23. Marshall, "Eighteenth-Century Empire," 180.
24. Carmagnani, *The Other West*, 76; Boxer, *Portuguese Society in the Tropics*, 9–10, 41; Boxer, *Golden Age*, 148–149.
25. Figures taken based on New Spain. See Cañeque, *King's Living Image*, 17; Parry, *Spanish Seaborne Empire;* Elliott, *Empires of the Atlantic World.*
26. On legal pluralism in general, see Benton, *Law and Colonial Cultures;* Premo, *Enlightenment on Trial*, 359; Hernández Chávez, *Mexico*, 38; Robert Travers, "Constitutions, Contact Zones, and Imperial Ricochets: Sovereignty and Law in British India," in Bowen, Mancke, and Reid, *British Oceanic Empire*, 98–129; Lehning, *European Colonialism*, 126.
27. Quotation in Darwin, *Unfinished Empire*, 75.
28. Ferreira, *Cross-Cultural Exchange*, 99; note that in the Quimbundu language, *mucano* means "litigation"; Lane and Restall, *Riddle of Colonial Latin America*, 77; Yannakakis, *Art of Being In-Between*, 29.

7. The Political Economy of Empire and Its Consequences

1. Raynal, *Philosophical and Political History*, vol. I, 1.
2. Russell-Wood, *Portuguese Empire*, 128.
3. Leonard Blussé, "Northern European Empire in Asia: The VOC," in Scott, *Oxford Handbook*, 236.

4. Colley, *Captives,* 246; Chaudhuri, *Trading World of Asia,* 96–97; Berg, *Luxury and Pleasure,* 56; Crosby, *Columbian Exchange,* 170; Norton, *Sacred Gifts, Profane Pleasures.*
5. Jorge Pedreira, "Costs and Financial Trends in the Portuguese Empire, 1415–1822," in Bethencourt and Curto, *Portuguese Oceanic Expansion,* 70; Elliott, *Empires of the Atlantic World,* 95, 100; Yun-Casalilla and Comín, "Spain," 263.
6. Quotation in McCusker and Menard, *Economy,* 119; Reid Andrews, *Afro-Latin America,* 19; Hoefte and Vrij, "Free Black and Colored Women," 146.
7. Steve Pincus has contested the view that there was ever a moment of unambiguous "mercantilist consensus": "The claim that early moderns believed that trade was a barbaric battle among competing nation-states . . . was only a partial truth." See Pincus, "Rethinking Mercantilism," 14–15, 32; Frost, *Global Reach of Empire,* 269–281 (quotation 281).
8. Davenant quotation in Nuala Zahedieh, "Economy," in Armitage and Braddick, *British Atlantic World,* 52; Darwin, *Unfinished Empire,* 14–15; Lynch, *Spain under the Habsburgs,* vol. I, 157; quotation in Lockhart and Schwartz, *Early Latin America,* 64.
9. Stein and Stein, *Silver, Trade, and War,* 57; Andrien and Kuethe, *Spanish Atlantic World,* 70.
10. Schwartz, *Sugar Plantations,* 183.
11. Parry, *European Hegemony,* 142; though note that England granted exceptions for the export of slaves as early as the 1660s and, a century later, created "free ports" where foreign subjects could legally purchase slaves and manufactured goods. See O'Malley, *Final Passages,* 13.
12. Findlay and O'Rourke, *Power and Plenty,* 183; Boxer, *Dutch Seaborne Empire,* 46; Levine, *British Empire,* 64.
13. On "improvement," economic botany, and scientific agriculture more generally, see Drayton, *Nature's Government;* Matsuda, *Pacific Worlds,* 141; Bleichmar, "Atlantic Competitions," 225–228.
14. Drayton, "Globalisation of France," 428; de Vries, "Limits of Globalization," 724–725.
15. Kwass, *Contraband,* 357; Kwass, "Global Underground," 18.
16. Kenneth Morgan, "Anglo-Dutch Economic Relations in the Atlantic World, 1688–1783," in Oostindie and Roitman, *Dutch Atlantic Connections,* 128–129, 134–135; Røge, "Why the Danes Got There First," 4; Dubois, *Colony of Citizens,* 48.

17. Richard Drayton, "The Collaboration of Labour: Slaves, Empires, and Globalizations in the Atlantic World, c. 1600–1850," in Hopkins, *Globalization,* 104; on the problem of "drawing up balance sheets of imperialism," see Adas, "'High' Imperialism," 326–327.
18. Williams, *From Columbus to Castro,* 163; Zahedieh, *Capital and Colonies,* 237.
19. De Vries, "Dutch Atlantic Economies," 12; Philip Boucher, "French and Dutch Caribbean 1600–1800," in Palmié and Scarano, *Caribbean,* 219.
20. Williams, *Capitalism and Slavery;* Draper, *Price of Emancipation,* 4, 103, 202; Port city populations taken from Doyle, *Old European Order,* 32.
21. Drayton, "Collaboration of Labour," 102. To these observations might be added that, "to the extent possible, the labor force was composed of interchangeable units." See Mintz, *Sweetness and Power,* 51; on Mexico, see Tutino, *Making a New World.*
22. Boxer, *Golden Age,* 189.
23. Havard and Vidal, *Histoire,* 461; Calloway, *New Worlds for All,* 16; Parker, *Global Interactions,* 174.
24. Melville, *Plague of Sheep;* Dean, *With Broadax and Firebrand.*
25. Miller, *Environmental History,* 81–82; quotation in Antonil, *Brazil,* 76.
26. Blussé, "Northern European Empire," 249; Cronon, *Changes in the Land,* 120–121; Calloway, *New Worlds for All,* 19; Parker, *Global Interactions,* 162.
27. Cronon, *Changes in the Land,* 126; Schwartz, *Sea of Storms,* 86–87, 96; McGregor, "Contemporary Caribbean Ecologies: The Weight of History," in Palmié and Scarano, *Caribbean,* 41.
28. Grove, *Green Imperialism,* 10–11; Pádua, *Sopro de destruição,* 67.

8. Imperial Migrations

1. Rodney, *How Europe Underdeveloped Africa,* 95; Eltis, "Coerced and Free Migrations," 36.
2. Klein, *Atlantic Slave Trade,* 56; Lovejoy, *Transformations,* 44.
3. Walvin, *Crossings,* 54, 125; Postma, *Atlantic Slave Trade,* 36–41; the various figures are constantly being updated (upward); for the most recent, see the Transatlantic Slave Trade Database (TSTD): http://www.slavevoyages.org.
4. Curtin, *Rise and Fall of the Plantation Complex.*
5. Russell-Wood, *Portuguese Empire;* Newitt, *Portuguese Overseas Empire;* Schmidt-Nowara, *Slavery, Freedom, and Abolition;* Green, *Rise of the Transatlantic Slave Trade;* Scammell, *First Imperial Age,* 228.
6. Schwartz, *Sugar Plantations;* Thornton, *Cultural History;* Schmidt-Nowara, *Slavery, Freedom, and Abolition.*

7. Reid Andrews, *Afro-Latin America*, 19; Klein and Vinson, *African Slavery*. It should be noted that Africa was not the only source of slaves. Enslaved people in South and Southeast Asia were transported to the Spanish Philippines from Mexico, where they were classified as "Chinos," as analyzed in Seijas, *Asian Slaves;* Joyce Chaplin, "The British Atlantic," in Morgan and Greene, *Oxford Handbook*, 222; Pritchard, *In Search of Empire*, 70; Silvia Marzagalli, "The French Atlantic World in the Seventeenth and Eighteenth Centuries," in Morgan and Greene, *Oxford Handbook*, 241.
8. Quotation in Thomas, *Slave Trade*, 324; note, however, as David Northrup has argued, that the "guns-for-slaves" transaction occurred largely in areas where African states were militarizing, and certainly was not prevalent everywhere. See Northrup, *Africa's Discovery of Europe*, 99; Lovejoy, *Transformations in Slavery*, 106; Davis, *Problem of Slavery*, 154.
9. Lovejoy, *Transformations in Slavery*, 104.
10. Thornton, *Africa and Africans*, 125; Thomas, *Slave Trade*, 344–345; Lovejoy, *Transformations in Slavery;* quotation in Sparks, *Where the Negroes Are Masters*, 196.
11. Quotation in Rushforth, *Bonds of Alliance*, 101; Lovejoy, *Transformations in Slavery*, 98–99.
12. The funereal comparison was also found in the Lusophone world, where slave ships were called *tumbeiros*, or hearses; Wilberforce quotation in Postma, *Atlantic Slave Trade*, 13; Thornton, *Africa and Africans*, 156; more generally, Rediker, *Slave Ship*.
13. This paragraph draws on Klein, *Atlantic Slave Trade*, Rediker, *Slave Ship*, Postma, *Atlantic Slave Trade*.
14. Rediker, *Slave Ship*, 227–229, 239; O'Malley, *Final Passages*, 7.
15. Beckles, "Plantation Production and White 'Proto-Slavery,'" 166; Elliott, *Empires of the Atlantic World*, 55; Boucher, *France and the American Tropics*, 145, 149.
16. Northrup, *Indentured Labor*, 63; Lai, *Indentured Labor*, 30–31; Yun, *The Coolie Speaks*, 7.
17. Coates, *Convicts and Orphans*, 183; Ekirch, *Bound for America*, 1, 27; Swingen, *Competing Visions of Empire*, 21.
18. Robertson, *History of America*, vol. I, 193.
19. Hoerder, *Cultures in Contact*, 231.
20. Anderson, "Convict Passages," 129; Taylor, "1848 Revolutions and the British Empire," 153–159; Clancy-Smith, *Mediterraneans*, 95–96.

21. Canny, "In Search of a Better Home?" 265, 269; Jan Lucassen, "Emigration to the Dutch Colonies and the USA," in Cohen, *Cambridge Survey of Migration,* 23–25; Michael Heffernan, "French Colonial Migration," in ibid., 34–35; Gainot, *L'empire colonial Français,* 24; Elliott, *Empires of the Atlantic World,* 56; Hoerder, *Cultures in Contact,* 222.
22. James Horn, "British Diaspora: Emigration from Britain, 1680–1815," in Marshall, *Oxford History,* vol. III, 49; Alison Games, "Migration," in Armitage and Braddick, *British Atlantic World,* 48.
23. Stern, *Company State,* 35–38; Cook, *Matters of Exchange,* 177–178; Boxer, *Dutch Seaborne Empire,* 81.
24. Jennifer M. Spear, "'They Need Wives': *Métissage* and the Regulation of Sexuality in French Louisiana, 1699–1730," in Hodes, *Sex, Love, Race,* 46; Clancy-Smith, *Mediterraneans,* 90.

9. Labor Regimes

1. Fisher, "Working across the Seas"; Amrith, *Crossing the Bay of Bengal;* Bonil Gómez, "Political Culture."
2. Hochschild, *Bury the Chains,* 223–225.
3. Burkholder and Johnson, *Colonial Latin America,* 14–59 passim; Sarreal, *Guaraní and Their Missions,* 3, 89; It should be noted that encomiendas were not hereditary without the permission of the Crown.
4. Reséndez, *The Other Slavery,* 137; Schwartz, *Sugar Plantations;* Metcalf, *Family and Frontier,* 45, 53; Hoerder, *Cultures in Contact,* 245; Hemming, *Red Gold,* 421.
5. Rushforth, *Bonds of Alliance,* 10, 70; Parker, *Global Interactions,* 115–116; Morgan, "Caribbean Slavery," 70; Warren, *New England Bound.*
6. These factors are discussed in Thornton, *Africa and Africans,* 135–137.
7. Bethencourt, *Racisms,* 6–8; Nirenberg, "Was There Race before Modernity?" 260; converso families were held in suspicion, as it was believed that their blood was tainted indelibly, thus foreclosing study at universities, positions in cathedral chapters, and membership in various military orders; see Ruiz, *Spanish Society;* Davis, *Inhuman Bondage,* 59; Wood, *Origins of American Slavery,* 10.
8. Wey Gómez, *Why Columbus Sailed South;* Russell-Wood, *Black Man;* Godwyn quotation in Wood, *Origins of American Slavery,* 5.
9. Stuart Schwartz, "Plantations and Peripheries, c. 1580–1750," in Bethell, *Colonial Brazil;* Greene, *Pursuits of Happiness,* 160; Morgan, *Slave Counterpoint,* 44, 101.

10. Berlin, *Many Thousands Gone;* Philip Boucher, "French and Dutch Caribbean, 1600–1800," in Palmié and Scarano, *Caribbean,* 219; Beckert, *Empire of Cotton,* 88–90; Morgan, "Caribbean Slavery," 76.
11. Elliott, *Empires of the Atlantic World,* 104, 100.
12. Johnson, *Workshop of Revolution,* 41–42; Berlin, *Many Thousands Gone,* 179; Bolster, *Black Jacks,* 18; Philip Morgan, "British Encounters with Africans and African-Americans, c. 1600–1780," in Bailyn and Morgan, *Strangers within the Realm,* 191–192.
13. Alden, *Making of an Enterprise,* 526; Heywood and Thornton, *Central Africans,* 186; Alden, *Making of an Enterprise,* held that this figure struck him as inflated, but he did not offer an alternative estimate, 515–516; St. Clair, *Grand Slave Emporium,* 242–243; Napoleon quotation in Dubois, *Avengers of the New World,* 259. Napoleon ultimately tried to reimpose slavery in Saint-Domingue, which hastened the final expulsion of the French.
14. Quotation in Hilary McD. Beckles, "Social and Political Control in the Slave Society," in Knight, *General History,* 201; more generally, Davis, *Problem of Slavery,* 248–253; Knight, *The Caribbean,* 119.
15. Schmidt-Nowara, *Slavery, Freedom, and Abolition;* Bryant, *Rivers of Gold,* 8.
16. Schmidt-Nowara, *Slavery, Freedom, and Abolition.*
17. Iliffe, *Africans,* 128; Gould, "Prelude," 34; Craton, *Testing the Chains,* 138.
18. Schmidt-Nowara, *Slavery, Freedom, and Abolition;* Klein and Vinson, *African Slavery in Latin America;* Russell-Wood, *Black Man;* Rowe, "'After Death Her Face Turned White'"; Morgan, *Short History,* 83–84; Seeman, *Death in the New World;* on "mortuary politics" in Jamaica, see Brown, *Reaper's Garden.*
19. Schmidt-Nowara, *Empire and Antislavery;* Bethell, *Abolition;* Murray, *Odious Commerce;* Blackburn, *Overthrow.*
20. Williams, *Capitalism and Slavery;* Drescher, *Abolition;* Christopher Brown, "The Politics of Slavery," in Armitage and Braddick, *British Atlantic World,* 230; see also Brown, *Moral Capital.*
21. Blackburn, *Overthrow of Colonial Slavery,* 520.
22. Franklin Knight, "The Disintegration of Caribbean Slave Systems, 1772–1886," in Knight, *General History;* Outram, *Enlightenment.*
23. Rik van Welie, "What Happened in the Colonies Stayed in the Colonies: The Dutch and the Slave-Free Paradox," in Misevich and Mann, *Rise and Demise of Slavery,* 115; Davis, *Inhuman Bondage,* 248; Christopher L. Brown, "Abolition of the Atlantic Slave Trade," in Burnard and Heuman, *Routledge History,* 285.

24. Lynch, *Simón Bolívar,* 108; Blanchard, *Under the Flags of Freedom,* 36; Reid Andrews, *Afro-Latin America.*
25. Drescher, *Abolition,* 257, 264; Walvin, *Crossings,* 162–163; Draper, *Price of Emancipation,* 106–107.

10. Creole Societies, Mestizaje, *and the Regulation of Hybridity*

1. Subrahmanyan, *Portuguese Empire,* 276; Green, *Rise of the Transatlantic Slave Trade;* Fisher, *First Indian Author in English,* 254–256; Morgan, "British Encounters," 205.
2. Quotation in Graubart, *With Our Labor and Sweat,* 13.
3. Quotation in Boxer, "The Problem of the Native Clergy," 181; Boxer, *Church Militant,* 9.
4. Jennifer Spear, "'They Need Wives': *Métissage* and the Regulation of Sexuality in French Louisiana, 1699–1730," in Hodes, *Sex, Love, Race,* 40–41; Ghosh, *Sex and the Family,* 40.
5. As historian Laurent Dubois noted, "Saint-Domingue was a schizophrenic society in which the law attacked relationships between those of European and African descent even as the whites who supported such laws continuously flouted them." See Dubois, *Avengers,* 68; Bethencourt, *Racisms,* 213, 215; Ghosh, *Sex and the Family,* 3, 30; Peter Bardaglio, "'Shameful Matches': The Regulation of Interracial Sex and Marriage in the South before 1900," in Hodes, *Sex, Love, Race,* 114–115; Fisher and O'Hara, *Imperial Subjects,* 3; quotation in Russell-Wood, *Black Man in Slavery and Freedom,* 31.
6. On the use of animal metaphors, see Bethencourt, *Racisms,* 165; Fradera traced the term "casta" to Portuguese Jesuits who used it to describe the social divisions of India in the sixteenth century, thus highlighting the interimperial genesis of racialized nomenclature. See Fradera, "Spain," 57; on the lesser-known castas, see Vinson, *Before Mestizaje;* Katzew, *Casta Painting,* 201.
7. Bethencourt, *Racisms,* 177; Schwartz noted that this term fell into disuse when Indian slavery ended, thus further sharpening the link between blackness and slavery in the Ibero-American mind. See Schwartz, *Sugar Plantations,* 52
8. An alleged taint could take many forms. As María Elena Martínez observed with regard to colonial Mexico, "Multiple, overlapping and even competing discourses of blood purity operated . . . some stressed Christian bloodlines, some Spanish ancestry and some skin color"; see Martínez, *Genealogical Fictions,* 270; John Garrigus, "Free Coloureds," in Burnard and Heuman, *Routledge History,* 239.

9. Quotation in Ralph Bauer and José Antonio Mazzotti, "Introduction: Creole Subjects in the Colonial Americas," in Bauer and Mazzotti, *Creole Subjects,* 4; Jefferson, "Notes on Virginia," in Jefferson, *Political Writings,* 506–507.
10. Russell-Wood, *Black Man,* 67–68; DuPlessis, *Material Atlantic,* 194.
11. Earle, *Body of the Conquistador,* 67–75 passim; Crosby, *Columbian Exchange,* 79, 89; Darwin, *Unfinished Empire,* 56.
12. Hoefte and Vrij, "Free Black and Colored Women," 147.
13. The material in the previous two paragraphs is derived, inter alia, from Berlin, *Many Thousands Gone,* 187; Morgan, "British Encounters," 192; Bethencourt, *Racisms,* 215; Geggus, "Slaves and Free People of Color," 104, 107; Garrigus, "Free Coloureds," 239; Bowser, "Colonial Spanish America," 52.
14. Landers, *Black Society,* 201; Russell-Wood, *Black Man,* 23–24, 44.
15. Vinson, *Bearing Arms for His Majesty;* Ferreira, *Cross-Cultural Exchange,* 154; Geggus, "Slaves and Free People of Color," 106; O'Shaughnessy, *Empire Divided,* 175; Landers, *Atlantic Creoles,* 145–147.
16. Israel, *Dutch Republic,* 952–955.
17. O'Shaughnessy, *An Empire Divided,* 30; Carla Gardina Pestana, "Religion," in Armitage and Braddick, *British Atlantic World,* 84.
18. Getz and Streets-Salter, *Empires and Colonies,* 148; Lyman Johnson and Susan Socolow, "Colonial Spanish South America," in Moya, *Oxford Handbook,* 68; Rachel S. O'Toole, "Religion, Society and Culture in the Colonial Era," in Holloway, *Companion,* 162–177; Pagden, *European Encounters,* 119.
19. Sweet, *Recreating Africa,* 227; This view is contested by Thornton: "Lacking the ethnic and cultural specificity necessary to maintain or recreate their African culture in the Americas, the slaves necessarily had to form a new culture." See Thornton, *Africa and Africans,* 184.
20. Mello e Souza, *Devil and the Land of the Holy Cross,* 130.
21. Hilton, *Kingdom of Kongo,* 93–94, 102; Heywood and Thornton, *Central Africans,* 188; Thornton, "Afro-Christian Syncretism," 77.
22. Gruzinski, *The Mestizo Mind,* 63.

11. Collaboration, Resistance, and the Fortunes of Empire

1. Taylor, "Two Shrines," 971; Scott, *Weapons of the Weak,* xvi.
2. Mark Meuwese, "The Opportunities and Limits of Ethnic Soldiering: The Tupis and the Dutch-Portuguese Struggle for the South Atlantic, 1630–1657," in Lee, *Empires and Indigenes,* 202–206; more generally, for the Caribbean, Whitehead, "Carib Ethnic Soldiering"; Thornton, "Kingdom of

Kongo and the Thirty Years' War"; Stuart B. Schwartz and Hal Langfur, "*Tapanhuns, Negros da Terra* and *Curibocas:* Common Cause and Confrontation between Blacks and Natives in Colonial Brazil," in Restall, *Beyond Black and Red,* 92–93; Lynch, *New Worlds,* 50.

3. Colley, *Captives,* 252–260 passim; Roy, *Oxford Companion;* Alavi, *Sepoys and the Company;* Bayly, *Empire and Information,* 365.
4. Kevin Terraciano, "Indigenous Peoples in Colonial Spanish American Society," in Holloway, *Companion,* 126 (quotation), 135; Garrett, "'His Majesty's Loyal Vassals,'" 580, 617; Owensby, *Empire of Law,* 300–301; such consciousness had important consequences in the Age of Revolutions; see Echeverri, *Indian and Slave Royalists.*
5. White, *Middle Ground,* 25–26; Steele, *Warpaths,* 76; Barr, *Peace Came in the Form of a Woman,* 88; since Amerindian-Spanish intermarriage was commonplace elsewhere, this case may be anomalous.
6. Egerton et al., *Atlantic World,* 160; Colley, *Captives,* 144.
7. Weber, *Bárbaros,* 12, 61, 72, 164–165; Hämäläinen, *Comanche Empire,* 7; Barr, *Peace Came in the Form of a Woman,* 8; Levaggi, *Diplomacia Hispano-Indígena.*
8. Carmagnani, *The Other West,* 78; Owensby, *Empire of Law,* 26.
9. Taylor, *American Colonies,* 92–93, quotation on 291.
10. Quotation in Darwin, *Unfinished Empire,* 82.
11. Duval, *Independence Lost,* 223, 258; Daniel Richter, "Native Peoples of North America in the Eighteenth-Century British Empire," in Marshall, *Oxford History,* vol. III, 368.
12. Farriss, *Maya Society,* 394; Graubart, *With Our Labor and Sweat,* 188; Bailyn, *Barbarous Years,* 30.
13. Stern, "Age of Andean Insurrection," 35; Bakewell, *Latin America,* 277; Thomson, "Sovereignty Disavowed"; Andrien, *Andean Worlds,* 193–225 passim.
14. Rediker, *Villains of All Nations,* 16–17, 29; Ogborn, *Global Lives,* 178; Matsuda, *Pacific Worlds,* 112–113; Frykman, "Pirates and Smugglers," 224.
15. Skidmore, *Brazil;* Fausto, *Brazil;* Lockhart and Schwartz, *Early Latin America.*
16. In a New World context, *cimarrón* originally referred to domesticated cattle that had escaped to the hills of Hispaniola. It soon became applied to Indian slaves who had absconded. By 1530, it was a description for refugee African slaves and carried strong negative connotations. See Price, "Introduction: The Maroons and Their Communities," in Price, *Maroon Societies,* 1–2, n. 1.

17. Klein and Vinson, *African Slavery,* 179–183; Boxer, *Golden Age,* 170; Schwartz, *Slaves, Peasants and Rebels,* 104–125 (quotation on 109).
18. Craton, *Testing the Chains,* 147; Michael Craton, "Forms of Resistance to Slavery," in Knight, *General History,* 257.
19. Gabriel Debien, "Marronage in the French Caribbean," in Price, *Maroon Societies,* 107–134; Andrew O'Shaughnessy, "Redcoats and Slaves in the British Caribbean," in Paquette and Engerman, *Lesser Antilles,* 112; Geggus, *A Turbulent Time.*
20. Colley, *Captives,* 273.
21. Morgan, "British Encounters," 195–196; Andrien, "Quito Insurrection"; Phelan, *The People and the King;* McFarlane, "Rebellion."
22. Maxwell, *Conflicts and Conspiracies;* Childs, "Secret and Spectral."
23. Maxwell, "The Idea of the Luso-Brazilian Empire," in Maxwell, *Naked Tropics.*
24. O'Shaughnessy, *An Empire Divided,* 9, 20–21, 29, 56–57.
25. Burkholder and Johnson, *Colonial Latin America,* 267–268; Wilder, *Ebony and Ivory;* on cultural efflorescence in eighteenth-century Spanish American cities, see Lucena-Giraldo, *A los quatro vientos.*
26. Paquette, *Enlightenment, Governance, and Reform,* 127–151; Wright, *Cultural Life,* 148; Gould, "Prelude," 27.
27. Brading, "Bourbon Spain"; Burkholder and Chandler, *From Impotence to Authority;* Walker, *Shaky Colonialism,* 13.
28. Manuel del Soccoro Rodríguez quotation in McFarlane, "American Revolution," 43–44.

12. The Age of Revolutions

1. Armitage, *Declaration of Independence,* 38–39 (Vattel quotation); 141.
2. Armitage, "American Revolution in Atlantic Perspective," in Morgan and Canny, *Oxford Handbook,* 528; Adelman, "An Age of Imperial Revolutions," 320, 332.
3. Elliott, *Empires of the Atlantic World,* 383.
4. R. R. Palmer, *Age of Democratic Revolution,* 21; Bayly, *Recovering Liberties,* 43–46, 71; Bayly, "The 'Revolutionary Age' in the Wider World," 30–31.
5. Levine, *British Empire,* 37–40; Marshall, *Remaking the British Atlantic,* 283 (quotation), 7; it should be recalled that leading British (and Irish) politicians, notably Edmund Burke, were sympathetic to the colonists' viewpoint, holding that the colonies could not be considered represented if the preferences of their assemblies were disregarded. See Bourke, *Empire and Revolution,* 297.

6. Black, *British Seaborne Empire,* 135–137; Scott, *British Foreign Policy;* Simms, *Three Victories,* 678.
7. Geggus, "Introduction," in Geggus, *Haitian Revolution;* Dubois, *Avengers of the New World;* James, *Black Jacobins;* "Free Citizens of Color. Address to the National Assembly" (October 22, 1789), in Dubois and Garrigus, *Slave Revolution,* 69.
8. Laurent Dubois, "The Haitian Revolution," in Palmié and Scarano, *The Caribbean,* 283.
9. "Dessalines' Proclamation" (April 28, 1804), in Geggus, *Haitian Revolution,* 182; the text of the 1805 constitution is found in Dubois and Garrigus, *Slave Revolution,* 192–194.
10. William Wordsworth, "To Toussaint L'Ouverture" (1803), in Geggus, *Haitian Revolution,* 202; Bethell, *Colonial Brazil.*
11. Quotation in Marks, "Confronting a Mercantile Elite," 525; Kuethe, *Cuba,* 5, 128, 149–151.
12. Adelman, *Sovereignty and Revolution;* for an overview of the historiography, see Paquette, "Dissolution"; Lucena-Giraldo, *Naciones de rebeldes;* Hamnett, *End of Iberian Rule;* McFarlane, *War and Independence,* 410.
13. Colley, "Empires of Writing."
14. This period is covered in Barman, *Brazil;* and Schultz, *Tropical Versailles.*
15. Reid Andrews, "Structural"; Maxwell, "Why Was Brazil Different?" in Maxwell, *Naked Tropics.*
16. Barman, *Brazil.*
17. Paquette, *Imperial Portugal.*
18. Jasanoff, *Liberty's Exiles,* 8–9, 201; Ferrer, *Freedom's Mirror,* 49.
19. Goldstone, *Revolution,* 4; Bayly, "Revolutionary Age," 40.
20. Edward Watts to George Canning, May 9, 1824, in Humphreys, *British Consular Reports,* 265; for an important study of the early postindependence period in northern South America, see Brown, *Struggle for Power.*

Epilogue. Continuities and Disjunctures

1. Headrick, *Tools of Empire,* 3, 177, 22; Black, *British Seaborne Empire,* 204.
2. Headrick, *Tools of Empire,* 64–67.
3. Harlow, *Founding of the Second British Empire;* Clarence-Smith, *Third Portuguese Empire.*
4. Bayly, *Imperial Meridian,* 8, 137; the new language of and belief in statistics, it should be noted, buttressed older aspirations to uniformity, centralization,

and efficiency, as shown in Laidlaw, *Colonial Connections,* 189–197 passim; Grab, *Napoleon,* x, 21; Coller, *Arab France,* 29.

5. Levine, *British Empire,* 51, 57; Metcalf and Metcalf, *Modern India,* 75.
6. Castlereagh and Canning, both quoted in Winn, "British Informal Empire," 102; on the utility of "informal empire" for British–Latin American relations more generally, see Brown, *Informal Empire.*
7. Dawson, *First Latin American Debt Crisis,* 1–2; Centeno, *Blood and Debt,* 132; more generally, Miller, *Britain and Latin America,* 34–41; Centeno, *Blood and Debt,* 132, 156–158; Gallagher and Robinson, "Imperialism of Free Trade," 7.
8. Cain and Hopkins, *British Imperialism,* 44.
9. Bethell, *Abolition,* 31, 46–60; on mixed commissions, see Martinez, "Anti-Slavery Courts"; on the British role in the abolition of the Brazilian slave trade, see Needell, "Abolition of the Brazilian Slave Trade"; Hyam, *Britain's Imperial Century,* 15.
10. Christopher L. Brown, "Abolition of the Atlantic Slave Trade," in Burnard and Heuman, *Routledge History,* 293; Hopkins, *Economic History of West Africa,* 128–129; Headrick, *Tools of Empire,* 106; Huzzey, "The Politics of Slave-Trade Suppression," 36; Lynn, "British Policy," 101–121.
11. Hyam, *Britain's Imperial Century,* 101; Palmerston quotation in Darwin, *Unfinished Empire,* 29; Matsuda, *Pacific Worlds,* 193; Bayly, *Birth of Modern World,* 151; Meyer-Fong, *What Remains.*
12. Matsuda, *Pacific Worlds,* 200; Wesseling, *European Colonial Empires,* 107–108; Geert Oostindie, "Dutch Atlantic Decline during the 'Age of Revolutions,'" in Oostindie and Roitman, *Dutch Atlantic Connections,* 316.
13. Todd, "French Imperial Meridian," 166, 168; Jennings, *French Anti-Slavery,* 26; Blackburn, *Overthrow of Colonial Slavery,* 501–503; Drescher, *Abolition,* 164; Aldrich, *Greater France,* 22–23.
14. Sessions, *By Sword and Plow,* 173, 201–202; Headrick, *Tools of Empire,* 92; Aldrich, *Greater France,* 94–95; Jennings, *French Anti-Slavery,* 207.
15. Costeloe, *Response to Revolution,* 150; Schmidt-Nowara, *"La España Ultramarina,"* 194; not all historians concur that the economic consequences of Spanish American independence were dire for peninsular Spain; see Prados de la Escosura, *De imperio a nación,* 27, 30–31, 93, 243.
16. Schmidt-Nowara, *"La España Ultramarina,"* 194; Schmidt-Nowara, *Slavery, Freedom, and Abolition,* 124.
17. Borucki, Eltis, and Wheat, "Atlantic History and the Slave Trade to Spanish America," 449; Schmidt-Nowara, *Empire and Anti-Slavery,* 4.

18. Fradera, *Colonias,* 232, 253, 325–326, 572; Tocqueville, "Second Letter on Algeria (22 August 1837)," in Tocqueville, *Writings on Empire and Slavery,* 23.
19. Eller, *We Dream Together;* Jacobson, "Imperial Ambitions."
20. Osterhammel, *Transformation,* 418.
21. Numerous works cover the post-1825 Portuguese Empire, including Paquette, *Imperial Portugal;* on the abolition of the slave trade, see Marques, *Sounds of Silence.*
22. Except where otherwise noted, the following paragraphs rely heavily on Macintyre, *Australia,* 15–90 passim.
23. On this process, see Ford, *Settler Sovereignty,* 28–29; Sinclair, *New Zealand,* 75.
24. Hughes, *Fatal Shore,* 162.
25. Hyam, *Britain's Imperial Century,* 43; on "settlerism," see Belich, *Replenishing the Earth.*
26. Shillington, *History of Africa,* 274; Wesseling, *European Colonial Empires,* 99.
27. Hyam, *Britain's Imperial Century,* 295.
28. Williams, *Capitalism and Slavery,* 211.
29. C. A. Bayly, "'Archaic' and 'Modern' Globalization in the Eurasian and African Arena, c. 1750–1850," in Hopkins, *Globalization,* 48.

Bibliography

Abernethy, David. *The Dynamics of Global Governance: European Overseas Empire, 1415–1980*. New Haven: Yale University Press, 2000.

Abulafia, David. *The Western Mediterranean Kingdoms: The Struggle for Dominion*. London: Longman, 1997.

———. *The Discovery of Mankind: Atlantic Encounters in the Age of Columbus*. New Haven: Yale University Press, 2008.

Abu-Lughod, Janet L. *Before European Hegemony: The World System A.D. 1250–1350*. Oxford: Oxford University Press, 1989.

Adas, Michael. *Machines as the Measure of Men: Science, Technology and Ideologies of Western Dominance*. Ithaca: Cornell University Press, 1989.

———. "'High' Imperialism and the 'New' History." In Adas, ed., *Islamic and European Expansion: The Forging of a Global Order*. Philadelphia: Temple University Press, 1993.

Adelman, Jeremy. *Sovereignty and Revolution in the Iberian Atlantic*. Princeton: Princeton University Press, 2006.

———. "An Age of Imperial Revolutions." *American Historical Review* 113, no. 2 (2008): 319–340.

Alavi, Seema. *The Sepoys and the Company: Tradition and Transition in Northern India, 1770–1830*. Delhi: Oxford University Press, 1995.

Alden, Dauril. *The Making of an Enterprise: The Society of Jesus in Portugal, Its Empire and Beyond, 1540–1750*. Stanford: Stanford University Press, 1996.

Aldrich, Robert. *Greater France: A History of French Overseas Expansion*. London: Macmillan, 1996.

Aldrich, Robert, and Kirsten McKenzie, eds. *The Routledge History of Western Empires*. London: Routledge, 2014.

Alencastro, Luiz Felipe de. *O trato dos viventes: Formação do Brasil no Atlântico Sul: Séculos XVI e XVII*. São Paulo: Companhia das Letras, 2000.

Altman, Ida, and James Horn. "Introduction." In Altman and Horn, eds., *"To Make America": European Emigration in the Early Modern Period*. Berkeley: University of California Press, 1991.

Ames, Glenn J. *Renascent Empire? The House of Braganza and the Quest for Stability in Portuguese Monsoon Asia, c. 1640–1683*. Amsterdam: University of Amsterdam Press, 2006.

Amrith, Sunil S. *Crossing the Bay of Bengal: The Furies of Nature and the Fortunes of Migrants*. Cambridge, Mass.: Harvard University Press, 2013.

Anderson, Clare. *Convicts in the Indian Ocean: Transportation from South Asia to Mauritius, 1815–1853*. Basingstoke: Macmillan, 2000.

———. "Convict Passages in the Indian Ocean." In Emma Christopher, Cassandra Pybus, and Marcus Rediker, eds., *Many Middle Passages: Forced Migration and the Making of the Modern World*. Berkeley: University of California Press, 2007.

Anderson, M. S. *War and Society in Europe of the Old Regime 1618–1789*. London: Fontana, 1988.

Andrews, Kenneth R. *The Spanish Caribbean: Trade and Plunder, 1530–1630*. New Haven: Yale University Press, 1978.

———. *Trade, Plunder and Settlement: Maritime Enterprise and the Genesis of the British Empire, 1480–1630*. Cambridge: Cambridge University Press, 1984.

Andrien, Kenneth J. "Economic Crisis, Taxes and the Quito Insurrection of 1765." *Past and Present* 129 (1990): 104–131.

———. *Andean Worlds: Indigenous History, Culture, and Consciousness under Spanish Rule, 1532–1825*. Albuquerque: University of New Mexico Press, 2001.

Andrien, Kenneth J., and Alan Kuethe. *The Spanish Atlantic World in the Eighteenth Century: War and the Bourbon Reforms, 1713–1796*. Cambridge: Cambridge University Press, 2013.

Antonil, André João. *Brazil at the Dawn of the Eighteenth Century*. Ed. Timothy J. Coates. Dartmouth: Tagus, 2012.

Archer, Christon I. *The Army in Bourbon Mexico, 1760–1810*. Albuquerque: University of New Mexico Press, 1977.

Armitage, David, ed. *Theories of Empire, 1450–1800*. Aldershot: Ashgate, 1998.

———. *The Ideological Origins of the British Empire*. Cambridge: Cambridge University Press, 2000.

———. *Greater Britain, 1516–1776. Essays in Atlantic History*. Aldershot: Ashgate/Variorum, 2004.

———. *The Declaration of Independence: A Global History*. Cambridge: Harvard University Press, 2007.

Armitage, David, and Alison Bashford, eds. *Pacific Histories: Ocean, Land, People.* New York: Palgrave Macmillan, 2014.

Armitage, David, and Michael Braddick, eds. *The British Atlantic World 1500–1800.* New York: Palgrave Macmillan, 2002.

Armitage, David, and Sanjay Subrahmanyan, eds. *The Age of Revolutions in Global Context, c. 1760–1840.* New York: Palgrave Macmillan, 2010.

Arrighi, Giovanni. *The Long Twentieth Century: Money, Power and the Origins of Our Times.* London: Verso, 2010 [1994].

Asher, Catherine B., and Cynthia Talbot. *India before Europe.* Cambridge: Cambridge University Press, 2006.

Avineri, Shlomo, ed. *Karl Marx on Colonialism and Modernization: His Despatches and Other Writings on China, India, Mexico, the Middle East and North Africa.* Garden City: Doubleday/Anchor, 1968.

Bailyn, Bernard. *The Peopling of British North America: An Introduction.* New York: Knopf, 1986.

———. *The Barbarous Years. The Conflict of Civilization, 1600–1675.* New York: Knopf, 2012.

Bailyn, Bernard, and Philip D. Morgan, eds. *Strangers within the Realm: Cultural Margins of the First British Empire.* Chapel Hill: University of North Carolina Press, 1991.

Bakewell, Peter. *A History of Latin America. Empires and Sequels, 1450–1930.* Oxford: Blackwell, 1997.

Barkey, Karen. *Empires of Difference: The Ottomans in Comparative Perspective.* Cambridge: Cambridge University Press, 2008.

Barman, Roderick J. *Brazil: The Forging of a Nation, 1798–1852.* Stanford: Stanford University Press, 1988.

Barr, Juliana. *Peace Came in the Form of a Woman: Indians and Spaniards in the Texas Borderlands.* Chapel Hill: University of North Carolina Press, 2007.

Bauer, Ralph, and José Antonio Mazzotti, eds. *Creole Subjects in the Colonial Americas: Empires, Texts and Identities.* Chapel Hill: University of North Carolina Press, 2009.

Bayly, Christopher A. *Indian Society and the Making of the British Empire.* Cambridge: Cambridge University Press, 1988.

———. *Imperial Meridian: The British Empire and the World 1780–1830.* New York: Longman, 1989.

———. *Empire and Information: Intelligence Gathering and Social Communication in India, 1780–1870.* Cambridge: Cambridge University Press, 1996.

———. *The Birth of the Modern World, 1780–1914: Global Connections and Comparisons.* Oxford: Blackwell, 2004.

———. "The 'Revolutionary Age' in the Wider World, c. 1790–1830." In Jane Rendell et al., eds., *War, Empire, and Slavery, 1770–1830.* New York: Palgrave Macmillan, 2010, pp. 21–43.

———. *Recovering Liberties: Indian Thought in the Age of Liberalism and Empire.* Cambridge: Cambridge University Press, 2012.

Beckert, Sven. *Empire of Cotton: A Global History.* New York: Knopf, 2014.

Beckles, Hilary McD. "Plantation Production and White 'Proto-Slavery': White Indentured Servants and the Colonisation of the English West Indies, 1624–1645." In Joyce Lorimer, ed., *Settlement Patterns in Early Modern Colonization, Sixteenth to Eighteenth Centuries: An Expanding World, the European Impact on World History, 1450–1800.* Aldershot: Ashgate, 1998.

Belich, James. *Making Peoples: A History of the New Zealanders from Polynesian Settlement to the End of the Nineteenth Century.* Honolulu: University of Hawaii Press, 1996.

———. *Replenishing the Earth: The Settler Revolution and the Rise of the Anglo-World, 1783–1939.* Oxford: Oxford University Press, 2009.

Bell, David A. *The Cult of the Nation in France: Inventing Nationalism, 1680–1800.* Cambridge, Mass.: Harvard University Press, 2001.

Benjamin, Thomas. *The Atlantic World: Europeans, Africans, Indians and Their Shared History, 1400–1900.* Cambridge: Cambridge University Press, 2009.

Bentham, Jeremy. "Rid Yourselves of Ultramaria" (1821/1830). In Bentham, *Colonies, Commerce and Constitutional Law: Rid Yourselves of Ultramaria and Other Writings on Spain and Spanish America,* ed. Philip Schofield. Oxford: Clarendon Press, 1995.

Bentley, Jerry H. *Oxford Handbook of World History.* Oxford: Oxford University Press, 2011.

Benton, Lauren. *Law and Colonial Cultures: Legal Regimes in World History, 1400–1900.* Cambridge: Cambridge University Press, 2002.

———. *A Search for Sovereignty: Law and Geography in European Empires, 1400–1900.* Cambridge: Cambridge University Press, 2010.

———. "Possessing Empire: Iberian Claims and Interpolity Law." In Saliha Belmessous, ed., *Native Claims: Indigenous Law against Empire, 1500–1900.* Oxford: Oxford University Press, 2012, pp. 19–40.

Berg, Maxine. *Luxury and Pleasure in Eighteenth-Century Britain.* Oxford: Oxford University Press, 2005.

Berkin, Carol. *First Generations: Women in Colonial America*. New York: Hill and Wang, 1996.

Berlin, Ira. *Many Thousands Gone: The First Two Centuries of Slavery in North America*. Cambridge, Mass.: Harvard University Press, 1998.

Bethell, Leslie. *The Abolition of the Brazilian Slave Trade: Britain, Brazil and the Slave Trade Question, 1807–1869*. Cambridge: Cambridge University Press, 1970.

———, ed. *Colonial Brazil*. Cambridge: Cambridge University Press, 1987.

Bethencourt, Francisco. *The Inquisition: A Global History, 1478–1834*. Trans. Jean Birrell. Cambridge: Cambridge University Press, 2009.

———. *Racisms: From the Crusades to the Twentieth Century*. Princeton: Princeton University Press, 2013.

Bethencourt, Francisco, and Diogo Ramada Curto, eds. *Portuguese Oceanic Expansion, 1400–1800*. Cambridge: Cambridge University Press, 2007.

Black, Jeremy. *The British Seaborne Empire*. New Haven: Yale University Press, 2004.

———. *Fighting for America: The Struggle for Mastery in North America, 1519–1871*. Bloomington: Indiana University Press, 2011.

———. *A History of the British Isles*. 3rd ed. New York: Palgrave, 2012.

———. *A Short History of Britain*. 2nd ed. London: Bloomsbury, 2015.

Blackburn, Robin. *The Overthrow of Colonial Slavery, 1776–1848*. London: Verso, 1988.

Blanchard, David. *Under the Flags of Freedom: Slave Soldiers and the Wars of Independence in Spanish South America*. Pittsburgh: Pittsburgh University Press, 2008.

Blanning, T. C. W. *The Pursuit of Glory: Europe 1648–1815*. London: Allen Lane, 2007.

Blaut, J. M. *The Colonizer's Model of the World: Geographical Diffusionism and Eurocentric History*. New York: Guilford, 1993.

Bleichmar, Daniela. "Atlantic Competitions: Botanical Trajectories in the Eighteenth-Century Spanish Empire." In Nicholas Dew and James Delbourgo, eds., *Science and Empire in the Atlantic World*. New York: Routledge, 2008, pp. 225–252.

———. *Visible Empire: Botanical Expeditions and Visions of Nature in the Hispanic Enlightenment*. Chicago: University of Chicago Press, 2012.

Blussé, Leonard. "Northern European Empires." In H. M. Scott, ed., *Oxford Handbook of Early Modern European History, 1350–1750*, vol. II: *Culture and Power*. Oxford: Oxford University Press, 2015, pp. 227–253.

Bolster, W. Jeffrey. *Black Jacks: African-American Seamen in the Age of Sail.* Cambridge, Mass.: Harvard University Press, 1997.

Bonil Gómez, Katherine. "The Political Culture of Free People of African Descent in Eighteenth-Century New Granada (1750–1810)." Unpublished Ph.D. dissertation, Johns Hopkins University, 2017.

Borucki, Alex, David Eltis, and David Wheat. "Atlantic History and the Slave Trade to Spanish America." *American Historical Review* 120, no. 2 (2015): 433–461.

Boucher, Philip. *France and the American Tropics to 1700. Tropics of Discontent?* Baltimore: Johns Hopkins University Press, 2008.

Bourke, Richard. *Empire and Revolution: The Political Life of Edmund Burke.* Princeton: Princeton University Press, 2015.

Bowen, H. V., Elizabeth Mancke, and John G. Reid, eds. *Britain's Oceanic Empire: Atlantic and Indian Ocean Worlds, c. 1550–1850.* Cambridge: Cambridge University Press, 2012.

Bowser, Frederick P. "Colonial Spanish America." In David W. Cohen and Jack P. Greene, eds., *Neither Slave nor Free: The Freedman of African Descent in the Slave Societies of the New World.* Baltimore: Johns Hopkins University Press, 1972, pp. 19–58.

Boxer, Charles Ralph. *The Dutch in Brazil, 1624–1654.* Oxford: Clarendon Press, 1957.

———. *The Golden Age of Brazil, 1695–1750: Growing Pains of a Colonial Society.* Berkeley: University of California Press, 1962.

———. *The Dutch Seaborne Empire: 1600–1800.* New York: Knopf, 1965.

———. *Portuguese Society in the Tropics: The Municipal Councils of Goa, Macao, Bahia and Luanda, 1510–1800.* Madison: University of Wisconsin Press, 1965.

———. *The Portuguese Seaborne Empire, 1415–1825.* London: Hutchinson, 1969.

———. *The Church Militant and Iberian Expansion, 1440–1770.* Baltimore and London: The Johns Hopkins University Press, 1978.

———. "The Problem of the Native Clergy in the Portuguese and Spanish Empires from the Sixteenth to the Eighteenth Centuries." In J. S. Cummins, ed., *Christianity and Missions, 1450–1800.* Aldershot: Ashgate, 1997.

Brading, David A. *Miners and Merchants in Bourbon Mexico, 1763–1810.* Cambridge: Cambridge University Press, 1973.

———. "Bourbon Spain and Its American Empire." In Leslie Bethell, ed., *The Cambridge History of Latin America.* Cambridge: Cambridge University Press, 1984, pp. 389–439.

———. "The Catholic Monarchy." In Serge Gruzinski and Nathan Wachtel, eds., *Le Nouveau Monde, mondes nouveaux: L'expérience Américaine.* Paris: Éditions de l'École des Hautes Études en Sciences Sociales, 1996, pp. 365–405.

———. *The First America: The Spanish Monarchy, Creole Patriots and the Liberal State, 1492–1867.* Cambridge: Cambridge University Press, 2001.

Breen, Benjamin, and Jorge Cañizares-Esguerra. "Hybrid Atlantics." *History Compass* 11, no. 8 (2013): 597–609.

Brewer, John. *The Sinews of Power: War, Money and the English State, 1688–1783.* New York: Knopf, 1989.

Briggs, Robin. *Early Modern France.* 2nd ed. Oxford: Oxford University Press, 1998.

Brooks, George E. *Eurafricans in Western Africa: Commerce, Social Status, Gender and Religious Observance from the Sixteenth to the Eighteenth Century.* Athens: Ohio University Press, 2003.

Brown, Christopher L. *Moral Capital: Foundations of British Abolitionism.* Chapel Hill: University of North Carolina Press, 2006.

Brown, Matthew, ed. *Informal Empire in Latin America: Culture, Commerce and Capital.* Oxford: Blackwell, 2008.

———. *The Struggle for Power in Post-Independence Colombia and Venezuela.* Basingstoke: Palgrave Macmillan, 2012.

Brown, Matthew, and Gabriel Paquette, eds. *Connections after Colonialism: Europe and Latin America in the 1820s.* Tuscaloosa: University of Alabama Press, 2013.

Brown, Vincent. *The Reaper's Garden: Death and Power in the World of Atlantic Slavery.* Cambridge, Mass.: Harvard University Press, 2008.

Bryant, Sherwin K. *Rivers of Gold, Lives of Bondage: Governing through Slavery in Colonial Quito.* Chapel Hill: University of North Carolina Press, 2014.

Burbank, Jane, and Frederick Cooper. *Empires in World History: Power and the Politics of Difference.* Princeton: Princeton University Press, 2010.

Burkholder, Mark, and D. S. Chandler. *From Impotence to Authority: The Spanish Crown and the American Audiencias, 1687–1808.* Columbia: University of Missouri Press, 1977.

Burkholder, Mark A., and Lyman L. Johnson. *Colonial Latin America.* 5th ed. New York: Oxford University Press, 2004.

Burnard, Trevor, and Gad Heuman, eds. *The Routledge History of Slavery.* London: Routledge, 2011.

Buschmann, Rainer, Edward R. Slack, and James B. Treller, eds. *Navigating the Spanish Lake: The Pacific in the Iberian World, 1521–1898*. Honolulu: University of Hawaii Press, 2014.

Butlin, Robin. *Geographies of Empire: European Empires and Colonialism, c. 1880–1960*. Cambridge: Cambridge University Press, 2009.

Cain, P. J., and A. G. Hopkins. *British Imperialism: 1688–2000*. 2nd ed. London: Routledge, 2000.

Calloway, Colin G. *New Worlds for All: Indians, Europeans and the Remaking of Early America*. Baltimore: Johns Hopkins University Press, 1997.

Campbell, Leon G. "The Changing Racial and Administrative Structure of the Peruvian Military under the Later Bourbons." *The Americas* 32, no. 1 (1975): 17–33.

Cañeque, Alejandro. *The King's Living Image: The Culture and Politics of Viceregal Power in Colonial Mexico*. New York: Routledge, 2004.

Cañizares-Esguerra, Jorge. *How to Write the History of the New World: Histories, Epistemologies, and Identities in the Eighteenth-Century Atlantic World*. Stanford: Stanford University Press, 2001.

———. *Puritan Conquistadors: Iberianizing the Atlantic, 1550–1700*. Stanford: Stanford University Press, 2006.

Canny, Nicholas. "In Search of a Better Home? European Overseas Migration, 1500–1800." In Nicholas Canny, ed., *Europeans on the Move: Studies on European Migration, 1500–1800*. Oxford: Oxford University Press, 1994, pp. 263–283.

Canny, Nicholas, ed. *Oxford History of the British Empire*, vol. II: *Origins of Empire*. Oxford: Oxford University Press, 1998.

Canny, Nicholas, and Anthony Pagden, eds. *Colonial Identity in the Atlantic World 1500–1800*. Princeton: Princeton University Press, 1987.

Canny, Nicholas, and Philip Morgan, eds. *The Oxford Handbook of the Atlantic World, 1450–1850*. Oxford: Oxford University Press, 2011.

Cardim, Pedro, et al., eds. *Polycentric Monarchies: How Did Early Modern Spain and Portugal Achieve and Maintain a Global Hegemony?* Brighton: Sussex Academic Press, 2012.

Carmagnani, Marcello. *The Other West: Latin America from Invasion to Globalization*. Berkeley: University of California Press, 2011.

Casale, Giancarlo. *The Ottoman Age of Exploration*. Oxford: Oxford University Press, 2010.

Centeno, Miguel Angel. *Blood and Debt: War and the Nation-State in Latin America*. University Park: Pennsylvania State University Press, 2002.

Charters, Erica. *Disease, War and the British State: The Welfare of the British Armed Forces during the Seven Years' War.* Chicago: University of Chicago Press, 2014.

Chaudhuri, K. N. *The Trading World of Asia and the English East India Company, 1660–1760.* Cambridge: Cambridge University Press, 1978.

———. *Trade and Civilization in the Indian Ocean: An Economic History of the Rise of Islam to 1750.* Cambridge: Cambridge University Press, 1985.

Cheney, Paul, and Loïc Charles. "The Colonial Machine Dismantled: Knowledge and Empire in the French Atlantic." *Past and Present* 219 (2013): 127–163.

Childs, Greg. "Secret and Spectral: Torture and Secrecy in the Archives of Slave Conspiracies." *Social Text* 33, no. 4 (2015): 35–57.

Clancy-Smith, Julia A. *Mediterraneans: North Africa and Europe in an Age of Migration, c. 1800–1900.* Berkeley: University of California Press, 2011.

Clarence-Smith, William Gervase. *The Third Portuguese Empire, 1825–1975: A Study in Economic Imperialism.* Manchester: Manchester University Press, 1985.

Clulow, Adam. *The Company and the Shogun: The Dutch Encounter with Tokugawa Japan.* New York: Columbia University Press, 2014.

Coates, Timothy J. *Convicts and Orphans: Forced and State-Sponsored Colonies in the Portuguese Empire, 1550–1750.* Stanford: Stanford University Press, 2001.

Cohen, Robin, ed. *The Cambridge Survey of Migration.* Cambridge: Cambridge University Press, 1995.

Cohen, Thomas M. *The Fire of Tongues: António Vieira and the Missionary Church in Brazil and Portugal.* Stanford: Stanford University Press, 1998.

Cohn, Bernard S. *Colonialism and Its Forms of Knowledge: The British in India.* Princeton: Princeton University Press, 1996.

Coller, Ian. *Arab France: Islam and the Making of Modern Europe, 1798–1831.* Berkeley: University of California Press, 2011.

Colley, Linda. *Captives: Britain, Empire, and the World, 1600–1850.* New York: Anchor, 2003.

———. *Britons: Forging the Nation 1707–1837.* 2nd ed. New Haven: Yale University Press, 2009.

———. "Empires of Writing: Britain, America and Constitutions, 1776–1848." *Law and History Review* 32, no. 2 (2014): 237–266.

Collins, James B. *The State in Early Modern France.* 2nd ed. Cambridge: Cambridge University Press, 2009.

Cook, Harold J. *Matters of Exchange: Commerce, Medicine and Science in the Dutch Golden Age*. New Haven: Yale University Press, 2007.

Cooper, Frederick. *Colonialism in Question. Theory, Knowledge and History*. Berkeley: University of California Press, 2005.

Costeloe, Michael P. *Response to Revolution: Imperial Spain and the Spanish American Revolutions, 1810–1840*. Cambridge: Cambridge University Press, 1986.

Cowan, Brian. *The Social Life of Coffee: The Emergence of the British Coffeehouse*. New Haven: Yale University Press, 2005.

Craton, Michael. *Testing the Chains: Resistance to Slavery in the British West Indies*. Ithaca: Cornell University Press, 1982.

Cronon, William. *Changes in the Land: Indians, Colonists and the Ecology of New England*. New York: Hill and Wang, 2003.

Crosby, Alfred W. *Ecological Imperialism: The Biological Expansion of Europe, 900–1900*. Cambridge: Cambridge University Press, 1986.

———. *The Columbian Exchange: Biological and Cultural Consequences of 1492*. Westport, Conn.: Praeger, 2003.

Curran, Andrew S. *The Anatomy of Blackness: Science and Slavery in the Age of Enlightenment*. Baltimore: Johns Hopkins University Press, 2011.

Curtin, Philip D. *The Tropical Atlantic in the Age of the Slave Trade*. Washington, D.C.: American Historical Association, 1991.

———. *The World and the West. The European Challenge and the Overseas Response in the Age of Empire*. Cambridge: Cambridge University Press, 1995.

———. *The Rise and Fall of the Plantation Complex: Essays in Atlantic History*. 2nd ed. Cambridge: Cambridge University Press, 1998.

Dale, Stephen Frederic. *The Muslim Empires of the Ottomans, Safavids and Mughals*. Cambridge: Cambridge University Press, 2010.

Dalrymple, William. *White Mughals: Love and Betrayal in Eighteenth-century India*. New York: Viking, 2002.

Dandelet, Thomas J. *The Renaissance of Empire in Early Modern Europe*. Cambridge: Cambridge University Press, 2014.

Darwin, John. *After Tamerlane: The Global History of Empire since 1405*. London: Allen Lane, 2007.

———. *The Empire Project: The Rise and Fall of the British World System, 1830–1870*. Cambridge: Cambridge University Press, 2011.

———. *Unfinished Empire: The Global Expansion of Britain*. New York: Bloomsbury, 2012.

Davis, David Brion. *The Problem of Slavery in the Age of Revolution, 1770–1823*. Ithaca: Cornell University Press, 1975.

———. *Inhuman Bondage: The Rise and Fall of Slavery in the New World*. Oxford: Oxford University Press, 2006.

Davis, Robert C. *Christian Slaves, Muslim Masters: White Slavery and the Mediterranean, the Barbary Coast and Italy, 1500–1800*. Basingstoke: Palgrave Macmillan, 2003.

Dawson, Frank Griffith. *The First Latin American Debt Crisis: The City of London and the 1822–25 Loan Bubble*. New Haven: Yale University Press, 1990.

de Vries, Jan. "The Dutch Atlantic Economies." In Peter Coclanis, ed., *The Atlantic Economy in the 17th and 18th Centuries*. Columbia: University of South Carolina Press, 2005, pp. 1–29.

de Vries, Jan, and Ad van der Woude. *The First Modern Economy: Success, Failure and Perseverance of the Dutch Economy, 1500–1815*. Cambridge: Cambridge University Press, 1997.

Dean, Warren. *With Broadax and Firebrand: The Destruction of the Brazilian Atlantic Forest*. Berkeley: University of California Press, 1995.

Delbourgo, James, and Nicholas Dew, eds. *Science and Empire in the Atlantic World*. New York: Routledge, 2008.

Disney, A. R. *A History of Portugal and the Portuguese Empire*, 2 vols. Cambridge: Cambridge University Press, 2009.

Doyle, Michael. *The Old European Order 1660–1800*. Oxford: Oxford University Press, 1978.

Doyle, Michael W. *Empires*. Ithaca: Cornell University Press, 1986.

Draper, Nicholas. *The Price of Emancipation: Slave Ownership, Compensation and British Society at the End of Slavery*. Cambridge: Cambridge University Press, 2010.

Drayton, Richard. *Nature's Government: Science, Imperial Britain and the "Improvement" of the World*. New Haven: Yale University Press, 2000.

———. "The Globalisation of France: Provincial Cities and French Expansion, c. 1500–1800." *History of European Ideas* 34 (2008): 424–430.

Drescher, Seymour. *Abolition: A History of Slavery and Anti-Slavery*. Cambridge: Cambridge University Press, 2009.

Dubois, Laurent. *Avengers of the New World: The Story of the Haitian Revolution*. Cambridge, Mass.: Belknap Press of Harvard University Press, 2004.

———. *A Colony of Citizens: Revolution and Slave Emancipation in the French Caribbean, 1787–1804*. Chapel Hill: University of North Carolina Press, 2004.

Dubois, Laurent, and John D. Garrigus, eds. *Slave Revolution in the Caribbean, 1789–1804: A Brief History with Documents.* Boston: Bedford/St. Martin's Press, 2006.

Dull, Jonathan R. *A Diplomatic History of the American Revolution.* New Haven: Yale University Press, 1985.

DuPlessis, Robert S. *The Material Atlantic: Clothing, Commerce, and Colonization in the Atlantic World, 1650–1800.* Cambridge: Cambridge University Press, 2016.

Duval, Kathleen. *Independence Lost: Lives on the Edge of the American Revolution.* New York: Random House, 2015.

Eakin, Marshall. *Brazil: The Once and Future Country.* New York: St. Martin's Press, 1997.

Earle, Rebecca. *The Body of the Conquistador: Food, Race and the Colonial Experience in Spanish America, 1492–1700.* Cambridge: Cambridge University Press, 2012.

Eccles, W. J. *The French in North America 1500–1783.* East Lansing: Michigan State University Press, 1998.

Echeverri, Marcela. *Indian and Slave Royalists in the Age of Revolution: Reform, Revolution and Royalism in the Northern Andes, 1780–1825.* Cambridge: Cambridge University Press, 2016.

Edney, Matthew. *Mapping and Empire: The Geographical Construction of British India, 1765–1843.* Chicago: University of Chicago Press, 1990.

Egerton, Douglas R., et al., eds. *The Atlantic World: A History, 1400–1888.* Wheeling: Harlan Davidson, 2007.

Ekirch, A. Roger. *Bound for America: The Transportation of British Convicts to the Colonies, 1718–1775.* Oxford: Clarendon Press, 1987.

Eller, Anne. *We Dream Together: Dominican Independence, Haiti, and the Fight for Caribbean Freedom.* Durham: Duke University Press, 2016.

Elliott, John H. *Imperial Spain, 1469–1716.* London: Penguin, 1970 [1963].

———. *Europe Divided 1559–1598.* New York: Harper Torchbooks, 1968.

———. *The Old World and the New 1492–1650.* Cambridge: Cambridge University Press, 1970.

———. *Richelieu and Olivares.* Cambridge: Cambridge University Press, 1984.

———. *The Count-Duke of Olivares: The Statesman in an Age of Decline.* New Haven: Yale University Press, 1986.

———. *Spain and Its World, 1500–1700.* New Haven: Yale University Press, 1989.

———. "A Europe of Composite Monarchies." *Past and Present* 137 (1992): 48–71.

———. *Empires of the Atlantic World: Spain and Britain in the Americas, 1492–1830*. New Haven: Yale University Press, 2006.

Elphick, Richard, and Hermann Giliomee, eds. *The Shaping of South African Society, 1652–1840*. 2nd ed. Middletown, Conn.: Wesleyan University Press, 1988.

Eltis, David. *The Rise of African Slavery in the Americas*. Cambridge: Cambridge University Press, 2000.

———. "Coerced and Free Migration from the Old World to the New." In Eltis, ed., *Coerced and Free Migration: Global Perspectives*. Stanford: Stanford University Press, 2002, pp. 33–74.

Engel, Barbara Alpern, and Janet Martin. *Russia in World History*. Oxford: Oxford University Press, 2015.

Falola, Toyin, and Kevin D. Roberts, eds. *The Atlantic World, 1450–2000*. Bloomington: Indiana University Press, 2008.

Farriss, Nancy. *Maya Society under Colonial Rule: The Collective Enterprise of Survival*. Princeton: Princeton University Press, 1984.

Fausto, Boris. *A Concise History of Brazil*. Cambridge: Cambridge University Press, 1999.

Fernández-Armesto, Felipe. *Before Columbus: Exploration and Colonization from the Mediterranean to the Atlantic, 1229–1492*. Philadelphia: University of Pennsylvania Press, 1987.

———. *Pathfinders: A Global History of Exploration*. New York: W. W. Norton, 2006.

Fernández-Armesto, Felipe, and Matthew Restall. *The Conquistadors: A Very Short Introduction*. Oxford: Oxford University Press, 2012.

Ferreira, Roquinaldo. *Cross-Cultural Exchange in the Atlantic World: Angola and Brazil in the Era of the Slave Trade*. Cambridge: Cambridge University Press, 2012.

Ferreiro, Larrie D. *Brothers at Arms: American Independence and the Men of France and Spain Who Saved It*. New York: Knopf, 2016.

Ferrer, Ada. *Freedom's Mirror: Cuba and Haiti in the Age of Revolution*. Cambridge: Cambridge University Press, 2014.

Findlay, Ronald, and Kevin H. O'Rourke. *Power and Plenty: Trade, War and the World Economy in the Second Millennium*. Princeton: Princeton University Press, 2007.

Fischer, David Hackett. *Albion's Seed: Four British Folkways in America*. Oxford: Oxford University Press, 1989.

Fisher, Andrew B., and Matthew D. O'Hara, eds. *Imperial Subjects: Race and Identity in Colonial Latin America*. Durham, N.C.: Duke University Press, 2009.

Fisher, John R. *The Economic Aspects of Spanish Imperialism in America, 1492–1810*. Liverpool: Liverpool University Press, 1997.

Fisher, Michael H. *The First Indian Author in English: Dean Mahomed (1759–1851) in India, Ireland and England*. Delhi: Oxford University Press, 1996.

———. "Working Across the Seas: Indian Maritime Laborers in India, Britain and in Between, 1600–1857." *International Review of Social History* 51 (supplement 14) (2006): 21–46.

Fitzmaurice, Andrew. "Discovery, Conquest and Occupation of Territory." In Bardo Fassbender and Anne Peters, eds., *The Oxford Handbook of International Law*. Oxford: Oxford University Press, 2012.

Ford, Lisa. *Settler Sovereignty: Jurisdiction and Indigenous People in America and Australia 1788–1836*. Cambridge, Mass.: Harvard University Press, 2010.

Fradera, Josep M. *Colonias para después de un imperio*. Barcelona: Bellaterra, 2005.

———. "Spain: The Genealogy of Modern Colonialism." In Robert Aldrich, ed., *The Age of Empires*. New York: Thames and Hudson, 2007, pp. 44–67.

Frank, Andre Gunder. *ReOrient: Global Economy in the Asian Age*. Berkeley: University of California Press, 1998.

Frost, Alan. *The Global Reach of Empire: Britain's Maritime Expansion in the Indian and Pacific Oceans, 1764–1815*. Melbourne: Miegunyah Press, 2003.

Frykman, Niklas. "Pirates and Smugglers: Political Economy in the Red Atlantic." In Carl Wennerlind and Philip Stern, eds., *Mercantilism Reimagined: Political Economy in Early Modern Britain and Its Empire*. New York: Oxford University Press, 2013, pp. 218–239.

Furber, Holden. *Rival Empires of Trade in the Orient, 1600–1800*. St. Paul: University of Minnesota Press, 1976.

Gaastra, Femme S. *The Dutch East India Company: Expansion and Decline*. Leiden: Walburg Pers, 2003.

Gainot, Bernard. *L'empire colonial Français de Richelieu à Napoléon (1630–1810)*. Paris: Armand Colin, 2015.

Gallagher, John, and Ronald Robinson. "The Imperialism of Free Trade." *Economic History Review*, 2nd series, 4 (1953): 1–15.

Gallay, Alan. *The Indian Slave Trade: The Rise of the English Empire in the American South*. New Haven: Yale University Press, 2002.

Garofalo, Leo J. "The Shape of a Diaspora: The Movement of Afro-Iberians to Colonial Spanish America." In Sherwin K. Bryant, Rachel-Sarah O'Toole, and Ben Vinson III, eds., *Africans to Spanish America*. Urbana: University of Illinois Press, 2012, pp. 27–49.

Garrett, David T. "'His Majesty's Loyal Vassals': The Indian Nobility and Túpac Amaru." *Hispanic American Historical Review* 84, no. 4 (2004): 575–617.

Garrigus, John. *Before Haiti: Race and Citizenship in French Saint-Domingue*. New York: Palgrave Macmillan, 2006.

Geggus, David. *A Turbulent Time: The French Revolution and the Greater Caribbean*. Bloomington: Indiana University Press, 1997.

———. "The Slaves and Free People of Color of Cap Français." In Jorge Cañizares-Esguerra et al., eds., *The Black Urban Atlantic in the Age of the Slave Trade*. Philadelphia: University of Pennsylvania Press, 2013, pp. 101–121.

———, ed. *The Haitian Revolution: A Documentary History*. Indianapolis: Hackett, 2014.

Gerbi, Antonello. *The Dispute of the New World: The History of a Polemic, 1750–1900*. Pittsburgh: University of Pittsburgh Press, 1973.

Getz, Trevor, and Heather Streets-Salter. *Empires and Colonies in the Modern World: A Global Perspective*. New York: Oxford University Press, 2016.

Ghosh, Durba. *Sex and the Family in Colonial India: The Making of Empire*. Cambridge: Cambridge University Press, 2006.

Gil Pujol, Xavier. "Un rey, una fe, muchas naciones: Patria y nación en la España de los siglos XVI y XVII." In Antonio Álvarez-Ossorio and Bernardo J. García, eds., *La monarquía de las naciones*. Madrid: Fundación Carlos Amberes, 2004, pp. 39–76.

———. "Spain and Portugal." In Howell A. Lloyd, Glenn Burgess, and Simon Hodson, eds., *European Political Thought, 1450–1700: Religion, Law and Philosophy*. New Haven: Yale University Press, 2006, pp. 416–457.

Glete, Jan. *Warfare at Sea, 1500–1650: Maritime Conflicts and the Transformation of Europe*. New York: Routledge, 2000.

———. *War and the State in Early Modern Europe: Spain, the Dutch Republic and Sweden as Fiscal-Military States, 1500–1650*. London: Routledge, 2002.

Goldstone, Jack A. *Revolution and Rebellion in the Early Modern World*. Berkeley: University of California Press, 1991.

Goodman, David. *Spanish Naval Power, 1589–1665. Reconstruction and Defeat*. Cambridge: Cambridge University Press, 1997.

Gould, Eliga H. "Zones of Law, Zones of Violence: The Legal Geography of the British Atlantic c. 1772." *William and Mary Quarterly* 60, no. 3 (2003): 471–510.

———. "Prelude: The Christianizing of British America." In Norman Etherington, ed., *Missions and Empire*. Oxford: Oxford University Press, 2005, pp. 19–39.

———. "Entangled Histories, Entangled Worlds: The English-Speaking Atlantic as a Spanish Periphery." *American Historical Review* 112, no. 3 (2007): 764–786.

Grab, Alexander. *Napoleon and the Transformation of Europe*. New York: Palgrave Macmillan, 2003.

Graubart, Karen. *With Our Labor and Sweat: Indigenous Women and the Formation of Colonial Society in Peru, 1550–1700*. Stanford: Stanford University Press, 2007.

Green, Toby. *Inquisition: The Reign of Fear*. New York: St. Martin's Press, 2007.

———. *The Rise of the Transatlantic Slave Trade in Western Africa, 1300–1589*. Cambridge: Cambridge University Press, 2012.

———. "Beyond an Imperial Atlantic: Trajectories of Africans from Upper Guinea and West-Central Africa in the Early Atlantic World." *Past and Present* 230 (2016): 91–122.

Greene, Jack P. *Pursuits of Happiness: The Social Development of the Early Modern British Colonies and the Formation of American Culture*. Chapel Hill: University of North Carolina Press, 1988.

Greene, Jack P., and Philip D. Morgan, eds., *Atlantic History: A Critical Appraisal*. Oxford: Oxford University Press, 2008.

Greengrass, Mark. *Christendom Destroyed: Europe 1517–1648*. New York: Viking, 2014.

Griffin, Patrick. *America's Revolution*. New York: Oxford University Press, 2012.

Grove, Richard. *Green Imperialism: Colonial Expansion, Tropical Island Edens and the Origins of Environmentalism, 1600–1860*. Cambridge: Cambridge University Press, 1995.

Gruzinski, Serge. *The Mestizo Mind: Intellectual Dynamics of Colonization and Globalization*. New York: Routledge, 2002.

Hale, J. R. *War and Society in Renaissance Europe, 1450–1620*. Baltimore: Johns Hopkins University Press, 1985.

Hämäläinen, Pekka. *The Comanche Empire*. New Haven: Yale University Press, 2008.

Hamnett, Brian R. *A Concise History of Mexico*, 2nd ed. Cambridge: Cambridge University Press, 2006.

———. *The End of Iberian Rule on the American Continent, 1770–1830*. Cambridge: Cambridge University Press, 2017.

Hancock, David. *Oceans of Wine. Madeira and the Emergence of American Trade and Taste.* New Haven: Yale University Press, 2009.

Hanioğlu, M. Şükrü. *A Brief History of the Late Ottoman Empire.* Princeton: Princeton University Press, 2008.

Hanna, Mark G. *Pirate Nests and the Rise of the British Empire, 1570–1740.* Chapel Hill: University of North Carolina Press, 2015.

Hardt, Michael, and Antonio Negri. *Empire.* Cambridge, Mass.: Harvard University Press, 2001.

Haring, Clarence Henry. *The Spanish Empire in America.* New York: Oxford University Press, 1947.

Harlow, Vincent T. *The Founding of the Second British Empire, 1763–1793.* 2 vols. London: Longmans, 1952–1964.

Harms, Robert, Bernard K. Freamon, and David W. Blight, eds. *Indian Ocean Slavery in the Age of Abolition.* New Haven: Yale University Press, 2013.

Harvey, L. P. *Islamic Spain, 1250–1500.* Chicago: University of Chicago Press, 1992.

Havard, Gilles, and Cécile Vidal. *Histoire de l'Amérique Française.* Paris: Flammarion, 2003.

Headrick, Daniel. *The Tools of Empire: Technology and European Imperialism in the 19th Century.* New York: Oxford University Press, 1981.

Hemming, John. *Red Gold: The Conquest of the Brazilian Indians.* Cambridge, Mass.: Harvard University Press, 1978.

Hernández Chávez, Alicia. *Mexico: A Brief History.* Berkeley: University of California Press, 2006.

Herzog, Tamar. *Frontiers of Possession: Spain and Portugal in Europe and the Americas.* Cambridge, Mass.: Harvard University Press, 2015.

Heywood, Linda M., ed. *Central Africans and Cultural Transformation in the American Diaspora.* Cambridge: Cambridge University Press, 2002.

Heywood, Linda M., and John. K. Thornton. *Central Africans, Atlantic Creoles and the Foundation of the Americas, 1585–1660.* Cambridge: Cambridge University Press, 2007.

Hilton, Anne. *The Kingdom of Kongo.* Oxford: Clarendon Press, 1985.

Hinsley, F. H. *Sovereignty.* 2nd ed. Cambridge: Cambridge University Press, 1986.

Hochschild, Adam. *Bury the Chains: Prophets and Rebels in the Fight to Free an Empire's Slaves.* Boston: Houghton Mifflin, 2005.

Hodes, Martha, ed. *Sex, Love, Race: Crossing Boundaries in North American History.* New York: NYU Press, 1999.

Hoefte, Rosemarijn, and Jean Jacques Vrij. "Free Black and Colored Women in Early Nineteenth-Century Paramaribo, Suriname." In David Barry Gaspar and Darlene Clarke Hine, eds., *Beyond Bondage: Free Women of Color in the Americas.* Urbana: University of Illinois Press, 2004, pp. 145–168.

Hoerder, Dirk. *Cultures in Contact: World Migrations in the Second Millennium.* Durham, N.C.: Duke University Press, 2002.

Holloway, Thomas, ed. *A Companion to Latin American History.* Oxford: Blackwell, 2008.

Hont, Istvan. *Jealousy of Trade: International Competition and the Nation-State in Historical Perspective.* Cambridge, Mass.: Harvard University Press, 2005.

Hopkins, A. G. *An Economic History of West Africa.* New York: Columbia University Press, 1973.

———. "Informal Empire in Argentina: An Alternative View." *Journal of Latin American Studies* 26 (1994): 469–484.

———, ed. *Globalization in World History.* London: Pimlico, 2002.

Hourani, Albert. *A History of the Arab Peoples.* New York: Grand Central, 1991.

Howe, Stephen. *Empire: A Very Short Introduction.* Oxford: Oxford University Press, 2002.

Humphreys, R. A. *British Consular Reports on the Trade and Politics of Latin America, 1824–26.* Camden, 3rd series, LXIII. London: Offices of the Royal Historical Society, 1940.

Hughes, Robert. *The Fatal Shore: A History of the Transportation of Convicts to Australia, 1787–1868.* New York: Vintage, 1986.

Huzzey, Richard. "The Politics of Slave-Trade Suppression." In Robert Burroughs and Richard Huzzey, eds., *The Suppression of the Atlantic Slave Trade: British Policies, Practices and Representations of Naval Coercion.* Manchester: Manchester University Press, 2015.

Hyam, Ronald. *Britain's Imperial Century, 1815–1914: A Study of Empire and Expansion.* 3rd ed. Basingstoke: Palgrave Macmillan, 2002.

Igler, David. *The Great Ocean: Pacific Worlds from Captain Cook to the Gold Rush.* Oxford: Oxford University Press, 2013.

Iliffe, John. *Africans: The History of a Continent.* 2nd ed. Cambridge: Cambridge University Press, 2007.

Irigoin, Alejandra, and Regina Grafe. "Bargaining for Absolutism: A Spanish Path to Nation-State and Empire Building." *Hispanic American Historical Review* 88, no. 2 (2008): 173–209.

Israel, Jonathan. *The Dutch Republic and the Hispanic World, 1606–1661.* Oxford: Clarendon Press, 1982.

———. *The Dutch Republic: Its Rise, Greatness, and Fall.* Oxford: Clarendon Press, 1995.

Jacobs, Jaap. *The Colony of New Netherland: A Dutch Settlement in Seventeenth-Century America.* Ithaca: Cornell University Press, 2009.

Jacobson, Stephen. "Imperial Ambitions in an Era of Decline: Micromilitarism and the Eclipse of the Spanish Empire, 1858–1923." In Alfred McCoy, Josep M. Fradera, and Stephen Jacobson, eds., *Endless Empire: Spain's Retreat, Europe's Eclipse and America's Decline.* Madison: University of Wisconsin Press, 2012, pp. 74–91.

Jaksíc, Iván. *The Hispanic World and American Intellectual Life, 1820–1880.* New York: Palgrave Macmillan, 2007.

James, C. L. R. *The Black Jacobins: Toussaint L'Ouverture and the San Domingo Revolution.* 2nd ed. New York: Vintage, 1989.

Jasanoff, Maya. *Edge of Empire: Lives, Culture and Conquest in the East, 1750–1850.* New York: Knopf, 2005.

———. *Liberty's Exiles: American Loyalists in the Revolutionary World.* New York: Vintage, 2012.

Jefferson, Thomas. *Political Writings.* Ed. Joyce Appleby and Terence Ball. Cambridge: Cambridge University Press, 1999.

Jennings, Lawrence C. *French Anti-Slavery: The Movement for the Abolition of Slavery in France 1802–1848.* Cambridge: Cambridge University Press, 2000.

Johnson, Lyman. *Workshop of Revolution: Plebeian Buenos Aires and the Atlantic World, 1776–1810.* Durham, N.C.: Duke University Press, 2011.

Jones, Colin. *The Great Nation: France from Louis XV to Napoleon.* London: Penguin, 2002.

Jones, E. L. *The European Miracle: Environments, Economies and Geopolitics in the History of Europe and Asia.* Cambridge: Cambridge University Press, 1981.

Kaczorowska-Ireland, Alina. *Public International Law.* 4th ed. London: Taylor and Francis, 2010.

Kagan, Richard. "Prescott's Paradigm: American Scholarship and the Decline of Spain." *American Historical Review* 101, no. 2 (1996): 423–446.

Kappeler, Andreas. *The Russian Empire: A Multi-Ethnic History.* Trans. Alfred Clayton. New York: Pearson Education, 2001.

Katzew, Ilona. *Casta Painting: Images of Race in Eighteenth-Century Mexico.* New Haven: Yale University Press, 2004.

Kearney, Hugh. *The British Isles: A History of Four Nations.* Cambridge: Cambridge University Press, 1989.

Kennedy, Dane. "Imperial History and Post-Colonial Theory." *Journal of Imperial and Commonwealth History* 24, no. 3 (1996): 345–363.

Kennedy, Paul. *The Rise and Fall of British Naval Mastery*. New York: Charles Scribner's Sons, 1976.

———. *The Rise and Fall of the Great Powers: Economic Change and Military Conflict from 1500–2000*. New York: Vintage, 1989.

Klein, Herbert S. *The Atlantic Slave Trade*. Cambridge: Cambridge University Press, 1999.

Klein, Herbert S., and Ben Vinson III. *African Slavery in Latin America and the Caribbean*. 2nd ed. Oxford: Oxford University Press, 2007.

Klooster, Wim. *Illicit Riches: Dutch Trade in the Caribbean 1648–1795*. Leiden: KITLV Press, 1991.

———. *Revolutions in the Atlantic World: A Comparative History*. New York: NYU Press, 2009.

———. *The Dutch Moment: War, Trade and Settlement in the Seventeenth-Century Atlantic World*. Ithaca: Cornell University Press, 2016.

Knight, Franklin W. *The Caribbean: The Genesis of a Fragmented Nationalism*. 2nd ed. Oxford: Oxford University Press, 1990.

———, ed. *General History of the Caribbean*. Vol. III: *The Slave Societies of the Caribbean*. London: UNESCO/Macmillan Education, 1997.

Koenigsberger, Helmut G. "*Dominium regale* or *dominium politicum et regale:* Monarchies and Parliaments in Early Modern Europe." In Koenigsberger, *Politicians and Virtuosi: Essays in Early Modern History*. London: Hambledon, 1986, pp. 1–25.

———. *Europe in the Sixteenth Century*. 2nd ed. London: Longman, 1989.

Kuethe, Allan J. *Cuba, 1753–1815: Crown, Military and Society*. Knoxville: University of Tennessee Press, 1986.

Kwass, Michael. "The Global Underground: Smuggling, Rebellion, and the Origins of the French Revolution." In Suzanne Desan, Lynn Hunt, and William Nelson, eds., *The French Revolution in Global Perspective*. Ithaca: Cornell University Press, 2013, pp. 15–31.

———. *Contraband: Louis Mandrin and the Making of a Global Underground*. Cambridge, Mass.: Harvard University Press, 2014.

Lai, Walton Look. *Indentured Labor, Caribbean Sugar: Chinese and Indian Migrants to the British West Indies, 1838–1918*. Baltimore: Johns Hopkins University Press, 1993.

Laidlaw, Zoe. *Colonial Connections 1815–1845: Patronage, the Informational Revolution and Colonial Government*. Manchester: Manchester University Press, 2005.

Lains, Pedro et al. *An Economic History of Portugal, 1143–2010*. Cambridge: Cambridge University Press, 2016.

Landers, Jane. *Black Society in Spanish Florida*. Urbana: University of Illinois Press, 1999.

———. *Atlantic Creoles in the Age of Revolutions*. Cambridge, Mass.: Harvard University Press, 2010.

Lane, Kris. *Colour of Paradise: The Emerald in the Age of Gunpowder Empires*. New Haven: Yale University Press, 2010.

Lane, Kris, and Matthew Restall. *The Riddle of Latin America*. Boston: Wadsworth/Cengage, 2012.

Lavrin, Asunción, ed. *Sexuality and Marriage in Colonial Latin America*. Lincoln: University of Nebraska Press, 1989.

Lee, Wayne E., ed. *Empires and Indigenes: Intercultural Alliance, Imperial Expansion and Warfare in the Early Modern World*. New York: NYU Press, 2011.

Lehning, James R. *European Colonialism since 1700*. Cambridge: Cambridge University Press, 2013.

Levaggi, Abelardo. *Diplomacia Hispano-Indígena en las fronteras de América: Historia de los tratados entre la monarquía Española y las comunidades aborígenes*. Madrid: Centro de Estudios Políticos y Constitucionales, 2002.

Levine, Philippa. *The British Empire: Sunrise to Sunset*. Harlow: Pearson Longman, 2007.

Lewis, Martin, and Kären Wigan. *The Myth of the Continents: A Critique of Metageography*. Berkeley: University of California Press, 1997.

Lieven, Dominic. *Empire: The Russian Empire and Its Rivals*. New Haven: Yale University Press, 2001.

Lockhart, James, and Stuart Schwartz. *Early Latin America: A History of Colonial Spanish America and Brazil*. Cambridge: Cambridge University Press, 1983.

Lovejoy, Paul E. *Transformations in Slavery: A History of Slavery in Africa*. Cambridge: Cambridge University Press, 2012.

Lucena-Giraldo, Manuel. *A los quatro vientos: Las ciudades de la América Hispánica*. Madrid: Marcial Pons Historia, 2006.

———. *Naciones de rebeldes: Las revoluciones de independencia Latinoamericanas*. Madrid: Taurus, 2010.

Lynch, John. *Spain under the Habsburgs*. Oxford: Oxford University Press, 1965.

———. *Simón Bolívar: A Life*. New Haven: Yale University Press, 2006.

———. *New Worlds: A Religious History of Latin America*. New Haven: Yale University Press, 2012.

Lynn, Martin. "British Policy, Trade, and Informal Empire in the Mid-Nineteenth Century." In Andrew Porter, ed., *Oxford History of the British Empire*, vol. 3: *The Nineteenth Century*. Oxford: Oxford University Press, pp. 101–121.

Macintyre, Stuart. *A Concise History of Australia*. 2nd ed. Cambridge: Cambridge University Press, 2004.

MacLeod, Roy, ed. *Nature and Empire: Science and the Colonial Enterprise. Osiris*, 2nd series, vol. 15. Chicago: University of Chicago Press Journals, 2000.

Mahoney, James, Matthew Lange, and Mattias vom Hau. "Colonialism and Development: A Comparative Analysis of British and Spanish Colonies." *American Journal of Sociology* 111, no. 5 (2006): 1412–1462.

Maltby, William S. *The Black Legend in England: The Development of Anti-Spanish Sentiment, 1558–1660*. Durham, N.C.: Duke University Press, 1971.

Marichal, Carlos. *Bankruptcy of Empire: Mexican Silver and the Wars between Spain, Britain and France, 1760–1810*. Cambridge: Cambridge University Press, 2007.

Marks, Patricia. "Confronting a Mercantile Elite: Bourbon Reformers and the Merchants of Lima, 1765–1796." *The Americas* 60, no. 4 (2004): 519–558.

Marks, Robert B. *The Origins of the Modern World: A Global and Ecological Narrative from the Fifteenth to the Twenty-First Century*. 2nd ed. Lanham, Md.: Rowman and Littlefield, 2007.

Marques, João Pedro. *The Sounds of Silence: Nineteenth-Century Portugal and the Abolition of the Slave Trade*. Trans. Richard Wall. New York: Berghahn, 2006.

Marshall, P. J. "The Eighteenth-Century Empire." In Jeremy Black, ed., *British Politics and Society from Walpole to Pitt*. Basingstoke: Macmillan, 1990, pp. 177–200.

———, ed. *The Oxford History of the British Empire*. Vol. II: *The Eighteenth Century*. Oxford: Oxford University Press, 1998.

———. *Remaking the British Atlantic: The United States and the British Empire after American Independence*. Oxford: Oxford University Press, 2012.

Marshall, P. J., and Glyndwr Williams. *The Great Map of Mankind: British Perceptions of the World in the Age of Enlightenment*. London: J. M. Dent and Sons, 1982.

Martinez, Jenny S. "Anti-Slavery Courts and the Dawn on International Human Rights Law." *Yale Law Journal* 117 (2008): 550–641.

Martínez, María Elena. *Genealogical Fictions: Limpieza de Sangre, Religion and Gender in Colonial Mexico*. Stanford: Stanford University Press, 2008.

Marzagalli, Silvia. "Atlantic Trade and the Sephardim Merchants in Eighteenth-Century France: The Case of Bordeaux." In Paolo Bernardini and Norman Fiering, eds., *The Jews and the Expansion of Europe to the West, 1450–1800*. New York: Berghahn, 2001, pp. 268–286.

Matsuda, Matt K. *Pacific Worlds: A History of Seas, Peoples and Cultures*. Cambridge: Cambridge University Press, 2012.

Maxwell, Kenneth R. "Pombal and the Nationalization of the Luso-Brazilian Economy." *Hispanic American Historical Review* 48, no. 4 (1968): 608–631.

———. *Pombal: Paradox of the Enlightenment*. Cambridge: Cambridge University Press, 1995.

———. *Naked Tropics: Essays on Empire and Other Rogues*. New York: Routledge, 2003.

———. *Conflicts and Conspiracies: Brazil and Portugal, 1750–1850*. New York: Routledge, 2004.

Mazower, Mark. *Dark Continent: Europe's Twentieth Century*. London: Penguin, 1998.

McAleer, John. *Britain's Maritime Empire: Southern Africa, the South Atlantic and the Indian Ocean, 1763–1820*. Cambridge: Cambridge University Press, 2017.

McCusker, John J., and Russell R. Menard. *The Economy of British America, 1607–1789*. Chapel Hill: University of North Carolina Press, 1985.

McFarlane, Anthony. *The British in the Americas, 1480–1815*. London: Longman, 1994.

———. *Colombia before Independence: Economy, Society and Politics under Bourbon Rule*. Cambridge: Cambridge University Press, 1993.

———. "Rebellion in Late Colonial Spanish America: A Comparative Perspective." *Bulletin of Latin American Research* 14, no. 3 (1995): 313–338.

———. *War and Independence in Spanish America*. London: Routledge, 2014.

McKay, Derek, and H. M. Scott. *The Rise of the Great Powers 1648–1815*. London: Macmillan, 1983.

McKinley, P. Michael. *Pre-Revolutionary Caracas: Politics, Economy and Society, 1777–1811*. Cambridge: Cambridge University Press, 1985.

McNeill, John Robert. *Atlantic Empires of Spain and France: Louisbourg and Havana, 1700–1763*. Chapel Hill: University of North Carolina Press, 1985.

———. *Mosquito Empires: Ecology and War in the Greater Caribbean, 1620–1914*. Cambridge: Cambridge University Press, 2010.

McNeill, John Robert, and William McNeill. *The Human Web: A Bird's Eye View of World History*. New York: W. W. Norton, 2003.

McNeill, William H. *The Rise of the West: A History of the Human Community.* Chicago: University of Chicago Press, 1963.

———. *Plagues and Peoples.* New York: Doubleday, 1977.

Meek, Ronald L. *Social Science and the Ignoble Savage.* Cambridge: Cambridge University Press, 1976.

Mello e Souza, Laura de. *The Devil and the Land of the Holy Cross: Witchcraft, Slavery and Popular Religion in Colonial Brazil.* Austin: University of Texas Press, 2003.

Melville, Elinor G. K. *A Plague of Sheep: The Environmental Consequences of the Conquest of Mexico.* Cambridge: Cambridge University Press, 1997.

Metcalf, Alida. *Family and Frontier in Colonial Brazil: Santana de Parnaíba, 1580–1822.* Austin: University of Texas Press, 1992.

———. *Go-Betweens and the Colonization of Brazil, 1500–1600.* Austin: University of Texas Press, 2005.

Metcalf, Barbara D., and Thomas R. Metcalf. *A Concise History of Modern India.* 2nd ed. Cambridge: Cambridge University Press, 2006.

Metcalf, Thomas R. *Ideologies of the Raj.* Cambridge: Cambridge University Press, 1994.

Meyer-Fong, Tobie. *What Remains: Coming to Terms with Civil War in Nineteenth-Century China.* Stanford: Stanford University Press, 2013.

Miller, Rory. *Britain and Latin America in the Nineteenth and Twentieth Centuries.* Longman, 1993.

Miller, Shawn. *An Environmental History of Latin America.* Cambridge: Cambridge University Press, 2007.

Mintz, Sidney W. *Sweetness and Power: The Place of Sugar in Modern History.* New York: Penguin, 1985.

Misevich, Philip, and Kristin Mann, eds. *The Rise and Demise of Slavery and the Slave Trade in the Atlantic World.* Rochester: University of Rochester Press, 2016.

Monteiro, Nuno G., Rui Ramos, and Bernardo Vasconcelos e Sousa. *História de Portugal.* Lisbon: A Esfera dos Livros, 2012.

Montesquieu, Baron de (Charles de Secondat). *The Spirit of the Laws.* Trans. and ed. A. M. Cohler, B. C. Miller, and H. S. Stone. Cambridge: Cambridge University Press, 1997.

Morgan, Kenneth. *A Short History of Transatlantic Slavery.* London: I. B. Tauris, 2016.

Morgan, Philip D. *Slave Counterpoint: Black Culture in the Eighteenth-Century Chesapeake and Low Country.* Chapel Hill: University of North Carolina Press, 1998.

———. "Caribbean Slavery." In Philip Misevich and Kristin Mann, eds., *The Rise and Demise of Slavery and the Slave Trade in the Atlantic World.* Rochester: University of Rochester Press, 2016, pp. 64–99.

Morgan, Philip D., and Christopher L. Brown, eds. *Arming Slaves: From Classical Times to the Modern Age.* New Haven: Yale University Press, 2006.

Morgan, Philip D., and Nicholas Canny, eds. *The Oxford Handbook of the Atlantic World, c. 1450–1850.* Oxford: Oxford University Press, 2011.

Morgan, Philip D., and Sean Hawkins, eds. *Black Experience and the Empire.* Oxford: Oxford University Press, 2004.

Moya, José C. *Oxford Handbook of Latin American History.* Oxford: Oxford University Press, 2011.

Munck, Thomas. *Seventeenth-Century Europe, 1598–1700.* London: Macmillan, 1990.

Mungello, D. E. *The Great Encounter of China and the West, 1500–1800.* Lanham, Md.: Rowman and Littlefield, 2009.

Murray, David R. *Odious Commerce: Britain, Spain and the Abolition of the Cuban Slave Trade.* Cambridge: Cambridge University Press, 1980.

Muthu, Sankar. *Enlightenment against Empire.* Princeton: Princeton University Press, 2003.

Needell, Jeffrey D. "The Abolition of the Brazilian Slave Trade: Historiography, Slave Agency and Statesmanship." *Journal of Latin American Studies* 33, no. 4 (2001): 681–711.

Nelson, Eric. *The Royalist Revolution: Monarchy and the American Founding.* Cambridge, Mass.: Belknap Press of Harvard University Press, 2014.

Newitt, Malyn. *A History of Mozambique.* London: Hurst, 1995.

———. *A History of Portuguese Overseas Expansion, 1400–1688.* London: Routledge, 2005.

———. *Portugal in European and World History.* London: Reaktion, 2009.

Nirenberg, David. "Was There Race before Modernity? The Example of 'Jewish' Blood in Late Medieval Spain." In Miriam Eliav-Feldon et al., eds., *The Origins of Racism in the West.* Cambridge: Cambridge University Press, 2009, pp. 232–264.

Northrup, David. *Indentured Labor in the Age of Imperialism, 1834–1927.* Cambridge: Cambridge University Press, 1995.

———. *Africa's Discovery of Europe, 1450–1850.* 3rd ed. Oxford: Oxford University Press, 2014.

Norton, Marcy. *Sacred Gifts, Profane Pleasures: A History of Tobacco and Chocolate in the Atlantic World.* Ithaca: Cornell University Press, 2008.

Norton, Mary Beth. *Founding Mothers and Fathers: Gendered Power and the Forming of American Society.* New York: Knopf, 1996.

Ogborn, Miles. *Global Lives: Britain and the World, 1550–1800.* Cambridge: Cambridge University Press, 2008.

Oliveira Marques, A. H. de. *History of Portugal.* Vol. I: *From Lusitania to Empire.* New York: Columbia University Press, 1972.

O'Malley, Gregory. *Final Passages: The Intercolonial Slave Trade of British America, 1619–1807.* Chapel Hill: University of North Carolina Press, 2014.

O'Shaughnessy, Andrew. "Redcoats and Slaves in the British Caribbean." In Robert Paquette and Stanley L. Engerman, eds., *The Lesser Antilles in the Age of European Expansion.* Gainesville: University of Florida Press, 1996, pp. 105–127.

———. *An Empire Divided: The American Revolution and the British Caribbean.* Philadelphia: University of Pennsylvania Press, 2000.

Oostindie, Gert, and Jessica Roitman, eds. *Dutch Atlantic Connections, 1680–1800: Linking Empires, Bridging Borders.* Leiden: Brill, 2014.

Operé, Fernando. *Indian Captivity in Spanish America: Frontier Narratives.* Trans. Gustavo Pellón. Charlottesville: University of Virginia Press, 2001.

Ormrod, David. *Rise of Commercial Empire: England and the Netherlands in the Age of Mercantilism, 1650–1770.* Cambridge: Cambridge University Press, 2003.

Osterhammel, Jürgen. *The Transformation of the World: A Global History of the Nineteenth Century.* Trans. Patrick Camiller. Princeton: Princeton University Press, 2014.

Outram, Dorinda. *The Enlightenment.* 2nd ed. Cambridge: Cambridge University Press, 2005.

Owensby, Brian P. *Empire of Law and Indian Justice in Colonial Mexico.* Stanford: Stanford University Press, 2008.

Oxford Dictionary of National Biography. "Yale, Elihu (1649–1721)." http://oxforddnb.com/article/30183, accessed July 23, 2016.

Pádua, José Augusto. *Um sopro de destruição: Pensamento político e crítica ambiental no Brasil escravista, 1786–1888.* 2nd ed. Rio de Janeiro: Jorge Zahar, 2002.

Pagden, Anthony. *Spanish Imperialism and the Political Imagination: Studies in European and Spanish American Social and Political Theory, 1513–1830.* New Haven: Yale University Press, 1990.

———. *European Encounters with the New World: From Renaissance to Romanticism.* New Haven: Yale University Press, 1993.

———. *Lords of All the World: Ideologies of Empire in Spain, Britain and France c. 1500–1800*. New Haven: Yale University Press, 1995.

———, ed. *The Idea of Europe from Antiquity to the European Union*. Cambridge: Wilson Center and Cambridge University Press, 2002.

———. *Peoples and Empires: A Short History of European Migration, Exploration and Conquest from Greece to the Present*. New York: Modern Library, 2003.

———. *The Burdens of Empire, 1539–Present*. Cambridge: Cambridge University Press, 2015.

Palmer, Jennifer. *Intimate Bonds: Family and Slavery in the French Atlantic*. Philadelphia: University of Pennsylvania Press, 2016.

Palmié, Stephan, and Francisco Scarano, eds. *The Caribbean: A History of the Region and Its People*. Chicago: University of Chicago Press, 2011.

Palmer, R. R. *The Age of the Democratic Revolution: A Political History of Europe and America, 1760-1800*. 2 vols. Princeton: Princeton University Press, 1959–1964.

Paquette, Gabriel. *Enlightenment, Governance, and Reform in Spain and Its Empire, 1759–1808*. Basingstoke: Palgrave Macmillan, 2008.

———. "The Dissolution of the Spanish Atlantic Monarchy." *Historical Journal* 52, no. 1 (2009): 175–212.

———. *Imperial Portugal in the Age of Atlantic Revolutions: The Luso-Brazilian World, c. 1770–1850*. Cambridge: Cambridge University Press, 2013.

Parker, Charles H. *Global Interactions in the Early Modern Age, 1400–1800*. Cambridge: Cambridge University Press, 2010.

Parker, Geoffrey. *Europe in Crisis, 1598–1648*. Ithaca: Cornell University Press, 1979.

———. *The Military Revolution: Military Innovation and the Rise of the West, 1500–1800*. Cambridge: Cambridge University Press, 1998.

———. *Empire, War and Faith in Early Modern Europe*. Clarendon: Allen Lane, 2002.

———. *Philip II*. 4th ed. Chicago: Open Court, 2002.

———. *Global Crisis: War, Climate Change, and Catastrophe in the Seventeenth Century*. New Haven: Yale University Press, 2013.

Parry, J. H. *The Establishment of European Hegemony 1415–1715: Trade and Exploration in the Age of the Renaissance*. New York: Harper Torchbooks, [1949] 1961.

———. *The Spanish Seaborne Empire*. Berkeley: University of California Press, [1966] 1990.

———. *Trade and Dominion: The European Overseas Empires in the Eighteenth Century*. London: Phoenix Press, 1971.

Parthasarathi, Prasannan. *The Transition to a Colonial Economy: Weavers, Merchants and Kings in South India, 1720–1800*. Cambridge: Cambridge University Press, 2001.

Patch, Robert W. *Indians and the Political Economy of Colonial Central America, 1670–1810*. Norman: University of Oklahoma Press, 2013.

Pearson, Michael. *The Indian Ocean*. London: Routledge, 2006.

Perdue, Peter C. *China Marches West: The Qing Conquest of Central Eurasia*. Cambridge: Belknap Press, 2005.

———. "Empires and Frontiers in Continental Eurasia." In Wolfgang Reinard, ed., *Empires and Encounters, 1350–1750*. Cambridge, Mass.: Belknap Press of Harvard University Press, 2005, pp. 67–218.

Pestana, Carla Gardina. *Protestant Empire: Religion and the Making of the British Atlantic World*. Philadelphia: University of Pennsylvania, 2009.

Pettigrew, William A. *Freedom's Debt: The Royal African Company and the Politics of the Atlantic Slave Trade, 1672–1752*. Chapel Hill: University of North Carolina Press, 2013.

Phelan, John Leddy. "Authority and Flexibility in Spanish Imperial Bureaucracy." *Administrative Science Quarterly* 5 (1960): 47–65.

———. *The Kingdom of Quito in the Seventeenth Century: Bureaucratic Politics in the Spanish Empire*. Madison: University of Wisconsin Press, 1967.

———. *The People and the King: The Comunero Revolution in Colombia, 1781*. Madison: University of Wisconsin Press, 1978.

Pinch, William R. "Same Difference in India and Europe." *History and Theory* 38, no. 3 (1999): 389–407.

Pincus, Steven C. *Protestantism and Patriotism: Ideologies and the Making of British Foreign Policy, 1650–1668*. Cambridge: Cambridge University Press, 1996.

———. *1688: The First Modern Revolution*. New Haven: Yale University Press, 2009.

———. "Rethinking Mercantilism: Political Economy, the British Empire and the Atlantic World in the Seventeenth and Eighteenth Centuries." *William and Mary Quarterly* 69, no. 1 (2012): 3–34.

Pomeranz, Kenneth. *The Great Divergence: China, Europe and the Making of the Modern World Economy*. Princeton: Princeton University Press, 2000.

Pomper, Philip. "The History and Theory of Empires." *History and Theory* 44, no. 4 (2005): 1–27.

Portuondo, María M. *Secret Science: Spanish Cosmography and the New World.* Chicago: University of Chicago Press, 2009.

Postma, Johannes. *The Atlantic Slave Trade.* London: Greenwood, 2003.

Prados de la Escosura, Leandro. *De imperio a nación: Crecimiento y atraso económico en España (1780–1930).* Madrid: Alianza, 1988.

Prakash, Gyan. "After Colonialism." In Prakash, ed., *After Colonialism: Imperial Histories and Postcolonial Displacements.* Princeton: Princeton University Press, 1995, pp. 3–20.

Prakash, Om. *European Commercial Enterprise in Pre-Colonial India.* Cambridge: Cambridge University Press, 1998.

Prange, Sebastian. "The Contested Sea: Regimes of Maritime Violence in the Pre-Modern Indian Ocean." *Journal of Early Modern History* 17 (2013): 9–33.

Premo, Bianca. *The Enlightenment on Trial: Ordinary Litigants and Colonialism in the Spanish Empire.* Oxford: Oxford University Press, 2017.

Price, J. L. *The Dutch Republic in the Seventeenth Century.* London: Macmillan, 1998.

Price, Richard. *Maroon Societies: Rebel Slave Communities in the Americas.* 2nd ed. Baltimore: Johns Hopkins University Press, 1979.

Pritchard, James. *In Search of Empire: The French in the Americas, 1670–1730.* Cambridge: Cambridge University Press, 2004.

Proctor, Frank T., III. *"Damned Notions of Liberty": Slavery, Culture and Power in Colonial Mexico, 1640–1769.* Albuquerque: University of New Mexico Press, 2010.

Quataert, Donald. *The Ottoman Empire, 1700–1922.* Cambridge: Cambridge University Press, 2000.

Quintero Saravia, Gonzalo M. *Bernardo de Gálvez: Spanish Hero of the American Revolution.* Chapel Hill: University of North Carolina Press, 2018.

Raynal, Abbé. *A Philosophical and Political History of the Settlements and Trade of the Europeans in the East and West Indies.* Trans. J. Justamond. 3rd ed. Dublin, 1779.

Rediker, Marcus. *Between the Devil and the Deep Blue Sea: Merchant Seamen, Pirates, and the Anglo-American Maritime World, 1700–1750.* Cambridge: Cambridge University Press, 1987.

———. *Villains of All Nations: Atlantic Pirates in the Golden Age.* Boston: Beacon, 2004.

———. *The Slave Ship: A Human History.* New York: Penguin, 2007.

Reid Andrews, George. "Spanish American Independence: A Structural Analysis." *Latin American Perspectives* 12, no. 1 (1985): 105–132.

———*Afro-Latin America 1800–2000*. New York: Oxford University Press, 2004.

Reinert, Sophus A. *Translating Empire: Emulation and the Origins of Political Economy*. Cambridge, Mass.: Harvard University Press, 2011.

Reinhard, Wolfgang. *A Short History of Colonialism*. Trans. Kate Sturge. Manchester: Manchester University Press, 2011.

Renton, David, ed. *Marx on Globalisation*. London: Lawrence and Wishart, 2001.

Reséndez, Andrés. *The Other Slavery: The Uncovered Story of Indian Enslavement in America*. Boston: Houghton Mifflin Harcourt, 2016.

Restall, Matthew. *Seven Myths of the Spanish Conquest*. Oxford: Oxford University Press, 2003.

———, ed. *Beyond Black and Red: African-Native Relations in Colonial Latin America*. Albuquerque: University of New Mexico Press, 2005.

Richards, John F. *The Unending Frontier: An Environmental History of the Early Modern World*. Berkeley: University of California Press, 2003.

Rieber, Alfred J. *The Struggle for the Eurasian Borderlands: From the Rise of Early Modern Empires to the End of the First World War*. Cambridge: Cambridge University Press, 2014.

Robertson, William. *The History of America*. 3 vols. 6th ed. London: A. Strahan, 1792.

Roca Barea, María Elvira. *Imperiofobia y la Leyenda Negra: Roma, Rusia, Estados Unidos y el Imperio Español*. Madrid: Siruela, 2016.

Rodney, Walter. *How Europe Underdeveloped Africa*. 2nd ed. Washington, D.C.: Howard University Press, 1982.

Røge, Pernille. "Why the Danes Got There First: A Trans-Imperial Study of the Abolition of the Slave Trade." *Slavery and Abolition* 35, no. 4 (2014): 576–592.

Rostworowski, María, and Craig Morris. "The Fourfold Domain: Inka Power and Its Social Foundations." In Frank Salomon and Stuart B. Schwartz, eds., *Cambridge History of the Native Peoples of the Americas*, vol. III. Cambridge: Cambridge University Press, 1999, pp. 769–863.

Rothschild, Emma. "Global Commerce and the Question of Sovereignty in the Eighteenth-century Provinces." *Modern Intellectual History* 1, no. 1 (2004): 3–25.

———. "'A Horrible Tragedy' in the French Atlantic." *Past and Present* 192 (2006): 67–108.

Rowe, Erin. "'After Death Her Face Turned White': Blackness and Sanctity in the Early Modern Hispanic World." *American Historical Review* 121, no. 3 (2016): 726–754.

Rowe, William T. *China's Last Empire: The Great Qing*. Cambridge, Mass.: Belknap Press of Harvard University Press, 2009.

Roy, Kaushik. *The Oxford Companion to Modern Warfare in India: From the Eighteenth Century to Present Times*. Oxford: Oxford University Press, 2009.

Ruiz, Teofilo. *Spanish Society, 1400–1600*. Harlow: Pearson Education, 2001.

Rushforth, Brett. *Bonds of Alliance: Indigenous and Atlantic Slaveries in New France*. Chapel Hill: University of North Carolina Press, 2012.

Russell-Wood, A. J. R. *Fidalgos and Philanthropists: The Santa Casa de Misericórdia of Bahia, 1550–1755*. Berkeley: University of California Press, 1968.

———. "Iberian Expansion and the Issue of Black Slavery: Changing Portuguese Attitudes, 1440–1770." *American Historical Review* 83, no. 1 (1978): 16–42.

———. *The Black Man in Slavery and Freedom in Colonial Brazil*. New York: St. Martin's Press, 1982.

———. "Ports of Colonial Brazil." In Franklin Knight and Peggy Liss, eds., *Atlantic Port Cities in the Atlantic World, 1650–1850*. Knoxville: University of Tennessee Press, 1991.

———. *The Portuguese Empire, 1415–1808: A World on the Move*. Baltimore: Johns Hopkins University Press, 1992.

Ryan, Mary P. *Womanhood in America: From Colonial Times to the Present*. 3rd ed. New York: Franklin Watts, 1983.

Safier, Neil. *Measuring the New World: Enlightenment Science and South America*. Chicago: University of Chicago Press, 2008.

Said, Edward. *Orientalism*. New York: Random House, 1994.

Salomon, Frank, and Stuart B. Schwartz, eds. *Cambridge History of Native Peoples of the Americas*. Vol. III: *South America, Part I*. Cambridge: Cambridge University Press, 1999.

Sarreal, Julia J. S. *The Guaraní and Their Missions: A Socioeconomic History*. Stanford: Stanford University Press, 2014.

Scammel, G. V. *The World Encompassed: The First European Maritime Empires c. 800–1650*. Berkeley: University of California Press, 1981.

———. *The First Imperial Age: European Overseas Expansion, c. 1400–1715*. London: Unwin Hyman, 1989.

Schiebinger, Londa, and Claudia Swan, eds. *Colonial Botany: Science, Commerce and Botany in the Early Modern World*. Philadelphia: University of Pennsylvania Press, 2005.

Schmidt, Benjamin. *Innocence Abroad: The Dutch Imagination and the New World, 1570–1670*. Cambridge: Cambridge University Press, 2001.

———. *Inventing Exoticism: Geography, Globalism and Europe's Early Modern World*. Philadelphia: University of Pennsylvania Press, 2015.

Schmidt-Nowara, Christopher. *Empire and Anti-Slavery: Spain, Cuba and Puerto Rico, 1833–74*. Pittsburgh: University of Pittsburgh Press, 1999.

———. "'*La España Ultramarina*': Colonialism and Nation-Building in Nineteenth-Century Spain." *European History Quarterly* 34 (2004): 191–214.

———. *Slavery, Freedom, and Abolition in Latin America and the Atlantic World*. Albuquerque: University of New Mexico Press, 2011.

Schultz, Kirsten. *Tropical Versailles: Empire, Monarchy, and the Portuguese Royal Court in Rio de Janeiro, 1808–21*. New York: Routledge, 2001.

Schwartz, Stuart B. *Sugar Plantations and the Formation of Brazilian Society: Bahia, 1550–1835*. Cambridge: Cambridge University Press, 1985.

———. *Slaves, Peasants and Rebels: Reconsidering Brazilian Slavery*. Urbana: University of Illinois Press, 1992.

———. *All Can Be Saved: Religious Tolerance and Salvation in the Iberian Atlantic*. New Haven: Yale University Press, 2008.

———, ed. *Early Brazil: A Documentary Collection to 1700*. Cambridge: Cambridge University Press, 2010.

———. *Sea of Storms: A History of Hurricanes in the Greater Caribbean from Columbus to Katrina*. Princeton: Princeton University Press, 2015.

Scott, Hamish M. *British Foreign Policy in the Age of the American Revolution*. Oxford: Clarendon Press, 1990.

———. *The Birth of a Great Power System, 1740–1815*. Harlow: Pearson Longman, 2006.

———, ed. *Oxford Handbook of Early Modern European History, 1350–1750*. Vol. II: *Culture and Power*. Oxford: Oxford University Press, 2015.

Scott, James C. *Weapons of the Weak: Everyday Forms of Peasant Resistance*. New Haven: Yale University Press, 1985.

Seeley, John R. *The Expansion of England: Two Courses of Lectures*. New York: Cosimo, 2005 [1891].

Seeman, Erik. *Death in the New World: Cross-Cultural Encounters, 1492–1800*. Philadelphia: University of Pennsylvania Press, 2010.

Seijas, Tatiana. *Asian Slaves in Colonial Mexico: From Chinos to Indians*. Cambridge: Cambridge University Press, 2014.

Sessions, Jennifer E. *By Sword and Plow: France and the Conquest of Algeria*. Ithaca: Cornell University Press, 2011.

Shillington, Kevin. *History of Africa*. 3rd ed. New York: Palgrave Macmillan, 2012.

Simms, Brendan. *Three Victories and a Defeat: The Rise and Fall of the First British Empire, 1714–1783*. New York: Basic Books, 2007.

Sinclair, Keith (with Raewyn Dalziel). *A History of New Zealand*. New York: Penguin, 2000.

Sinha, Manisha. *The Slave's Cause: A History of Abolition*. New Haven: Yale University Press, 2016.

Skidmore, Thomas. *Brazil: Five Centuries of Change*. 2nd ed. Oxford: Oxford University Press, 2009.

Smith, Adam. *An Inquiry into the Nature and Causes of the Wealth of Nations*. Ed. R. H. Campbell and A. S. Skinner. 2 vols. Oxford: Clarendon Press, 1976.

Socolow, Susan M. *The Women of Colonial Latin America*. Cambridge: Cambridge University Press, 2000.

Soll, Jacob. *The Reckoning: Financial Accountability and the Rise and Fall of Nations*. New York: Basic Books, 2014.

Sparks, Randy J. *Where the Negroes Are Masters: An African Port in the Era of the Slave Trade*. Cambridge, Mass.: Harvard University Press, 2014.

Spence, Jonathan. *The Search for Modern China*. 2nd ed. New York: W. W. Norton, 1999.

St. Clair, William. *The Grand Slave Emporium: Cape Coast Castle and the British Slave Trade*. London: Profile, 2006.

Steele, Ian K. The *English Atlantic, 1675–1740: An Explanation of Communication and Community*. Oxford: Oxford University Press, 1986.

———. *Warpaths: Invasions of North America*. Oxford: Oxford University Press, 1994.

Stein, Stanley J., and Barbara H. Stein. *Silver, Trade, and War: Spain and America in the Making of Early Modern Europe*. Baltimore: Johns Hopkins University Press, 2000.

Stern, Philip J. *The Company State: Corporate Sovereignty and the Early Modern Foundations of the British Empire in India*. Oxford: Oxford University Press, 2011.

Stern, Philip J., and Carl Wennerlind, eds. *Mercantilism Reimagined: Political Economy in Early Modern Britain and Its Empire*. Oxford: Oxford University Press, 2014.

Stern, Steve. "The Age of Andean Insurrection, 1742–1782: A Reappraisal." In Stern, ed., *Resistance, Rebellion and Consciousness in the Andean Peasant World, 18th–20th Centuries*. Madison: University of Wisconsin Press, 1987, pp. 34–93.

Storrs, Christopher. *The Resilience of the Spanish Monarchy, 1665–1700*. Oxford: Oxford University Press, 2006.

———. *The Spanish Resurgence, 1713–1748*. New Haven: Yale University Press, 2016.

Subrahmanyan, Sanjay. *The Portuguese Empire in Asia, 1500–1700: A Political and Economic History*. New York: Longman, 1993.

Sundkler, Bengt, and Christopher Steed. *A History of the Church in Africa*. Cambridge: Cambridge University Press, 2000.

Sweet, James H. *Recreating Africa: Culture, Kinship and Religion in the African-Portuguese World, 1441–1770*. Chapel Hill: University of North Carolina Press, 2003.

Swingen, Abigail L. *Competing Visions of Empire: Labor, Slavery and the Origins of the British Atlantic Empire*. New Haven: Yale University Press, 2015.

Tallett, Frank. *War and Society in Early Modern Europe, 1495–1715*. London: Routledge, 1992.

Tannenbaum, Frank. *Slave and Citizen*. Boston: Beacon, 1974 [1947].

Taylor, Alan. *American Colonies*. New York: Viking, 2001.

Taylor, Jean Gelman. *The Social World of Batavia: European and Eurasian in Dutch Asia*. Madison: University of Wisconsin Press, 1983.

Taylor, Miles. "The 1848 Revolutions and the British Empire." *Past and Present* 166 (2000): 146–180.

Taylor, William. "Two Shrines of the *Cristo Renovado:* Religion and Peasant Politics in Late Colonial Mexico." *American Historical Review* 110, no. 4 (2005): 945–974.

Teschke, Benno. *The Myth of 1648: Class, Geopolitics and the Making of Modern International Relations*. London: Verso, 2003.

Thomas, Hugh. *The Slave Trade: The History of the Atlantic Slave Trade*. London: Picador, 1977.

———. *Conquest: Cortés, Montezuma, and the Fall of Old Mexico*. New York: Simon and Schuster, 1995.

———. *Rivers of Gold: The Rise of the Spanish Empire, from Columbus to Magellan*. New York: Random House, 2005.

Thompson, I. A. A. "Castile." In John Miller, ed., *Absolutism in Seventeenth-Century Europe*. Basingstoke: Macmillan, 1990, pp. 69–98.

Thomson, Janice E. *Mercenaries, Pirates and Sovereigns: State Building and Extraterritorial Violence in Early Modern Europe*. Princeton: Princeton University Press, 1994.

Thomson, Sinclair. *We Alone Will Rule: Native Andean Politics in the Age of Insurgency.* Madison: University of Wisconsin Press, 2002.

———. "Sovereignty Disavowed: The Tupac Amaru Revolution in the Atlantic World." *Atlantic Studies* 13, no. 3 (2016): 407–431.

Thornton, John K. *The Kingdom of Kongo: Civil War and Transition, 1641–1718.* Madison: University of Wisconsin Press, 1983.

———. *Africa and Africans in the Making of the Atlantic World, 1400–1800.* 2nd ed. Cambridge: Cambridge University Press, 1998.

———. *A Cultural History of the Atlantic World, 1250–1820.* Cambridge: Cambridge University Press, 2012.

———. "Afro-Christian Syncretism in the Kingdom of Kongo." *Journal of African History* 54 (2013): 53–77.

———. "The Kingdom of Kongo and the Thirty Years' War." *Journal of World History* 27, no. 2 (2016): 189–213.

Tilly, Charles. *Coercion, Capital and European States, A.D. 990–1992.* Oxford: Blackwell, 1992.

Tocqueville, Alexis de. *Writings on Empire and Slavery.* Ed. and trans. Jennifer Pitts. Baltimore: Johns Hopkins University Press, 2001.

Todd, David. "A French Imperial Meridian, 1814–1870." *Past and Present* 210 (2011): 155–186.

———. "Transnational Projects of Empire in France, c. 1815–1870." *Modern Intellectual History* 12, no. 2 (2015): 265–293.

Tombs, Robert and Isabelle. *That Sweet Enemy: The French and the British from the Sun King to the Present.* London: William Heinemann, 2006.

Tomich, Dale. "Slavery in Martinique and the French Caribbean." In Verene Sheperd and Hilary McD. Beckles, eds., *Caribbean Slavery and the Atlantic World.* Kingston: Ian Randle, 2000, pp. 413–436.

Tracy, James D. *The Political Economy of Merchant Empires.* Cambridge: Cambridge University Press, 1991.

Trouillot, Michel-Rolph. *Silencing the Past: Power and the Production of History.* Boston: Beacon, 1995.

Tuck, Richard. *The Rights of War and Peace: Political Thought and the International Order from Grotius to Kant.* Oxford: Oxford University Press, 1999.

Tutino, John. *Making a New World: Founding Capitalism in the Bajío and Spanish North America.* Durham, N.C.: Duke University Press, 2011.

Twinam, Ann. *Public Lives, Private Secrets: Gender, Honor, Sexuality and Illegitimacy in Colonial Spanish America.* Stanford: Stanford University Press, 1999.

Valladares, Rafael. *Portugal y la monarquía Hispánica 1580–1668*. Madrid: Arcolibros, 2000.

Verlinden, Charles. "The Transfer of Colonial Techniques from the Mediterranean to the Atlantic." In Verlinden, *The Beginnings of Modern Colonization: Eleven Essays with an Introduction*, trans. Yvonne Freccero. Ithaca: Cornell University Press, 1970, pp. 3–32.

Vinson, Ben, III. *Bearing Arms for His Majesty: The Free-Colored Militia in Colonial Mexico*. Stanford: Stanford University Press, 2001.

———. *Before Mestizaje: The Frontiers of Race and Caste in Colonial Mexico*. Cambridge: Cambridge University Press, 2017.

Walker, Charles F. *Shaky Colonialism: The 1746 Earthquake-Tsunami in Lima, Peru, and Its Long Aftermath*. Durham, N.C.: Duke University Press, 2008.

Walvin, James. *Crossings: Africa, the Americas and the Atlantic Slave Trade*. London: Reaktion, 2013.

Ward, Kerry. *Networks of Empire: Forced Migration in the Dutch East India Company*. Cambridge: Cambridge University Press, 2009.

Warren, Wendy. *New England Bound: Slavery and Colonization in Early America*. New York: Liverlight, 2016.

Weber, David. *Bárbaros: Spaniards and Their Savages in the Age of Enlightenment*. New Haven: Yale University Press, 2005.

Wesseling, H. L. *The European Colonial Empires, 1815–1919*. Trans. Diane Webb. Harlow: Pearson Education, 2004.

Wey Gómez, Nicolás. *The Tropics of Empire: Why Columbus Sailed South to the Indies*. Cambridge: MIT Press, 2007.

Wheat, David. *Atlantic Africa and the Spanish Caribbean, 1570–1640*. Chapel Hill: University of North Carolina Press, 2016.

White, Richard. *The Middle Ground: Indians, Empires and Republics in the Great Lakes Region, 1650–1815*. Cambridge: Cambridge University Press, 1991.

Whitehead, Neil L. "Carib Ethnic Soldiering in Venezuela, the Guianas and the Antilles, 1492–1800." *Ethnohistory* 37, no. 4 (1990): 357–389.

Wilder, Craig Steven. *Ebony and Ivy: Race, Slavery, and the Troubled History of America's Universities*. New York: Bloomsbury, 2013.

Williams, Eric. *Capitalism and Slavery*. Chapel Hill: University of North Carolina Press, 1994 [1944].

———. *From Columbus to Castro: The History of the Caribbean, 1492–1969*. New York: Harper and Row, 1970.

Winch, Donald. *Classical Political Economy and Colonies*. London: G. Bell and Sons, 1965.

Winius, George D. "India or Brazil? Priority for Imperial Survival in the Wars of the Restauração." In Winius, *Studies on Portuguese Asia, 1495–1689*. Aldershot: Ashgate, 2001, pp. 1–9.

Winn, Peter. "British Informal Empire in Uruguay in the Nineteenth Century." *Past and Present* 73 (1976): 100–126.

Wolff, Larry. *The Singing Turk: Ottoman Power and Operatic Emotions on the European Stage from the Siege of Vienna to the Age of Napoleon*. Stanford: Stanford University Press, 2016.

Wood, Betty. *The Origins of American Slavery: Freedom and Bondage in the English Colonies*. New York: Hill and Wang, 1997.

Wood, Gordon S. *The Radicalism of the American Revolution*. New York: Knopf, 1992.

Wright, Louis B. *The Cultural Life of American Colonies, 1607–1763*. New York: Harper and Bros., 1957.

Yannakakis, Yanna. *The Art of Being In-Between: Native Intermediaries, Indian Identity, and Local Rule in Colonial Oaxaca*. Durham, N.C.: Duke University Press, 2008.

———. "Making Law Intelligible: Networks of Translation in Mid-Colonial Oaxaca." In Yannakakis and Gabriela Ramos, eds., *Indigenous Intellectuals: Knowledge, Power and Colonial Culture in Mexico and the Andes*. Durham, N.C.: Duke University Press, 2014, pp. 79–106.

Yun, Lisa. *The Coolie Speaks: Chinese Indentured Laborers and African Slaves in Cuba*. Philadelphia: Temple University Press, 2008.

Yun-Casalilla, Bartolomé, and Francisco Comín. "Spain: From Composite Monarchy to Nation State, 1492–1914. An Exceptional Case?" In Yun-Casalilla and Patrick O'Brien, eds. *The Rise of Fiscal States. A Global History, 1500–1914*. Cambridge: Cambridge University Press, 2012, pp. 233–266.

Zahedieh, Nuala. *The Capital and the Colonies: London and the Atlantic Economy, 1660–1700*. Cambridge: Cambridge University Press, 2010.

Index

Page numbers in *italic* type indicate illustrations or maps.

Abbas I, Shah of Persia, 34
Abd-el Kader, Emir, 214–215
Aboriginals, 219
absolutism, 65, 126, 192
acculturation, 39–41
Act of Union (1707), 65
Africa: American slave syncretism with, 171–172; incursions into interior of, 207–208; linguistic borrowing from, 161; littoral trading posts and, 28–29; racial bias toward, 148. *See also* North Africa; South Africa; West Africa; *specific countries*
African slave trade. *See* slavery; transatlantic slave trade
Afrikaners (Boers), 220
agriculture, 53, 68, 69, 74, 150, 201; Dutch "cultivation system" and, 213–214; ecological impact of, 128, 129; scientific, 122; Spanish America and, 167–168. *See also* coerced labor; foods; plantation system; *specific crops*
Aix-la-Chapelle, Treaty of (1748), 87
Akbar, Mughal emperor, 34
Alcácer Quibir, battle of (1578), 59
Alcoçovas, Treaty of (1479), 52
alcohol, 31, 136
Alexander VI, Pope, 51
Algarve region (Portugal), 49, 133
Algeria, 12, 24, 144, 208, 214–215, *215*, 217
Algonquians, 41, 147, 177
Aljubarrota, Battle of (1385), 49, 53
Álvaro I, king of Kongo, 37
Amazon Delta, 12, 91
American Colonization Society, 221
American Mutiny Act (1765), 194
American Revolution, 145, 156, 157, 158, 179, 189, 191, 199; British loyalists and, 204–205; European interventions in, 92–94; phases of, 194–195
Americas, 2, 12–15, 16, 51, 68, 121; basis of British and Dutch claims to, 74; contrasted Spanish vs. British rule in, 21; decimation of indigenous societies in, 40–41 (*see also* Amerindians); environmental damages in 127–130; expulsion of Jesuits from, 109; French first forays into, 68; map of, *88*; papal donation and, 52; Spanish-Portuguese division of, 29, 30, 52, 91; types of migrants to, 131. *See also* British America; New France; Spanish America
Amerindians, 13, 30, 36, 177–182, 202; British encroachment on, 179; Christian conversion of, 108–109, 146, 161, 171, 175; disease decimation of, 40–41, 58, 134, 178; enslavement and, 134, 146–147, 156, 158–159; European cultural influences on, 180; European intermarriages with, 182; French alliances with, 89, 163; kinship systems of, 163; languages of, 178; racial inferiority beliefs about, 26, 148; resistance by, 4, 147, 177–180
Amsterdam, 63, 70
ancient empires, 19–20, 25
Andes, 36, 58, 90, 171, 176, 180
Anglicanism, 7, 62, 64, 154–155, 187
Anglo-Dutch Wars, 79

Angola, 7, 23, 24, 30, 40, 87, 114, 172; Dutch and, 82,175; Portuguese and, 80, 169, 217, 218; slave ownership in, 151; transatlantic slave trade from, 133, 202
Antipodes, 116, 141
António I, king of Kongo, 80
Aragon, kingdom of, 48, 50
Araucanians, 13, 178
Archive of the Indies (Seville), 22
Aristotle, 25
armies. *See* military
Armitage, David, 191
Asia: civilizations of, 26, 27, 38; Dutch VOC and, 28, 32, 38, 82–83, 106–107, 179; international economic system and, 29, 31, 32, 37, 116–117; land-based empires in 32-35, map of, *33*; overland and sea routes to, 55. *See also* South Asia; *specific countries*
asiento concession, 85
Atlantic islands, 50, 53, 54, 134
Atlantic Ocean, 8, 69, 85, 89, 125; Dutch corsairs and, 72–73; "golden age" of piracy and, 181; voyages of exploration and, 50–51
Atlantic slave trade. *See* transatlantic slave trade
audiencias, 100, 113, 188
Augsburg, Peace of (1555), 78
Aurangzeb, Mughal emperor, 34, 43
Australia, 30, 74, 141, 209, 213, 218–220
Ayacucho, Battle of (1824), 200
Azores, 53, 146
Aztec Empire, 8, 36, 58

Bacon's Rebellion (1676), 185–186
Bahamas, 204, 205
Bahia, 80, 86, 108, 117, 203–204; Tailors' Revolt (1798), 186
balance of power, 61–75, 95–96
balance of trade, 31, 105, 119, 120, 122–123
Balta Liman, Treaty of (1830), 212
Baltimore, 2nd Baron (Cecil Calvert), 103–104
Banda Oriental (modern Paraguay), 202
"Baptist War" (Jamaica), 158
Barbados, 29, *71*, 72, 121, 135, 139; slave code, 152, 167
Barlow, Edward, 13
Batavia (modern Indonesia), 23, 28, 98–99, 142, 214, 218; deforestation of, 128; Dutch VOC and, 106; failed migration to, 144; intermarriage and, 163; malaria deaths in, 128; map of, *106*; value of spices from, 32
battles. *See key word*
Bayly, Christopher, 43, 176, 193, 205; *Imperial Meridian,* 208
Belize, 30, 72, 93
Benedict, St., 172
Bengal, 43, 45, 95
Benguela, 133
Benin, Bight of, 133
Bentham, Jeremy, 14–15
Bentick, Lord, 45–46
Benton, Lauren, 19, 23
Berbice, 104; slave rebellion, 185
Bermuda, 68, 141
Bethencourt, Francisco, 110
Biafra, Bight of, 133
Bible, 148
black codes, 152
Black Legend, 21–22, 26, 61
Black Sea, 42, 133
black skin, 148, 149
Blackstone, William, 233n2
Blome, Richard, *A New and Exact Mapp of the Isle of Jamaica, 80*
Blood River, Battle of (1838), 220
Bodin, Jean, *Les six livres de la république,* 19
Boers (Afrikaners), 220
Bolívar, Simón, 158
Bombay, 80, 107, 193
Boston, 150, 151
botany, 75–76, 122, 129, 161
Botany Bay (Australia), 30, 141, 218, 219
Bougainville, Louis-Antoine de, 75
Bounty, H.M.S., 122
Bourbon dynasty, 85, 86, 93, 94, 199
Boxer, C. R., 5–6
Brading, David, 109
Braganza dynasty, 73, 80, 204
Brazil: British credit with, 210; cattle ranchers in, 181–182; continuance of Old Regime in, 206; deforestation of, 128; Dutch incursion in, 24, 30, 70–71, 72, 81, *81*, 82, 175, 184; economic development of, 92; elevated status of, 203; export variety and, 105, 116,

198; female migrants to, 144; free blacks and, 169; fugitive slave communities and, 182, 184; hybrid language and, 161, 178; independence of (1825), 203, 205, 206, 211, 217; indigenous people of, 41, 57, 91, 103, 147, 165, 175; Jesuits and, 108; Pombal's power in, 92; Portuguese colonizing of, 24, 29, 39, 57, 80–82, *81*, 86–98, 102–103, 105, 186, 187; Portuguese royalty and, 201, 202–203, 204; racial categories and, 165, 202; religious syncretism and, 172; revolts in, 186, 205; slavery and, 8, 87, 92, 133, 134–135, 147, 149, 151, 153–156, 158, 192, 193, 197–198, 202, 205, 211, 218; slave syncretism and, 171–172; slave trade abolishment by, 212, 218; sugar production and, 72, *81*, 86, 117, *118*, 121, 128, 147, 197–198, 201; sumptuary laws of, 166, 167; viceroy's power in, 101; wealth of, 87. *See also* Rio de Janeiro

brazilwood, 57, 128

breadfruit trees, 122

British America: Amerindians and, 36, 41, 146, 177–180; colonial charters and, 103–104; colonies of, 29, 30, 68, 69, 71, 72, 89, 94, 98; culture and learning in, 7, 187–188; Dutch displacement from, 71, 82, 170; early failures in, 12; environmental damage in, 127, 129; first settlements in, 12, 67–68, 98; free blacks and, 168; French losses to, 24, 87, 89 (*see also* Seven Years' War); governance of, 74, 98, 103–105, 110–111, 113–114, 141, 233n2; imperial breakdown in, 111, 187, 190, 191, 194 (*see also* American Revolution); indentured labor and, 139–140; intermarriage in, 163, 164; map of, *88*; nationalities in, 23; Proclamation Line (1763) and, 179; Protestantism and, 7, 110, 170–171; slavery and, 133, 135, 139, 147, 149–151, 154, 156, 185–186, 194; Spanish incursions in, 12, 29, 93, 179; spheres of influence of, 30; sumptuary laws and, 166–167; taxation of, 194. *See also* Canada

British Caribbean, 10, 12, 30, 69, 72, 74, 86, 141, 166, 194, 204; Amerindian resistance in, 178; closed trading and, 121; continued British ties with, 186–187; dominance of, 89, 122; free black militia of, 169–170; indentured servitude and, 139; islands of, 24, 29, 79; naval losses and, 94; race relations and, 187; slave labor and, 11, 135, 150, 152; slave rebellions and, 158, 184–185

British Empire, 11–12, 30, 42, 77–96; Act of Union (1707) and, 65; America and (*see* British America; Canada); Amerindians and, 147, 175, 177–178, 179; centralization and, 62; Chinese trade and, 7, 11, 38, 213; coercive tactics of, 212–213; commercial focus of, 21, 124, 218; common law and, 98, 141, 194, 233n2; commonwealth of, 65; concept of empire of, 21, 22, 25, 73–74, 98; deportations from, 30, 140–142, 218; Dutch rivalry with, 79; EIC autonomy and, 95 (*see also* English East India Company); emergence of, 8, 15, 47, 64–68; fiscal bureaucracy of, 83–84; Gibraltar and, 28, 85, 94; global power of, 94–95, 96; Glorious Revolution and, 84–85, 104; gunboat diplomacy of, 212–213, 218; historical legacy of, 22; individual proprietor model and, 103–104; industrialization and, 38, 155–156; map of (1750), *3*, 6; military expenditures of, 83–84; naval dominance of, 79, 93, 211; opium trade and, 11, 38; population (1800) of, 35; Portuguese alliance with, 80–81, 85, 87, 91–92, 201, 218; Protestantism of, 7, 21, 29, 64–65, 67–68, 72; reform of 1780s and, 84; religious dissent and, 64–65; reorientation after American Revolution of, 208–210, 218–220; revenue collection by, 83–84; Saint-Domingue slave rebellion and, 195–196; scientific expedition and, 75; seafaring tradition of, 7; slave emancipation and, 154–158, 221; slavery and, 125–126, 135, 136, 147, 151, 152, 153; slave trade opposition and, 37, 137–138, 155, 157, 211–212; South Africa and, 220; South Asia and (*see* English East India Company; India); Spain and, 10, 12, 28, 29, 61, 69, 74–75, 85, 198; supremacy of, 89; technological advances and, 207; theorists of, 73–74; trade regulation and, 119, 121; Turkish culture fad and, 38–39

Buffon, Comte de (Georges-Louis Leclerc), 25–26

bullion, 85–86, 90, 116, 117, 120, 123; political significance of, 126. *See also* gold; silver
Burke, Edmund, 14, 107, 243n5
Burma, 34, 141–142
Buxar, Battle of (1764), 44–45, 95

cabildo (town council), 112, 114, 170
Cabral, Pedro Álvares, 52, 57, 133, 134
cacao, 90, 117, 123, 125, 215
Cádiz, 54, 69, 90, 120, 126, 198, 216; constitution of, 199–200
Calcutta, 46, 107, 140, 193, 221
Calvert, Cecil, 2nd Baron Baltimore, 103–104
Canada: Amerindians and, 177, 179; British claims to, 30, 94, 194; French interests in, 29, 30, 68, 89, 104, 114, 127, 163, 177, 180; migrants to, 143, 204; model self-government in, 209
Canada Act (1791), 204
Canary Islands, 50–53, 57, 134
Canning, George, 210, 211
Canton (modern Guangzhou), 38, 213
Cape Coast Castle (modern Ghana), 141
Cape Colony, 114, 153–154, 170, 220
Cape of Good Hope, 55, 220
Cape St. Vincent, 198
Cape Town, 28
Cape Verde, 29, 52, 53, 72, 134, 161, 217
Cap Français, 133, 168
capitalism, 2, 17, 46, 115, 126
Caribbean, 12, 13, 41, 123, 140, 163, 170; African slave trade ports in, 133; climate change in, 129; colonial councils and, 111–112; colonization of, 57–58; Columbus's landfall in, 29, 52; free ports in, 84; interimperial conflict impact in, 23–24; justification for colonization of, 74; slave labor and, 147, 150; slave rebellions and, 157, 184–185; sugar plantations, 117, 150; sumptuary laws and, 167. *See also* British Caribbean; Dutch Caribbean; French Caribbean
Carib Indians, 178
Cartagena, 12, 13, 110, 150
cartaz system, 56, 119
Cartier, Jacques, 68
casta, 164, 168, 240n6
Castile, kingdom of, 20, 48–49, 70, 97–98
Castlereagh, Viscount, 210
Catalonia, 48, 50, 70
Cateau-Cambrésis, Peace of (1559), 78
Cathedral of San Juan, Puerto Rico, 71
Catherine of Braganza, 80
Catholic Church, 25, 56, 104, 146, 162, 170; converts to (*see under* Christianity); Inquisition and, 109–110, 172; Maryland colony and,103; Protestant challenges to, 21, 62–63, 64–66; secular power of, 51, 97, 107–110; slave ownership by, 151, 154–155, 156; syncretism and, 171, 172. *See also* Jesuits; papacy
cattle ranchers, 181–182
cayote, 164–165
Ceuta, 53, 55
Ceylon (modern Sri Lanka), 29, 72, 82, 170, 185
Champlain, Samuel de, 68
Charles I, king of England, 65, 72
Charles II, king of England, 80
Charles V, Holy Roman Emperor, 20
Charleston (S.C.), 127, 133, 168, 194
charters, 97, 104–105. *See also* trading companies
Chesapeake region, 72, 149, 163
Chile, 13, 178, 210, 217
China: as British trade market, 7, 11, 38, 213; contract laborers from, 140, 216–217; dynasty empires of, 8, 32-35, 43–44; European fascination with, 26, 39; eviction of VOC from, 82; export products of, 31, 38, 39, 116–117; map of, *33*; as opium market, 11, 38, 213; Portuguese in, 54–55
Chincha Islands, 217
chinchona bark ("Jesuit bark"), 208
Choiseul, Duke of, 89
Christianity: converts to, 51, 54, 64, 103, 109, 146, 154–155, 161, 171; racial views and, 148, 165, 169; syncretic forms of, 172. *See also* Catholic Church; Protestantism
Christophe, Henri, 197
coastal enclaves, 28–29, 30, 37, 215
coerced labor, 18, 21, 139–149, 159, 176, 216–217. *See also* convict labor; indentured servitude; slavery
coerced migration, 131, 139–144. *See also* transatlantic slave trade

coffee, 32, 105, 116–117, 123, 125, 150, 198
Coimbra, 87, 186, 201
Colbert, Jean-Baptiste, 78, 105
Colley, Linda, 22
Colombo, 55, 82
colonies, 1–2, 9, 116, 191, 192; derivation of term, 20; justifications for, 74–76; law and, 97–98, 106, 194, 217; self-government and, 209–210; subordinate position of, 144; trading companies and, 126; typologies of, 20, 105
Columbus, Christopher, 29, 51, 52, 55, 57
Comanches, 36, 178
common law, 98, 141, 194, 233n2
Comunero Revolt, 186, 189
Condorcanqui, José (Túpac Amaru), 176, 180
confraternities, 170
Connecticut, 7, 170
conquistadors, 58–59, 99, 101, 146, 163
constitutions, 193, 196, 197, 199–200, 204, 205
contract laborers ("coolies"), 140, 216–217
convict labor, 30, 131, 134, 140–142, 145, 147, 218–220
Cook, James, 75
Cortes, 49, 59, 126–127, 203
Cortés, Hernán, 58, 146
cotton, 69, 79, 105, 125, 128, 150, 198, 213, 215. *See also* textiles
Council of the Indies, 99–100, 101
credit, 70, 71, 82, 83, 210–211
creole, 4, 9, 15, 165–171, 176, 187–189, 198–199; consciousness of, 187, 192, 193; derivation of term, 165–166; languages, 160–161; rebellions, 158, 186, 188
Cromwell, Oliver, 65, 79
Crown Colony, 209, 220
Cuba, 12, 89, 140, 158, 200, 205, 216–218; colonizing of, 57; slave trade and, 133, 155, 216. *See also* Havana
Curaçao, 28, 30, 104, 123, 161, 170, 185
Curtain, Philip, 8
customs duties, 49, 216
Cyprus, 28, 133

Darwin, John, 2, 18
Davenant, Charles, 119
Declaration of Independence (1776), 191
Declaratory Act (1766), 194
Defoe, Daniel, 38
deforestation, 128–129
Demerara (modern Guyana), 29, 123, 125, 158
Dessalines, Jean-Jacques, 197
Dias, Bartolomeu, 55
Diderot, Denis, 13–14, 156
disease, 12, 30, 59, 128; Amerindian deaths from, 40–41, 58, 134, 178; medical advances and, 207–208; transatlantic slave trade and, 137, 138, 139
dissent: political, 36, 140, 141, 142, 202; religious, 62, 64–65
diwani (land grant revenue rights), 45, 95
Dom João, prince regent of Portugal, 201, 202, 203
Dom Pedro, prince of Portugal, 203, 204
donatary captains, 102–103, 105
Drake, Sir Francis, 10, 67
Drayton, Richard, 27, 74, 75, 84, 124, 126
Dundas, Henry, 96
Dutch Caribbean, 28, 30, 71, 74, 82, 123; French rivalry with, 78; Jewish settlers in, 170; language of, 160–161. *See also* Dutch West India Company
Dutch East India Company (VOC), 23, 37, 82–83, 116, 126, 170, 179; business model of, 32, 121–122; charter provisions of, 105–107; coastal trading posts of, 28; decline of, 94; environmental degradation by, 128; intermarriage bans and, 164; intra-Asian trade and, 32, 38; law and, 98–99; rebellion against, 185; reinvestment of shares in, 122; sovereignty concept of, 19; voluntary migration and, 144
Dutch East Indies. *See* Batavia
Dutch Empire, 6, 10, 12, 13, 22, 28, 78–84; American Revolution and, 92, 94; ascendancy of, 78; Brazil and, 24, 30, 70–71, 72, 81, *81*, 82, 175, 184; British rivalry with, 79; clandestine trade and, 123; commercial advantages of, 82–83; "cultivation system" of, 213–214; emergence of, 8, 15, 47, 63–64, 66, 72–73; financial successes of, 63, 71, 124–125; freedom of conscience and, 170; Grotius justification of, 73, 74; Holland and, 82, 231n7; law and, 98–99; map of (1750), *3*; migrants from, 142–144; naval strength of,

Dutch Empire *(continued)*
72–73; North America and, 23, 30, 71, 82, 170; patroonship and, 104; Portugal and, 80, 81, 72–73; Protestantism of, 21, 23, 29, 63, 170; slave rebellions and, 185; slavery and, 153–154, 156–157; slave trade and, 27, 133, 135, 136, 155; in South Africa, 28, 114, 220; Spain and, 27, 61, 63, 69, 70–75, 78; Surinam and, 30, 117, 123, 125, 168, 170; wealth of, 63, 72
Dutch Reformed Church, 23, 71, 170
Dutch West India Company (WIC), 23, 27, 70–71, 72, 104, 175

East Africa, 29, 40
East India Company. *See* Dutch East India Company; English East India Company; French East India Company
economic systems. *See* political economy
Egypt, 42, 209, 212
EIC. *See* English East India Company
Elizabeth I, queen of England, 10, 67, 68
Elliott, John H., 62, 70, 97–98, 111, 192
El Mina castle, 54, 55, 137
El Niño, 129
Emancipation Act (1833), 154, 158
empire: definitions of, 15, 17–30; justifications for, 73–76. *See also* colonies; *specific empires*
encomiendas, 58–59, 99, 146, 176, 238n3
England. *See* British Empire
English Civil War (1660), 65, 79, 140
English East India Company (EIC), 7, 32, 37, 40, 82, 119, 126, 145, 205; abuses by, 14; evolution of, 11; functions of, 95, 107; new charter (1657) of, 79; overseas penal colonies and, 141–142; power of, 45, 94–95, 107; profitability of, 122; rebellions against, 185; South Asia and, 28–29, 44–45, 94–95, 105, 143, 175–176; trade goods and, 116
English language, 161
English Royal African Company, 10
environmental damage, 116, 127–130
epidemics. *See* disease
Estado da Índia, 29, 37, 55–56, 59–60, 81–82
Eurasian empires, 8, 30, 32, 35–37, 41–45; map of, *33*
European seaborne empires: map (1750) of, *3*. *See also* British Empire; Dutch Empire; French Empire; Portuguese Empire; Spanish Empire
evangelization, 51, 101, 108, 131, 171, 172. *See also* missionaries
exclusif, 78–79, 121, 123
exogamy, 162–163, 164
exploration, 49–50, 55, 58–60, 64, 68; global circumnavigation and, 67; secular legal basis for, 52

factories (forts), 54, 55, 56, 57, 134, 135, 136–137
Ferdinand II of Aragon, king of Spain, 48
Fernando VII, king of Spain, 200
filles du roi, 144
firearms, 37, 90, 136, 177, 212
First Dutch Church (New Amsterdam), 71
fiscal military state, 83
fishing, 49, 64
Florida, 12, 30, 93, 169, 179
flota system, 86, 119–121
foods, 117, 128–129, 167–168
forts. *See* factories
"Four Stages Theory," 26
Fradera, Josep, 21
France. *See* French *headings*
Francis I, king of France, 68
Franklin, Benjamin, 188
free blacks, 167, 168–170, 196, 202, 220–221
freedom of conscience, 170
free trade, 90, 208, 211, 212
French Caribbean, 29, 30, 69, 89, 93, 111–112, 123, 125, 133, 142, 215; African slaves and, 135, 147, 150, 197; Dutch rivalry with, 78; expulsion of Jews from, 170; indentured servants and, 149
French East India Company, 31, 78–79
French Empire, 6, 8, 12, 15, 19, 22, 27, 30, 35, 47, 77–96, 147, 163; in Algeria, 24, 208, 214–215, *215*, 217; American Revolution and, 92–93, 94, 195; ascendancy of, 78–79; Atlantic ports of, 125; governance and, 104, 105, 111–112, 114; Haitian independence and, 197–198; Jesuit expulsion from, 109; map of (1750), *3*; religious civil war and, 62, 66, 68; scientific expedition and, 75; Seven Years' War and, 89; trade and, 68, 78–79, 104, 105, 121, 123, 124, 135. *See also* Napoleon

French North America. *See* New France
French Revolution, 186, 190, 195, 199
French Revolutionary Wars, 151, 152, 175–176, 208
Fronde (1648), 66
fugitive slave communities, 157, 175, 182–185, *183*
fur trade, 68, 127, 163, 177, 180

Gabon, 215, 220
Gálvez, José de, 90
Gama, Vasco da, 55, 57
George III, king of Great Britain, 38
Ghana, 52, 141
Gibraltar, 12, 28, 85, 94
Gilbert, Sir Humphrey, 67–68
Glorious Revolution (1688), 84–85, 104, 111
Goa, 29, 55, 72, 98, 151, 193, 217
Godwyn, Morgan, 149
gold, 2, 13, 56, 86–87, 90, 120; "royal fifth" and, 127; as trading currency, 31, 54, 134
Gold Coast, 52, 133; map of, *132*
Goldstone, Jack, 205
Gould, Eliga, 26
governance models, 97–114, 192, 208–210
Granada, 47–48
Grasse, Comte de, 94
Great Awakening (1740s), 154
Great Lakes, 68–69, 178
Great Northern War, 35
Great Trek (1835–1837), 220
Greece, 41, 42, 50–51; ancient, 25
Grenada, 93, 185
Grotius, Hugo, 73, 74; *De Indis*, 73; *Mare liberum*, 73
Guadeloupe, 29, 69, 89, 94, 123, 129, 150, 197
guano, 217
Guaraní missions, 109, 146, 175
Guiana, 12, 68, 140, 197
Gulf Coast (North America), 93, 179
gunboat diplomacy, 212–213, 218
gunpowder. *See* firearms
Guyana, 29, 123, 125, 158

Habsburg dynasty, 13, 20, 21, 34, 41, 69, 94; defeat of, 77, 78, 85; power of, 60, 61
Hadar Ali, 185
Haitian Revolution, 157, 158, 182, 186, 190, 195–197
Hakluyt, Richard, 67
Han Chinese, 34
Hanoverian Succession, 22, 85
Harvard College, 187
Hastings, Warren, 45
Havana, 12, 13, 89, 91, *91*, 216
Hawaii, 37, 75
Henry IV, king of France, 66, 68
Henry XVIII, king of England, 61
Henry the Navigator, Prince of Portugal, 53
Heren XVII (Seventeen Gentlemen), 32, 122
Hispaniola, 52, 57, 182
Holy Alliance, 200, 208
Holy League, 41
Holy Roman Emperor, 20, 41, 94
Hong Kong, 213
Hormuz, 55
Howe, Stephen, 18
Hudson Bay Company, 177
Huguenots, 66, 68
hybridity, 9, 160–173

Iberian Peninsula, 29, 47–48, 51, 54. *See also* Portuguese Empire; Spanish Empire
imperium/imperator, 19–20
Inca Empire, 8, 36, 58, 146, 176, 180
indentured servitude, 131, 134, 135, 139–140, 145, 147, 159, 185
India, 26, 31, 34, 39, 208, 209; Britain and, 30, 44–46, 213, 221; British-French disputes over, 87, 94; British migrants to, 143, 204; EIC power and, 7, 11, 14, 40, 94–95, 107, 175; French trading posts in, 79, 80; legal pluralism and, 113–114; opium trade and, 11, 38, 213; provincial governors of, 43; sepoy mutinies and, 185; spice trade and, 127; tea from, 213; textiles from, 31, 32, 37, 38, 116–117. *See also* Mughal Empire
India Act (1784), 95
Indian Ocean, 8, 28, 30, 161, 204; British and Dutch trading companies and, 30, 145; Dutch interests in, 73, 81–82; French interests in, 78–79, 215; as pirate haven, 181; Portuguese interests in, 30, 49, 55–57, 73, 81–82, 119; slave trade and, 37, 131, 136

indigenous people, 2, 4, 9, 17, 58, 104, 113, 114, 162, 163, 175–177; Australia and New Zealand and, 219–220; Christian conversion of, 51, 172; encomendero system and, 146; European acculturation to, 39–41; European colonization claims and, 74; factors in decimation of, 40–41, 58, 134; imperial exploitation of, 127; intermarriage with, 163; as labor force, 146–147; natural knowledge and, 75; rights of, 52; Spanish "Black Legend" and, 21, 22; Spanish "conquests" of, 58, 98, 101, 146–147, 161–162, 178; syncretic religious forms and, 110; tribute collected from, 90. *See also* Amerindians; *under* Brazil; *under* Spanish America
indigo, 69, 124, 125, 213
Indonesia. *See* Batavia
Industrial Revolution, 125, 155–156
Inquisition, 109–110, 170, 172
intermarriage, 40, 71, 163–165, 177, 182, 184
Ireland, 35, 64, 65, 142, 143
Iroquois, 178–179, 180
Irving, Washington, 21
Isabel of Castile, 48
Islamic world: 8, 28, 31-34, *33*, 36, 41–44, 113, 114; Christian conquests of, 47–50; Christian racial theories and, 148, 165, 169; map of, *33;* slave labor in, 131

Jahangir, Mughal emperor, 44
Jamaica, 24, 29, 121, 133, 140, 149, 168, 204–205; "Baptist War" and, 158; British capture of, 79, 86; Jewish status in, 170; map (1687) of, *80*; mixed-race children and, 165; Tackey's Revolt in, 152, 154, 184–185
Jamestown (Va.), 68, 186
Japan, 38, 82
Java, 28, 162, 163, 185, 213–214
Jefferson, Thomas, 166
Jesuits, 68, 92, 108–109, 146, 151, 162, 175
Jews, 148, 169, 170
joint-stock company, 107, 121–122, 126
Joseph II, Holy Roman Emperor, 94

Kamehameha, Chief (Hawaii), 37
Kandy Revolt (1817–1818), 185
Kang-Xi, emperor of China, 39, 44
Karlowitz, Treaty of (1699), 41–42
King Philip's (Metacom's) War, 147, 177
Kongo, kingdom of, 8, 37, 54, 80, 175

labor regimes, 15, 18, 21, 53, 127, 131, 206. *See also* coerced labor
La Condamine, Charles-Marie de, 75
land grants, 45, 59, 95, 99, 102–103, 105
languages, 45, 160–161, 164–165, 171, 178
La Salle, Robert de, 69
Las Casas, Bartolomé de, 13
law, 9, 15, 22, 36, 43, 51, 74, 97–114, 141, 146, 153, 194, 217, 233n2
Laws of Burgos (1512), 146
Lepanto, Battle of (1571), 34
libraries, 87, 188
Lima, 110, 150, 168, 187; earthquake (1746), 188
Lisbon, 49, 54, 87, 98, 116; earthquake (1755), 92
Locke, John, *Second Treatise of Government,* 73–74
London Abolition Society, 157
Longfellow, Henry Wadsworth, 21
López de Velasco, Juan, 166
Lords of Trade (Britain), 98, 111
Louis XIV, king of France, 78, 83
Louisiana, 24, 30, 114, 163
Louverture, Toussaint, 196–197
Luanda, 23, 72, 87, 133, 172, 175

Macaulay, Thomas Babington, 45
Macquarie, Lachlan, 219
Madagascar, 12, 37, 79, 153, 181
Madeira, 24, 53, 134
Madras, 94, 107, 140, 175, 185, 193
Madrid, Treaty of (1670), 79
Madrid, Treaty of (Treaty of Limits) (1750), 91
Malacca, 55, 72, 141, 170, 213
malaria, 12, 128, 138, 207–208
Manchu Empire, 31
Manikongo, king of Kongo, 54
Manuel, king of Portugal, 49–50
Maoris, 219
Maranhão (Brazil), 147, 175, 203
maroons (escaped slaves), 157, 182, *183*

marriage, 23, 107, 143, 154, 171; dynastic, 48, 66, 73, 80, 81; slave, 154. *See also* intermarriage
Martínez de la Rosa, Francisco, 22
Martinique, 29, 69, 89, 123, 129, 150, 197
Marx, Karl, 2, 17, 46, 115, 126, 130
Maryland, 72, 103–104, 117, 170
Massachusetts, 29, 163, 170, 194
Massachusetts Bay Colony, 68, 98, 111
Mauritius, 79, 140, 141
Maya culture, 180
Mayall Creek massacre (1838), 219
Mazarin, Cardinal, 78
Mbwila, Battle of (1665), 80
Mediterranean region, 28, 34, 50, 54, 85, 204
mercantilism, 119, 208
mercury pollution, 127
mestizo, 15, 160, 162, 163–165, 168–173, 205
Metacom's War, 147
Methuen Treaty (1703), 85, 91, 92
Mexico: 13, 69, 90, 114, 150, 162, 187, 210, 217; Aztec power and, 36, 58; encomiendas and, 99, 146, 176; expulsion of Jesuits from, 109; expulsion of Spaniards from, 205; first Spanish incursions into, 58; map of, *88;* mercury-polluted rivers of, 127; mythic narratives about, 58; Pueblo revolt and, 177; religious syncretism and, 171; silver from, 29, 127
Middle Passage, 68, 137–138, 149
military, 54, 63, 131, 169, 213, 217; creoles and, 198–199; expenditures for, 53, 61–62, 83–84; forced labor and, 145, 151–152; free blacks and, 169–170; mercenaries and, 22–23; South Asians and,175–176
Mill, James, 15; *History of British India*, 45
Minas Gerais, 86–87, 186, 201
Ming dynasty, 32-34, map of, *33*
mining. *See* gold; silver
Minorca, 12, 28, 50, 85, 93, 94
missionaries, 7, 44, 108–109, 146, 154–155, 188
mita (forced labor), 146
mocambo community, 175, 182, 184
monopoly, 14, 19, 56, 68, 78–79, 83, 86, 90, 102, 104, 105, 116, 119, 121–122, 126, 127, 135. *See also* trading companies
Montesquieu, 13, 156
Morgan, Henry, 10
Morocco, 11, 12, 59, 217
Mosquito Coast, 72, 93
Mozambique, 151, 153, 217
Mughal Empire: 8, 31-34, 42–45, 95, 185; European trade and, 37, 38, 56–57; map of, *33*; power of, 55
Muhammad Ali, 42, 212
mulatto, 163, 164, 165, 169, 202
Münster, Treaty of (1658), 77
Muslims. *See* Islamic world

Nadir Shah, king of Iran, 43
Nahuatl language, 164–165, 171, 178
Nanjing, Treaty of (1842), 213
Nantes, Edict of (1648), 66
Napoleon, 42, 152, 196–197, 198, 202, 208–209
Nasrid dynasty, 47, 49
Natal, 220
nationalism, 21, 22–23
natural law, 51, 74
Navarino, Battle of (1827), 42
navies, 7, 10, 37, 41, 53; British, 7, 10, 11, 27, 28, 37, 69, 79, 93–94, 129, 198, 211, 218; Dutch, 63, 78, 94; French, 93, 94; impressments and, 131, 145; Spanish, 10, 69, 70, 86
Navigation Acts (1651), 79, 118, 121, 167
Netherlands. *See* Dutch Empire
New Amsterdam, 71, 170
New England, 72, 111, 128–129, 157; Amerindians and, 147, 177, 179; interracial marriage and, 163
Newfoundland, 65, 68
New France: 29, 68-69, 87-89, 104, 142–143, 147; Amerindian relations, 177, 178–179; British acquisition of, 194; French losses and, 24, 87, 179; fur trade and, 68, 127, 163, 177, 180; interethnic marriage and, 163; map of, *88;* migrants to, 144
New Granada (modern Colombia), map of, *88*, 90, 145, 168
New Laws (Spain, 1542), 146
New Netherland, 23, 170
New Spain. *See* Spanish America
newspapers, 187–188
New York, 23, 30, 170, 194
New Zealand, 75, 209, 213, 218, 219, 220

North Africa, 32, 47; French in, 24, 208, 214–215, *215*, 217; imperial failures in, 11–12; Portuguese in, 53, 55, 59, 80; Spaniards in, 53, 86, 142
North America. *See* British America; Canada; New France
Nova Scotia, 68, 204

Oaxaca (Mexico), 114, 180
Olivares, Count-Duke of, 62, 70, 73, 77
opium trade, 11, 38, 213
Orange-Nassau dynasty, 63, 84
Orientalism, 45
Osnabrück, Treaty of (1658), 77
Ottoman Empire, 8, 28, 31–34, 37–39, 41–42, 55; map of, *33*

Pacific Ocean, 8, 28–30, 37, 49, 181; European discovery of, 58; scientific expeditions to, 75, 122
padroado real, 103, 108
Pagden, Anthony, 19, 20, 21, 27
Palmares, 182, 184
Palmer, R. R., 192–193
Palmerston, Lord, 212–213
Panama, Isthmus of, 57–58, 120
papacy, 51–52, 62, 63, 67, 102, 103, 108, 109, 148
Papamiento language, 160–161
Pará, 182, 203
Paraguay, 108–109, 146
Paris, Peace of (1783), 95–96
Parry, J. H., 5–6
patronato real, 51, 107–108
Paul III, Pope, 156
Pauw, Cornelius de, 25–26
Pax Hispanica, 60
Pedro II, king of Kongo, 175
penal colonies. *See* convict labor
Penang, 141, 213
Pennsylvania, 157, 170
Pernambuco, 71, 80, 203–204
Peru, 59, 83, 100, 127, 136, 140, 146, 162, 167, 168, 180, 200, 217. *See also* Inca Empire; Lima
Peruvian bark trees, 75
Peter the Great, emperor of Russia, 35
Pétion, Alexandre, 158
Philadelphia, 150, 194
Philip II, king of Spain, 66, 97–98
Philippines, 7, 29, 89, 91, 100, 162
philosophes, 13–14, 156
piracy, 10, 68, 72–73, 181
Pius II, Pope, 156
Pizarro, Francisco, 58
Plantation Act (1764), 194
plantation system, 72, 124–125, 161, 196; investments in, 123; slave labor basis of, 53, 87, 117, 134–135, 145, 147, 149, 150, 157, 216–217. *See also* sugar; tobacco
Plassey, Battle of (1757), 44, 95
political economy, 15, 31, 115–130, 216; basis of, 127, 211–213; political ramifications of, 126–127; three aspects of, 116. *See also* trading companies
Pombal, Marquis de, 26, 92, 105, 198
Pomeranz, Kenneth, 2
Pomper, Philip, 17
Pondicherry, 89
Pontiac's Rebellion (1763), 178
porcelain, 38, 116–117
Portuguese Empire, 6, 8, 14, 15, 22, 23, 30, 37–40, 46, 48, 78, 117, 150, 200–204; British alliance with, 80–81, 85, 91–92, 201, 211, 218; *cartaz* (pass system), 56, 119; Catholic Church and, 21, 51, 107–110, 162; Civil War (1830s) in, 217–218; creole languages and, 161; Dutch threat to, 73, 82, 83; factory (fort) system of, 54–57, 134–137; Golden Age of, 49–57; governance of, 92, 101–103, 112, 114, 126–127; independence from Spain (1648) of, 73; Indian spice trade monopoly of, 127; Inquisition in, 110; Jesuit expulsion from, 92, 109; legal system of, 98; losses of, 11, 72–73, 77, 190, 217–218; map (1750) of, *3*; maritime trade routes and, 7, 30, 49, 51–57, 81–82, 92, 102, 105, 119, 127; migrations from, 142, 144; population (1800) of, 35, 217; scientific expeditions and, 122; slavery and, 153, 154, 156; Spanish union with, 59–60, 69, 70, 72–73; transatlantic slave trade and, 133–136, 211; as unitary kingdom, 49–50. *See also* Brazil; Tordesillas, Treaty of
Prescott, William H., 21
presidios, 13, 142

printing press, 187
Proclamation Line (1763), 179
protectorates, 209
Protestantism, 23, 25, 71; ascendant power of, 21, 29, 62–65, 67–68; Britain and, 7, 79, 110, 154–155, 170–171, 187; British dissenters and 62, 64–65; Dutch Empire and, 21, 23, 29, 63, 79, 170; French religious war and, 66, 68
Puerto Rico, 57, 71, 200, 216, 217
Puritans, 65, 72, 177

Qing dynasty, 8, 31-35, 38, 43–44, 213; map of, *33*
Quakers, 156, 170
Quartering Act (1765), 187, 194
Quebec, 29, 68, 89, 104, 114, 204
Quebec Act (1774), 194
quinine, 75, 208
Quito Insurrection (1765), 18

race, 25–26, 202, 208; blackness and, 148, 149, 152, 154, 172; purity of blood statutes and, 164–165, 169. *See also* intermarriage
Raleigh, Sir Walter, 67–68
Raynal, Abbé, 13–14, 115; *History of the Two Indies*, 39
Reconquista, 47
Reformation. *See* Protestantism
religion, *See* evangelization; *specific religions*
revolutions, 4, 8, 16, 92–93, 94, 180, 186–206; characteristics of, 205; four factors leading to, 192–193. *See also* slave rebellions
rice, 69, 149
Richelieu, Cardinal, 62
Rio de Janeiro, 57, 87, 92, 117, 133, 193, 212; political ascendancy of, 201, 202, 204
Río de la Plata (modern Argentina), 13, 91, 109, 146; map of, *88*
Roanoke settlement, 12, 68
Robertson, William, 14, 141, 211; *History of America*, 39
Rodney, Walter, 131
Roman Empire, 19, 25
Roman law, 51, 74, 153
Romanov dynasty, 8, 31, 35–36
Rowe, Erin, 154
Rowe, William, 44
Roy, Rammohun, 46
Russell-Wood, John, 169
Russian Empire, 8, 31, 35–36, 42, 64, 83
Ryswick, Treaty of (1697), 85

Safavid Empire, 34, 37, 42; map of, *88*
Said, Edward, 45
St. Croix, 23–24, 123, 150
Saint-Domingue (modern Haiti), 29, 69, 89, 133, 150, 168–169; imperial breakdown in, 190, 192–197 (*see also* Haitian Revolution); refugees in Cuba, 205; view of Cap François, *196*
St. Eustatius, 28, 123, 170
St. Kitts, 72, 187
St. Lucia, 23–24, 30
St. Vincent, 93, 152
salt, 49, 83, 128, 149, 150, 158
Salvador da Bahia, 57, 70–71, 92, 98, 103
San Ildefonso, Treaty of (1777), 91–92
Santo Domingo, 187, 217
São Tomé, 63, 72, 134, 163, 175
São Vicente (modern São Paulo), 86, 181–182
scientific expeditions, 74–76, 122
Scotland, 62, 64, 65, 141, 143
scurvy, 138
Sebastian, king of Portugal, 11, 59
Senegal, 30, 78, 137
sepoys, 175, 185
Seven Years' War, 15, 92–95, 179, 188, 194; consequences of, 24, 89, 94, 114
Seville, 54, 120
sharia law, 36, 43, 113, 114
sheep raising, 218–219
Sierra Leone, 204, 220
silk, 31, 37, 38, 90
silver, 2, 13, 27, 37, 38, 58, 69, 120; Dutch plunder of, 70, 71; export market for, 117; Japanese embargo on, 82; river pollution from mining of, 127; Spanish Empire and, 29, 90–91; as trade currency, 31–32
Singapore, 141, 213
sistema de castas, 164–165
Slave Emancipation Act (1833), 154, 155–156, 158
slave rebellions, 139, 152, 154, 157, 158, 184–186. *See also* fugitive slave communities; Haitian Revolution

slavery, 2, 8, 11, 15, 18, 28, 54, 95, 122, 123, 129, 131–139, *132*, 146–159, 167, 187, 193–194, 212; American Revolution and, 204; of Amerindians, 134, 146–147, 156, 158–159; British Emancipation Act (1833), 154, 158; Cuban/Puerto Rican expansion of, 216, 217; Cuban "second," 216; French Code Noir and, 152; fugitives from (*see* fugitive slave communities); as imperial economic basis, 127; justifications for, 148–149; manumission and, 153–154, 168; opponents of, 137–138, 156–157, 192, 195, 197, 221; profitability of, 125–127; self-purchase and, 153–154, 169; social variations in, 150–151; Spanish America and, 27, 82, 85, 90, 133, 134, 150–153, 192, 216–217; syncretism and, 171–172. *See also* free blacks; plantation system

"slaves by nature" ideology, 25, 148

slave trade. *See* transatlantic slave trade

smallpox, 41, 58

Smith, Adam, 14, 115, 156; *The Wealth of Nations*, 2

Society for Promoting Christian Knowledge, 188

Society for the Propagation of the Gospel (SPG), 7, 154–155

Society of Jesus. *See* Jesuits

Solórzano Pereira, Juan de, *Política Indiana*, 100–101

Somerset case (1772), 154, 156

South Africa, 28, 114, 163, 220

South America. *See* Brazil; Spanish America

South Asia, 89, 106–107, 185, 193, 209; desired trading products of, 31, 32, 116; early history of, 46; interethnic unions in, 163, 164; Portuguese symbiosis and, 29, 56–57. *See also* English East India Company; India; Mughal Empire

South Carolina, 127, 133, 149, 168

South Pacific, 41, 75, 122

South Sea Company, 85

sovereignty, 19, 23, 78, 97, 99, 192; defining feature of, 191

Spanish America: audiencias and, 100, 113, 188; British challenges to, 210–211; citizenship and, 199–200; conquistadors and, 58–59, 99, 101, 146, 163; Council of the Indies and, 99–100, 101; creoles and, 187–189; defense expenditures for, 66–67, 69; economic resurgence of, 90–91, 117, 198–199; encomiendas and, 58–59, 99, 146, 176, 238n3; exogamy and, 164–165; foods and, 167–168; independence of, 199–200, 215–216; indigenous people and, 36, 58, 98, 101, 134, 146–147, 161–162, 175, 177, 178, 180–182; Inquisition in, 109–110; laws and institutions of, 97–98; map of, *88*; mestizo societies and, 15, 160, 162–165; religious orders and, 107–109; royal governance of, 99–101, 112–113; silver mining and, 27, 29, 31, 90–91; slavery and, 27, 82, 85, 133, 134, 150–155, 192; trade and, 27, 86, 90, 119–121

Spanish armadas (1688), 10, 69, 70

Spanish Caribbean, 10, 12, 30, 57–58, 69, 85, 200. *See also* Cuba; Puerto Rico

Spanish Empire, 6, 8, 11–13, 15, 20–26, 46, 62, 85, 89; American Revolution and, 92, 93–94, 195; balance of power and, 61–62, 66–75, 81; Black Legend and, 21–22, 26, 61; Britain and, 10, 12, 28, 29, 61, 69, 74–75, 85, 198; Castilian nucleus of, 48–49; Catholicism of, 21, 63, 107–109; colonial typologies of, 20–21; Columbus's voyages and, 51, 55, 57; constitutions of, 193, 199–200; Council of the Indies and, 99–100, 101; first overseas forays of, 50, 51, 55, 57–59; flota system of, 86, 119–121; governance of, 99–101, 105; growth of, 90–91; Haitian slave rebellion and, 195–196; Inquisition and, 110; Jesuit expulsion from, 109; losses of, 77, 78, 190, 198–200, 210, 215–217; map (1750) of, *3*; military expenditures of, 61, 83; New Laws (1542) of, 146; nineteenth-century economics of, 216–217; North Africa and, 53, 86, 142; overseas possessions of, 97–98 (*see also* Spanish America); papacy and, 51, 102; Pax Hispanica and, 60; population (1800) of, 35; Portugal and, 59–60, 69, 70, 72–73, 80; purity of blood statutes and, 165, 169; resurgence of, 90–91; revolutionary 1790s and, 198–200; royal absolutism and, 126–127; scientific expeditions and, 75, 122; Seven Years' War and, 89; silver trade and, 29, 90–91; societal segregation and,

161–162; Thirty Years' War losses of, 77–78; trade and, 95, 119–121; vulnerability of, 69–71, 83, 198. *See also* Tordesillas, Treaty of
specie. *See* gold; silver
spices, 7, 31, 32, 54, 56, 75, 82, 116, 117, 127
Stamp Act (1765), 194
Staple Act (1622), 121
steamships, 207, 216
Straits Settlements, 213
Stuart monarchy, 84, 103–104
sugar: African slave labor and, 53, 134; Brazil and, 72, *81*, 86, *118*, 121, 128, 147, 197, 201; British taxes on, 194; capitalist economy and, 126; Caribbean and, 69, 89, 117, 150; Dutch merchants of, 27; European taste for, 117; trade in, 78, 123, 125, 213, 216
Suleyman the Magnificent, Sultan, 34
sumptuary laws, 166–167
Surat, 43, 44, 107
Surinam, 30, 117, 123, 125, 168, 170
syncretism, 9, 110, 114, 160, 171–172, 193

Tacky's Revolt, 152, 154, 184–185
Tailors' Revolt, 186
Taiping Rebellion, 213
Tangier, 23, 80
Tanzimat decrees (1839), 42
tariffs, 78, 212
taxation, 36, 37, 49, 83, 111, 124, 194, 216
tea, 31, 38, 39, 116–117, 146, 213
Tea Act (1773), 194
technological advances, 207, 216
textiles, 31, 32, 37, 38, 90, 116–117, 212
Thirty Years' War, 69, 72, 76, 77–78
timber, 119, 129, 218
Tipu Sultan, 185
tobacco, 69, 72, 86, 90, 116, 123, 124, 128, 136, 213; European rage for, 117; slave labor and, 149
Tobago, 30, 93, 187
Tocqueville, Alexis de, 217
Todd, David, 27
Tordesillas, Treaty of (1494), 29, 62, 74, 98, 135; clarified borders of, 91; key feature of, 52
trade. *See* balance of trade; tariffs; transatlantic slave trade; *specific commodities and regions*
trading companies, 10, 11, 28, 32, 84, 92, 97, 103–106; monopoly and, 116–117, 121–122, 126; slave trade regulation by, 135–136. *See also specific companies*
Trafalgar, Battle of (1805), 198
transatlantic slave trade, 8, 131–139, 148, 181; abolition of, 8, 155, 218; African agents and, 137; Brazil and, 92, 105, 218; British suppression of, 37, 157, 211–212; coastal fortresses and, 30; condemnations of, 156; cruelty of, 68, 137–139, 149; to Cuba and Puerto Rico, 216; Dutch ships and, 27, 82, 85; mortality rates, 138; Portugal and, 37, 54, 87, 202, 218; profits from, 125–126; Spain and, 90, 133, 216; from West African coast, 132, map of, *132;* 135–137, 202
Transvaal, 220
treaties, 210, 211, 212, 218, 221. *See also key word*
triangular trade, 116
tribute, 36, 146
Trinidad, 30, 114, 140, 198, 209
Trouillot, Michel-Rolph, 6
Túpac Amaru rebellion, 176, 180
Turkish culture, 38–39

Uighurs, 34, 44
United States, 8, 21, 143, 155, 156, 157, 205
universities, 7, 46, 87, 186, 187, 201
Utrecht, Treaty of (1713), 85, 181

Van Dieman's Land (modern Tasmania), 220
Vattel, Emer de, *Law of Nations*, 191
venereal diseases, 41
Venice, 55, 133
Vergennes, Count of, 92–93
Verlinden, Charles, 24–25
viceroy, 50, 100–101, 112–113
Virginia, 12, 29, 68, 72, 135, 164, 166; Bacon's Rebellion, 185–186; charter (1606), 98; slave population, 135
Virginia Company, 104–105, 143
Vitoria, Francisco de, 52, 74
VOC. *See* Dutch East India Company
Voltaire, 39, 156

Wahhabi Muslims, 42
Waitaingi, Treaty of (1840), 219

War of Spanish Succession, 83–84, 85, 190
wealth creation, 115–130; coerced labor and, 159; Dutch Empire and, 63; geopolitical power from, 119
West Africa, 36, 82, 133, 139, 212; coast of, 52, map of, *132;* Portuguese symbiosis with, 55, 56, 57; slave trade posts and, 135–137, 202
West Indies. *See* Caribbean
Westminster model of government, 209
Westphalia, Peace of (1648), 77–78, 83, 84, 231n1
whaling products, 116, 218
WIC. *See* Dutch West India Company
Wilberforce, William, 137–138
William and Mary, College of, 187
Williams, Eric, 125, 155–156, 221
wine, 24, 49, 92, 167
witchcraft, 110
wool, 119, 218
Wordsworth, William, 197

Yale, Elihu,
Yale University, 7
yellow fever, 12, 41, 138
yerba maté, 146
Yorktown, Battle of (1781), 93

Zululand, 220